The Diary
of
Elizabeth Drinker

The Diary
of
Elizabeth Drinker

The Life Cycle of an Eighteenth-Century Woman

EDITED AND ABRIDGED BY

Elaine Forman Crane

Sarah Blank Dine

ASSOCIATE EDITOR

Alison Duncan Hirsch
Arthur Scherr

ASSISTANT EDITORS

Anita J. Rapone

CO-EDITOR, 1982–1986

Northeastern University Press
Boston

Northeastern University Press

Library of Congress Cataloging-in-Publication Data

Drinker, Elizabeth Sandwith, 1734–1807.
The diary of Elizabeth Drinker : the life cycle of an eighteenth-
century woman / edited and abridged by Elaine Forman Crane.
p.   cm.
Includes bibliographical references and index.
ISBN 1-55553-190-3—ISBN 1-55553-191-1 (pbk.)
1. Quakers—Pennsylvania—Philadelphia—Social life and customs.
2. Philadelphia (Pa.)—Social life and customs.   3. Drinker,
Elizabeth Sandwith, 1734–1807—Diaries.   4. Quakers—Pennsylvania—
Philadelphia—Diaries.   I. Crane, Elaine Forman.   II. Title.
F158.9.F89D752   1994
305.6'86074811—dc20   94-4525

Designed by David Ford

Composed in Plantin by Coghill Composition, Richmond, Virginia. Printed and bound
by Edwards Brothers, Ann Arbor, Michigan. The paper is Glatfelter Offset,
an acid-free sheet.

MANUFACTURED IN THE UNITED STATES OF AMERICA
99 98 97 96 95 94   5 4 3 2 1

Contents

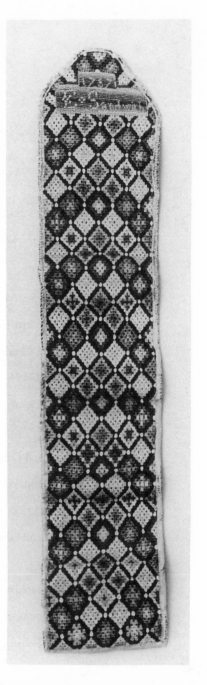

Sewing pocket (front and back) worked by Elizabeth Sandwith in 1757. Courtesy of the Rye Historical Society, Rye, New York.

Acknowledgments

In addition to the many people whose contributions to the unabridged edition of *The Diary of Elizabeth Drinker* are reflected in this volume, I would like to thank Steven Spishak, Gilbert Stack, and Bowen Smith, graduate assistants at Fordham University who helped with this version of the diary. I am also grateful to John Weingartner and Jill Bahcall at Northeastern University Press, for their assistance. Last, but perhaps most important, I would like to express my appreciation to Ann Twombly, Larry Hamberlin, and John Kaminski for their efforts this second time around. Their expertise has been essential to the editorial process.

Valentine, watercolor on cut paper, mounted on velvet. Sent to Elizabeth Sandwith by an unknown admirer and dated February 14, 1753. Courtesy of the Abby Aldrich Rockefeller Folk Art Center, Williamsburg, Virginia.

Introduction

After a particularly stressful day in the fall of 1798, Elizabeth Sandwith Drinker, a Quaker Philadelphian whose lifetime pill intake made her an expert on the subject, concluded that "a mixture of good with the bad, makes the pill of life go down."[1] And even if this was not one of her more astute observations, it does imply that at age sixty-three she assessed her own life in terms of such a balance. Elizabeth Drinker's life, most certainly a mixture of good and bad, is the focus of this abridged edition of her diary.

Because she was female, the stages of Drinker's life (1735–1807) differed greatly from the experiences of her male contemporaries, and her diary reflects those differences. Where male progress was defined by youth, career, public life, and material success, a woman's life was inextricably linked to marriage, children, domesticity, and, frequently, widowhood. Although Drinker's education and affluence distinguished her from most women (and men), the pattern of her life was quite typical of other women sharing that time and place. This edition of her diary thus mirrors what was central to her life by highlighting four critical phases of its cycle: her youth and courtship (1758–61), her years as young wife and mother (1762–75), her middle age in years of crisis (1776–93), and her role as grandmother and Grand Mother (1794–1807). Each of these phases conforms proportionately to the length of the same section in the 2,100-page unabridged version of Drinker's diary.

Elizabeth herself had vaguely defined ideas about women and the cycle of life. Sally Dawson, just under twenty, was "in the bloom of youth," while Esther Smith at fifty-five was "not much past the prime of life." At sixty-nine, Drinker reflected that she had "grown old." And only once—from the vantage point of her sixty-second year—did she make a pronouncement on female expectations and the quality of life: "I have often thought that women who live to get over the time of Child-bareing, if other things are favourable to them,

---

experience more comfort and satisfaction than at any other period of their lives."[2] What Drinker already knew, and what the last ten years of her life were to confirm, was that in a "world of trouble" the scales tipped as often toward unfavorable as they did to "favourable."[3]

The earliest chapter of Elizabeth Drinker's story is distinct from the later ones, which reflect a more settled life-style. Her unmarried years offered far more mobility than her marital and maternal commitments permitted, and once she was ensconced as wife and mother, her roles changed subtly rather than sharply over the remainder of her life.

Drinker's "beloved family" is always the focus of her attention, but different members advance or recede in literary importance as the years accumulate.[4] Her sister, Mary Sandwith, is Elizabeth's constant companion and confidante as the diary opens—not surprisingly, since the young women's bond must have been strengthened by the sudden death of both parents two years earlier. In the late 1750s Elizabeth occasionally penned an elaborately intertwined MES when referring to her sister and herself.

After Elizabeth's marriage in 1761, however, the young merchant Henry Drinker displaces Mary as Elizabeth's closest friend, although Mary, who never wed, lived the rest of her life as a member of the Drinker household. It is unlikely that either Elizabeth or Henry anticipated, much less encouraged, Mary's long-term residence given the existence of a "Sweet-heart" in 1764 and the unsolicited advice offered by her brother-in-law. Temporarily away from home, Henry seemed mildly anxious to further the courtship: "I want to know how you spend your Evenings together—Learn Sal to go to Sleep in good Time that she mayn't interrupt." As late as 1771, Henry Drinker still wrote as if he expected the thirty-nine-year-old Mary Sandwith to enter "into the Bands" of matrimony.[5]

Eventually, the Drinkers' five surviving children eclipse both their aunt and father and dominate the diary, as the early glow of marriage dims and the obligations of motherhood demand more attention. In the last two decades of her life, grandchildren take up nearly as much space in the diary's entries as Elizabeth's beloved children. Wife, mother, grandmother: these are the relationships that shaped Elizabeth Drinker's identity. "My Children are as dear to me, seemingly, as my existance—I believe no wife or mother, is more attach'd to her near relative[s] than myself."[6]

Drinker may have used the word "relatives" deliberately in a conscious effort to distinguish them from her family, or household, which consisted of considerably more people than those related to her by blood or marriage. Drinker's family included the household servants, several of whom played active roles in her life. Drinker was responsible for obtaining, hiring, paying, caring for, and disciplining them, and although her frequent references to them by their first names (Betsy, Rosie, John, Peter, Pompey) indicate class differences, paternalism, and lack of respect, Drinker clearly regarded them as family members under her jurisdiction. Although she exhibits no affection toward her servants in the diary, there is evidence of at least short-term sadness, remorse, and even guilt if some misfortune befell a longtime live-in servant.[7]

Because Elizabeth Drinker's life cycle is so intimately interwoven with sister, husband, children, grandchildren, and servants, the diary is not merely a record of events from Drinker's perspective but also a re-creation of ongoing relationships between and among these family members. An analysis of the journal enhances our understanding of the various roles women played through-out their lives as well as the dynamics of familial interaction.

The diary opens on the eve of Henry and Elizabeth's courtship, and if Henry's suit appears to lack passion, it may be due more to Elizabeth's literary reticence than to Henry's inadequate ardor. By her own admission, Elizabeth strayed from propriety at least once when Henry stayed unseasonably late one night, and her "judgment" was at odds with her "Actions."[8] Elizabeth's circumspect comments only hint at the emotional upheaval surrounding her engagement to Henry later that month, but after their wedding in January 1761, evidence of her devotion to her husband flows freely from her quill.

Mercantile and Quaker business took Henry from home with a frequency that Elizabeth initially resented but eventually adjusted to, and if ever a companionate or affectionate marriage existed in fact, Elizabeth and Henry Drinker shared such a union. This is not to say that she was aware of all of his dealings, or that she consistently participated in his decision making. Yet they did discuss business matters regarding the Atsion ironworks, cargoes, and property transfer, and Henry was privy to the servants' frequent transgressions and children's crises. If the two occupied distinct spheres, those worlds were not totally separate. As primary caregiver, Elizabeth was greatly concerned about Henry's health, the more so as the couple aged.

Elizabeth respected her husband as "a man of good judgment," albeit "venterous," an assessment that remained constant throughout their years together. She thought him more "honest" than most men. And if she was never completely reconciled to the business and public concerns that occupied "ten twelfths" of HD's time, Elizabeth knew that the "benevolence and beneficence" he showed to others were steppingstones to heaven. If Henry demeaned her interest in nature, if he told her "not to stir in the affair" of their daughter's elopement, if he did not consult her before the sale of their summer home, his other qualities nevertheless made up for an occasional thoughtless remark or paternalistic act.[9]

From the time her first child was born, Elizabeth Drinker's life revolved around her children; their well-being, both in youth and maturity, was her prime concern. She continually worried about their health—a valid preoccupa-tion, given the host of diseases that carried off even the healthiest people on short notice. Still, Drinker's excessive anxiety may have stemmed from the death of her own parents within months of each other when she was twenty-one. Drinker's acknowledgment of the anniversary of their deaths each year is testament to the blow she experienced as a young adult—a blow that may have compounded her fear that her own children would be taken from her just as unceremoniously. At the death of Robert Morgan, "oldest Child of Thos. and Nancy Morgan," Drinker identified with the grieving mother: "Poor Nancy! I really feel much for her, knowing her to be a very affectionate Mother."[10]

Elizabeth Drinker encouraged harmony and affection among her children. She knew that it was a "favour" for "a young woman to have a good Brother or brothers," and she was "always pleased" to see her married daughters united under her roof. In 1802 she expressed a "sencere desire" that her children's bond might give them strength and that they might be "councellours and helps to each other," without neglecting their spouses.[11]

Elizabeth described her adult children as favoring either herself or Henry in temperament: "Sally is her fathers own Child; Ann and William belong to me—Henry and Molly to us both, but reather incline to my side."[12] By appraising them in such a way, Elizabeth bound four out of five closer to her than to their father. How close Drinker's children felt to their mother is reflected in the names they chose for each of their own firstborn children. Both Sally Drinker Downing and Nancy Drinker Skyrin named their oldest children Elizabeth. Molly Drinker, whose elopement with Samuel Rhoads was condemned by her parents and condoned by her mother-in-law, named her first daughter Sarah, presumably after her husband's mother.

The bond between Sarah Rhoads and Molly Drinker Rhoads was strong—for reasons that may have been intensified by the loss of Sarah's only two daughters (Mary and Elizabeth) when they were in their late twenties. Her son and only surviving child, Samuel, married Molly Drinker in 1796, the same year his sister Elizabeth died. These maternal dynamics fostered a competition between Sally Rhoads and Elizabeth Drinker for Molly's affection and attention, a contest that festered and then erupted over issues of health. Health care, after all, was power—probably the most powerful function a woman performed. It would not be surprising if Elizabeth Drinker sought to retain a strong relationship with her children through her capacity as caregiver.

Thus, when Molly was "blooded" during her pregnancy in 1798, Drinker found it "very extraordinary" that she was "not sent for," especially since "Sally Rhoads has been there all day."[13] And some days later, Drinker added unhappily that Molly "has taken pills composed of Assafatida and Opium, which I had advised against . . . Sally Rhoads had procribed Assifatida."[14] A year later, Molly and Sammy took up residence at Sarah Rhoads's house during the yellow fever epidemic rather than at the Drinkers', prompting Mother Drinker to assert, "I would rather they had come to us." At Mother Rhoads's, Molly was "very near" Drinker's heart, although (and more to the point) "very much" out of her "jurisdiction."[15]

Against their grandmother Drinker's advice, Molly Rhoads's children were inoculated rather than vaccinated for the smallpox, since "SR" (either Sammy or his mother) was in favor of the former procedure. Less than a week later,

Drinker recorded that "Henrys little Son is bravely—he has vaccinated 4 of his Children."[16] Elizabeth could claim that victory, at least.

This is not to imply that Elizabeth Drinker and her daughter Molly were estranged in any way. Elizabeth attended her "dear Child" during childbirth, and they grieved together over the loss of Molly's firstborn son.[17] Indeed, Elizabeth was at the bedside of all of her daughters during labor and delivery as long as she was physically able. She also knew the most intimate details of her daughters' married life in order to calculate the stages of pregnancy with such precision: "it is ten months this day since she [Molly] was unwell as the women call it," and "had Nancy gone out her full time, this would have been the time of her reckoning."[18]

The shared experience of childbirth forged the most natural bonds between mother and daughter, but there were other means by which Elizabeth Drinker either intentionally or unintentionally prolonged maternal control over her married children who threatened to weaken the natal ties by establishing households of their own. One child, William, never married and remained at home, an invalid under his mother's direct supervision. Health permitting, they took long walks together on summer evenings.

Medicines were prepared in the Drinker household; Drinker's children sent servants for the proper remedies from their mother instead of concocting them in their own homes. "Nancys Patience came in this evening for some lavender Compound, said her Mistress was sick at her Stomach."[19] They constantly sought medical advice from her; she just as constantly gave it—even without being asked. Children at a distance, even married children, heightened anxiety: "a letter from HSD. to WD. desiring him to send a pound of good pale bark, as he has had a severe fitt of the Ague; dear Henry, I wish he was here, that I might nurse him."[20] Presumably, Henry's wife was not equal to the task.

In 1797 both Nancy and Sally borrowed their mother's copy of William Buchan's *Domestic Medicine*, although the popular book had gone through at least fifteen American editions by that time and was a common household item that they themselves could have bought. Seven years later, Drinker was still dispensing remedies, this time for her grandchildren: "Mollys Dan was here, he says the 2 oldest Children have the Chills and fever, I sent them Century."[21] Yet if, in fact, Drinker deliberately retained an exclusivity over her medical expertise, she did so at the expense of her daughters. They were precluded from developing the same skills and thus relied not only on her but on professional male physicians, who were beginning to dominate the practice of medicine.

As members of the Drinker family, servants received much the same medical care as everyone else in the household—treatment that was either advantageous or not, depending on one's assessment of eighteenth-century medicine. The renowned physician Benjamin Rush favored Sally Dawson with a prescription for castor oil, just as he did his other Drinker patients. Elizabeth's personal physician, Dr. Kuhn, attended Nancy's "black girl" Patience Gibbs and diagnosed Sally Dawson's yellow fever.[22] A favorable recommendation from Elizabeth Drinker permitted a servant, former servant, or relative of a servant to obtain free medication from the Philadelphia dispensary, thus extending Drinker's influence over the health of her extended family and reinforcing the deferential nature of eighteenth-century society.[23]

Other, more subtle scenarios suggest that Elizabeth Drinker consciously or unconsciously extended her role as matriarch:

> sent Paul yesterday to the Library with a list, none were to be had but the last on the list, which was "Bolinbroke on the study and use of History." Nancy put it down, and tho' I like'd not the Authors name, I had no objection to the title . . . but found on looking it over, that it set at nought the Holy scriptures . . . I sent it back unread, and did not let Nancy have it. how pernicious are such writings to young people.

Nancy, a married woman with two children, was thirty-six years old. In theory, Drinker also disapproved of novels and tried to discourage her adult children from "doing much of that business," although Drinker shaded the truth considerably when she asserted " 'tis seldom I listen to a romance."[24]

Elizabeth Drinker's married children often took meals at their parents' home, but although Elizabeth was a frequent visitor in her children's homes, she did not ordinarily share meals at their tables. She baby-sat for her grandchildren, but watched them in her home rather than theirs. Indeed, one or two of the granddaughters spent months at a time at the Drinker residence. And Drinker's daughters stored furniture and clothing, as well as children, at their mother's house.

Drinker's married daughters shopped, visited, and enjoyed tea with her quite often; her son Henry stopped in less frequently only because of the greater distance separating them. If the time between visits seemed excessive, Drinker made a note: "S. Downing has not been here for near seven weeks," and more precisely, "It is 4 months and 11 days since our Son HSD. was here."[25] If Drinker, as journal writer, constructed a world with herself at center, she was neither obscuring reality nor deceiving herself. Her sons and daughters gravitated toward her out of affection, duty, respect, and probably guilt, the relative proportions of each component depending on the particular offspring.

Elizabeth Drinker was never as close to her one daughter-in-law, Hannah Smith Drinker, as she was to her own daughters, nor for that matter was the relationship as warm as it was with her son-in-law Jacob Downing. "Henry S. and Hannah Drinker, sup'd here . . . have not seen Hannah for a long time past." It was HSD (Henry) who wrote to his mother, until he sailed for India in 1806, and only then did Elizabeth occasionally correspond with Hannah. Drinker felt compelled to announce prior to the event that she would not attend the birth of Hannah's first child in October 1795 "if the weather was unfair . . . or in the night," conditions that would not have deterred her from her own daughter's travails. She was not always aware of Hannah's pregnancies even as Hannah approached the end of her term, and in 1805 Elizabeth noted that she had just seen her eight-month-old granddaughter, Henry and Hannah's eighth child, for the first time.[26]

If the data distilled by historians in the 1960s and 1970s have argued for the early preeminence of the nuclear household, it is still true that eighteenth-century Americans formed temporary extended families that consisted of grandparents and grandchildren. In 1794 Elizabeth Downing lived with her Drinker grandparents for six months; she took up residence again in 1799. On a short-term basis Elizabeth Drinker welcomed several granddaughters at once. Elizabeth and Mary Downing joined Elizabeth Skyrin in June 1800.[27] Not only did these residential patterns strengthen the bonds between grandparents and grandchildren, but they also seem to have enhanced the relationship between cousins, who saw more of each other under these conditions than otherwise might have been the case.

Given the fungible nature of time in a society where production was household oriented, uncles and aunts could also turn up at unexpected times for equally unexpected outings with their nieces and nephews. Seven-year-old William Drinker appeared at his grandparents' home one February afternoon in 1803, "his Aunt Betsy Smith, and Uncle James, with little Esther" with him. "He took a ride, on his Uncle Williams little Horse. . . . he was very much pleased with his short ride."[28] As a testament to the role their Aunt Mary played in their lives a generation earlier, each of the Drinker children named a daughter after her.

In her roles as mother and grandmother, Elizabeth Drinker relied heavily on the assistance of servants. Servants sought information on the health of family members who lived elsewhere in the city. And just as they cared for the five young Drinker children, they watched over the Drinker grandchildren decades later. Invested with responsibility, if not authority, servants took children and grandchildren visiting, sledding, and horseback riding.[29] In turn, Elizabeth Drinker played mother to her servants, advising, advocating, indeed demanding, a code of behavior appropriate to her family's station. And if household hierarchy was less pronounced when it came to medical care, it was fairly obvious in other situations. Three servants were soaked during a thunderstorm so that Nancy Drinker Skyrin could stay dry. Besides, as competitors for hot water in the household tub, servants had the last bath.[30]

It is hardly surprising that Elizabeth Drinker saw her needs and those of her immediate family as taking precedence over those of her servants. This attitude was reflected by her preference for unmarried employees who were on perpetual call by living under the Drinker roof: "A Negro woman named Mary, who was hear on & off, for a week or upwards, we dismist last seventh day, not for any fault, but she could not be here but when it suited herself, being a married woman."[31] Since Elizabeth Drinker felt it was her province to determine when and how often a servant might visit his or her family of birth or marriage, an independent stance was not a particularly desirable characteristic from Drinker's perspective. Nevertheless, Mary's attributes appear to have persuaded Drinker to rehire her: "black Mary who has been at work here some months, went home sick this morning she never lodges here having a husband."[32] If Elizabeth was forced to capitulate to the needs of an otherwise capable servant on this occasion, she held the upper hand at other times. Drinker was the matriarch of a prominent, prosperous Philadelphia family in a society that hired people on the basis of recommendations. By giving "characters," Drinker determined the employment potential and future well-being of former servants and their families.[33]

Interestingly, servants were the family members who responded most directly to Drinker's intellectual curiosity. Knowing that she was fascinated by the natural world, Peter and Patience brought Drinker unusual insects and drew astronomical phenomena to her attention—thus revealing something of their own interests as well.[34]

If the diary confirms that Elizabeth Drinker's life cycle fit the stereotypical portrait of upper-class white women, it also suggests that gender roles may have been more strictly applied to women of her standing than to upper-class men or less affluent women and men. Drinker knew and did what her class and upbringing prescribed. She was as skilled with the needle as any eighteenth-century woman could hope to be. She crafted elegant embroideries, knit warm stockings, and cut, stitched, and mended clothing. She was a capable cook and baker, although these tasks were delegated to servants on a daily basis, leaving Drinker free to preserve jelly and bake an occasional pie. Only as a young married woman did she actually clean house or iron. As she aged, servants took over these chores, leaving Elizabeth or Sister to supervise the household workers. In these later years she read continually, an activity accompanied by guilt, but apart from a few romantic novels, few could criticize her choice of reading matter.

Yet if female servants in the Drinker household washed clothes and linens, with an outside washwoman on call, and men drove the horse and carriage, it is not true that other domestic activities were as gender specific. It is clear from Elizabeth's complaints that not all women seeking domestic employment could cook, whereas men were often capable kitchen workers who could be put to work salting meat or preparing meals.[35] Female employees whitewashed the house and delivered milk by horse and cart.

In the early years of their marriage, Elizabeth Drinker accompanied her husband on an occasional business trip, and the constant flow of visitors in and out of "the" office (never "his" office) indicates that Elizabeth must have possessed some knowledge of her husband's business ventures, especially when those same associates stayed for dinner and continued their conversation at the table.[36] Nevertheless, even if she engaged in small shipping transactions before her marriage, her role in her husband's business affairs was distinctly modest.

Conversely, Henry did not distance himself from family concerns and activities as much as the historical male image suggests. HD took his children and grandchildren fishing and sleighriding. They went to Quaker meetings together. The children and grandchildren accompanied him to business appointments, and their health was a matter of concern to him. "My husband is gone this evening to visit our dear little Eleanor," who was "very unwell with something like the bloody flux."[37] During the day, both HD and his son William visited friends and Friends to inquire about their health. They both arrived to be on hand for the labor and delivery of Henry's daughter-in-law, Hannah Smith Drinker.[38] Indeed, William was apparently on the short list to attend his sister, although because of inclement weather "poor Molly . . . near her time, if she should be taken ill" would have "No mother, no Sister, no brother to go near her."[39]

Other incidents, casually acknowledged by Elizabeth Drinker, indicate that if women were at times deputy husbands, men could be similarly employed as deputy wives. In his wife's absence, Elizabeth's son-in-law John Skyrin dressed his daughter's head wound with brandy and brown paper—a remedy suggesting an appalling lack of familiarity with nursery rhymes, and a mistake that Elizabeth Drinker soon rectified. Joseph Scott went "to New York to look after his Grand-Children" who had "lately lost their Mother."[40] Jacob Downing, another son-in-law, sat up all night with his ailing cousin by marriage, Israel Whelan, even though Whelan's wife was alive and well.[41]

In short, only in extraordinary circumstances such as wartime did Elizabeth Drinker transgress her culturally defined boundaries as a woman, whereas other members of her family were more likely to do so on a regular basis. Did Drinker resent the perimeters of her life? Did she aspire to more than her roles as wife, mother, and grandmother permitted? Although on the whole she seemed satisfied, there were times that she admitted to some ambivalence: "I have read a large Octava volume, intitled the Rights of Woman, By Mary Wolstonecroft. in very many of her sentiments, she, as some of our friends say, *speaks my mind*, in others, I do not, altogether coincide with her—I am not for quite so much independance."[42]

In both editions of Drinker's diary public events are always seen from the perspective of family, which emphasizes Drinker's point of reference as a woman. Yet if this abridged volume highlights Elizabeth Drinker's life cycle by focusing on different stages of her personal development within the context of her family, it does, by necessity, exclude many other aspects of her life and life in Philadelphia. Elizabeth Drinker was a voracious reader, to a degree only hinted at in this edition. She was politically sensitive and knowledgeable, qualities that are evident in the unabridged version, but less so here given the deliberately selective nature of the entries.

The repetitiveness of daily activities has been minimized in this volume, and it is therefore not as obvious just how frequently Drinker takes an evening walk or visits friends. The parade of people in and out of the Drinker home in this edition is also considerably contracted. HD's activities, including his social and business calls, his attendance at weddings and funerals, have been abbreviated as well. Sickness and pain are pervasive; this version of the diary is suggestive rather than comprehensive.

The complete diary is a compendium of aberrational as well as normal behavior in eighteenth-century Philadelphia, and includes instances of stress, suicide, delusions, fantasy, and murder (including an attempted regicide), few of which are retained in this edition. In the full edition, each entry records the day's weather and wind direction, information that had meaning for Drinker but does not further our understanding of her life.

Lacking in this abridgement also are the sights and sounds of eighteenth-century Philadelphia: the watchman's rattle, church bells, fire alarms, burning buildings, carriage accidents, runaway horses, and the fruits and flowers of a city that could accommodate more of such civilized delights. Most of Philadelphia's smells will not be missed: raw sewage, spoiled food, burning rubbish, and unwashed bodies. These deletions have all been modern editorial choices, but the entries have already been edited by Drinker herself. Hers is a particularly private and unemotional diary, and for all her openness about bodily functions, Drinker has nothing to say directly about sex—a minor point, of course, given the voluminous amount she has to say about everything else. Nevertheless, her silence is testimony to what was proper subject matter, even within the confines of her journal.

In some ways the pattern of Elizabeth Drinker's life was slightly different from that of her daughters. Although her two oldest daughters married at approximately the same age as their mother (twenty-six and twenty-seven), the youngest, Molly, eloped at twenty-two. Each had fewer children than Elizabeth, probably as a result of long-term breast-feeding, which retarded pregnancy. Sally gave birth to six children, Nancy three, and Molly five. The firstborn children of both Sally and Molly died at birth. Elizabeth encouraged family limitation, and was dismayed by the fecundity of her son and daughter-in-law (eight children in ten years). Because of Hannah's perceived derelictions, Elizabeth even saw her son's role as different from his father's: "My poor Son Henry, I believe must be a Nurse, which his father never was."[43] Eventually, both Nancy and Molly were widowed, Molly as early as 1810. HD survived Elizabeth by two years. Sally predeceased her husband and parents when she died of cancer in the early fall of 1807, just before her forty-sixth birthday.

Since her children's welfare was, as she admitted, "the thing next to my heart," Elizabeth Drinker never really recovered from the death of her cherished daughter, and she herself succumbed two months later, in November 1807, to what the Arch Street Meeting Burial Book referred to as "lethargy."[44] Her diary was her legacy to her children, and if some of the lines they read after her death were designed to evoke remorse ("I see my Children much seldomer than I could wish . . . they dont consider that they will not have their mother long to visit"), there could be no doubt how much they meant to her during her life, or how central they, and their father, were to her life cycle.[45]

Notes

1. Oct. 22, 1798 (2:1100). All volume and page numbers refer to the unabridged edition of the Drinker diary.

2. Oct. 3, 1803 (3:1691); Mar. 26, 1807 (3:2020); Mar. 4, 1804 (3:1731), Feb. 26, 1797 (2:893).

3. Feb. 21, 1803 (3:1628).

4. Nov. 3, 1794 (1:614).

5. Henry Drinker to Mary Sandwith, Sept. 7, 1764, and Aug. 24, 1771, Drinker-Sandwith papers, Historical Society of Pennsylvania.

6. Dec. 2, 1802 (2:1595).

7. See Nov. 30, 1759 (1:40); Dec. 7, 1777 (1:262); Aug. 9, 1779 (1:358); May 27, 1794 (1:561); and Jan. 27, 1804 (3:1726), for references to servants as family. Drinker was not among those mistresses in the second half of the eighteenth century who altered their definition of family to exclude servants. See Jacquelyn C. Miller, "The Body Politic: Disease and Political Culture in the Age of the American Revolution," paper presented at the Philadelphia Center for Early American Studies, Dec. 4, 1992. For servants' misfortunes see July 14, 1795 (1:704–5), when Sally Brant's illegitimate child died, and Dec. 12, 1803 (3:1712), after Sally Dawson's death.

8. July 4, 1760 (1:64); July 23, 26, 27, 28, 30, 1760 (1:67).

9. Sept. 24, 1800 (2:1342); Jan. 17, 1803 (3:1618); Dec. 12, 1795 (1:759–60); May 23, 1806 (3:1932); Aug. 10, 1796 (2:830); Jan. 19, 1796 (2:771).

10. Feb. 21, 1803 (3:1628).

11. Mar. 15, 1795 (1:658); Mar. 5, 1801 (2:1391); July 25, 1802 (2:1537).

12. Oct. 16, 1798 (2:1098).

13. July 18, 1798 (2:1055).

14. July 24, 1798 (2:1057).

15. July 1, 1799 (2:1185); July 9, 1799 (2:1188).

16. March 23, 31, 1805 (3:1819, 1821); Apr. 2, 1805 (3:1822).

17. June 14, 1797 (2:929).

18. Oct. 7, 1801 (2:1453); Aug. 23, 1801 (2:1438). See also Jan. 14, 1807 (3:2002), and Sept. 16, 1801 (2:1446).

19. Dec. 25, 1800 (2:1364). See also Mar. 8, 1798 (2:1010).

20. May 2, 1797 (2:913).

21. Aug. 6, 1804 (3:1760).

22. June 23, 1795 (1:695); May 24, 1799 (2:1171); Sept. 29, 1803 (3:1688).

23. May 2, 1807 (3:2032).

24. Sept. 23, 1800 (2:1342); June 20, 1795 (1:694).

25. Feb. 6, 1796 (2:775); July 27, 1803 (3:1671).

26. Dec. 26, 1804 (3:1787); Oct. 11, 1795 (1:739); Apr. 18, 1805 (3:1826).

27. June 14, 1794 (1:565); Jan. 12, 15, 1799 (2:1129, 1130); June 18, 1800 (2:1310).

28. Feb. 14, 1803 (3:1627).

29. Jan. 14, 1805 (3:1800); Feb. 14, 1803 (3:1627).

30. July 18, 1806 (3:1948); Aug. 7, 1806 (3:1955).

31. Nov. 18, 1799 (2:1239).

32. June 20, 1800 (2:1311).

33. June 15, 1798 (2:1044).

34. Aug. 3, 1800 (2:1326); Dec. 15, 1796 (2:867).

35. See, for example, Aug. 28, 1794 (1:586); Sept. 8, 1804 (3:1766); July 2, 1804 (3:1753); May 30, 1806 (3:1934); June 26, 1806 (3:1941); and Dec. 24, 1806 (3:1992).

36. Mar. 22, 1804 (3:1734).

37. Apr. 20, 18, 1803 (3:1644, 1643).

38. Oct. 14, 1795 (1:742).

39. Dec. 3, 1806 (3:1986).

40. Apr. 17, 1799 (2:1157); May 29, 1781 (1:388).

41. Oct. 8, 1806 (3:1971).

42. Apr. 22, 1796 (2:795).

43. Aug. 13, 1804 (3:1761); Sept. 4, 1797 (2:960).

44. Dec. 5, 1803 (3:1709).

45. May 15, 1806 (3:1929–30).

Editorial Note

Elizabeth Drinker's diary falls somewhere between a historical and a literary document. Although its primary value is historical, readers can enjoy both content and form. Similarly, it falls somewhere between a private and a public document: private in the sense that it was not meant to be published, public because the volumes were open to the scrutiny of others, both in her time and ours.

The journal, like any other document, presents the usual problems with regard to editorial procedure. The primary task was to ensure a faithful reproduction of the unabridged text without sacrificing readability. This balance required certain textual modifications, but the result is a nearly literal transcription of the original manuscript that retains, with minor exceptions, Elizabeth Drinker's spelling and punctuation.

The modifications are as follows:

Superscript letters have been brought down to the baseline, and common nouns abbreviated in this manner have been silently expanded, with the period below the superscript letter omitted. The words so altered are *about, account, appeared, company, could, daughter, dear, deceased, ditto, doctor, dollars, evening, friend, instant, meeting, morning, neighbor, o'clock, paid, pair, quarter, received, said, should, supped, testimony, ultimo, with, would.*

The superscript letters of proper nouns, including titles such as *Nr.* (Neighbor), *Fd.* (Friend), and *Dr.* (Doctor), have been dropped to the baseline, but the words have not been expanded, on the theory that abbreviated names are ambiguous ("Jos.," for example, could refer to Joseph, Josiah, or Joshua); also, it seems more reasonable to apply a consistent rule to all proper nouns than to expand some and not others.

The few abbreviated words within the text that contain no superscript letters have not been expanded.

The thorn (*ye, yt*) has been replaced by *th* (*the, that*).

Punctuation has been retained exactly as it appears in the original manuscript with the following exceptions:

1. A period completes each daily entry no matter what punctuation mark Drinker used.

2. All dashes within the text that indicate a pause or change of thought are reproduced as em dashes (—) regardless of their size in the manuscript. Dashes to fill an incomplete line or to mark the end of an entry have been eliminated.

3. A colon or comma after the first initial of a name has been replaced with a period. Thus "J: Logan" in the manuscript appears as "J. Logan" in the published version. In the case of names such as *McKean* where Drinker wrote a superscript *c*, the letter has been brought down to the baseline and the period under the *c* eliminated.

4. The period following the *s* in possessive superscript names such as *Jamess* has been deleted.

Elizabeth Drinker's handwriting is extremely legible, and the manuscript volumes are generally in good condition. Nevertheless, use has taken its toll, and there are the usual smudges, holes, and even an occasional tooth mark where a mouse has sampled a page corner. In such cases, letters or words transcribed with difficulty are surrounded by a bracket, and totally illegible ones are represented by an empty bracket. Regretfully, the reader will not know how many letters or words are missing in the latter situation, since this was often impossible to determine. Since ED's capital *I, J, T,* and *S* are almost totally indistinguishable from one another, they frequently appear in brackets when used as initials in place of a name.

Entries on loose pages that were erroneously inserted in the manuscript volumes at some undetermined time have been silently placed in their proper chronological order.

Annotation

The focus of the annotation is explanatory rather than interpretive, the assumption being that the editor's role is to present the text with as little bias and as much neutrality as possible. Toward that end, the annotation seeks to clarify entries where the meaning is elusive, and to expand where the information ED relays is insufficient for the reader to understand a situation. Only words omitted from standard English dictionaries are defined. Since the annotation is intended merely to support, the notes have been written and edited with an eye toward brevity. Many notes, however, include citations that allow the reader to explore a subject in greater detail.

Except for those occasions where Drinker corrects herself by crossing out a word inadvertently misspelled or repeated, her deletions have been restored in the form of annotation, since they represent information that she chose to remove from the reader's view for one reason or another. The deleted words, phrases, and sentences appear in a note rather than at their original place in the body of the entry in order to avoid any interruption to the flow of the text.

In addition to the silent corrections already noted, two sorts of deletions appear in the original text. In the first case, Drinker merely excised a word or statement with a line through it in order to rephrase a thought, apply a synonym, or change a name. It created minimal difficulty to decipher these deletions. In the second instance, however, she attempted to completely obliterate what she had written. Every effort has been made to reconstruct accurately what in many cases Drinker took great pains to conceal. Where this proved impossible, the editor has noted that material has been crossed out. Words within brackets indicate the editor's best guess as to what they had been. Empty brackets indicate word(s) that the editor was unable to decipher at all. Although the reader will share the editor's frustration at not being able to tell with precision how many words belong within that bracket, the reader may assume that the missing words comprise less than a full line of text. Deletions of a line or more are so indicated.

The note number to indicate deleted material has been placed immediately preceding the expunged text.

Drinker's French phrases are an attempt at concealment as well, and translations of these phrases appear in the notes. ED's French spelling is even more arbitrary than her English; her French grammar and sentence structure are nonstandard, to say the least. Some "French" words seem to be her own invention. No attempt has been made to standardize or correct any of her French phrases, and in many instances the English equivalents are merely approximations of what she probably meant.

In this abridged version, ellipses represent text deleted by the editor. Bracketed months have been added in some instances to clarify dates.

For purposes of easy reference, people are identified in a biographical directory at the end of this volume.

Abbreviations and Short Titles

Annals of Congress
>U.S. Congress. *Annals of the Congress of the United States.* 42 vols. Washington, D.C.: Gales and Seaton, 1834–56.

APS   American Philosophical Society.

Augustin. *Yellow Fever*
>George Augustin. *History of Yellow Fever.* New Orleans: Searcy & Pfaff, 1909.

Bailey. *Universal Etymological Dictionary*
>N. Bailey. *A Universal Etymological English Dictionary.* 4th ed. London: 1728.

Barbour and Frost. *Quakers*
>Hugh Barbour and William J. Frost. *The Quakers.* New York: Greenwood Press, 1988.

Bard. *Compendium of Midwifery*
>Samuel Bard. *A Compendium of the Theory and Practice of Midwifery.* New York: Collins and Perkins, 1807.

Blackwell. *Curious Herbal*
>Elizabeth Blackwell. *A Curious Herbal Containing Five Hundred Cuts of the Most Useful Plants. Which Are Now Used in the Practice of Physick. Engraved on Folio Copper Plates, after Drawings Taken from the Life.* 2 vols. London: John Nourse, 1739.

Boatner. *American Revolution*
>Mark M. Boatner III. *The Encyclopedia of the American Revolution.* New York: McKay 1966.

Bridenbaugh and Bridenbaugh. *Rebels and Gentlemen*
>Carl Bridenbaugh and Jessica Bridenbaugh. *Rebels and Gentlemen: Philadelphia in the Age of Franklin.* 1940. Reprint. New York: Oxford University Press, 1962.

Brinton. *Quaker Practice*
>Howard H. Brinton. *Guide to Quaker Practice.* Pendle Hill Pamphlets 20. Wallingford, Pa: Pendle Hill Pamphlets 1943.

Brissot de Warville. *New Travels*

J. P. Brissot de Warville. *New Travels in the United States of America, 1788.* Translated by Maria Soceanu Vamos and Durand Echeverria. Edited by Durand Echeverria. Cambridge, Mass.: Belknap Press of Harvard University Press, 1964.

Bronner. "Quaker Landmarks"

Edwin Bronner. "Quaker Landmarks in Early Philadelphia." In *Historic Philadelphia: From the Founding until the Early Nineteenth Century, 210–16* Transactions of the American Philosophical Society, n.s., 43, pt. 1. Philadelphia, 1953.

Brooke. *George III*

John Brooke. *King George III*. New York: McGraw Hill, 1972.

Buchan. *Domestic Medicine* (1793)

William Buchan. *Domestic Medicine: Or a Treatise on the Prevention and Cure of Diseases by Regimen and Simple Medicines*. 14th ed. Boston: Printed for Joseph Bumstead by James White and Ebenezer Larkin, jun., 1793.

Buchan. *Domestic Medicine* (1799)

William Buchan, *Domestic Medicine: Or, a Treatise on the Prevention and Cure of Diseases by Regimen and Simple Medicines Adapted to the Climate and Diseases of America, by Isaac Cathrall*. Philadelphia: Richard Folwell, 1799.

Carey. *Short Account*

Mathew Carey. *A Short Account of the Malignant Fever, Lately Prevalent in Philadelphia*. Philadelphia: Printed by the author, 1793.

Carroll and Ashworth. *George Washington*

John Alexander Carroll and Mary Wells Ashworth. *George Washington*. Vol. 7, *First in Peace*. Completes biography by Douglas Southall Freeman. New York: Scribner, 1957.

Clement. *Welfare and the Poor*

Priscilla Ferguson Clement. *Welfare and the Poor in the Nineteenth-Century City: Philadelphia, 1800–1854*. Rutherford, N.J.: Fairleigh Dickinson University Press, 1985.

Col. Recs. Pa.

Commonwealth of Pennsylvania. *The Colonial Records of Pennsylvania*. 14 vols. Harrisburg, 1852. Reprint. New York: AMS Press, 1968.

Comly. *Comly Family*

George Norwood Comly, comp. *Comly Family in America*. Philadelphia: Lippincott, 1939.

Cope. *Smedley Family*

Gilbert Cope, comp. *Genealogy of the Smedley Family*. Lancaster, Pa.: Wickersham Printing Co., 1901.

Cullen. *Practice of Physic*

William Cullen. *First Lines of the Practice of Physic. With Practical and Explanatory Notes by John Rothermel*. 4 vols. Edinburgh: Bell & Bradfute, and William Creech, 1791.

DAB   *Dictionary of American Biography* (1928–58). New York: Scribner, 1964.

Davis, A., and Appel. *Bloodletting Instruments*
  Audrey Davis and Toby Appel. *Bloodletting Instruments in the National Museum of History*. Smithsonian Studies in History and Technology 41. Washington, D.C.: Smithsonian Institution, 1979.
Dewees and Dewees. *Centennial of Westtown*
  Watson W. Dewees and Sarah B. Dewees. *Centennial History of the Westtown Boarding School 1799–1899*. Westtown, Pa.: Westtown Alumni Association and Sherman & Co., 1899.
DNB   *Dictionary of National Biography*. Oxford: Oxford University Press, 1967–68.
Drinker, C. K. *Not So Long Ago*
  Cecil K. Drinker. *Not So Long Ago: A Chronicle of Medicine and Doctors in Colonial Philadelphia*. New York: Oxford University Press, 1937.
Drinker, H. S. *Drinker Family*
  Henry S. Drinker. *History of the Drinker Family*. Merion, Pa.: Privately printed, 1961.
Duffy. *Epidemics*
  John Duffy. *Epidemics in Colonial America*. Baton Rouge: Louisiana State University, 1953.
Estes. "Therapeutic Practice"
  J. Worth Estes. "Therapeutic Practice in New England." In *Medicine in Colonial Massachusetts*, 289–383. *Publications of the Colonial Society of Massachusetts* 57. Boston, 1980.
Fisher, S. R. "Fisher Journal"
  "Journal of Samuel Rowland Fisher, of Philadelphia, 1779–1781." Contributed by Anna Wharton Morris. *Pennsylvania Magazine of History and Biography* 41 (1917): 145–97, 274–333, 399–457.
Franklin. *Papers*
  The Papers of Benjamin Franklin. Edited by Leonard Labaree et al. New Haven: Yale University Press, 1959–.
Frost. *Quaker Family*
  J. William Frost. *The Quaker Family in Colonial America*. New York: St. Martin's Press, 1973.
Gardner. *New Medical Dictionary*
  D. Pereira Gardner. *A New Medical Dictionary*. New York: Harper & Brothers, 1855.
Gifford. "Botanic Remedies"
  George E. Gifford, Jr. "Botanic Remedies in Colonial Massachusetts, 1620–1820." In *Medicine in Colonial Massachusetts*, 263–88. *Publications of the Colonial Society of Massachusetts* 57. Boston, 1980.
Gilpin. *Exiles in Virginia*
  Thomas Gilpin. *Exiles in Virginia*. Philadelphia: n.p., 1848.
Gould. *Dictionary of Medicine*
  George M. Gould. *An Illustrated Dictionary of Medicine, Biology and Allied Sciences*. Philadelphia: P. Blackiston's Son, 1901.

Griffenhagen and Young. *Patent Medicines*
George B. Griffenhagen and James Harvey Young. "Old English Patent Medicines in America." In *Contributions from The Museum of History and Technology,* 218. United States National Museum Bulletin 10. Washington, D.C.: Smithsonian Institution, 1959.

Haller. "Tartar Emetic"
John S. Haller. "The Use and Abuse of Tartar Emetic in the 19th-Century Materia Medica." *Bulletin of the History of Medicine* 49 (1975): 235–57.

Harrison. *Thomas P. Cope*
Eliza Cope Harrison, ed. *Philadelphia Merchant: The Diary of Thomas P. Cope, 1800–1851.* South Bend, Ind.: Gateway Editions, 1978.

Harvey. *Wilkes-Barré*
Oscar Jewel Harvey. *A History of Wilkes-Barré, Luzerne County, Pennsylvania.* 6 vols. Wilkes-Barre: Kaeder Press, 1909–30.

Historic Philadelphia
Historic Philadelphia: From the Founding until the Early Nineteenth Century. Transactions of the American Philosophical Society, n.s. 43, pt. 1. Philadelphia, 1953.

Hole. *Westtown*
Helen G. Hole. *Westtown Through the Years.* Westtown, Pa.: Westtown Alumni Association, 1942.

Hopkins. *Princes and Peasants*
Donald R. Hopkins. *Princes and Peasants: Smallpox in History.* Chicago: University of Chicago Press, 1983.

HSP   Historical Society of Pennsylvania.

Jackson. *Pennsylvania Navy*
John W. Jackson. *The Pennsylvania Navy 1775–1781: The Defense of the Delaware.* New Brunswick, N.J.: Rutgers University Press, 1974.

Jackson. *With the British Army*
John W. Jackson. *With the British Army in Philadelphia 1777–1778.* San Rafael, Calif.: Presidio Press, 1979.

James. *Quaker Benevolence*
Sydney V. James, *A People among Peoples: Quaker Benevolence in Eighteenth-Century America.* Cambridge: Harvard University Press, 1963.

JCC   U.S. Congress. *Journals of the Continental Congress, 1774–1789.* Edited by Worthington C. Ford et al. 34 vols. Washington, D.C., 1903–37. Reprint. New York: Johnson Reprint Co., 1968.

JHMAS
Journal of the History of Medicine and Allied Sciences.

Jones. *Later Periods of Quakerism*
Rufus M. Jones. *The Later Periods of Quakerism.* 2 vols. London: Macmillan, 1921.

Jordan. *Col. Fam. Phila.*
John W. Jordan. *Colonial Families of Philadelphia.* 2 vols. New York: Lewis, 1911.

Kelsey. *Friends and the Indians*
 Rayner W. Kelsey. *Friends and the Indians.* Philadelphia: The Associated
 Executive Committee of Friends on Indian Affairs, 1917.
King. *Medical World of the Eighteenth Century*
 Lester S. King. *The Medical World of the Eighteenth Century.* Chicago: Univer-
 sity of Chicago Press, 1958.
Labaree. *Boston Tea Party*
 Benjamin Woods Labaree. *The Boston Tea Party.* New York: Oxford University
 Press, 1966.
LaWall. *Pharmacy*
 Charles H. LaWall. *Four Thousand Years of Pharmacy.* Philadelphia: Lippin-
 cott, 1927.
Laws Enacted in the Second Sitting
 *Laws Enacted in Second Sitting of the General Assembly of the Commonwealth of
 Pennsylvania Which Began at Lancaster . . . (February 18, 1778).* Lancaster, Pa.,
 1778.
Lewis, W. *New Dispensatory*
 W. Lewis. *The New Dispensatory.* 5th ed. London, 1785.
Marshall. *Diary Extracts*
 Extracts from the Diary of Christopher Marshall 1774–1781. Edited by William
 Duane. Albany, 1877. Reprint. New York: The New York Times and Arno
 Press, 1969.
Mekeel. "Founding Years"
 Arthur J. Mekeel. "The Founding Years, 1681–1789." In *Friends in the
 Delaware Valley: Philadelphia Yearly Meeting 1681–1981,* ed. John M. Moore,
 14–55. Haverford, Pa.: Friends Historical Association, 1981.
Mekeel. *Relation of the Quakers*
 Arthur J. Mekeel. *The Relation of the Quakers to the American Revolution.*
 Washington, D.C.: University Press of America, 1979.
Miller, R. G. *Federalist City*
 Richard G. Miller. *Philadelphia, the Federalist City: A Study of Urban Politics
 1789–1801.* Port Washington, N.Y.: Kennikat Press, 1976.
Millspaugh. *Medicinal Plants*
 Charles F. Millspaugh. *American Medicinal Plants.* New York: Dover, 1974.
Montgomery. *Textiles*
 Florence M. Montgomery. *Textiles in America 1650–1870: A Dictionary Based
 on Original Documents, Prints and Paintings, Commercial Records, American
 Merchant Papers, Shopkeepers' Advertisements, and Pattern Books with Original
 Swatches of Clothes.* New York: Norton, 1984.
Moore, J. "Moore's Journal"
 "Joseph Moore's Journal." Michigan Pioneer and Historical Society. *Historical
 Collections* 17 (1892): 632–71.
Moore, J. M. *Friends in the Delaware Valley*
 John M. Moore, ed. *Friends in the Delaware Valley: Philadelphia Yearly Meeting
 1681–1981.* Haverford, Pa.: Friends Historical Association, 1981.

Moreau de St. Méry. *Journey*

 Médéric Louis Élle Moreau de Saint-Méry. *Moreau de St. Mery's American Journey (1793–1798)*. Translated and edited by Kenneth Roberts and Anna M. Roberts. Garden City, N.Y.: Doubleday, 1947.

Nash. *Forging Freedom*

 Gary Nash. *Forging Freedom. The Formation of Philadelphia's Black Community.* Cambridge: Harvard University Press, 1988.

NUC *National Union Catalog. Pre-1956 Imprints*. London: Mansell, 1968.

Oaks. "Philadelphians in Exile"

 Robert F. Oaks. "Philadelphians in Exile: The Problem of Loyalty during the American Revolution." *Pennsylvania Magazine of History and Biography* 96 (1972): 298–325.

Oberholtzer. *Robert Morris*

 Ellis Paxson Oberholtzer. *Robert Morris, Patriot and Financier.* New York: Macmillan, 1903.

OED *Oxford English Dictionary*. Oxford, 1933. 2d ed. Oxford: Clarendon Press, 1989.

Ott. *Haitian Revolution*

 Thomas O. Ott. *The Haitian Revolution 1789–1804.* Knoxville: University of Tennessee Press, 1973.

Pa. Archives

 Samuel Hazard et al., eds. *Pennsylvania Archives: Selected and Arranged from Original Documents in the Office of the Secretary of the Commonwealth.* Harrisburg and Philadelphia, 1825–1935.

Pa. Ev. Post

 Pennsylvania Evening Post.

Pa. Gaz.

 Pennsylvania Gazette.

Pa. Hist.

 Pennsylvania History.

Pa. Journal

 Pennsylvania Journal and Weekly Advertiser.

Pa. Packet

 Pennsylvania Packet.

Parr. *London Medical Dictionary*

 Bartholomew Parr. *The London Medical Dictionary.* 2 vols. Philadelphia: Mitchell, Ames, and White, 1819.

Peale. *Selected Papers*

 The Selected Papers of Charles Willson Peale and His Family. Edited by Lillian B. Miller. New Haven: Yale University Press for the National Portrait Gallery, Smithsonian Institution, 1983–.

Philadelphia Yearly Meeting. *Rules of Discipline* (1797)

 Society of Friends. *Rules of Discipline and Christian Advices of the Yearly Meeting of Friends for Pennsylvania and New Jersey.* Philadelphia: Samuel Sansom, 1797.

Philadelphia Yearly Meeting. *Rules of Discipline* (1806)
   Philadelphia Yearly Meeting. *Rules of Discipline of the Yearly Meeting of Friends Held in Philadelphia*. Philadelphia: Kimber, Conrad, 1806.
PMHB   *Pennsylvania Magazine of History and Biography*.
Powell. *Bring Out Your Dead*
   John Harvey Powell. *"Bring Out Your Dead": The Great Plague of Yellow Fever in Philadelphia in 1793*. Philadelphia: University of Pennsylvania Press, 1949.
Powers. "Historic Bridges"
   Fred. Perry Powers. "The Historic Bridges of Philadelphia." *City Historical Society of Philadelphia* 1 (1908–16): 265–316.
Redman. *Account of the Yellow Fever, 1762*
   John Redman. *An Account of the Yellow Fever as it prevailed in Philadelphia in the Autumn of 1762*. Philadelphia, 1865.
Reed. *Joseph Reed*
   William B. Reed. *Life and Correspondence of Joseph Reed*. 2 vols. Philadelphia: Lindsay and Blackiston, 1847.
Rhoads. *Catawissa*
   Willard R. Rhoads. *History of the Catawissa Quaker Meeting at Catawissa, Columbia County, Pa. and the Roaring Creek Quaker Meeting near Numidia, Columbia County, Pa*. Numidia, Pa.: n.p., 1963.
Ritter. *Moravian Church*
   Abraham Ritter. *History of the Moravian Church in Philadelphia from Its Foundation in 1742 to the Present Time*. Philadelphia: Haynes & Zell, 1857.
Rosenbach. *Early American Children's Books*
   A. S. W. Rosenbach. *Early American Children's Books*. Portland, Maine, 1933. Reprint. New York: Kraus Reprint Corporation, 1966.
Rosswurm. *Arms, Country, and Class*
   Steven Rosswurm. *Arms, Country, and Class: The Philadelphia Militia and "Lower Sort" during the American Revolution, 1775–1783*. New Brunswick, N.J.: Rutgers University Press, 1987.
Rucker. "Pain Relief in Obstetrics"
   M. Pierce Rucker. "An Eigththeenth-Century Method of Pain Relief in Obstetrics." *Journal of the History of Medicine and Allied Sciences* 5 (1950): 101–8.
Rush. *Inquiries and Observations*
   Benjamin Rush. *Medical Inquiries and Observations*. 1st ed. 5 vols. Philadelphia: Thomas Dobson, 1794–98; 2d ed., rev. 4 vols. Philadelphia: J. Conrad, 1805; 3d ed., rev. 4 vols. Philadelphia: 1809.
Rush. "Yellow Fever, 1797"
   Benjamin Rush. "An Account of the Bilious Yellow Fever, as It Appeared in Philadelphia in 1797." In *Inquiries and Observations*. 2d ed. 4:1–62.
Rush. "Yellow Fever, 1803"
   Bejamin Rush. "An Account of the Bilious Yellow Fever, as It Appeared in Philadelphia, in 1803." In *Inquiries and Observations*. 2d ed. 4:131–43.
Ryerson. *Revolution Is Now Begun*
   Richard Alan Ryerson. *The Revolution Is Now Begun: The Radical Committees of Philadelphia, 1765–1776*. Philadelphia: University of Pennsylvania Press, 1978.

Salinger. *Labor and Indentured Servants*
Sharon V. Salinger. *"To Serve Well and Faithfully": Labor and Indentured Servants in Pennsylvania 1682–1800.* Cambridge: Cambridge University Press, 1987.

Scharf and Westcott. *Philadelphia*
J. Thomas Scharf and Thompson Westcott. *History of Philadelphia 1609–1884.* 3 vols. Philadelphia: Everts, 1884.

Scholten. *Childbearing*
Catherine M. Scholten. *Childbearing in American Society 1650–1850.* New York: New York University Press, 1985.

Sellers. *Charles Willson Peale*
Charles Coleman Sellers. *Charles Willson Peale.* Memoirs of the American Philosophical Society 23, pts. 1–2, Philadelphia, 1947.

Sellers. *Mr. Peale's Museum*
Charles Coleman Sellers. *Mr. Peale's Museum: Charles Willson Peale and the First Popular Museum of Natural Science and Art.* New York: Norton, 1980.

Siddall. "Bloodletting"
A. Clair Siddall. "Bloodletting in American Obstetrical Practice 1800–1945." *Bulletin of the History of Medicine* 54 (1980): 101–10.

Skinner. *Medical Terms*
Henry Alan Skinner. *The Origin of Medical Terms.* 2d ed. New York: Hafner, 1970.

Smedley. *Catalog of Westtown*
Susanna Smedley. *Catalog of Westtown through the Years.* Westtown, Pa.: Westtown Alumni Association, 1945.

Smith, P. H. *Letters of the Delegates*
Paul H. Smith, ed. *Letters of the Delegates to Congress.* Washington, D.C.: Library of Congress, 1976–.

Smith, W. G. *English Proverbs*
William George Smith, comp. *The Oxford Dictionary of English Proverbs.* 3d ed. revised by F. P. Wilson. Oxford: Clarendon Press, 1970.

Statutes at Large
Commonwealth of Pennsylvania. *The Statutes at Large of Philadelphia from 1682 to 1801.* Compiled by James T. Mitchell and Henry Flanders. 16 vols. Harrisburg, Pa.: 1896–1911.

Stoneburner and Stoneburner. *Quaker Women*
Carol Stoneburner and John Stoneburner, eds. *The Influence of Quaker Women on American History.* Biographical Studies. Lewiston, N.Y.: Mellen Press, 1986.

Stryker. *Forts on the Delaware*
William S. Stryker. *The Forts on the Delaware in the Revolutionary War.* Trenton, N.J.: Murphy, 1901.

Swan. *Plain & Fancy*
Susan Burrows Swan. *Plain & Fancy: American Women and Their Needlework 1700–1850.* New York: Holt, Rinehart & Winston, 1977.

Teeters. *Cradle of the Penitentiary*
  Negley K. Teeters. *The Cradle of the Penitentiary: The Walnut Street Jail at Philadelphia 1773–1835*. Philadelphia: Temple University Press, 1955.
Thacher. *New American Dispensatory*
  James Thacher. *The New American Dispensatory*. 2d ed. Boston: Wait and Williams, 1813.
Thayer. *Israel Pemberton*
  Theodore Thayer. *Israel Pemberton, King of the Quakers*. Philadelphia: Historical Society of Pennsylvania, 1943.
Thomas, K. *Religion and Decline of Magic*
  Keith Thomas. *Religion and the Decline of Magic*. New York: Scribners, 1971.
Thomas, R. *Modern Domestic Medicine*
  Robert Thomas. *Modern Domestic Medicine: Being a Treatise Divested of Professional Terms on the Nature, Causes, Symptoms, and Treatment of the Diseases of Men, Women, and Children, in Both Cold and Warm Climates: With Appropriate Prescriptions in English*. New York: Collins, 1829.
Toner, *Inoculation in Pa.*
  J. M. Toner. "Inoculation in Pennsylvania." *Transactions of the Medical Society of the State of Pennsylvania*, 16th annual sess. 4th ser. 1 (1865): 163–82.
Watson, G. *New Cambridge Bibliography*
  George Watson, ed. *The New Cambridge Bibliography of English Literature*. 4 vols. Cambridge: Cambridge University Press, 1971.
Watson, J. F. *Annals*
  John F. Watson. *Annals of Philadelphia and Pennsylvania in the Olden Time*. 3 vols. Philadelphia: Stuart, 1891.
Weiss. "More's Cheap Repository Tracts"
  Harry B. Weiss, "Hannah More's Cheap Repository Tracts in America." *Bulletin of the New York Public Library* 50 (1946): 539–49, 634–39.
Weiss and Weiss. *Snuff Mills of New Jersey*
  Henry B. Weiss and Frances M. Weiss. *The Early Snuff Mills of New Jersey*. Trenton, N.J.: New Jersey Agricultural Society, 1962.
White, *Management of Pregnant and Lying-In Women*
  Charles White. *A Treatise on the Management of Pregnant and Lying-in Women* . . . Worcester, Mass.: Isaiah Thomas, 1793.
Wolman. *"Tale of Two Colonial Cities"*
  Roslyn S. Wolman. "A Tale of Two Colonial Cities: Inoculation against Smallpox in Philadelphia and Boston." *Transactions and Studies of the College of Physicians of Philadelphia*. 4th ser., 45 (1978): 338–47.

Henry and Elizabeth Drinker: Their Children and Grandchildren

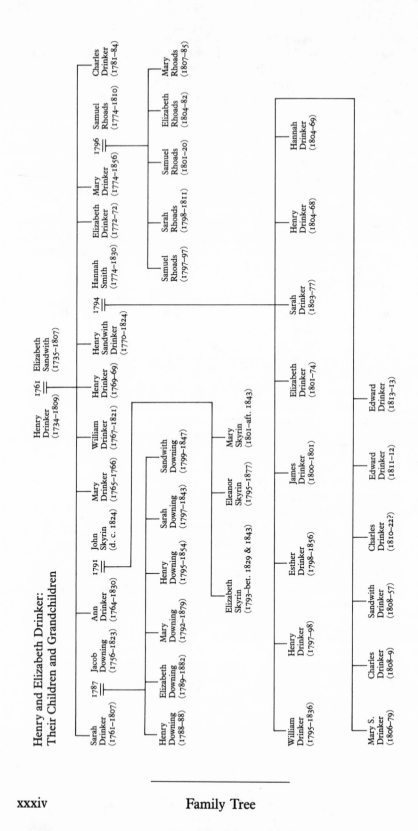

The Diary
of
Elizabeth Drinker

Silhouettes of Elizabeth Sandwith Drinker (courtesy of the Historical Society of Pennsylvania) and Henry Drinker, at age 57 (from History of the Drinker Family *by Henry S. Drinker [1961]; used by permission of the Drinker family).*

1. Youth and Courtship, 1758–1761

Elizabeth Sandwith introduces herself through her needlework. Preceding her chronological entries, and not reproduced here, is a compilation of hand-wrought accomplishments for the years 1757–60. The list of nearly one hundred items presents a young woman who was both skilled and productive. Elizabeth knitted stockings, plaited watchstrings and whipstrings, and worked pincushions, pocketbooks, and purses, most of which she either gave or perhaps sold to friends.

Her literary entries begin on October 8, 1758, when the orphaned Sandwith sisters were already living with Ann Warner and her daughters. Daily life revolved around Quaker meetings, socializing, and shopping, activities that were interspersed with country outings where she and her friends picked flowers and sampled strawberries. While an occasional toothache punctuated the sweetness of life, and a not so occasional funeral attested to its uncertain duration, the constant round of activities—and the absence of complaints—suggests that Elizabeth Sandwith led a busy, happy, and satisfying life.

Although she had known Henry Drinker even before he had married her dear friend Ann Swett, the young widower entered Elizabeth's life as a potential suitor on November 6, 1758, a little less than six months after the death of his wife. In three weeks Henry began to spend evenings at the Warners, and after his ten-month trip to England, which ended on June 20, 1760, the courtship intensified. Henry visited Elizabeth nearly every day or evening thereafter, and Elizabeth made watchstrings and garters for her beau. Elizabeth's "distress'd" mind as well as the "memoriable" evening of July 26, 1760, indicate that she and Henry were committed to each other by the summer of that year, and their wedding on January 13, 1761, comes as a happy ending to this chapter of her life.

1758

1758 Octor. the 8   First Day, drank Tea at Jos. Howell's; call'd to see M. Foulk, who was lyeing in; with her Daughter Elizabeth.

9   Stay'd at Home all Day: M Parr Drank Tea with us.

12   Went to Meeting[1] in the Morning, spent the Afternoon with S. Sansom, at Robt. Lewis's: call'd in the Evening at Danl. Stanton's: and at S. Plumly's.

16   Spent the Afternoon at Isreal Pemberton's, call'd in the Evening at Saml. Sansom's & at J. Foulk's.

1758 Octor. the 17   Went to Meeting in the Morning, spent the Afternoon at S. Sansom's.

[Nov.] 6   Stay'd at Home all Day; H Drinker drank Tea with us.

7   Went to Youths Meeting;[2] spent part of the Evening at S. Sansom's.

1758 Novemr the 18   Stay'd at Home in the Morning; took a walk in the

1. The Society of Friends was organized around a series of meetings, the smallest being a particular meeting, consisting of a group of individuals who came together for worship at regularly scheduled times (at least once a week on Sunday—or First Day, as Quakers called it—and often more frequently) and to transact corporate business. These local meetings were also called preparative meetings when they had permanent status and indulged meetings when they had temporary status. The members of two or more preparative meetings constituted a monthly meeting, which kept the membership records and had the power to establish preparative and indulged meetings and to receive, disown, and discipline members (Rhoads, *Catawissa*, 8–9; Brinton, *Quaker Practice;* Barbour and Frost, *Quakers,* 77).

2. As the Quaker population in Pennsylvania grew, the Society of Friends became especially concerned with overseeing the behavior of their young, particularly with instructing them in the tenets of the Society of Friends and keeping them from misbehaving at meeting. Following the advice of the Philadelphia Yearly Meeting in 1694, Philadelphia Friends established a special youths' meeting in 1696. The plan called for meetings four times a year, where regular Quaker worship would be augmented by special readings and advice to youth concerning their behavior (Sydney V. James, "Quaker Meetings and Education in the Eighteenth Century," *Quaker History* 51 (1962): 95–99; Philadelphia Yearly Meeting, *Rules of Discipline of the Yearly Meeting of Friends Held in Philadelphia*. [Philadelphia: Kimber, Conrad, 1806], 27).

Afternoon with Reb. Rawle; in the Evening Rec'd a Letter from Jamacia; by HDr.

20 Took a Walk in the Morning to Sarah Plumly's; call'd at Uncles; at C. Nicholdson's; & at J. Richardson's; Dine'd and spent the Afternoon at Betsy Moodes: help'd to Quilt: spent the Evening at F. Rawle's.

[Dec.] 4 Spent the Afternoon at Neighr. Shoemaker Betsy Moode & HD spent the Evening with us.

1759

[Jan.] 5 Went to Frankford Meeting; W Parr, M Parr, MES: Testimonies[1] borne by Sarah Morris, S. Spavold, and two other Friends. Heny. Drinkr. came after Meeting to WP's.

16 Went to Meeting in the Morning; went After Dinner to buy Wosted; call'd at T Say's; HD spent the Evening.

20 W & N Parr call'd in the Morning; went with N Parr to Shops; stay'd at home in the Afternoon & Evening.

[Feb.] 5 Went to Meeting in the Morning; it being Quarterly Meeting;[2] call'd at C. Nicholdson, and at Uncle Jervis's; spent the Afternoon at S Plumly's, with E. White, J Kearney, H Hicks; & MS; it being a visit to the Bride, Mary Searson, formerly Lord; S Plumly sick in Bed;—call'd in the Evening at S Sansom's & at R Rawle's.

25 First Day; Stay'd at home all Day.—had one Tooth drawn, in the Morning, and another attempted; suffer'd much thereby.

1759 March the 1 Stay'd at Home all Day.—Benja. Swett Senr. Saml. Sansom Senr. and Hannah Callender; spent the Afternoon, at Fd. Warners.— pull'd out a Tooth in the Evening; which the Tooth-drawer had drawn, before and replaced.[3]

1. ED uses the word *testimony* in several different yet related ways. In general, Quaker testimony and concerns were public statements that defined the behavioral code required of Society members. Such rules included, but were not limited to, plain dress, pacifism, and the eschewal of oath taking. During meeting, one member might appear in testimony to offer a personal statement of belief (or a concern over the widespread breach of Quaker guidelines), while another member might present a testimonial regarding the exemplary conduct of a particular person. Sentiments could also be expressed by way of testimony at home among Friends or in the form of a letter (explanation courtesy of J. William Frost, Director, Friends Historical Library, Swarthmore College).

2. All the monthly meetings in a given area met together four times a year for worship, fellowship, the transaction of business, and the discussion of common problems. They also would undertake projects that needed more support than a local or monthly meeting could muster (Brinton, *Quaker Practice*; Barbour and Frost, *Quakers*, 77).

3. This was a common practice in early American dentistry. A toothdrawer would reimplant the original tooth into the patient's mouth in the hope that it had enough life to make a good implant and would fit the socket better than an artificial tooth (Samuel H. Willens, "Dr. Nathaniel Peabody and His Book *The Art of Preserving Teeth*," *Bulletin of the History of Dentistry* 28 [1980]: 85).

3 Stay'd at Home all Day. B. Moode came home with Polly in the Afternoon, haveing been to the Burial of Sally Howell, seacond Daughter of Jos. Howell; who Dye'd of a Mortification[4] in her Mouth.

5 Stay'd at home all Day; sore Throat so bad, was oblige'd to send for the Doctor after 10 o'clock at Night.

1759 March the 25 First Day, stay'd at home in the Morning; had a bad Cold;—went to Meeting in the Afternoon and Evening; half Year Meeting;[5] Jacob Howell & Sarah Wamsley drank Tea at Fd. Warner's.

[Apr.] 2 Took a walk in the Afternoon call'd at H, Robinson's; at Uncle Jervis's; drank Tea at Betsy Moode's, call'd at S. Sansom's, Sammy Sansom spent the Evening with us.

11 Stay'd at home all Day; was let Blood[6] in the Morning, for a Cough, and cold on the Stomach.

4. In medical terms, *mortification* meant the loss of vitality, death, and subsequent putrefaction of a part of the body while the rest of the body was still alive. Medical writers differed on the causes and types of mortifications, but agreed that when preceded by inflammation, mortification often meant the forming of gangrene on the affected part, followed by sphacelus, which occurred when the part became brown or black, flaccid, and putrid. Mortification of the mouth, the phrase used here, often referred to pleurisy, an inflammation of membranes around the lungs (Robert Hooper, *Quincy's Lexicon Medicum* [Philadelphia: E. & R. Parker, M. Carey & Son, & Benjamin Warner, 1817]; Parr, *London Medical Dictionary*; King, *Medical World of the Eighteenth Century*, 85–88, 107).

5. In 1712 the Philadelphia Yearly Meeting decided to hold a two-day public worship meeting annually in the spring. The meeting was held just for worship and not for the administrative business of the Society of Friends. It was first held in May, but was soon changed to March, six months before the yearly meeting, and thus became known as the Half Yearly Meeting (Mekeel, "Founding Years," 25; Frost, *Quaker Family*, 4).

6. Bloodletting was a standard treatment for various inflammations, particularly of the lungs, as well as for pneumonia and related illnesses. It was also used as a prophylactic device at certain times of the year such as the spring and fall to maintain the body's balance. In late eighteenth-century Philadelphia it was also used to treat pregnant women. As the tools available to the bleeder became more sophisticated, bloodletting became a widely used therapy in the eighteenth century.

There were two major categories of bloodletting: *general bloodletting*, which involved opening an artery or, more commonly, a vein (usually in the elbow) with a lancet, and *local bloodletting*, which severed only the capillaries and used suction provided by heated cups or leeches to withdraw blood. Each cup held four or five ounces of blood, and several were generally used in any procedure. Because American leech species were considered inferior, Americans frequently imported leeches from Europe. A Swedish leech at maximum efficiency could take an ounce of blood; small children were treated with two leeches, adults with twenty or more.

In England bloodletting had been the special province of barber-surgeons. In the absence of guilds in the American colonies, specialists such as the Hailer family in Philadelphia, often used by the Drinkers, advertised their skills as bleeders. Doctors Kuhn, Rush, and others bled members of the Drinker household themselves or recommended bloodletting specialists (A. Davis and Appel, *Bloodletting Instruments*; King, *Medical World of the Eighteenth Century*, 318–20; Rucker, "Pain Relief in Obstetrics," 101–8; Siddall, "Bloodletting," 101–10).

15 First Day; went to Meeting 3 times, HD, call'd after Evening Meeting;—
we were Allarm'd by the Cry of Fire at 11 o'clock at Night; (have this last
Winter been very much Favour'd on the Acct of Fire).

16 Stay'd at home all Day.

1759 April the 17 . . .
  The Fire which happn'd on the 15th. Instant; was a Bake-House of Mark
Cooles; which was burn'd down, and a large quantity of Bread distroy'd.

[May] 5 M Parr spent part of the Morning with us, and drank Tea in the
Afternoon, W Parr call'd. Betsy Moode drank Tea, and spent part of the
Evening, went part of the way home with her; had a long discourse with B
Moode upstairs, in the Dark.

14 Breakfast'd, dinn'd, and drank Tea, at Betsy Moodes; she came home
with me towards Evening; went to Sarah Browns silk dyer, return'd to A
Warners, spent part of the Evening togeather; A Warner, Polly, &c, return'd
from Buybary; this evening.

15 Went to Meeting in the Morning, took a walk after Tea in the Afternoon;
with A Warner Senr. A Warner Junr. B. Warner MES; to the Church Burying
Ground, read the Tomb Stones.

25 Went to Monthly Meeting, saw Jacob Lewis, and Sarah Mifflin pass;[7]
went home with Betsy Moode, dinn'd and spent the Afternoon there; taken
very sick there; H Drinker spent the Evening Chez nous.

31 MS, came home early in the Morning after seting up all night with M.
Foulk. I Went to Meeting in the Forenoon; spent the afternoon at J. Searsons;
call'd towards Evening at Uncles; and at Abrahm. Mitchell's, to see Jos.
Hicks, who lay ill of the Nerverous Fever:[8] . . .

  7. Friends who wished to marry needed the approval of both parents or guardians and their
Quaker meeting. The couple was required to appear before two monthly meetings before the
marriage was approved. This was called *passing the meeting*. (Frost, *Quaker Family*, 172–73).
  8. The nervous fever was generally associated with typhus, after William Cullen, an
eighteenth-century British physician famed for his classification of diseases, so described it.
The symptoms included a quick, low pulse, chilliness and flushing in turn, giddiness and pain
in the head, nausea, and vomiting. There were, however, many descriptions of nervous fevers,
not all of which were typhus, and there were also illnesses that presented certain nervous
symptoms but were not considered the nervous fever (Cullen, *Practice of Physic*, 1:109–15;
Benjamin Rush, "Outlines of a Theory of Fever," in Rush, *Inquiries and Observations*, 1:48–
49; Buchan, *Domestic Medicine* [1799], 137–41; Parr, *London Medical Dictionary*; King, *Medical
World of the Eighteenth Century*, 130–31).

[July] 13, HD; call'd at dinner-time, to ask us to go to Wm. Callenders place at Point which we declin'd; went to R Steels to buy Silk—Spent the Afternoon at T Says, HD spent the E.

27 Went after Dinner with Becky Rawle, to Buy Chinia, at Peter Thomsons—was awake almost all Night with a bad Tooth Ake.

Augt. the 1 Took a dose of Salts;[9] stay'd at home all Day; Aunt Jervis, Betsy and Polly, with Hannah Ward; spent the After-noon with us.

22 Stay'd at home all Day; Wm. Parr, call'd in the Morning,—had a bad spell of the sick Head-Ake;—Hannah Moode came after Tea and stay'd 'till Night,—Fd. Warner came from Germantown, where she had been 2 or 3 days—with Becky Rawles, and Katty Howell who had spent part of the Summer there, with their Children, as the Small Pox is in Town,[10] and the Weather has been very warm; Joshua Howell sup'd Chez nous; HD. call'd but went away unwell.

Sepr. the 1 Stay'd at home all Day: Henry Drinker came at Noon, and bid us Adieu. he left Philada. after Dinner; several of his Friends accompanying him to Chester or Marcus-Hook, where he designs on the Morrow, with Sammy Sansom & Benny Swett, to embark in the Snow Recovery, Nathanel[11] Falconer Master for Bristol.—Betsy Moode spent part of the Evening with us.

9 First Day. Frans. Rawle, with his Cousin Sally Rawle, came to Germantown, in the Morning. MESand. could not go to Meeting, for want of Clean

9. Many kinds of salts were used medicinally in the eighteenth century. Most, such as Glauber's salt (sodium sulfate), introduced into medical use by Johann Glauber in the seventeenth century, had a cathartic effect on the body, inducing the intestines and neighboring organs to purge their contents. Other salts used similarly were Rochelle salt (sodium potassium tartrate) and Epsom salt (magnesium sulfate). Cathartics were used to treat constipation, colic, dysentery, fevers, and many other ailments. Dr. John Redman used saline purges to treat yellow fever victims in 1762 (Estes, "Therapeutic Practice," 365–83; Redman, *Account of the Yellow Fever, 1762*).

10. A smallpox epidemic struck Philadelphia in 1759. Mortality was particularly high among those not inoculated, and it was estimated that five hundred to six hundred deaths were caused by the disease that year. Philadelphia was especially prone to outbreaks of smallpox during the French and Indian War (1756–63) because of the many unimmunized troops and refugees who streamed through the city. During the war years alone there were three major outbreaks, and between 1712 and 1773 Philadelphia suffered ten major outbreaks. According to Benjamin Franklin, there were five "visitations of smallpox" between 1730 and 1752, and Drinker noted several others between 1759 and 1775 (Toner, "Inoculation in Pa."; Wolman, "Tale of Two Colonial Cities"; Hopkins, *Princes and Peasants*," 257; Benjamin Franklin to John Perkins, August 13, 1752, in Franklin, *Papers*, 340–41).

11. The name "Fortuner" crossed out. Although "Falconer" is correct, the latter name may not be in ED's handwriting.

Cloaths. Molly Foulk, & Betsy Bringhurst, drank tea with us.—came to Philada. this Evening.

13   Went to Meeting in the Morning, call'd at M Burrows, went after Meeting to Hustons Store with H. Callender &c. call'd after-dinner at R Steels, and at H Steels, to see his son Jemmy who was this Week inoculated for the Small Pox,[12] spent the After-noon at J. Searsons, call'd towards Evening at Wido. Maddoxs. . . .

22   Polly Sandwith sat up last Night, with Neighr. Callender. ES. had Nancy Warner for a Bed Fellow.—Wm. & Sarah Walmsley came to Town this Morning, Breakfast'd and Dinn'd at AWs—went after Tea with Sarah Wamsley to Shops; Betsy Moode spent part of the Evening with us. went part of the way home with her—Wm. & Sarah Walmsley Lodg'd at AWs.

25   Went to Meeting in the Morning, and in the Afternoon to Meeting of Discipline[13]—Drank Tea at James James's, where we went to see Hannah Hicks, who is unwell with the Ague and Feaver. . . .

26   Stay'd at home all Day. Eight Women Friends dinn'd at AWs which made 14 of the best sort, our selves included.—H. Ward & R. Knight call'd in the Evening.

28   Stay'd at home all Day; Polly and Nancy, went this after-noon to the

12. Smallpox inoculation began in the American colonies in 1721 when Zabdiel Boylston, a Boston physician, learned about the practice from Cotton Mather, who had read about it in the Levant and also learned of it from an African servant. Over half of Boston's nearly eleven thousand persons contracted the disease that year, and almost 15 percent of those infected died. Although only six of the 287 persons Boylston inoculated died, his work excited much opposition on both religious and socioeconomic grounds.

In inoculation, matter taken from a pustule of someone who had caught the disease naturally was placed on several small cuts made by a needle or a lancet in the arm or leg muscles of the person receiving the inoculation. This method produced a milder, less fatal form of smallpox, although the person was still a carrier of the disease. (John B. Blake, *Public Health in the Town of Boston 1630–1822* [Cambridge: Harvard University Press, 1959], chapter two; Kenneth Silverman, *The Life and Times of Cotton Mather* [New York: Harper & Row, 1984], 339–40; Franklin, *Papers*, 4:341–42; Toner, "Inoculation in Pa."; Wolman, "Tale of Two Colonial Cities").

13. The meeting for discipline or the committee for discipline met at the Philadelphia Yearly Meeting to compile the Book of Discipline, the formal compendium of Quaker belief and practice. While work on the book was usually limited to committee members, their meetings were open to all Friends who wanted to attend (Richard Bauman, *For the Reputation of Truth: Politics, Religion, and Conflict among the Pennsylvania Quakers, 1750–1800* [Baltimore: Johns Hopkins University Press, 1971], 50; Society of Friends, *Rules of Discipline and Christian Advices of the Yearly Meeting of Friends for Pennsylvania and New Jersey* [Philadelphia: Samuel Sansom, 1797]; earlier manuscript books of discipline are owned by the Friends Historical Library, Swarthmore College, Swarthmore, Pa.).

Burial of Sally Lloyd, Daughter of Hannah Lloyd,—Hannah Ward, & R Knight, call'd this Evening.

[Oct.] 24th   Went this Morning to Thos. Says, whose Daughter Becky, lays ill, in the Small Pox, which she has taken in the Natural way; and to most that take it Naturaly (at this time) it proves mortal.[14] . . .

1759, Octor. the 26 . . . spent this After-noon at S Sansom's, Esther Mifflen & Daughter there, went in the Evening to Thos. Say's, whoes little Becky dyed this Morning: Frans. & Becky Rawle sup'd with us.

[Nov.] 9   This Morning Rachel Budd brought us a noat from R Say, requireing (if we had a desire to see Tommy Say in this World) we would come Immeadatly, which we did, and found him very ill, tho in his Senses, he continued untill Evening—when he departed this Life in the 20th year of his age, Rachel Wells spent this afternoon with us.

1759: Novr. the 10,   William Parr call'd this Morning M Winter fitted a Body Lining,[15] Betsy & Nelly Moode spent this Afternoon and part of the Evening with us,—Betsy went with me to T Says to see Tommy's corps.—We were Alarmm'd this evening by the cry of Fire, prov'd a Chimney directly oppisite to AWs.

1759. Decr. the 3   Stay'd at home all Day, very cold Weather A Carpenter's Shop, on Society Hill, took Fire,[16] this Morning at about 9 o'clock, the Wind blowing Violently at N W; severel Houses were burnt down.

4th   Went to Meeting this Morning. Phebe Broom from NewPort, call'd to see us this After-noon—begun to read Pope's Homer; the Iliad.[17]

---

14. While most patients who suffered from smallpox eventually recovered, ED was correct in noting the differences in mortality between those who contracted it naturally and those who were inoculated. Accurate statistics do not exist for Philadelphia, but in the Boston epidemic of 1752 almost 10 percent of those who caught the disease naturally died, and in the 1764 epidemic that figure was close to 18 percent. The comparable mortality figures for those inoculated were 1.4 and .9 percent (for a comparative view of English cities see Peter Razzell, *The Conquest of Smallpox: The Impact of Inoculation on Smallpox Mortality in Eighteenth-Century Britain* [Firle: Caliban Books, 1977], 113–37; Hopkins, *Princes and Peasants*, 41).

15. *Body* or *bodies* was the original form of the word *bodice*, the undergarment also known as a corset, worn by American women in the eighteenth century (Estelle Ansley Worrell, *Early American Costume* [Harrisburg: Stackpole Books, 1975], 73).

16. See *Pa. Gaz.*, Dec. 6, 1759.

17. Alexander Pope, *The Iliad of Homer* (London: W. Boyer, Bernard Lintott, 1715–20 [*Brit. Mus. Cat.*]).

1760

1760: Jenry. the 7   Stay'd at home all Day: T Moore, call'd this Morning to know, if we would go, to the Accadamy,[1] to hear the Lectures upon Electricity, did not suit us to go—Johney Searson drank Tea with us.

11th.   Stay'd within all Day. Jos. & Katty Howell, Frans and Becky Rawle, drank tea at AWs Nancy, went out to set up with the Corps of Hannah Lynn.

19th   Went out this Morning after Breakfast—calld at Patty Powell's, for mittens, stop'd at C Jones's, call'd at S Whartons, dinn'd and spent the Afternoon at B Moodes—call'd in the Evening at Uncle Jerviss—Charles came home with me.

20th   First Day: went to Meeting this Morning—Daniel Stanton, and John Pemberton, appeard in Testimony, S Morris in Prayer; In the Afternoon, Becky Jones, [H] Willims & David Estaugh, preach'd—Wm. & Sarah Fisher drank Tea at AWs Joshua & Katty Howell spent the Evening—stay'd from Meeting this Evening, it being very dark & the Streets dirty.

27   First Day: B Trotter, and Becky Jones, appeard in testimony, this morning; had a Silent Meeting[2] in the Afternoon;—we were detaind from Meeting this Evening, by rain.

[Feb.] 8th.   Spent this Afternoon, with Molly Foulk at the Widdow Brin-

---

1. The College and Academy of Philadelphia was offering a series of lectures and experiments on electricity. A professor of English and oratory, Ebenezer Kinnersley, was the main speaker; admission to each lecture was a half a dollar (*Pa. Gaz.*, Dec. 27, 1759).

2. The purpose of the Quaker meeting was to allow the community of Quaker believers to experience the inner light, a spiritual state not attainable by such earthly means as speech and prayer. Quakers distrusted set prayers and an ordained ministry—creations of man's reasoning powers, an earthly faculty—because the personal experiencing of God through the inner light required the suppression of those very qualities. Persons who entered the Quaker ministry did so because they believed they had been moved by the divine spirit to speak; though they both preached and prayed at meetings, their sermons and prayers were expected to be spontaneous and from the heart. Ideally all Quaker meetings would have been held in silence, but in practice only a minority were (Richard Bauman, "Speaking in the Light: The Role of the Quaker Minister," in *Explorations in the Ethnography of Speaking*, ed. Richard Bauman and Joel Sherzer [Cambridge: Cambridge University Press, 1974], 144–60).

ghursts, where we were entertain'd with divers objects in a Micrescope; and with several expediments in Electricity.

1760. Febry. the 11. Billy Parr, and his Boy Sipteo, came for us with the Chaise, before 4 o'clock, this Afternoon, Arriv'd at Point[3] before 6 o'clock, roades very bad, found Peggy, and the Children well.

17th. First Day, Stay'd within all Day, John Drinker, Junr. came to Point this Afternoon, he with Thos. Bowlsbys drank Tea with us.—Received two letters from HD, one from Bristol, the other from London.

March the 15th. 1760 Went out this Afternoon with sister, called at Widdow Maddoxs, then went to Isaac Howells, to leave silk with Polly Parrish to make a Bonnit—call'd at Uncles, then went to Betsy Moodes, drank Tea there, with Sally Morris and Ra. Reave; spent part of the Evening avac les Filles.[4]

[Apr.] 3d Stay'd from Meeting within all Day—unwell with a cold,—read in this Days Paper, an account of a Terrible Fire, which happn'd in Boston.[5] . . .

April the 11th. 1760 Went this Morning after Breakfast, to Betsy Moodes, who was gone out, the Girls busy in the Garden, went from thence to S Whartons, stay'd a short time there, then came back to EMs. who was not yet return'd, went to Uncle Jerviss, stay'd some time there, went again to Betsys, where I stay'd dinner, and spent the Afternoon, and part of the Evening.

13. First Day: went to Meeting as usual—B[T], DS, &c, spoke this Morning, Daniel was led in a particular manner, to speak of tryeing times which Would come upon the people, if they did not soon repent,—in the Afternoon we had silence, went home with B Rawle, drank tea there, with S Fisher— went to Evening meeting, where Polly Pussey, Elizth. Morgan, Ann Widdowfield, J. Storor, and D Stanton, appeard in testimony.

April the 23: 1760 Went out after dinner, call'd at Widw. Childs, spent the Afternoon at C. Morgans, H Ward drank tea with us,—call'd at John Knights where HW boards, and at R Wellss.

28 Went this morning to Neighr. Callenders, who are busy, moveing to Point no Point, haveing sold their House to Thos. Richee,—spent this Afternoon at

3. Point No Point, a bulge of land on the Delaware River. Formerly northeast of Philadelphia, today it is within the city limits, north of Kensington (Scharf and Westcott, *Philadelphia*, vol. 1, endpaper).
4. With the girls.
5. Accounts of the fire that destroyed much of Boston on Mar. 20, 1760, appeared in *Pa. Gaz.* and *Pa. Journal*, Apr. 3, 1760.

Richd. Wellss, Mary Pemberton, Senr and Nanny Lloyd there, call'd in the Evening at Willm. Callenders, Hannah Callendr. and Katty Smith, sup'd and loged at our House,—one Wm. Ricketts, a man, who serv'd Joshua Howells, was this Afternoon drown'd, endeavouring to git up a Hoggshead of Sugar, which had[6] fell in the River—On First Day last, was Buried, Peter Pappin, de pre fountaine, our Frence Master.

May the 1.   One John Jackman, a young man from Barbadoes, Breakfasted, with us, he log'd here last night,—call'd this Morning at S Sansom's, went to meeting, went after meeting, home with B Moode, came home to dinner.— Molly Searson, Polly and Sally Pemberton, and Black Jude, spent the After- noon with us—John Searson call'd after tea, FR, call'd this Evening.

8th.   Call'd this morning at Joshua Howells, and at Frans. Rawles, then went to meeting, John ——— something, and Susanna Townsend, were married,— call'd after meeting to see Sarah Fisher, who lays-in, with her Daughter, Elizabeth,—spent this Afternoon, at Jonathan Zanes, who has been disabled, (next October will be five years) by a fall from his Horse,—went towards Evening, to Betsy Moodes, stayd a while there, Betsy and Nelly, came part of the way home with us. I had the Sick Head Ake, after I came home.

1760 May the 14.   K, & H, Callender, breakfast'd and Dinn'd with us, went out after dinner with Hannah, call'd at S Sansoms, from thence went to Wm. Coopers, came back to S Sansoms—drank tea there, went after Hannah left me, to Betsy Moodes, stop'd at Billy Morriss—found sister at Betsys, went up stairs with BM, where we read part of Samy Sansoms journal, which he lent me, went from Betsys with Sally Parrish left her, and call'd at Uncles, Charles, came home with us—Margt. Allen, Wife to our Chief Justice, and sister to our present Governour, was this Afternoon, interr'd.

1760: May the 20.   Went this Morning to Meeting, Peggy Parr, with her children, call'd while we were out,—call'd after Dinner, at J Foulks, to see Peggy—left sister there, and went to Betsy Moodes—who is still unwell, Polly came there to us, sat up stairs, where Betsy read, to Hannah, Nelly, Sister, and self,—Sammy Sansoms Journal.

31   Stay'd at home all Day: John Paul, call'd in the Afternoon, Sister busy ironing—myself makeing up Pincushons.

[June] 2d.   Hannah Callender came this Morning, dinn'd with us, was so kind as to leave her diary with sister,—spent this Afternoon at Widdow Dowars's, our old Neighbour a hansome young widdow, saw a large peice of a

6. The word "falling" crossed out.

---

bone, which was taken out of the Leg of a little Girl, who boards with her, an extraordinary cure. . . .

7   Stay'd within all Day, Betsy Parker, came in the Morning, Becky Rawle, and Catty Howell, in the afternoon—imploy'd many ways[7] this day.

June the 9: 1760   Stay'd at home all Day: dull Weather, cold weather for the Season Betsy Parker came in the Afternoon to fitt Gowns, Betsy Moode, came in the Evening, stay'd but a short time.

20th.   Stay'd within all Day: work'd in the Morning at my Purse, Henry Drinker call'd this afternoon, he arrived here, since dinner from London, in the James & Mary Capt. Friend.

23d.   Stay'd at home all Day, rainy weather, work'd at my Purse in the Morning, help'd quilt Nancy Warners Peticoat in the Afternoon.

24   Went to Meeting this Morning B Moode came home with me, Kate. and Hannah Callender, dinn'd at AWs—I went this Afternoon to Betsy Moodes drank tea there, Hannah and Nelly gone out—Betsy and self took a walk after tea by the Negros Burying Ground,[8] Numbers of People out, came home with Betsy stay'd but a short time, call'd at Uncle Jerviss found when I came home Becky Rawle, Francis and B supd—HD. came.

June the 25: 1760   Spent this Morning with sister, up stairs, looking over accounts. B. Moode came after dinner, stay'd till 5 o'clock Molly Foulk sent to desire we would drink tea with her, did so, came home in the Evening, a Gust of Thunder and Lightning, HD, spent part of the Evening.

30   Stay'd at home all Day, Jude came this Morning to see us, I am ready to think she has run away, says her Master uses her ill, poor Child. . . .

[July] 4   Spent the greatest part of this Day up stairs with sister, looking over accounts, HD, came at 10 o'clock, stay'd till past 11, unseasonable hours, my judgment dont coincide with my Actions, tis a pity, but I hope to mend.

7   . . . Sister and self left home before tea, with Judath Foulks chair and Horse, Arrived at Wm Parr, Point by 6 o'clock, Peggy well, Billy from home,—Many agreeable hours have I spent at this delightfull place—this

7. The word "to" crossed out.
8. The Negro burial ground, a separate section of the Strangers' Burial Ground, located at what is now Washington Square in Philadelphia, was a popular meeting place for the city's black population, both free and enslaved (Nash, *Forging Freedom*, 13; J. F. Watson, *Annals*, 2:265).

Morning was bury'd from Neigr. Mountgomerys a Man who with several others, was drown'd on sixth Day last.

13th.   First Day: Billy came home last night or rather this Morning: John Wright, his Daughter, and Capt. Roberson came to Point before breakfast, HD, came also, they all spent this day with us, took a walk after dinner to the Summer-House, round the bank as far as the Boat House, some one propos'd going into the boat, which we being of our guard comply'd with, row'd a little way up the Creek, landed at the Horse-Shoe, I don't like such doings on a First Day. walk'd home by the retreat, after tea, our coumpany all but HD— departed, I took a walk with him in the Gardins, to the Summer-House, round the Meadow banks &c—he left Point between 9 and 10.

14   Billy went to Town this Morning with his 3 Children, in the Boat, Peggy, Sister and self minded our work, till after Tea then found ourselves inclin'd to take another ride in the Cart, which we did, Polly and black Arch took turns to drive,—when we had road about 2 miles from home, we had like to have been cast away, by reason of the gears brakeing—thought we should have been oblig'd to walk back, but 2 or 3 honest dutchmen, (for ought I know) who overtook us on the road were so kind as to rectify Matters, and we proceed'd to Wm. Callenders. . . .

15   Awoke this Morning before 4, Arose at 5, which is not my usual Costom, took a solitary walk in the Gardens, found Billy up, when I return'd, went with him to see his people Mow Barley—he went to Town before dinner with Crosston, HD, came to Point towards Evening—Peggy, Sister, Henry and self, walk'd in the Gardens, eat Currants and Pares, Henry stay'd all Night. After he was gone to Bed, (which was not till past 12 o'clock) we had a Washing Frolick, for which we had prepar'd beforehand, took the oppertunity of Billys absence, went to Bed between one and two.

July the 23   HD,—call'd this Morning, B. Trapnal, brought some Pine-Appels HD, call'd this Afternoon went out this Evening, call'd at T Says, at Uncles, at S Whartons, Sally gone out, went from thence to B. Moodes, mett Sally Wharton there, came home before 10, Henry over took us, he stay'd till after 11—my Mind has been much distress'd all this day.

26   Stay'd at home all Day, Betsy Moode came this Evening, she stay'd till after Super, HD, (who I thought was gone to Burlington) came after she was gone; this Evening I shall never forget.—for tis a memoriable one.

27   First Day: slept none last night, HD, came this Morning, before I was up, had a conferance with sister, he went to Burlington—there is a great

similitude this day, between the Elements and my Mind,—stay'd at home all day.

[Sept.] 3   Stay'd at home all Day: Nancy Morgan, and Peggy Ross, drank tea with us—Sister went out this Evening Sammy Sansom came home with her—Henry Drinker, is as I fear'd ill, of a Feaver.

5   Stay'd at home all Day: Sammy Emlen drank tea with us, our people gone out, H Moode call'd in the Evening—to tell me, Betsy goes tomorrow to Plymouth,—Sister went this Evening with[9] Sarah Sansom, to see Henry who is very weak and low.

First Day Sepr. the 7: 1760.   Went 3 times to Meeting—Joshua and Caty Howell, drank tea with us, this Afternoon; Sarah Sansom, informs us this Evening that HD. is so much mended, that he rode out this Morning,—Wm. and Sarah Fisher here this Evening—just as we had sat down to supper, Betsy Warner, came in to acquaint us, that Fire was cry'd;—it prov'd to be a House next the Frds. Burying Ground, at the Sign of the Spread Eagle; a Pot House,[10] and Stable, adjacent, were burnt down.

10   Stay'd at home all Day: rainy weather Benny Swett, came to see us this afternoon, he arriv'd yesterday at New-Castle, from London, in the Philada. Packet Capt. Buden, with whome came Passengers, George Mason, Jane Crossfield, and Susannah Hatton, all Publick Fds.[11] (Susy Hatton is an Irish woman) H Drinker and Benny Swett drank tea with us Henry came again in the Evening—I hope he is Haply recover'd—he went away before super,—Wm. and Sarah Fisher supped at AWs.

17   Stay'd within all Day: unwell with the Tooth-ach—dull Weather—saw Nobody but our People.

21   First Day: my Face ach'd badly in the night:—stay'd from meeting, rainy weather:—HD—call'd after Morning Meeting he spent the Evening with me.

[Oct.] 22d.   Spent this Afternoon at S Whartons—Sally unwell, keeps her Room—call'd in our way home at Uncle Jervis's, and at S Sansom's—found when we came home Benny Swett—Beny has a mind to our Nancy—No Henry this Evening.

9. "Sammy" crossed out.
10. Either a house where pottery was made or where pots of beer were retailed (*OED*).
11. These Public Friends were Quakers authorized to travel in the ministry. See below, Aug. 15, 1762.

Novr. the 1   Peggy Parr, and Caley, call'd this Morning—went with her to several shops call'd in my way home at F Rawles. HD—call'd before dinner— he spent the Evening with us—he's unwell with a cold.

3   Polly received a Letter this Morning from HD informing us—his cold is so bad, he's obliged to lose Blood—spent this Morning at home with sister—she at work, myself writeing—our people gone to quarterly meeting—from whence they did not return till late—dinn'd at 4 o'clock—Sammy Sansom spent part of this Evening.

10   Stay'd at home all Day, Sammy Emlen, calld after dinner, I had a conference with him, in the Bleu Parlor—touchant Baubette[12]—HD, spent the Evening avac moy[13] hes still unwell.

18   Stay'd from Meeting this Morning, within all Day: spent this Morning solas, writeing—Betsy Moode and HD—call'd after meeting—Henry's Brother Daniel, married this Morning A Warner Senr. and Molly Sandwith, went this Afternoon to the Burial of Caleb Parr,—Billys Brother—HD, call'd this Afternoon, Benny Swett spent part of the Evening, HD came after he was gone.

27   Stay'd at home all Day: dull weather—Betsy Parker, and HD. call'd this Morning—Betsy Moode spent this Afternoon, HD. the Evening—Sister this Evening at Uncles—they are all offend'd.

November the 28: 1760   HD. breakfasted, with us—Went to Monthly Meeting this Morning—A Warner Senr. and Sister, with me, diclare'd my intentions of Marriage with my Friend HD—Sarah Sansom and Sarah Morris, accompany'd us, to the Mens Meeting—Stephen Colling, and Polly Parish, and 2 other couples—past—Betsy Moode, came home with us, she and Henry, dinn'd at AWs and spent the Afternoon, Betsy went home[14] towards Evening.

Decemr the 6: 1760.   Stay'd within all Day: A Warner Senr. from home,— the greatest part of the Day, with Becky Rawle,[15] who was brought to Bed, this Afternoon, of a Daughter,[16] which she calls Peggy.—the 7th. Child born in the Family, since our abode in it.—B Moode spent an hour this Evening, after she was gone Henry came he spent the rest of the Evening.

12. About Baubette (a nickname for Betsy Moode).
13. With me.
14. The words "in the" crossed out.
15. Becky Rawle, born Rebecca Warner, was a daughter of Quakers Anne and Edward Warner. This was the Warner family with whom Elizabeth and Mary Sandwith resided after the death of their parents (Jordan, *Col. Fam. Phila.*, 151).
16. The word "whome" crossed out.

14 First Day: Went to Meeting this Morning—Molly at home, her throat not well—The Burlington yearly Meeting epistle[17] was read—HD. call'd while we were at dinner—I stay'd at home this Afternoon with sister being unwell myself, which I think is frequently the case—Hannah Callender, drank tea at AWs she, HD, and self, went to Evening Meeting togeather—Henry came home with me, spent the rest of the Evening.

18th.   . . . I stop'd in the Afternoon to see B Rawle, went back to tea to Joshuas, Henry Drinker drank tea with us—Molly and Henry went down Town, towards Evening—I came home—B——y Swett came, I think he wont succead—Sister came home, Betsy Moode and HD. with her they spent the Evening.

Decemr. the 19—1760   Stay'd within all Day: T Williams measur'd me for a pair[18] shoes, HD. call'd and drank tea, he expects to be busy this Evening chez lui[19]—therefore I expect not to see him untill tomorrow.

24 Stay'd at home all Day: Henry call'd—Hannah Hicks, drank tea with us—she came to town on account of her Father's being ill of the Pleurisy—she designs to stay in town till I have changed my Name—Henry Drinker spent the Evening.

26 Henry call'd twice this Morning—I went to Monthly Meeting, A Warner Senr. and Sister with me—inform'd Friends that I continued my intentions &c.—Sarah Sansom, Sarah Morris, A Warner, and Sister, went up to the Mens meeting with us—Betsy Moode came home with us. she and HD. dinned at AWs—they spent the Afternoon, Henry the Evening—Stephen Collins, and Mary Parish,—one Wells—and—I dont know the Womans name—Henry and myself past the Seacond meeting—Isreal Morris, and Phebe Brown; Molly Holloway, and I know not who, past their first—HD. informs us this Evening of the Death of our good Old King, George the 2d,[20] who departed this life

17. The Epistle was the annual report drawn up at the yearly meeting in September to be sent to the London Yearly Meeting, which noted the spiritual condition of the Society of Friends, its achievements for the year, and its future goals; it also contained requests to British Friends for help on certain political issues pertaining to colonial affairs (Mekeel, "Founding Years," 17; see also the appendix in J. M. Moore, *Friends in the Delaware Valley*, 250).

18. Words crossed out.

19. At his house.

20. George II had died Oct. 25, and George III was proclaimed king the next day, first at Savile House and then at other places in and around London. News of the death of George II and the ascension of George III reached the American colonies on Dec. 26 (Brooke, *George III*, 73–74, 79; *Pa. Gaz.*, Jan. 8, 1761).

October the 25. 1760,—his grand-son George the 3d. was proclaim'd at Bristol the 27.

30th. . . . Betsy Moode came from meeting home with sister—she stay'd but a short time—Sister went out this Afternoon of arrents[21]—S Fisher here—HD. spent this Evening with me.

21. To collect rents (*OED*).

1761

Jany. the 1: 1761   Went to Meeting this Morning, call'd after Meeting at Uncle Jervis's, had a dialogue at the Door, with Aunt, no very agreeable one, call'd to see Becky Rawle—came home to dinner—HD. call'd—Betsy, Hannah, and Nelly Moode, Sammy Emlen, and H——y Drinker, drank tea with us—Henry came again and spent the Evening.

Bad accounts of James Tasker.

6th.   Molly Newport call'd this Morning—I stay'd at home all Day: HD. here several times, Sister busy, down at the House in Water-street[1]—this day we began to move our Goods from AWs—Polly went down-town this Evening, Henry spent the Evening with me; went home much tir'd.

7th.   Henry call'd 3 times this Morning, Sister gone to Market &c—A Warner Senr. Nancy Warner, Polly Sandwith, Betsy Warner, and HD. went after Breakfast in A James's Sleygh to Frankford, Henry drove—they came home to Dinner—Sister in Water-Street this Afternoon. Aunt Jervis, A Warner Senr. there. Polly and Henry came to AWs to Tea, they went back to the House in the Evening, no body left at home but R Coleman, and myself, knit at my mittins—Throat sore—wish it was well—I know not what B Moode means, by Absenting herself thus—Henry and Sister, came home after 8 o'clock, he spent the rest of the Evening.

9   This Day 5 Years, and on the same day of the Week, my Mind was much agatated, tho on a very different Occasion,[2]—May I so conduct myself, in this state of perpetual change, as to arrive at last, to that state of Bliss, never to be again seperated from my dear Parents. Sister and Fd. Warner the greatest part of the Day in Water-Street, prepareing for the important Day—AW came home to Dinner, Pollys sent to her.—HD. call'd several times, he spent the Evening with us—Sister and self, were to have lodg'd this night in the Bleu Chamber (our Bed being remov'd) but Polly had inadvertantly put the Key of the door on the inside, and pull'd it too, which prevented our enterance, were oblig'd to go into AWs Chamber, and sleep, or lay, there—Sister in a little Bed on the Floor, myself between AW, and Nancy.

1. The Drinkers occupied a house on Water Street for the first ten years of their marriage; they then moved to 110 North Front Street.
2. ED's mother had died five years earlier, after "a lingering illness."

10   My Throat continues very bad, which gives me great uneasaness, Sister
and AW. Senr. busy in Water street, Betsy Moode spent this Afternoon & part
of the Evening—Rachel Drinker call'd this Afternoon—Henry went home
this Evening with Betsy—Nurse Peggy Grigory came this Afternoon to put up
my Pallet,[3] have found no relief thereby—Henry came home with Sister after
11 o'clock, did not go to Bed till near 12.

12   HD. informs that the River's fast—Pollys gone in Water-street—My
Throat not quite well—Betsy Moode, and Hannah Hicks, here this Afternoon—Henry Several times.[4]

3. By "pallet" ED means the soft palate, or uvula, which in a viral illness could become
inflamed and interfere with swallowing. The seventeenth-century German surgeon Wilhelm
Fabry (Fabricius Hiladanus) fashioned several devices that could be thrust in the mouth either
to place an astringent powder on the swollen uvula or to give the patient nourishment when
the organs of the mouth were very swollen. See also below, Apr. 14 and Dec. 19, 1806 (Parr,
London Medical Dictionary, s.v. "palate" and "uvula"; *Oeuvres chirurgies die Hierosome Fabrioe*
[Lyon: Chez Pierre Ravaud, 1659], 594–95).
4. ED and HD were married on Jan. 13, 1761.

2. Wife and Mother, 1762–1775

Life for Elizabeth Sandwith Drinker was very different from what it had been for Elizabeth Sandwith. Love overcame restraint, and Henry Drinker became "mon chere," "my best friend," or "my Sweet-Heart." Yet these endearments were the only indicators of her marital relationship. Except for one entry on May 12, 1761, silence shields the seventeen months following her marriage, during which time her first child, Sarah (affectionately called Sally), was born. Elizabeth confided nothing to her diary about sex or pregnancies, apart from oblique references to several miscarriages.

Between 1761 and 1775 Elizabeth Drinker gave birth to eight children, five of whom reached adulthood. Of the other three, none survived beyond fourteen months. Elizabeth Drinker shared her grief sparingly on these occasions, and did not even record her two-week-old namesake's death in December 1772. By the end of 1775 her youngest surviving child was not quite two years old.

In addition to Elizabeth, Henry, and the children, the Drinker household contained Mary Sandwith (Elizabeth's unmarried sister) and several servants. Sister and servants relieved Elizabeth of some of the burdens of housework and child care, and although the responsibilities of motherhood consumed most of her waking hours, her limited mobility still permitted a few extended trips with her husband some distance from Philadelphia. At home, she and Henry took walks together, visited friends and Friends, and rode with the children. Elizabeth summered at their home in Frankford, where entries lengthened in proportion to Henry's frequent absences. During these years she continued to socialize with or without the children, one or more of whom were usually breeding, battling, or recovering from one or more of the relentless eighteenth-century maladies.

The children's own life cycles take form in this decade as they teethe, prattle, toddle, attend school, shed baby clothes, learn to ride, and enter their teens. Only a short entry on September 6, 1775, when increasingly militant Philadelphians vented their wrath on two friends, suggests the fury and disruption that lay just ahead.

1762

[June] 17 AJ, call'd, this Morning Sister & Self went this Afternoon to Frankford,[1] to notre place,[2] with Sally,[3] Sally Emlen, Hannah Moode, Call'd this Evening—I wrote this Morning a mon Chere.[4]

19. Abel here, I at Abels, B. Oxon brought his Account, let him have 20 S— Sister, Sally, John and self, went this Afternoon, to Quarry-Bank, or Airy-Hill—saw Richd. Wells preparing his Carriage to take a ride, invited him with us—he follow'd with Rachel, they stay'd an hour at our Place, visited the Spring-House &c then left us for Blooms-Berry,—we came home too late, tho I hope no ways injur'd, several to see us while we were out. Betty knows not who—wrote to my H——Y.

23 Anna Warner Senr., Saml. and Sarah Sansom, drank tea with us, B. Walln here with the Child, Richd. came in, Silvia Spicer, Patty, Becky, James, call'd, sister out this Evening looking for a Maid—Nanny Silas Iron'd here, Betty behaves Badly—some talk of an Earth-quake last seventh-Day Night I remember to have heard a Strange Noise—John Drinker Abel Js.—here.

1762 7 mo. July 22 took up our Aboad during the warm weather, at our place near Frankford, from 22d. to 28th. kept no account. saw but little Company— Sister went to Town the 24th. 28th. She went again in the Morning with my H——y she came back to dine with me, took a ride in the Afternoon, John and Sally with her to B. Parrs, came back to Tea with me. HD. stay'd in Town all Night the first time since we came up; I have my Sister, my Sally; John Burket and Hannah Broom; with me, and did it suit HD, to be constantly here also, I think I could be very happy in the Country.

[Aug.] 3d. HD. and MS. left me for Town this Morning after Breakfast, between 7 & 8 o'clock, John went with them, he return'd at 11 o'clock.—the first time of my dining alone since I came to Frankford—Thos. and Rebecca Say with Benny came up this Afternoon, HD. and MS, came home before Tea took a Walk round the Place, TS. &c went home towards Evening.

1. The Drinkers owned a country home near Frankford.
2. Our place.
3. Sarah Drinker was born on Oct. 23, 1761.
4. To my dear.

4th. Ma Chere went to Town Early this Morn—Samey and Betsy Emlen Hannah and Nelly Moode, spent this Day with us, the Day as Agreeably spent as could be in the absence of my best Friend.

9th. HD. went to Town, [agin] this Morning saw no Company to Day, clean'd House.

12 Sister and John went to Town this afternoon, ma Chere came back with them drank, coffee with me, they took Sally to ride a little way—Abel Jamess little Son George was Yesterday Buryed—HD. in Town last Night.

13 HD. stay'd Breakfast with us this Morning, went to Town after, he brought Nancy Warner up in the Chaise after Dinner, A Warner Senr. and Betsy with them, they spent the After-noon with us Peggy Parr, Nancy and Polly also here, We all took a Walk after Tea round by the Creek, HD. went to Town with them, I dont Expect him back to Night, Peggy Parr &c went away soon after them.

15th. First Day. HD, and self went to Meeting this Morning, no Publick Friends⁵ there, took a Nap in the Afternoon, then went with the Child to ride, round by Willings Place and to the River, came home to Coffee—no Body to see us from Town to Day.

23 My H——y and Sister went to Town this Morning, I have been alone all Day they came home late; Isaac Worrels Wife and Sister here this Evening.

30, A great quantity of rain fell, last Night and this Morning, [in] so much, that the Road by the Mill was rendred impassable, the Fresh was so great, Oswin Sutton says, the like has not been since his time, at Frankford, which is 40 odd Years—HD, Sister and self, took a walk after Dinner to the Mill, People were oblig'd to swim their Horses, [accross] the road—HD, stay'd with us till this Afternoon—tis an ill wind,⁶ &c.

Septr. 3: Jacob brought me a Letter this Morning from HD. giveing us an

---

5. Public Friends originally were Quakers, both male and female, who expressed their faith by preaching to and attempting to convert and reform the larger society. Later the term came to designate the authorized traveling public ministry of the Society of Friends (Stoneburner and Stoneburner, *Quaker Women*, xv; Carol Stoneburner, "Drawing a Profile of American Female Public Friends as Shapers of Human Space," in Stoneburner and Stoneburner, *Quaker Women*, 61; Thomas D. Hamm, *The Transformation of American Quakerism: Orthodox Friends, 1800–1907* [Bloomington: Indiana University Press, 1988], 8–9; Jones, *Later Periods of Quakerism*, 1:230–31).
6. Word crossed out.

account of the Reduction of the Havannah, by the English;[7]—and of the safe delivery of Hannah Jones who was brought to Bed, on First-Day last of a Son:—Samey & Hannah Sansom, Peggy Parr, Nancy, Polly and Caleb, spent this Afternoon with us—HD. came home to Tea—Isaac Worrel here this Evening.

9   left Frankford this Afternoon Bag and Bagage—found our Frds. at Philaa. generaly well—Hannah Moode, Here this Evening.

1762 Septr.   A Sickley time at Philada.[8] many Persons are taken down, with Something very like the Yellow-Feaver.

Septr. 23[9]   Received a Letter this Evening—from Samuel Emlen junr. intimating his Wife's indisposition, went there about 9 o'clock & stay'd till near 3 in the morning,[10] when H.D. came to inform of Sal's being Saucy, so came Home, about 5 in the morning (the 24th) E.[11] Emlen was delivered of a fine Boy Joshua junr.

Octor. 11: 1762   My little Sally taken unwell with a vomitting and Purging, Doctors Redman and Evans tended her, seems now recover'd, the 26th.

Molly Searson departed this Life Octor. the 23: 1762, her Body carri'd to Church, Sister at the Burial—she died of a Consumption.
     A Negro of Patty Craddocks, dead at Abel James's of the Small Pox, it proves Mortal to Many. Octor 26: 1762.

Decemr. 24   Sally Fisher dead of the Small-Pox, her Brother Johny bury'd last Week of the same disorder.

7. England and Spain were then at war. In June an expedition headed by the earl of Albemarle captured Havana (Howard H. Peckham, *The Colonial Wars, 1689–1762* [Chicago: University of Chicago Press, 1964], 207).
8. Yellow fever struck Philadelphia in August and did not subside until October. The city did not experience another major outbreak until the disastrous epidemics in the 1790s. Philadelphia's first experience with epidemic yellow fever occurred in 1699, when 220 persons, approximately 5 percent of the population, died (Redman, *Account of the Yellow Fever*, 1762; Duffy, *Epidemics*, 142–61; Augustin, *Yellow Fever*, 986–87).
9. The entries dated Sept. 23 and 24 do not appear to be in ED's handwriting.
10. Word crossed out.
11. The word "Moode" crossed out.

1763

Febry. 6: 1763—First-Day Afternoon very unwell, Miscarried;[1] Sally, Inoculated, last sixth-Day.

8 Weeks gone, when it happn'd.

March 31: 1763, began this Morning to Ween my Sally,—the Struggle seems now (April 2) partly over.—tho it can scarcely be call'd a Struggle she is such a good-natur'd patient Child.

Nancy Jones came to work. May 3: 1763 the 3 day of the Week.

May 23:1763, at home as usual, Rebecca Say here this Afternoon Abel here to day; mis'd an oppertunity of Writeing to my Henry. very unwel, Elizth. Pines here this Evening partly Engag'd to[2] hier her.

25 Went this Afternoon, with Sally, in the Waggon to Frankford, with Abel, Becky and Children, David Franks and Wife, drank Tea with us there; came home towards Evening, Abel received a letter to Day from HD—white Washers here.

June 20, 1763, little Joshua Emlen was this Afternoon buried, he dyed the 19 of a vomitting purging and cutting Teeth &c.

1763: July 1st. sixth Day afternoon came to Quarry-Bank myself with Abel James in the Chaise John behind, HD. MS, the Child and Hannah in Abels Waggon,—left Elizabeth Pines, and B Trapnel, to keep House in Town—Judah Foulks Family moveing up to Widdow Mc. Vaughs new House, so that we shall have Molly for a Neighbour—Abels Family at their Place—myself and Child unwell.

12 HD. went to Town, he came back, early this Afternoon, AJ with him HD. went Guning, Doctor Evans call'd, Richd. Waln drank Coffee with us—Made Currant Jelly.

1. Word(s) crossed out.
2. Word crossed out.

14 Went to Town this Morning, all of us, did not go from home, busy—came back to Frankford before Tea time, Charles West Junr. & Wife drank tea with us, my Henry at Abels, he came from Town with him.

17 First Day HD. and self went to meeting this Morning call'd at Judaths door, I rode with M Parr, walk'd back Joyce Benezett and Sally Morris Preach'd, they din'd at Abels—HD. MS. and self, John & the Child took a walk towards Evening—Abel and Becky James, Molly Foulk sup'd with us.

23 Molly and self went to Market this Morning, call'd at Uncles, and at Reeves, Silver-smith,—bought little Books at Rivengtons—came home found Phebe Broom there. she went away this Morning—we are very busy giting ready to return to the Country—lock'd up the House this Afternoon—HD. MS, the Child and Hannah, went in our Chaise, myself with Abel in his Waggon—& our John &c—call'd at Abels, Edmd. Carneys Wife and Nurse Lloyd there—HD, came for me, came home to Tea.

29. Ma Chere went after Breakfast. Sister and self stay'd at home all Day Rain with Thunder this Afternoon and Evening—I dont expect to see my Sweet-Heart to Night.

[Aug.] 4. HD. stay'd with us all day—Molly, Sally, John and my-self took a ride this Morning to Wm. Parr's, calld in our return at Abels. came home by 11 o'clock—John Drinker and Jos. Penock here this Afternoon,—HD & MS went this Evening to M Foulks, Phebe Morris here—James Bringhursts Child dy'd[3] this Afternoon.

15 HD. went to Town this Morning. MS. John the Child and myself went to School, which is held at the Meeting House—A Jamess, W Parr's and J. Foulks, Children go there. tis a large School—We call'd in our way home at M. Foulk's—Thos. Bolsbey and Wife there, drank Tea with them; HD. came home—while we were there—the Weather is very cool and Pleasent.

23. HD. went to Town—Patty James dinn'd and spent the Afternoon with us—Peggy Parr call'd, several of hir Family unwell, little black Nedd dyed last week of the Flux, which disorder, many are troubled with. . . .

26. HD. MS. and John went to Town this Morning, after Breakfast, MS. and John, return'd by 11 o'clock Noon—put a Gown skirt in the Frame, to Quilt this Afternoon—HD came up this Evening unexpectedly.

31 HD. went to Town this Morning—Sammy and Betsy Emlen, Molly Foulk

3. The word "Yesterday" crossed out.

and Children, here this Afternoon, a large number of the People about
Frankford troubled with sore-Eyes—another of Billy Parrs little Negros, dead
of the Flux;—Abel James here this Evening: says I need not expect my Henry
up to Night—the Weather grows cool—expect soon to return to Town.

> Such quick regards his Sparkling eyes bestow:—
> Such wavy ringlets o'er his shoulders flow!

Sally Drinker's Mouth was sore from the time she was a fortnight old, until
she was five months—discover'd her first Tooth November 17th. 1762—she
being then near 13 months old.

[Sept.] 10   HD. gone to Town this Morning he came up after dinner, John
Drinker with him—Abel James here,—My Henry left us this Afternoon
on Horse-back at 5 o'clock—designing for Burlington to Night; toMorrow to
proceed towards Brunswick, Elizabeth-Town, and New-York.

11   First Day—Benn. Trapnel came up this Morning: he went with me to
Meeting—silent meeting, which is very common here—this has appear'd
a long day—Ben went away in the Afternoon, wrote by him to E. Emlen, I
call'd after Meeting at M Foulks.

Sepr. the 19: 1763;   Busy all Day: Cleaning House, went this Evening to see
Catty Howell, who, Miscarried last seventh Day, and has been very ill.

October 28,   was called up in the Night to Betsy Waln, who was, brought to
Bed this Morning, of her Son Nicholas.—1763 sixth Day.

1764

My Dear Friend Bettsy Emlen, with her Husband—left Philada. after dinner, for Chester, intending there to embark or board the Ann, George Fortune Master for Bristol—I took leave of them at the Ferry—My Henry and Sister with Several other Friends gone with them to Chester, dont expect them home 'till Tomorrow—June the 6. 1764.

Our dear Nancy[1] was left at Sammy Harpers at Frankford, July 3: 1764.

July 4.   took a ride this Afternoon to see our little Dear,—drank Tea at A James'.

July 10: 1764,   My Henry on Horse-back, Sister, Sally and myself, in the Chaise, went to GermanTown, to Doctor Witts, for Worm-Powder for Sally, the old man sick, got the Powder of a young Man in the Shop—drank Tea with the Widdow Vanaken who I think is in a poor way—then went to Mackenetts where we put up, and than home.

Augt. 8: 1764.   sent Benny this Morning for Nanny Harper, and our dear Nancy they spent the Day with us, went back in the Evening.

1764 October 23,   sent for Nancy home to Wean, Nanny Harper came with her she stay'd all Night the child takes her weaning Extroydinary well so far.

1764 Octor. 29   Phebe Morris came to Work—stay'd 11 Days.

1. Ann (Nancy) Drinker was born on Jan. 11, 1764.

1765

Febry. 5. 1765. the Carcase of an Ox or Cow, was this Day roasted on the River, which has been fast 5 Weeks past and seems likely to continue so 5 Weeks to come, this being a remarkable hard Winter. the river open'd the 17 Instant Feby.

Sally Drinker went first to School April the 8. 1765, to Becky Jones, and Hannah Cathrall.

June 12. 1765. Came to Frankford, all except BJ, in the Evening, fourth Day.

17 HD. MS, John and Hannah went this Morning to Town—so that I have none with me at Present but Agnis and my three Children.[1] Sally, who has been unwell several days past, grew worse this Afternoon, Complains of her Throat, and has a Fever, which increas'd as night came on. I sent to AJs for Nurse who did not come till 11 o'clock.—A James and Patty Accompanied her. the Child bad all night, vomited, freaquently—this has been a tedious long and anxious Day.

18 Sister, John and Hannah came this Morning; Nurse went away before Dinner; MS, John and Hannah went to Town after dinner and took my dear sick Child with them, and now I seem in a manner forsaken: my dear Henry engag'd in Town geting Roberson away—Booths Man Robart came this Evening informing that, there was no reason but to think Sally was better, which seems a mesage calcalated to make me easy—but misses having that effect.

20 Sally so bad this Morning that we thought it best to consult Docter Evans, who with Docr. Redman, who before attended her, concluded in the Evening to clap on a Blister,[2] and a large one it was, which we laid on her back, Betsy Jervis sat up with us.

1. Mary Drinker was born on April 20, 1765.
2. A substance applied to the skin to stimulate and promote redness and inflammation and eventually to produce a discharge. Bringing an inflammation to the surface of the skin was thought to have beneficial effects in a variety of illnesses and conditions including fevers, smallpox, measles, hemorrhages, diarrhea, and kidney and bladder problems. One of the most widely used substances in eighteenth-century blisters were cantharides, or Spanish flies (Parr, *London Medical Dictionary*, 254–55).

21st. Sally continues much the same. the Blister drawn and runs finely. her disorder the Doctors calls an Apthea Fever,[3] something of the nature of the Melignent sore Throat—her Mouth having several soars in it: she continued bad for several days, when the disorder took a turn for the better: and on the 30 Instant we came back to Frankford: First Day. afternoon.

[July] 2   HD. MS. Sally, John and Hannah, left me this Morning after breakfast. so that my Family is again reduced to myself, Agnis, and my two little ones. Nancy very poorly all the Morning with a bad lax. she was taken, before we left Town with a vomiting and Purging—the former went of, but the latter continues, she cuts her Teeth with more difficultey then some Children; she seems better this Afternoon—the Widdow Commins and Lizey Ashbridge drank Tea with me—HD. came up this Evening.

7   First Day: HD. MS, gone to Meeting—J Foulk and B Booth call'd while they were gone:—dinn'd alone only Benny—I mean our own Family. Stephen Collins and John Drinker with little Henry, spent this Afternoon here, Abel James & Isaiah Worrel call'd—HD and my self took a ride this Morning with our little Nance, who continues unwell, we went up Busbys road, where I had never been before. were HD. MS. constantly here Frankford would be very agreeable to me.

9   Robart Waln and Wife and little Son came here this Morning, and Abel James—Robart, Abel and HD went to the Burial of Robart Harper, Sister and Sally went to meeting. Becky Waln stay'd with me untill they came back—AJ. stay'd dinner with us, then went to Town with my Henry:—Sister gave the Children a little Airing in the Chaise this Afternoon—Nancy continues poorly, which with the care of 2 Houses, occasions us a good deal of Trouble.

15   HD. &c gone to Town this Morning Phebe Morris here this Afternoon fitting a Gown for me, Molly Worrel with Sitgreaves's Baby who she Nurses, were also here: HD. came towards Evening.

16   HD. went to Town early this Morning Phebe with him: she is I expect at Work at our House for Sister: John came by himself this Evening to my great disapointment, many and various, are the Occasions, that will communicate Sorrow to a Susseptable mind.

18   HD. went to Town Solas this Morning leaving Sister &c with me; he came

3. *Apthae* was the term used to describe white inflammations and ulcers of the mucous membranes in the throat. *Apthae* or *aptha fever* was most often used to describe the illness still called thrush, but was sometimes used to denote other common childhood illnesses involving the throat, such as diphtheria (Skinner, *Medical Terms*, 35–36).

up again this Afternoon, B Booth with him, they went Fishing: Nany Harper here—HD. BB. came back to Tea: Abel James, Capt Rose, Capt. Rees, and John Parrock here this Afternoon, they went away soon—how exceeding agreeable the Country is when we are all togeather.

30 HD. gone to Town this Morning: Sister and Sally. Sally Wharton and her Son Dicky came before 11 o'clock. they spent the Day with me; wint home in the Evening: I took a run to the end of the lane at 9 o'clock to look for my best beloved; but saw him not: as the Moon shone bright, I was in hopes it would induce him to come; tho late.

[Aug.] 11 First Day: rain'd all last Night, a heavy rain. HD. gone to Meeting this Morning no Coumpany at Dinner—Abel James and Booth here in the Afternoon—they say that the rain has done considerable damage in Town: tore up the pavement in some places and spoiled goods, that were in Cellers in Market-Street.

15 Sally fell this Morning against a Tub. and cut the back part of her Head. and I am afraid she has fractur'd the Bone—we stop'd the Blood with Turlington;[4]—HD. came this Evening.

20 HD. and John went to Town this Morning:—We gave Nancy a Clyster,[5] composed of Worm-wood, and Tansey,[6] made into a strong Tea; to a Gill of it: put a table Spoon full of Lynseed Oyl,[7] and a little Venice-

4. A British patent medicine, Turlington's Balsam, patented in 1744 by Robert Turlington. Its maker claimed it would cure kidney and bladder stones, colic, and inward weaknesses. The ingredients used in the preparation, a compound tincture of benzoin, had entered into European pharmaceutical practice in the seventeenth century. Similar, if not patented, medications in the pharmacopeia of the time were Traumatic Balsam, Jesuit Drops, and Commander's Balsam. The Drinkers were using it externally to clean and heal a wound (Griffenhagen and Young, "Patent Medicines," 160–61; La Wall, *Pharmarcy*, 414, 282; W. Lewis, *New Dispensatory*, 323–24).

5. *Clysters, glysters, lavements,* and *injections* are terms used in the diary to refer to enemas, or more technically, rectal injections for therapeutic or nutritive purposes. There were many types of glysters in use in the eighteenth century, the more common ones including a starch glyster made of starch and linseed oil, opiate glysters made of liquid laudanum, common glysters made with chamomile flowers, and simple glysters made with warm water. Because they purged the intestines of their contents, glysters were often used to treat cases of flux and dysentery. They were also a useful way of introducing a medication, such as cinchona bark, into the body of a person unable to swallow an oral dose (Gould, *Dictionary of Medicine*; W. Lewis, *New Dispensatory*, 618–20, 289; Buchan, *Domestic Medicine* [1799], 445).

6. Wormwood and tansy, perennial plants flowering in August, are noted for their bitter taste. Both were used singly or in conjunction to expel worms from the intestinal tract. Wormwood was also considered a tonic (Thacher, *New American Dispensatory*, 156, 356; R. Eglesfeld Griffith, *A Universal Formulary: Containing the Methods of Preparing and Administering Officinal and Other Medicines, The Whole Adapted to Physicians and Pharmaceutists* [Philadelphia: Blanchard & Lea, 1850], 397).

7. Linseed oil, cold-drawn oil from the flax or linen plant, was a popular remedy for both chest and stomach disorders. It could be administered by mouth or in glysters (Blackwell, *Curious Herbal*, vol. 1, plate 160).

Treacle;[8]—it is gave with a design of killing the little Worms, that she is troubled with; which the Doctor says, are a sort, that always lay at the lower part of the Bowels—HD. returnd in the Evening.

29 We stay'd at home, saw no Coumpany till towards Evening. we went after John came up to Abel Jamess: John draw'd the Children in the little Coach. Sister and self walk'd.

[Sept.] 10 MS. SD, AD. John and Hannah went to Town this Morning: HD. came for me and little Polly after Dinner. I went over to see the Widdow McVough who is unwel, came soon back, and between 3 and 4 o'clock bid Adieu to Frankford for a Season.

8. Venice treacle was typical of the elaborate preparations popular in the seventeenth century but not as widely used in the eighteenth. Among its ingredients (fifty-five to sixty in all) were alcohol, opium, honey, and squill (J. Worth Estes, "John Jones' *Mysteries of Opium Reveal'd* [1701]: Key to Historical Opiates," *JHMAS* 39 [1984]: 204, 206; W. Lewis, *New Dispensatory*, 582–92).

1766

[Jan.] 24, my little Poll very much broke out like the small Pox—Sally better—Nancy broke out—Becky James, Betsy Waln, [J] Redman, call'd this Morning—Received a Letter from Sammy Harper informing that Nanny had got the Small Pox; Becky James, and Sister went to Frankford to see her, found her bad: they return'd to Tea; snow this Afternoon, weather raw and cold.

[Feb.] 3 Elferth's Boy. came this morning to tell us of the death of Nanny Harper who dyed last night—Hannah Jones, and Nancy Mitchel, Sally Parrish and little Nancy Parrish spent this Afternoon with us. My dear little Nancy was taken this Afternoon with a Fever;—Abels Family came today from Bybarry where they have been since sixth day last.

22 took a Walk this Morning, with Sister, Sally, Nancy, and Hannah; call'd at W Parrs, at Uncle Jerviss, at S Pleasents, and at A Warners—came home before dinner,—the Prince-George sail'd after dinner, Capt. Roberson call'd to bid us farewell; I step'd into Wallns—Becky James here this Afternoon, My Nancy still unwell. . . .

began to wean my Polly, April 21. 1766 she being a Year and day old, not one Tooth bears weaning extrodinary well—she cut her first tooth July 1 or 2d., being 14 months and 11 or 12 days old, 4 or 5 days before she dyed[1]—could almost go alone, and speak many Words very plain.

21st May. Sally began her Seacond Quarter at School—August 12. 1765.

May 19 a Vessel from Pool brought the Account of the Repeal of the Stamp Act, the 20th. the Town Illuminated upon the occasion.

May the 25. HD. and MS. went to Darby, to the Burial of Sarah Fordam, who dyed of a Cancer in her Breast.

1. Mary Drinker died on July 7, 1766.

May 27. 1766.   Sister gone to sit up to Night with Peggy Parr, who has been ill for 3 days past, bleeding at the Nose, & Vomitting Blood.

[Aug.] 10   First Day: took a ride with my H——y this Morning to the river side—came back a little after 7. Sister and the Children not up when we return'd: Dicky Waln stop'd, in his Way to Abington to inform us, of Jammy Smiths being very ill occasiond by drinking cold Water last Evening. . . .

Novr. the 24   Sally was let Blood, and took a Vomitt, 25 she took a purge—for a bad cold, Docr. Redman tend her—the 28 the Child much better—1766.

1767

Janry. 13. 1767. ED. was let Blood.[1]

1767 May: Billy[2] unwell, a Cold and Fever with disordered Bowels, Docr. Redman tends him—June 4 the Child better: weather very hott.

Agnis Fergusong went away May 3. 1767.

Rosanna came June 16. 1767 at £8—p Ann.

Agnis came again June the 20. wint away [Augt.] the 2. 1767.

[July] 3   HD. came this Evening our Kitchen Chimney took fire Yesterday before dinner but by the help of Isah. and his Men, it was soon put out. Cool Weather.

7   Henry D went to Town this Morning one of our Neighbor Children dead of the Hooping Cough, almost all the Children in the Neighborhood bad with it mine in pretty good health, which makes me think of going to Town. HD. Sister, and Betsy Waln here this Afternoon.

8   HD. here most of the day, Sammy and Hannah Sansom spent the Afternoon with us, after they were gone, we shut up Frankford House, and came away. John, Agnis and Sally in the Cart, HD. myself and Billy in the Chair. by Norriss Woods we [mett] the Company returning from Ludys Childs burying. a Yound Fellow on a mad Colt gallop'd against our Mare, with such force as occasion'd my falling out of the Chair, having the Child in my arms, asleep,[3] in endeavouring to save the Child, I fell with all my weight on my right foot and hurt it so much that I was unabel to set it to the Ground for upwards of 3 Weeks, the Child through mercy escap'd unhurt. I have lately mett with so many frights, that I can[4] not [bear] to think of riding with any satisfaction.

1. ED was frequently bled in the later stages of pregnancy.
2. William Drinker was born on Jan. 28, 1767.
3. Three lines crossed out.
4. Word crossed out.

My very dear Friend, Betsy Emlen, departed this life, Janry. the 1767 in Bristol, Old England, leaving behind her 2 little Sons.

Nancy Drinker cut one of her little fore-Teeth, when she was, between 3 and 4 years of age.

1768

ED. was let Blood March 23. 1768.

May 26. 1768 ED. miscarried.

in the fall 1767 the Children took the Hooping-Cough, it continued some time in the Winter.

[July] 21.   I was call'd up last night between 12 and 1. by B. Waln, who made a falls alarm, came home at day break, Billy road out this Morning with Nurse—went thice into Walns to day. Becky Waln here to Night. Weather very hott Billy much better.

Betsy Waln brought to Bed, with her Daughter Elizath. July 30: 1768.

July 31. 1768   Sister went to Frankford with Billy: who is very unwell, Sally Drinker, Eve, and Sally Gardner with her, I stay'd in Town, with my H——y, who is unwell with the Chills and Fever.

[Aug.] 6   clean'd house this Morning John Hunt Junr. here, HD. and MS. and Sally came up this Afternoon in James's Waggon, Becky James and 3 of her Children drank Tea with us, HD, MS. &c went to Town this Evening weather very hott.

27.   HD. and MS. went to Town this Morning Agnis went away. she has been with us 3 or 4 days upon a Visit. HD. and MS. came up this Evening after 9 o'clock, the Moon shone bright.

[Sept.] 13.   Sally and Nancy both very ill this Afternoon, high fevers and delarious; Billy but poorly.

14   this is Nancy well day as we call it; Sally was so much better this Morning as to be taken up, to have her Bed made, she was very chearfull and eat some toast and Chocolate, the fever came on towards Evening[1] and by 10 o'clock she was very ill Patty James sat up.

1. The word "with" crossed out.

15   Nancy has taken 13 doses of the Bark[2] since yesterday Morning and has mist her fitt to Day—Sally was Chearful this Morning but in a high fever and lightheadd, in the Afternoon; several here—Abby Spicer sat up.

16   move'd Sally this Morning into my Chamber, Docr. Redman call'd on Docr. Evans, he came with him to Visit our dear little Girl; Her Fever has never intermitted but remitts; she has what the Doctors call a double tourchen; every other day it comes on at about 2 or 3 o'clock and every other at 7 or 8 in the Evening[3]—I sat up with her.

23.   The Children through Mercy are now on the recovery; tho Sally's very weak[4] HD. came home before dinner in the rain.

1768 Novr. 13.   went to the Burial of Danl. Drinkers little Daughter Betsy.

1768 Novr. the 17.   our good Friend Sarah Sansom, departed this life.

Novr. 20   Sarah Sansom's Corps was taken to the Bank Meeting-House this Afternoon, from thence to the [Buring] Ground:—Snow all Day: HD. and Sister were at the funeral.

---

2. Medication derived from the bark of the cinchona tree, native to Peru. Also known as Peruvian bark, Jesuits' bark, red bark, and yellow bark, it is the basis for quinine, used in the treatment of malaria. First imported into Europe in 1638, it achieved swift popularity because of its efficacy in treating stubborn recurring fevers. It did not become available in the American colonies until the 1720s and then via Europe rather than South America. Sometimes European pharmacopeias included preparations made with barks of other trees in the hope they would prove as useful as cinchona (LaWall, *Pharmacy*, 283–85; Richard Harrison Shryock, *Medicine and Society in America 1660–1860* [New York: New York University Press, 1960], 48; Buchan, *Domestic Medicine* [1799], 115).

3. Intermittent fevers recur at short, regular periods, remittent fevers at longer, irregular periods. A fever with a three-day cycle was called tertian, one with a four-day cycle quartan. Though the doctors labeled Sally's fever a double tertian, ED seems to describe a two-day double cycle. Sometimes called agues, some of these recurring fevers were probably various forms of malaria. Medical writers of the era such as William Buchan recognized the connection between the prevalence of these fevers and low marshy areas, stagnant water, and tropical climates. The most common form of treatment was with Peruvian bark (Buchan, *Domestic Medicine* [1799], 112–18, 150–52; Gould, *Dictionary of Medicine*, 468–69).

4. The words "and low" crossed out.

1769

1769 April the 25   My Henry gone to Burlington to the Burial of Sally Dwyling, daughter of John Smith. she dy'd in Child-Bed, of her first Child. HD. return'd the 26.

[June] 25   First Day, The weather very hott our Family very unwell;—ED. was taken at 11 at Night with the Collick and Cramp in the Bowels and Stomach to such a degree that at 2 in the Morning we were oblig'd to send for Docr. Redman who administered an anodyne Pill[1] and Mixture of the same Nature, which Lull'd the pain by day brack—the disorder was accompanyed with a violent lax and vomiting insomuch that in 2 or 3 hours I was unable to stand on my feet or hold up my head.

26   lay all day under the effects of the Anodyne;—Nancy bad with the Fever.

27   ED took a dose Rheubarb, and through mercy is much better than could be expected, considering the voiolence of the disorder.

July 7. 1769,   came to Frankford with our 3 Youngest Children:[2] Sally in Town with her Aunt: Molly Moore, with me, Eve, and Sally Gardner—My Henry came up with me in the Chaise, the rest in the Waggon: HD stay'd all Night.

1. ED generally uses *anodyne* to refer to any medication containing opium or laudanum (tincture of opium) in pill, liquid, or glyster form (Gould, *Dictionary of Medicine*; W. Lewis, *New Dispensatory*, 315–16, 618–19).
2. Henry (Harry) Drinker was born May 24, 1769. He died Aug. 20, 1769.

1770

ED had a Tooth drawn Feby. 5. 1771.

Spent 6 weeks of the Summer 70, at S. Merriotts Bristol.

1771

1771 March 9   Removed from John Smiths House in Water Street, (where we had lived 10 Years and near 2 Months)—to our House in Front Street.

27   Docr. Redman call'd this Morning.—Susanna Jaquet call'd—Neighrs. Swift and Waln, with Sucky spent this Afternoon. with us—Polly Ritche Reynolds came in the Evening—she went with us to enquire for a Maid, came back and sup'd with us—We were invited this Afternoon to the Burial of John Smith of Burlington.

28   Betsy Parker here this Morning—Abel James call'd, he intends, with his Wife &c this Afternoon for Burlington—Widow Mountgomerys Maid call'd—Nany Carlisle call'd—our Nancy little Henrys[1] maid lift us this Morning.

1771 June 22   seventh Day—came to Bristol HD. ED. HD Junr. John Drinker with us—din'd at John Kidds: George Baker drove up Polly Campbell, whome I have hir'd this day to tind my little Henry; George [return'd] to Philada. from Kidds: came to the Widdow Merriotts to Tea—Boarders there at this time; Parson Carter and Wife—Parson Peters—David Halls Wife and Son; Thos. Cash's Wife—their Servants—my self, my little Son, and Maid.—went to the Bath[2] this Evening.

27   Capt. Williams's Child, Nurse, and Negro Girl, took up their aboad with us this Morning The Mornings have been Foggy most of this Week which renders it improper to go out I took a short ride this Afternoon with Anna Sarah Large here, and several others this Day.

30   . . . went this Afternoon into the Bath, I found the shock much greater than I expected; road the 7 miles round afterwards; came home rather late, our dear little ones went to Bed, this and last Night, very much tired.

---

1. Henry Sandwith Drinker was born October 30, 1770.
2. Bristol, Pa., was noted for its bath springs, located just outside the borough limits. Hotels and boarding houses were built in the 1760s to accommodate summer guests who came for the waters and eventually transformed Bristol into one of the most fashionable watering places in the United States in the years following the Revolutionary War (Doron Green, *A History of Bristol Borough in the County of Bucks, State of Pennsylvania* [Camden, N.J.: Magrath, 1911], 67–68, 73).

[July] 4   went to Bath this Morning Patty Merriott drove, I carried the Child; we road to the Ferry. at 11 o'clock I went into the Bath; with Fear and trembling, but felt cleaver after it. . . .

10   WP. gone this Morning before I was up—Peggy went with me to B, to drink—at Noon I went again with Anna, took a dip, drank a pint and then home. . . .

13   My Henry left me this Morning I have been unwell all Day: I went into the Bath this Morning Dr. D. says I must wean by little Henry or get a nurse for him, either seems hard—but I must submitt. Billy Parr, and Caleb, came up this Afternoon, Billy went to Trent town: I wrote this Afternoon to sister; went to B. saw in my return, R and E. Waln—there is a great number of People in Bristol at present. Pollys Mother call'd here.

22   HD. and myself, took our little Lamb, after Breakfast to S. Oats, whose Breast he willingly suck'd; stay'd there an hour or 2, then went to Bath, came home to Dinner; went in the Afternoon to see our little dear; found him asleep, he waked in high good humour—but has a little Cough. . . .

Augt. 22. 1771. left home after dinner fifth Day HD. ED. and John, stop'd at [Roben] Hoods—waited there half an hour for Robt. and Hannah Stevenson, who accompanys us on our tour to Lancaster &c. baited at the Nags Head 12 Miles from Philada. came to Rowland Evanss before 7 o'clock.—wrote to Sister this Evening sent back my Keys, which I had unknowingly brought from home: sup'd lodg'd and Breakfasted at REs road 23 long miles this Day.

23   . . . we rode upwards of 18 miles this day and 23 Yesterday, tho we are at present but 32 miles from Philaa. weather very fine, roads very hilly & Stony. RS. HS. HD. and ED—sleep'd all in one Chamber.

24   left Chainys Pennsburg this Morning rode 8 miles to the Waggon Breakfasted there, then went 12½ to the Hat. Jacobss: din'd there—left it at 3 o'clock, rode on, were overtaken by rain but not wett, went 12½ miles father, to Lancaster, were we arrived about 6 o'clock. . . .

27   left Sloughs Lancaster, after Breakfast cloudy morning rode 10 miles to the Glass-House, at Manheim, saw them make a Wine-Glass &c—din'd at Jarome Hazelmans, near the Glass-House, then set of for Lititz. . . .

29   . . . discoverd the Young Horse, (rode up the Hill by HD) had broke loose and that the inner part of his Thigh was badly wounded; probably by the Spur of a Tree, it bled fast, which hurry'd us back to the Tavern where a Bath and suitable applications were made: here we dined, and about 3 o'clock after

paying an extravagent Bill, we set forward to David Levans 18 Miles from Reding, a Tavern in Manatawny, to this place we got about Dusk, the Wounded Horse soon became stiff and his Thigh swell'd much—This Evening our Landlady, a dirty old Dutch Woman, refused Changing very dirty, for Clean Sheets, tho after much intreaty, she pretend'd to comply, but to our mortification found she had taken the same sheets, sprinkled them, then Iron'd and hung 'em by the fire and placed them again on the Bed; so that we were necessitated to use our cloaks &c & this Night slepp'd without sheets.— with the assistance of our two Servants cooking, we sup'd pretty Well and slep'd better than we had any Reason to expect, all in one Room. . . .

30 HS and self each folded a dirty Sheet Nutmeg fashion, and left then cover'd up in the Beds, for the old Woman.[3] . . . we forded the Lehigh first from the Shore to an Island and from thence over the broad and stony part to the other Shore—from hence we had 5 or 6 miles bad and stony Road to Bethleham, which however we reach'd in good time to eat a hearty Dinner— this Afternoon walk'd thro' several parts of the settlement with J.F Oberlin, examined the Single Brothers House, single sisters and Widdows Houses— Water Works &c—and then return'd to our lodgings at the Tavern in Bethleham.[4]

3. Words crossed out.

4. Moravians settled in Bethlehem in 1740 and dominated the community for nearly a century thereafter. Their society was based on the concept of a joint economy in which members resided in communal living quarters and pooled their income to support the missionaries among them. In 1744 a house for single brothers was completed, and four years later when the men were removed to a larger building in order to accommodate their growing numbers, unmarried women made their home in the older structure.

By 1754 the Bethlehem waterworks was in operation. Among the first of its kind in the colonies, the system consisted of a waterwheel that provided power for pumps, which directed the water into a holding tank (information courtesy of Judith B. Claps, Board Member, Burnside Plantation, Bethlehem, Pa.; William J. Murtagh, *Moravian Architecture and Town Planning: Bethlehem, Pennsylvania, and Other Eighteenth-Century American Settlements* [Chapel Hill: University of North Carolina Press, 1967], 36–37, 73).

1772

1772 Janry. 1. . . . Sister and self. went this Evining to see our poor Friend Peggy Parr, who was taken this Afternoon with a fit of the Appoplexey; in which she lays: (A very affecting Scene)—Sister sat up all Night with her.

1772 Janry. 3 Peggy Parr, departed this life, between 38 & 39 Years of Age— dull weather this day—We stayd at home all day, nobody here.

Febry. 1. 1772. seventh Day—HD. and MS left home between 11 and 12 near Noon, in a Sleigh for George Oats,—Conrade drove—they return'd the 2, left our dear baby well—ordred Sally Oat to begin to wean him on Second day the 3 Instant.

Febry. the 12 we heard from our baby this Day, and several times by the Post Boy since he has been weaning; he takes it pritty well; and is bravely.

Feby. 17 1772 Benjn. Ardey; Abel Jamess Man was taken up, and put into Jail for taken Goods out of the Store &c. to a large Amount.

April 15. 1772 HD. was let Blood.

April 25. 1772 ED. was let Blood.

Billy Drinker put on Coat and Britches[1] May 12, 1772.

Sally Drinker went to Writing School April 22. 1772. to B. Jones.

1772. June 13. HD. ED. AD. WD. HD Junr. [h]arry and Nany; set of in the Waggon for Frankford, but could not get the Horses' cross Race Street corner,

---

1. In the eighteenth-century Anglo-American world, boys and girls wore similar tunics or dresses from infancy until age six or seven, when the boys began donning breeches or jackets and trousers. At age five, Billy Drinker first wore breeches a little earlier than most boys, as did his brother, Henry (Karen Calvert, "Children in American Family Portraiture, 1670 to 1810," *William and Mary Quarterly*, 3d ser., 39 [1982]: 87–113; Philip Greven, *The Protestant Temperament: Patterns of Child-Rearing, Religious Experience, and the Self in Early America* [New York: Knopf, 1977], 282–86; see below, June 25, 1775).

---

they run back and behav'd so ill that we were oblidg'd to get out and stay at home.

July 27. 1772   I was call'd up between 12 and one, this Morning by Richd. Waln Betsy was brought to Bed about. four with her Daughter Rebecca, Second Day Morning.

July 28, 1772   Richard Jolloff was Drownd'd, he was playing in the River, but knew not how to swim.

the 29.   MS. Betty Davis, my Nancy and Jacob, went to Frankford, to clean the House, they came home in the Evening—Sally Oat went away this after-noon. My little Henry has voided nine worms this Day. 20 since he came home from Nurse. he has taken the Caro. pink-Root;[2] Rheubarb,[3] and Bark for disordred Bowels.

1772 Octor. 2   the Measels came out on Sally, after being 5 days very unwell she has been for 3 days past, much Afflicted with a reaching to vomitt, &c.

1772 Octor. 15   Nancy has the Measels coming out on her, tho not so kindly as could be wish'd, little Henry they are just appearing on 'tho he has been very unwell for a week past, they are both very poorly; Sally took a dose Physick to Day, and seems, thro' Mercy bravely—Nany Oat, beginning to grow unwell—Docr. Evans very unwell, Docr. Redman tends us.

28   Billy very full of the Measels, little Henry continues very poorly.

1772 Novr. 24   third day. the first Monthly Meeting up Town. HD. chose Clark.

1772 Novr. 30,   ED. was let Blood.

2. Carolina pink root or Indian pink root, native to the southern United States, was effective in treating worms in children. Long used by Native Americans and adopted by southern colonists in the mid-eighteenth century, the root was administered in powders or infusions (W. Lewis, *New Dispensatory*, 231–32; Millspaugh, *Medicinal Plants*, 522–23).

3. Rhubarb was used in the Drinker household for constipation and indigestion. According to one contemporary manual, rhubarb helped purge the stomach, but was also "celebrated for its astringent [quality] by which it strengthens the tone of the stomach and intestines, and proves useful in diarrhorea and disorders proceeding from a laxity of fibers" (C. K. Drinker, *Not So Long Ago*, 9; W. Lewis, *New Dispensatory*, 210).

1773

1773 April 9   HD. and Daughter Sally went round the Race Ground on Horse Back; Sally on the oldest of our Brack Mares, the first of her riding alone, unless, 2 or 3 times up and down our Alley.

1773 April the 11   First Day—After Dinner—HD. Josey James, and myself, cross'd Delaware, the wind pretty high at N W, did not sail—ED. road on the Old Mare as far as Moores-Town, had not been on Horse back for 15 years past—drank tea, sup'd and lodg'd at Josh. Smiths—a good Deal shaken; Breakfasted there next Morning, then set of in a Borrow'd Waggon, with our 2 Mares. for Ansiunc[1] at the Iron-Works, Polly Smith with us; stop'd at Charles Reeds Iron Works 10 miles from Moorestown; then went on 10 miles further to Lawrence Salters, dined there late:—went in the afternoon to the Forge, saw then make Barr-Iron; Lodg'd there at LS.[2]

Henry Drinker Junr. cut his first Tooth the beginning of Sepr. 1771 at G. Oats.

Henry Drinker Junr. walk'd alone, the beginning of Novr. 1771; just turn'd of 12 Months at George Oats.

HD. junr. began to Chatter in the Spring 1772.

Decr. 2, 1773.   AJ. and HD. sent a paper to the Coffee-House this Evening conserning the Tea.[3]

1. The Atsion ironworks in the Pine Barrens of New Jersey, near Shamong Township, were first developed by Charles Read, a lawyer and political leader of Burlington County, N.J. In 1766 in conjunction with two other partners Read built a forge to convert pig iron into bar iron. He ran into financial difficulties in 1773 and on Mar. 16 sold his interest in the forge to Henry Drinker and Abel James. In a financial reorganization on Apr. 2 Drinker and James became owners of 50.1 percent of the forge and Lawrence Salter, one of Read's original partners, the owner of the remainder. In 1774 the owners expanded the furnace of the forge, making it independent of other forges and allowing the ironworks to exploit the bog ore at the site (Arthur D. Pierce, *Iron in the Pines: The Story of New Jersey's Ghost Towns and Bog Iron* [New Brunswick, N.J.: Rutgers University Press, 1957], 20–35).
2. ED returned to Philadelphia on April 16.
3. James and Drinker, like other agents, had posted a bond enabling them to sell dutied British East India tea, the object of great opposition in the colonies. During the autumn of 1773 a popularly chosen extralegal committee of twelve (later augmented to twenty-four)

Decr. 14   HD. ED. took a ride before dinner, as far as the 3 M Stone, return'd home by [the front] of Kingsington, where they are just begining to build a Ship for James & Drinker—6 Miles.

Decr. 24.   an account from Boston, of 342 Chests of Tea, being thrown into the Sea.[4]

Decr. 25.   John Parrock call'd this Evining to inform that the Tea Ship, was at Chester.

Decr. [27.]   The Tea Ship, and Cargo, sent of this Morning.

---

pressured the agents not to sell the tea. Agents Thomas and Isaac Wharton, despite a previous agreement to stand together, yielded to the committee's demands sooner than did James and Drinker, who were caught between their business obligations, their bond, and the popular opposition in Philadelphia to landing the tea. Finally on Dec. 2 the committee of twenty-four secured a pledge from James and Drinker that they would not insist on landing the tea from the ship *Polly* (Ryerson, *Revolution Is Now Begun*, 34–37; Labaree, *Boston Tea Party*, 97–103; *Statement of Philadelphia Consignees to the Committee*, Dec. 2, 1773, in Mss. Relating to Non-Importation Agreements, 1766–75, *APS*; James & Drinker Statement, Dec. 2, 1773, in Drinker Papers [1739–79] at HSP).

4. A special postscript edition of the *Pennsylvania Gazette* on this date brought Philadelphians their first published accounts of the Boston Tea Party of Dec. 16 (*Pa. Gaz.*, Dec. 24, 1773; for further account of the Boston Tea Party, its background, and its consequences, see Labaree, *Boston Tea Party*).

1774

March 1. My little Henry, went first to School; to, R. Jones, and H. Catheral—& Nancy went to Drawing-School—to Ty. Barret.

March 4. HD. ED. took a ride before dinner round part of the Town—1½ Mile.

from March the 7 to April the 12, HD. went to Atsion JD. with him, and to Burlington, AJ. with him, while ED—was up stairs.[1]

April 14. Sucky James Departed this Life—she pass'd the first meeting, with R S Smith the 22 ultimo—Age'd 17 years.

1774 April 25 HD. MS. went to the Burial of Charles Jerviss Son John, aged 5 months.

April 27 HD. ED. took a ride to Kingsington, clim'd up to the side of our new Ship which is building there—came home by Charles Wests place—4 Miles.

May 3. Govr. H——h——n, &c, carted round the Town hang'd and burnt in Effigie.[2]

May 27. Sally Drinker and Nany Oat, took a dose Physick; Docr. Redman tends 'em for a rash and soar Throat,—which great numbers are afflicted with at this time, in town—, several have been taken of, with the Putrid soar Throat,[3] of which number were, Abey Howel, and Sucky James.

1. ED gave birth to Mary (Molly) Drinker Mar. 14, 1774.
2. Massachusetts Governor Thomas Hutchinson's failure to oppose British taxation policies aroused hostility in the major colonial port cities. On May 2 residents of Philadelphia constructed a wooden effigy of him, to which was affixed a plaque describing him as a traitor to his native country. The likeness was placed in a cart, conducted through the streets, and finally burned (*Pa. Gaz.*, May 4, 1774).
3. A serious inflammation of the mucous membrane of the pharynx, the tonsils, and the folds of the palate that resulted in the formation of gangrenous patches in the throat. The illness could be fatal if the eroded blood vessels in this area hemorrhaged (Gould, *Dictionary of Medicine*, 1220, 1063).

June 14. we were knockd up before Day this Morning by Portugease, his Mistress, Hannah Stevenson, being ill, Sister waited on her; I could not leave my little Molly she being unwell—Hannah Was brought to Bed, about 5 this Morning of her Daughter Hannah.

1774 June 22, Our 4 Children, Nancy Oat, and Nancy Waln, Hannah and Polly Drinker, went in our Waggon to Kingsington, Jacob, and Harry, went afoot to see the New Ship Chalkley Lanch'd, the Seacond of that Name, Belonging to James & Drinker HD. din'd there—the Children return'd and all din'd with us.

July 3 B. Trapnel taken unwell—the 4 and 5–6 continues very unwell keeps his Room, with a sick stomach and Fever Docr. Park tends him.—he continued the same till the Morning of the 9th without our being apprehensive of the danger he was in or Docr. Parke; tho' Benny had desir'd him to call in Dr. Kearsley, who did not see him till the 9th. when he was much changed for the worse his fever had chang'd to Billious.[4] he departed this Life about 4 o'clock the Morning of the 10th. First Day—and was so much chang'd by 9 o'clock that the Doctors advis'd by all means to bury him that day which was accordingly done between 7 and 8 in the Evening—Benny was in his 27th. or 8th. year; much lamented by all of us.

25: HD. and Sally, took a ride on Horse-back—to Frankford.

30. MS. Billy little Henry, Harry, and Nanny, (who they took up out of Town,) went in the Chaise to Frankford, HD. and Sally on Horse back, Sally rode her Daddys Horse for the first time—they clean'd the House, drank Coffee there, came home by dusk in the Evening.

Augt. 12. MS. Billy and little Henry, in the New Chaise, J Drinkers Horse; ED. Hannah Dingee and little Molly in the old Chaise and Mare—Jacob on Britton—went after Breakfast to Frankford.—HD. and Sally came up on Horse back after dinner; Sally on Noble, HD. on Wilddear the Children and Daddy, went Fishing to the Creeck—came home all togeather after Tea—10 Miles.

Augt. 19 fifth Day: HD. Sally and Nancy, in the New Chaise, MS. Billy and Henry in the Old Chaise, went after Breakfast to Frankford,—Rachel Drinker, her Son Josey and Daughter Polly—Sammy Sanson and Hannah, with their

---

4. *Bilious fever* in its simplest definition meant a fever accompanied by a copious discharge of bile. Many writers found this to be a symptom of intermittent and remittant (malarial) fevers, occurring in the summer and fall, but it was also used to describe other fevers (Cullen, *Practice of Physic*, 111–12; Buchan, *Domestic Medicine* [1799], 187–88; Gould, *Dictionary of Medicine*, s.v. "fevers").

Daughter—John Drinker on Horse back—went after dinner to our Foulks at Frankford, Becky James with her daughters, and son Tommy and Sally Dukes, drank Coffee with them—the Children were much delighted catching Fish—Jacob and Herry there.

Augt. 26. Reba. Waln and her Daughter Nancy—MS. ED. Sally, Nancy and Billy, went to see the Wax-Work made by Mrs. Wells,[5] opposit the Royal white Oak.

Sepr. 7. Sally and Nancy went to Mrs Woods Kniting School.

Octor. 7. R Walln, her daughter Nancy and Son Boby. ED. Sally, Nancy, and Billy, & MS—took a walk this afternoon, to the new Prison:[6] workman very busy there—walk'd in the Negros Burying Grownd, and went in to J Dickinson's new House, came home to Coffee.

Novr. 1. HD. and Nancy went out on Horseback, road 6 or 7 Miles Nany on Noble.

5. Rachel Lovell Wells (d. 1795), born a Quaker, was the widow of Philadelphia shipwright James Wells. In the early 1770s she and her sister, Patience Lovell Wright, began making portraits in wax. The two sisters toured the South with their portraits during the winter months and displayed their work the rest of the year at the Wells's home in Philadelphia and at Wright's home in New York City, until Wright left for London (E. J. Pyke, *A Biographical Dictionary of Wax Modellers* [Oxford: Clarendon Press, 1973]; For a description of Wells's work from 1776 see John Adams's account in Charles Coleman Sellers, *Patience Wright: American Artist and Spy in George III's London* [Middletown, Conn.: Wesleyan University Press, 1976], 119–20, 13–14, 24–43).

6. The construction site of Philadelphia's new jail was at Walnut Street near Sixth Street. The old city jail at Third and High streets was overcrowded and underfunded, and it lacked security. While the new jail was able to receive some prisoners in 1775, it was still only partially completed when the British entered the city in 1777 (Bridenbaugh and Bridenbaugh, *Rebels and Gentlemen*, 250–53; Teeters, *Cradle of the Penitentiary*, 17–27).

1775

March 8.   New-Ship Chalkley, arriv'd here with servants—in Ballist.[1]

April 13.   Susannah Swett came to Live with us.[2]

May 3.   Billy Drinker, went to Shool to. Wm. Dickinson, the first of his going to a Mans School.

25   Molly fell out of Bed last Night an attemt was made last Night to break open the Jail, to resque one Steuart, who is condem'd for foarging Mony[3]—Molly Gosnold here this Morning for to Borrow Sheets—Sarah Mitchel and Molly Stretch, drank Tea with us—A Lad call'd for HD. to make up a Board. at the School Corporation Saml. Hopkins, call'd for a paper I step'd over to R Walns.

28th.   First Day: S Swett went to Meeting with the Children this Morning myself wint with them this afternoon—R Waln, J. Drinker here.

30   went this Morning to A. Taylors—Amos here—I received a Letter from HD. by Post, wrote to him John Drinker call'd—Wm. Brown drank Coffee[4] with us— A James call'd this Evening.

June 25.   little Henry put on Coat and Britches.

July 9   HD. self and 4 Children went this afternoon, to the Burial of little Hannah Drinker, daughter of Jos. Drinker—not 10 months old—they bury'd last week a Son and Daughter (twins) who were born the week before—Aquila & Prissila.

Sepr. 6.   Isaac Hunt, and Docr. John Kearsley were exposed in a Cart, through some parts of the City[5]—the Doctors Hand much wounded with a Bayyonet.

1. Henry Drinker engaged in the German servant trade (Salinger, *Labor and Indentured Servants*, 76).
2. Susannah Swett was the widow of Benjamin Swett, who had been the father of HD's first wife, Ann Swett.
3. *Pa. Ev. Post*, May 25, 1775.
4. "Coffee" written over the word "Tea."
5. Isaac Hunt was an attorney who had represented a dry goods retailer before the Philadelphia Committee of Observation and Inspection. The retailer was accused of selling goods contrary to rules set up by the Continental Association, which promoted a boycott of British goods, and Hunt, who had Tory leanings, challenged the committee's right to regulate commerce. Hunt was forced to submit to popular pressure, however, and agreed to make a public confession on Sept. 6, when he was carted around the city in an orderly fashion apologizing to groups of residents. Dr. John Kearsley, also a loyalist, observed this procession and fired on the militiamen escorting Hunt. The militiamen then released Hunt and seized Kearsley, who was then carted around the city and subjected to taunts and abuse by its residents (Ryerson, *Revolution Is Now Begun*, 128–32).

3. Middle Age in Years of Crisis, 1776–1793

Two major public events bookend the central phase of Elizabeth Drinker's life: a violent War for Independence and a virulent yellow fever epidemic. Both episodes threatened the Drinkers' well-being, although neither claimed the life of immediate family members.

During the Revolution, zealous rebel leaders banished Henry Drinker and other fellow Quakers to Virginia, leaving Elizabeth and "Aunty" to cope as best they could. With the children's health at an all-time low and inflationary prices at an all-time high, servants running away and armies drawing near, Elizabeth found it difficult to maintain her equanimity in a war zone and occupied city. Nevertheless, she dealt with each potential disaster as it arose, and in the spring of 1778 she and several other wives journeyed to Lancaster to confront the radical leaders and plead for their husbands' release. Elizabeth's passion for privacy prevented her from revealing the intimate nature of Henry's homecoming, but the Drinker children doubtless welcomed their affectionate "Daddy" with great joy.

Ten years after the war's end, yellow fever struck Philadelphia with such force that Drinker titled her journal for that half year the "Book of Mortality." The disease claimed at least 10 percent of the city's population of forty thousand, while seventeen thousand terrified citizens fled until the epidemic subsided—the Drinkers among them.

When Elizabeth Drinker's oldest daughter was nearly twenty, Elizabeth gave birth to her last child, a son who died in 1784 at age two and a half. Four years later, she became a grandmother. Entries for the 1780s are sparse, but despite their meagerness recount the progression of Sally's and Nancy's courtships. Suitors visited the two older Drinker sisters on a regular basis and spoke to

Henry Drinker "on account of" his daughters. Sally and Jacob Downing married in 1787, and John Skyrin became Nancy's husband in 1791. Both Sally and Nancy named their first daughters after their mother, and by the end of 1793 Elizabeth Drinker was a grandmother three times over.

It is at the end of this chapter, when Drinker was in her late fifties, that now and then she found herself free from the continual beck and call of others—a circumstance reflected by the notation "no of our Children at home . . . myself alone."

1776

Janry. 25   ED—M.

Janry. 30.   JD. call'd before the Committee.[1]

[Feb.] 12   had a very bad Night, got up with my Forehead very much swel'd discover'd it to be St. Antoys Fire[2]—sent for Dr. Redman—Jacob Shoemaker call'd, a man for poor Tax—H Sanson, Becky Waln, Rachel and Henry Drinker here to Day:—fine Weather.

15th.   John Drinkers Store shet up by the Committe[3]—. HD. JD. return'd the 18th.

1776 March 2.   HD. left home Sammy Sansom—call'd,[4] din'd A Benezet; Salors Wife, G. Churchman, call'd—Cheese from Burlington, fell on Sisters Toes—Ellection[5]—MS. out this Morning at R Stevensons &c.

May 8th.   HD. this Morning Henry Mitchel and Jos James went to Atsion— the Town has been in Confusion this afternoon on account of an engagement

1. John Drinker and Thomas and Samuel Fisher were called before the Committee of Observation and Inspection for the City and Liberties of Philadelphia on Jan. 30 for refusing to accept continental bills of credit. On Feb. 5 the committee issued a statement condemning them as enemies of their country; the three men neither denied nor appealed the charges. The committee also precluded them from all trade with the inhabitants of the colonies (*Pa. Journal*, Feb. 7, 1776; *Col. Recs. Pa.* 10:486–87).

2. St. Anthony's Fire, also known as erysipelas or the rose, is characterized by red swellings on the face, the legs and face, or the whole body, and is caused by streptococci. Some forms attacked women in childbearing years (Buchan, *Domestic Medicine* [1799], 188–91; Gould, *Dictionary of Medicine*).

3. On Feb. 15 the Council of Safety directed the Philadelphia Committee of Observation and Inspection to seize all of John Drinker's books and papers and deposit them in a locked and sealed chest or trunk in his ship and to lock up the windows and doors of his stores and warehouses and nail them shut (*Col. Recs. Pa.* 10:486–87).

4. The name "Tommy James" crossed out.

5. A by-election for the seat held by Benjamin Franklin in the Pennsylvania Assembly. Franklin, who had never occupied the seat, resigned on Feb. 27, giving Philadelphians an opportunity to elect another representative to the assembly in his place (Ryerson, *Revolution Is Now Begun*, 159).

between the Rowbuck Man of War and the Gondelows[6]—the 9 another fight below, without much Damage—HD, return'd the 10th—sixth Day.

July 16. Friends Meeting-House at Market-Street Corner broke open by the American Soldiers, where they have taken up their Abode.[7]

Augt. 13. third Day—HD. Nancy and, little Henry—in the Chaise, George James on Horse-back.—left home for the Iron, Works—Nancy to be left at J. Hopkins Haddonfield—An Account this afternoon of 104 sail of Vessels having joyn'd Lord How[8]—Sister went this Afternoon with S Wharton to Visit Joseph Whartons Widdow HD return'd the 17th—Nancy stay'd at Haddonfield 'till the 21st—then came home, with Betsy Mickel and Hannah Hopkins, who, went back in the Afternoon.

Augt. 28. fourth day, Susanna Swett, left us, and went to House-Keeping near Cabble Lane.

6. On this day two heavily armed British ships, the *Roebuck*, a man of war, and the *Liverpool*, a frigate, were prevented from sailing up the Delaware River to Pennsylvania by colonial forces stationed at Fort Island. Fire was exchanged, but neither side was able to inflict much damage (*Pa. Gaz.*, May 15, 1776).

7. In 1776 several Friends' meetinghouses in the Philadelphia area were seized by local agencies and used to quarter soldiers and for other military purposes. American soldiers en route to New York from Maryland broke into the Market Street Meetinghouse and seized it for their quarters. After discussions, the officer in charge allowed Quakers to use the meetinghouse for worship, but the army retained possession of it (Mekeel, *Relation of the Quakers*, 167).

8. Philadelphia newspapers reported various sightings of British and Hessian ships off Perth Amboy, Bermuda, and Annapolis in August. Some of these vessels carried the remnants of the British army following its defeat in Charleston and survivors of Lord Dunmore's raids in Virginia. The ships were bound for New York to join Gen. William Howe and Adm. Richard Howe, whose forces had arrived in New York in July (*Pa. Journal*, Aug. 14, 1776; *Pa. Gaz.*, Aug. 14, 1776; Boatner, *American Revolution*, 472–73, 798).

1777

1777 Janry. 25.   We had 5 American Soliders quartered upon us by order of the Counsel of Safty[1]—the Soliders named Adam Wise, Henry Feating, these two stay'd 2 or 3 days with us, the rest went of in an hour or two after they came.

March 5.   Thos. Wharton, was proclaimed; Esqr., President of the Supreme Executive Council of the commonwealth of Pennsylvania,[2] Capt. General and Commander in Chief in and over the Same—some call him Governour.

March   a Young Man of the Name of Molsworth was hang'd on the Commons by order of our present ruling Gentr'y.[3]

March   Our little Henry was run over by a Horse in the Street, his Knee was Brused, but not meterially hurt.

April 12   Bill Gardiner push'd little Henry of a Carpenters Bench, in Car-lilse's Shop, and hurt his arm very much—we sent for Docr. Redman who

1. In the winter of 1777 various colonial militia groups passed through Philadelphia. As the available barracks in Philadelphia filled up, the Council of Safety on Jan. 22 directed the barracks master to quarter the militia in the private homes of people who had not joined the campaign against England. Quarters in private homes were to be based on the size of the house and the convenience of the families (*Pa. Ev. Post*, Jan. 25, 1777).
2. On Mar. 5 Thomas Wharton, Jr., was elected president of Pennsylvania's Supreme Executive Council. Wharton, a merchant, was a younger cousin of Thomas Wharton, Sr., a Quaker who was later exiled to Virginia with HD. Wharton Jr., unlike his cousin, was an enthusiastic supporter of the rebel cause and had been the head of Pennsylvania's Council of Safety, which ran the state from July 1776 until this date, when the new constitution went into effect. The 1776 state constitution created a plural executive branch called the Supreme Executive Council, made up of one representative of the city of Philadelphia and one representative from each county. The representatives served three-year terms. At the head of the council was a president elected jointly by the council and the assembly. Wharton was its first elected president, and George Bryan was the vice president. Five members of the Supreme Executive Council constituted a quorum (*DAB*, s.v. "Thomas Wharton"; Robert L. Brunhouse, *The Counter-Revolution in Pennsylvania 1776–1790* [1942; 2d ptg. Harrisburg, Pa.: The Pennsylvania Historical and Museum Commission, 1971], 10–15, 22).
3. James Molesworth was hanged following his conviction for treasonable practices against the state. He was accused of trying to hire men to pilot the British fleet up the Delaware River (Reed, *Joseph Reed*, 2:30–34; Marshall, *Diary Extracts*, 118, 201; *Pa. Archives*, ser. 1, 5:270–82; *Col. Recs. Pa.*, 11:197).

after examineing it, found the Bones were not broak but the Arm badly strain'd.

June the 5   an Officer with 2 Constables call'd on us for Blankets,[4] went away without any—as others had done 3 or 4 times before.

1777 July 4—the Town Illuminated and a great number of Windows Broke on the Anniversary of Independence and Freedom.[5]

Augt. 20 or 21   our dear little Henry was taken ill with a vomiting and disordred Bowels, occasion'd by eating watermellon too close to the Rine—he voided in the course of his Sickness, (which turnd out to be an inviterate Bloody and white Flux) 3 large Worms, and vomited one alive—for 12 Days he eat nothing—and is now Sepr. the 6 in a very poor way, reduced almost to a Skelaton with a constant fever hanging about him, tho' the disorder seems to be somewhat check'd, and he has an appetite in the Morning—he has taken 8 Clysters and many doses of Physick—his Body comes down and he is so weak that he cannot sit up alone.

Some day since the illness of our Child, we had a valuable pair of large End-Irons seazed and taken from us, by Philip Mause.

1777 Sepr. the 2   third Day—HD. having been, and continuing to be unwell, stay'd from meeting this morning. he went towards Noon into the front Parlor to copy the Monthly meeting minuits—the Book on the Desk—and the Desk unlock'd, when Wm. Bradford; one [Bluser] and Ervin, entred, offering a Parole for him to sign—which was refus'd. they then seiz'd on the Book and took several papers out of the Desk and carried them off; intimating their design of calling the next morning at 9 o'clock; and desireing HD to stay at home for that time, which as he was unwell, was necessary; they according calld the 4th, in the morning and took my Henry to the [Massons] lodge—in an illegeal, unpredesented manner—where are several, other Friends with some of other proswasions, made prisoners;—Isreal Pemberton, John Hunt, James Pemberton, John Pemberton, Henry Drinker, Saml. Pleasants, Thos.

4. On Mar. 12 the Continental Congress had passed a resolution requesting the states to supply blankets to colonial troops. The commissary of the continental army then requested the Pennsylvania Board of War to supply blankets, and on May 2 Pennsylvania's ruling body, the Supreme Executive Council, authorized the requisition of 4,000 blankets from the state, 667 of them to come from the city of Philadelphia, where twelve men, including the artist Charles Willson Peale, were appointed commissioners to collect the blankets. Quakers were apparently singled out for this and other requisitions (*Pa. Ev. Post*, Mar. 13, 1777; *Pa. Gaz.*, May 7, 1777; Mekeel, *Relation of the Quakers*, 167).

5. Quaker shopkeepers refused to close their shops on holidays like July 4 or days appointed to celebrate American military victories. In retaliation, Philadelphians broke the windows of many Quaker shops (Mekeel, *Relation of Quakers*, 167).

Fisher, Saml. Fisher, Thos. Gillpin, Edward Penington; Thos. Wharton, Charles Jervis, Ellijah Brown, Thos. Afflick, Phineas Bond, Wm. Pike, Mires Fisher, Charles Eddy, Wm. Smith, Broker—Wm. D Smith, Thos. Comb, &c I went this Even'g to see my HD. where I mett with the Wives & Children of our dear Friends and other visitors in great numbers—upwards of 20 of our Friends call'd to see us this Day—my little Henry very low and Feverish.

8th. my little Henry very unwell this Day could not go to see his Daddy untill the Afternoon, who I found with the other Friends pritty-well. they have sent several Remonsterances to the Congress and Consel.[6] . . .

9 . . . My self Sally and little Molly went this Afternoon to the Lodge, during my stay there, word was brought from the Conscil that their Banish-ment was concluded to be on the Morrow,[7] the Waggons were preparing to carry them off—I came home in great distress. . . .

11 The sending off our Friends is put of till 3 this Afternoon, they find it difficult to procure Waggons and Men—My Henry Breakfasted with us; then went to the Lodge. I went there about 10 o'clock, R Drinker with me, I step'd over to S. Pleasants, then back to the Lodge HD—not there when I return'd—the Town is in great Confusion at present a great fireing heard below[8] it is supos'd the Armies are Engag'd, 'tis also reported that several Men of War are [ ] up the River—Jos. Howell, R. Scattergood, S Swett, R Drinker &c here this Morning.—Some time after dinner Harry came in a hurry for his Master Horse for a Servent to ride, informing me that the waggons were waiting at the Lodge to take our dear Friends away. I quickly went there; and as quickly came away finding great a number of People there but few women, bid my dearest Husband farewell, and went in great distress to James Pembertons, Sally with me. . . .

6. The prisoners sent remonstrances to the Continental Congress and the Supreme Execu-tive Council, protesting that their arrests were arbitrary, unjust, and illegal. Upon receiving the remonstrances, the Continental Congress requested that the Supreme Executive Council give the prisoners a hearing. The council replied that in the press of events it had no time to listen to the prisoners' claims. The Congress then disassociated itself from the matter by saying that the prisoners were subject to the Supreme Executive Council and that Congress would not interfere in the state's internal affairs (the remonstrances are printed in Gilpin, *Exiles in Virginia*, 77–85, 96–97, 103–4; Congress's response is in *JCC*, 8:718–19, 722–23; for a discussion of the confusion regarding authority over the prisoners, see Thayer, *Israel Pemberton*, 225–31).

7. The instructions of the Continental Congress to Pennsylvania were only to secure and disarm disaffected persons. On September 3, however, Congress noted a letter from George Bryan, vice president of the Supreme Executive Council of Pennsylvania, requesting the approval of Congress for Pennsylvania's plan to send those arrested, particularly Quakers who refused to make any promises or affirmations of allegiance, to Staunton, Virginia. Congress approved the request (*JCC*, 8:707–8; *Col. Recs. Pa.* 11:264, 265; Oaks, "Philadelphians in Exile," 309).

8. A reference to the Battle of Brandywine, at which Washington unsuccessfully attempted to halt the British advance on Philadelphia (Boatner, *American Revolution*, 104–10).

12   . . . this has been a day of Great Confusion to many in this City; which I have in great measure been kept out of by my constant attension on my sick Child. part of Washingtons Army has been routed, and have been seen coming into Town in Great Numbers; the perticulars of the Battle, I have not attended to, the slain is said to be very numerous.—hundreds of their muskets laying in the road, which those that made off have thrown down . . . the Wounded have been brought in this Afternoon, to what amount I have not learnt. . . .

13   Wrote to HD. by Isaac Zane Junr.—our Child appears to be better.—they have Chang'd the place of Banishment of our Friends to Winchester, as I understand. . . .

15, I have heard no News from abroad this Morning but Carriages constantly passing with the Inhabitants going away . . . last night I heard of several Friends having lost their Horses, taken from the Stables,—for which reason I ordred our Horse, and Cow to be put into the Washhouse, where they at present remain—several of my Sisters in Affliction, have this Day received Letters from their Husbands, I make no doubt but I should also have had one, but for some good reason. . . .

16   I read a letter this Morning from my HD to JD—our Stable seller was last Night broak open, and several of Jos. Scotts Barrels of Flour stolen—I rote to my HD. this Morning by Nisbet—our child seem'd better, this forenoon, but more unwell towards Evening a great weight upon my Spirits most of this day: Nancy and little Molly both complaining—this is a Sickly season, many taken down with Fevers. May it please kind Providence to preserve my dearest Husband. . . .

19   Jenny awoke us this Morning about 7 o'clock, with the News that the English were near; we find that most of our Neighbors and almost all the Town have been up since one in the Morning The account is that the British Army cross'd the [S]weeds-Foard last night, and are now on their way heather; Congress, Counsil &c are flown,[9] Boats, Carriages, and foot Padds going off all Night; Town in great Confusion. . . .

20   The Town has been very quiet all this day, I believe; it is said that Washingtons Army has cross'd the Foard and are at present on this side— some expect a battle hourly; as the English are on the opposite side—I received a Letter this Evening from my dear, a long letter . . . all the boats,

9. Members of the Continental Congress, expecting Philadelphia to fall to the British, left Philadelphia on Sept. 19 for Lancaster, Pa. (Boatner, *American Revolution*, 860).

Ferry boats excepted, are put away—and the Shiping all ordred up the River, the next tide, on pain of being burnt, should G. Howes Vesels approach. . . .

21.   . . . Sammy read aloud my dear Henrys long letter of the 17th Instant and was very much affected thereby.—after which we had a setting togeather, and Sammy was led to speak comfort to us. . . . this Evening our little sick Son received a letter from his dear Father, which is well worth the store he sits by it, he has ordred it to be put in his Pocket-Book Wile he larns to read writeing. . . .

22   . . . Nanny Oat call'd to day, to demand her freedom dues,[10] and was very impertinent and Saucy. . . .

23.   . . . Our dear Child has walk'd several times across the Room, with Jennys help to day. those men that collected Blankets &c in our Ward, were this Afternoon at each of our Neighbours, but did not call on us. it is reported and gains credit, that the English have actually cross'd Schuylkill and are on their way towards us,[11]—I received two letters after meeting from my dear Husband; which at the same time that they made my Heart ake, gave me comfort. . . .

24.   . . . the Sign (Over the Way) of G. Washingn. taken down this Afternoon—talk of the City being set on fire—Joseph Ingel, call'd to pay, for 2 or 3 Tonns of Hay, but as I had not my Husbands papers, could not receive the money. . . .

25   . . . most of our warm people are gone of, tho there are many continue here that I should not have expected. Things seem very quiate and still, and if we come of so, we shall have great cause of thankfullness—should any be so wicked as to attempt fireing the Town, Rain which seems to be coming on, may Providentially, prevent it—a great number of the lower sort of the People are gone out to them. . . .

26.   Well, here are the English in earnest,[12] about 2 or 3000, came in, through

10. Legislation passed in 1700 by the colonial assembly gave indentured servants two suits of clothes, a new axe, a grubbing hoe, and a weeding hoe as freedom dues (the axe and hoes were eliminated in 1771 legislation), but the actual composition of freedom dues varied greatly over time and place in eighteenth-century Pennsylvania. By the 1770s many indentured servants in Philadelphia received clothes and a cash settlement upon the completion of their service (Cheesman A. Herrick, *White Servitude in Pennsylvania* [Philadelphia, 1926; reprint, New York: Negro Universities Press, 1969], 205-11, 293; *Statutes at Large*, 8:30-31; Salinger, *Labor and Indentured Servants*, 134-35).

11. The word "they" crossed out.

12. On Sept. 26 three thousand British troops under Lord Charles Cornwallis took possession of Philadelphia. The main body of the British army remained in Germantown, five miles north of the city, where they had camped on Sept. 25 with their commander-in-chief, General Howe (Frederick D. Stone, "The Struggle for the Delaware: Philadelphia under Howe and Arnold," in *Narrative and Critical History of America*, ed. Justin Winsor [Boston: Houghton Mifflin, 1887], 6:383-84).

second street, without oppossition or interruption, no plundering on the one side or the other, what a satisfaction would it be to our dear Absent Friends, could they but be inform'd of it. . . .

27   About 9 o'clock this Morning the Province, and Delaware Frigets, with several Gondelows came up the River, with a design to fire on the[13] they were attac'd by a Battry[14] which the English have errected[15] the engagement lasted about half an hour when many shots were exchang'd; one House struck, but not much damaged; no body, that I have heard, hurt on shore. . . .

28   First Day: Sister and the Children went to Meeting this Morning this is our Yearly Meeting, and many more Friends in Town than could have been expected, the Situation of things considred. . . . I hear this Evening that they are building Battrys on the Jersey shore, opposite Arch and Market Streets. The Ameriacans I mean.

29   . . . a Number of the [Citysans] taken up, and imprison'd.[16] . . .

[Oct.] 6   . . . The heaviest fireing that I think I ever heard, was this Evening, for upwards of two hours, thought to be the English troops, engag'd with the Mud-Island Battry,[17]—an Officer call'd this Afternoon to ask if we could take in a Sick or Wounded Captain; I put him off by saying that as my Husband was from me, I should be pleas'd if he could provide some other convenient place, he hop'd no offence, and departed. . . . two of the Presby-

13. "Town" crossed out.
14. On Sept. 27, a day after the British occupation of Philadelphia, British soldiers began erecting batteries to protect the city against the American navy anchored a short distance below in the Delaware River. The British succeeded in mounting only four guns when the American frigate *Delaware*, with Capt. Charles Alexander in command, the ship *Montgomery*, the sloop *Fly*, and four galleys began firing on the British at nine in the morning. The battle lasted about an hour, when the *Delaware*'s foremast was shot away and the ship ran aground. The *Fly* also ran aground shortly thereafter. The other American vessels slipped away safely. The British boarded the *Delaware* and captured those of the crew who did not escape to other vessels or the Jersey shore (Stryker, *Forts on the Delaware*, 3–4).
15. The words "at the upper lower end of the Town" crossed out.
16. Loyalists were rounding up American sympathizers, subjecting them to a "Loyalist citizen arrest," and incarcerating them in the Walnut Street jail. After questioning, British authorities released most of the several hundred persons arrested (Jackson, *With the British Army*, 17).
17. Mud Island, situated in the Delaware River a little below the mouth of the Schuylkill River, south of Philadelphia, had a commanding position over the navigable channel between the island and the Pennsylvania shore. American forces built Fort Mifflin there and placed barricades in the river to hinder British vessels. The British, who had entered the lower Delaware on Oct. 4, knew they had to incapacitate the American batteries and river barricades to advance. The gunfire to which ED refers may have had some connection with the British troops who began building batteries on nearby Province Island in the Schuylkill River on Oct. 7. The British hoped that the Province Island location would give them a commanding position over Mud Island so they could silence the batteries at Fort Mifflin and remove the barricades (Stryker, *Forts on the Delaware*, 7–11).

tearan Meeting Houses, are made Hospitals of, for the Wounded Soliders, of which there are a great Number.

8 . . . Sister with Billy and the two Hannah Catherels & M Pleasants, went to the Play-House, the State-House, and one of the Presbytearn's Meeting Houses, to see the Wounded Soliders.

9 fireing last night, and heavey fireing this Morning from 5 o'clock 'till between 6 & 7, it was the Frigit and Gondelows, playing upon the English, who were errecting a Battry on, or near the Banks of Schuylkill,[18] one Englishman slain and two Wounded, 2 Horses kill'd—Jenney and Harry went this Afternoon in the rain, to the Play House &c. with a Jugg of Wine-Whey and a Tea-Kittle of Coffee, for the Wounded Men. . . .

12 First Day: We were awaked this Morning at about 2 o'clock, by H Drinker, knocking at my Chamber door, and asking for a light, as there was a cry of fire, it prov'd to be a Stable at the upper end of Second Street, where 3 or 4 Horses were burnt to Death. . . .

16 . . . 5 Weeks this day since my dearest Henry left us, the thoughts of the approaching cold season, and the uncertainty when we shall meet again, is at times hard to bare; yet at other times I am sustain'd with a Lively hope, that I shall see that time, and prehaps it may be sooner than we seem to expect. . . .

our little Molly went alone when she was, between 14 and 15 months—May— 1775.[19]

little Molly began to Chatter, when she was about 20 months old.

Novr. the 20. 1775. second Day, I began to Wean my little Molly—she is very good natur'd, and bares it well, tho' she seems in trouble about it—20 months old and upwards, when she was Wean'd.

18th. . . . The Troops at Germington are coming within 2 or 3 miles of this City to encamp—provisions are so scarce with us now, that Jenney gave 2/6 p. lb. for mutton this Morning—The people round the Country dose not come near us with any thing, what little butter is brought is 7/6—The fleet not yet up, nor likely to be soon, I [fear]. Jenney and Billy, went this Afternoon, with coffee and whey for the Soliders.

18. An attack by nine American galleys on British grenadiers who were building batteries at Webb's Ferry, a crossing point of the Schuylkill River to Province Island (Jackson, *Pennsylvania Navy*, 143, 139).

19. The three entries "our little Molly . . . when she was wean'd" were written on loose, mispaginated leaves in the manuscript volume.

20th. Chalkley James Breakfasted with us—Billy began a quarters Schooling, whole Days, at Joseph Yerkess the first of his going since his dear Daddy left us, and for a long time before, Henry went this morning for the first time since his illness, little Molly also, I put to school with Henry, to H. Catheral, the first of her ever going unless on a visit . . . if things dont change 'eer long, we shall be in poor plight, everything scarce and dear, and nothing suffer'd to be brought in to us. . . .

23 this day will be remember'd by many; the 2500 Hessions who cross'd the River the day before yesterday, were last Night driven back 2 or 3 times, in endeavouring to Storm the fort on Red Bank,[20] 200 slain and great Numbers wounded, the fireing this Morning seem'd to be incesant, from the Battry, the Gondelows, and the Augustia Man of War, of 64 Guns, she took fire, and after burning near 2 hours, blew up . . . The Hessians and other of the British Troops are encamp'd in the Jersyes, this Night, we can see their fiers for a considerable distance along the shore. . . .

25 . . . An Officer call'd to Day to know if Genl. Grant could have quarters with us; I told him as my Husband was from me, and a Number of Young Children round me, I should be glad to be excus'd—he reply'd, as I desir'd it, it should be so. . . .

Novr 1. . . . a poor Solider was hang'd this Afternoon on the Common, for striking his Officer; The Hessians go on plundring at a great rate, such things as, Wood, Potatoes, Turnips &c—Provisions are scarce among us. . . .

5 . . . A Solider came to demand Blankets, which I did not in any wise agree to, notwithstanding my refusial he went up stairs and took one, and with seeming good Nature beg'd I would excuse his borrowing it, as it was G. Howes orders. . . .

8 We had a Stove put up in the back Parlor; this Morning Wood is so very scarce, that unless thing mend there is no likelyhood of a Supply, and we have no more then 4 or 5 Cord, in the Celler. . . .

11 . . . it is two months this day since my dear Henry left me, and I have not

20. A reference to the Battle of Fort Mercer on Oct. 22. Fort Mercer, another of the Delaware River fortifications (see above, Oct. 6), was located at Red Bank in Gloucester County, N.J. Four hundred American troops led by Col. Christopher Greene repulsed an attack by three battalions and one artillery regiment of Hessian soldiers. The Hessians suffered many casualties. The naval action concerning the *Augusta* took place on Oct. 23 in the vicinity of Fort Mifflin at Mud Island, where a five-hour battle transpired between the British and American fleets (Stryker, *Forts on the Delaware*, 15–26).

heard directly from himself since he left Reading, except one Letter from Carlile to J Drinker. . . .

12   great part of last Night and most of this day at times, we have heard the Cannon below; Mud-Island Battry not yet taken.—they say that it is reported in the Country that 5/– is given here for a Rat: it is bad enough indeed, but far from being so, I trust it will not. . . .

15   . . . I had the great Satisfaction this Evening of receiving two Letters from my dearest Henry, the first I have received from him since he left Reading, he mentions 2 others, wrote before these, that have not come to hand, several since I doubt not,—if I can judge of my dear by his Letters, he is in good Spirits, which thought is pleasing to me. . . .

18   . . . Nanny Oat came while I was out, to ask pardon for her former conduct, which has been vastly impudent. . . .

19   . . . G. Corn Walace left this City the Day before Yesterday at 2 o'clock in the Morning with 3000 men.[21] . . .

20   . . . Wm. Jackson and Benjn. Mason call'd and brought me two letters from my dear Henry—dated the 1 and 11th. Instant—tis a great comfort to know that he was so lately well—they left others litters for us poor women. . . .

22   . . . one thousand Men, attack'd the Picquet guard this Morning about 11 o'clock, they drove them off, when some took Shelter in J. Dickensons House, and other Houses thereabouts, the English immeadatly set fire to said Houses and burnt them to the Ground,—the burning those Houses tis said is a premeditated thing, as they serve for skulking places; and much anoy the Guards. . . .

23   . . . William Jackson proposes, paying a visit to Winchester next month, he leaves Town tomorrow Morning I gave him this Afternoon £61. 11. 3. Continenl. Cury.—and 2 pair of worsted Stockings for my dear Henry. . . .

24   Wm. Jackson call'd this Morning to let me know, that he was not free to take the continental money with him, I must therefore seek another

21. Lord Cornwallis left Philadelphia with two thousand troops to attempt another assault on Fort Mercer (see above, Oct. 23). After the fall of Fort Mifflin on Nov. 16 further defense of Fort Mercer was untenable, and Col. Christopher Greene evacuated the fort the night of Nov. 20-21, thus opening the Delaware River to British shipping (Boatner, *American Revolution*, 383).

conveyance. . . . the poor people have been allow'd for some time past to go to Frankford Mill, and other Mills that way, for Flour, Abraham Carlile who gives them passes, has his Door very much crouded every morning. . . .

25 . . . We were very much affrighted this Evening before 9 o'clock, Jenney happen'd to go into the Yard, where she saw a Man with Ann—she came in and wisper'd to Sister, who immediately went out, and discoverd a Young Officer with Ann coming out from the little House, Sister held the Candle up to his Face and ask'd him who he was, his answer was whats that to you, the Gate was lock'd and he followd Ann and Sister into the Kitchen, where he swore he had mistaken the House, but we could not get him out,—Chalkley James who happen'd to be here, came into the Kitchen and ask'd him what busyness he had there he dam'd him and ask'd whats that to you, shook his Sword, which he held in his Hand and seem'd to threaten, when Chalkly with great resolution twisted it out of his Hands and Collor'd him—Sister took the Sword from Chalkly and lock'd it up in the draw in the parlor, all his outcry was for his Sword, and swore he would not stir a foot untill he had it. I then sent in for Josa. Howel, when he declar'd that he knew we were peaceable people, and that he gave up his Sword on that account out of pure good natur'd, which he had said to us before. he told Chalkley in the Kitchen that he would be the death of him tomorrow,—Josa. got him to the door, and then gave him his Sword, expecting he would go of, but he continu'd swaring there, where Josa. left him and went to call Abel James; in the mean time the impudent Fellow came in again swareing in the entry with the Sword in his hand. Sister had lock'd Chalkly up in the Middle Room, and we shut ourselves in the parlor, where he knock'd, and swore desireing entrance, our poor dear Children was never so frightend, to have an enrag'd, drunken Man, as I believe he was, with a Sword in his Hand swareing about the House, after going to or 3 times up and down the Entry, desireing we would let him in to drink a Glass of Wine with us—he went to the end of the Alley—when Harry lock'd the Front door on him, he knock and desir'd to come in, when J. Howel, and A James whome Josa. had been for, came to him, they had some talk with him, and he went off as I supose'd—I had all the back doors boulted, the Gate and[22] Front door lock'd, when in about 10 minuts after Harry came out of the Kitchen, and told us he was there I then lock'd the parlor door, and would not let Chalkley go out, Harry run into Howels for Josa. who did not come 'till some time after the Fellow was gone, and Ann with him he came over the Fence, and they went out the same way; 'tis not near one in the Morning and I have not yet recoverd the fright,—Ann call'd him Capt. Tape, or John Tape. . . .

28 sent Harry to M. Hains, with 9 Bottls of Sider for Thos. Gothrope, Sally

22. The word "back" crossed out.

Logan spent this Afternoon with us—Nr. Waln and myself took a walk this Morning to see Polly Brown, we call'd at Sally Lewiss at Eliza Armitts, came home to dinner, I took a walk in the Afternoon to Uncle Jerviss came home to Coffee. . . .

[Dec.] 2 . . . Our Saucy Ann came while I was at meeting desereing to know what I would take for hir time and she would bring the money in a minuit Sister told her she did not know, but that she heard me talk of puting her in the Work House, she reply'd if you talk so, you shall neither have me nor the Money, Sister then ordred her to come again at 12 o'clock, but she has not been since. . . .

4th. . . . I went with Nancy to H Pembertons, to carry my Letter &c to T Lightfoot, I sent lap'd up in[23] HDs Shirts £61. 11. 3 in Conti. . . .

7 . . . I drank Tea at Neigr. Howell's who was last Night Robed of a Bed from one of their 2 [p'r.] Stairs Chambers, the Fellow being surpris'd got of, without the rest of the Bootey which he had lay'd out of the Drawers ready to take away—there has been many roberies committed lately in Town. . . . we have but [9] Persons in Family this Winter we have not had less then 13 or 14 for many years past.

11 Catty Howell came in to show us, some things that she had purchas'd, Sister went out upon the Strength of it and bought a piece of Lennen &c, its a long time since we have done such a thing—goods will soon be plenty in all probobility, nothing but hard mony will pass; 40 or 50 Sail below with goods . . . Isaac Zane call'd here this Morning to see us. he is going to Winchester to see our dear Frds. he takes no letters, I sent by him a under Jacket and pair Gloves, and lap a letter up in them from Billy. . . . these are sad times for Thiveing & plundering, tis hardly safe to leave the door open a minuet. . . .

13 . . . John Gillingham was lately stop'd in the Street, after Night, and his Watch taken from him. we daily hear of enormitys of one kind or other, being committed by those from whome, we ought to find protection.

18th. . . . An Officer who calls himself Major Carmon or Carmant, call'd this Afternoon, to look for Quarters for some Oiffecer of distinction, I plead off, he would have preswaded me that it was a necessary protiction at these times to have one in the House; said I must consider of it, that he would call in a day or two, I desir'd to be excus'd, and after some more talk we parted, he behaved with much politeness, which has not been the case at many other places; they have been very rude and impudent at some houses,—I wish I may

23. The word "his" crossed out.

---

come of so; but at same time fear we must have some with us, as many Friends have them, and it seems likely to be a general thing. This has been a trying day to my Spirits—E. Edwards had a number of Letters stolen from him, which was for us poor destitutes. I have just finish'd a Letter to my dearest tis now past 12 o'clock, and Watch has put me in a flutter, by his violent barking, as if some one was in the Alley, which I believe was the case—hail since Night.

22 . . . Thos. Pleasants and Ezekill Edwards, came this Morning stayed [above] an hour, conferms the Sorrowful account that my dear is to be sent further from me. . . . the night before, I heard somebody down stairs, upon enquiry found it was Harry who had been up; every[24] noise now seems alarming, that happns in the Night.

23 . . . the Soliders Wife who lives in our House in Water Street came to me this Morning to inform that some were taring down the Shed &c. Sister went down after Meeting and desir'd 'em to desist, they said they would not for it was a Rebels House, she assur'd 'em it was not, and after more talk, proms'd if she would let 'em take the large Gate they would desist, she agreed thereto, and came [away]. . . .

29 very clear and cold, Cramond here this morning, we have at last agreed on his coming to take up his aboud with us, I hope it will be no great inconvenience, tho I have many fears, he came again in the Afternoon with a servant to look at the Stable, stay'd Tea, Thos. Masterman also, C. West and Reba. Waln here, the Troops are all return'd from Forageing—tis now 19 days since the date of my dears last letter; my mind is greatly troubled.

31st. J. Cramond who is now become one of our Family, appears to be a thoughtful sober young man, his Servant also sober and orderly; which is a great favour to us. . . .

24. The word "thing" crossed out.

1778

[Jan.] 4   First Day: I forgot to mention Yesterday, that I had a conferance with the officer who took away Ann; I stop'd him as he past the door—and after desiring him to stand still, 'till a noisey Waggon which was going by had past, (as he said he was in a hurry) I then adress'd him; if thee has no sense of Religion or Virtue, I should think that what you Soliders call Honor would have dictated to thee what was thy duty after thy behavour some time ago in this House, who me! Yes I know thee very well, I have as yet been carefull of exposeing thee, but if thee dont very soon pay me for my Servants time; as there is officers quarterd among Numbers of my acquaintance, I will tell all I meet with, he stutter'd and said I han't got your Servant, I dont care who has her, it was thee that stole her; well said he a little impudently if you'l come up to my quarters up Town, I told him If he did not bring the Mony or send it soon he should hear further from me; well, well well said he and away he went seemingly confus'd. . . .

10th.   I went this Morning to H Pembertons found her smokeing her pipe with 2 officers one of 'em is quarter'd there, after they were gone Hannah and myself were comparing notes, and reading our last Letters, we were neither of us so happy in our expectations as some others—I left Hannah near 1 o'clock and as I was returning I mett Susanna Jones and Richd. Wister talking together. I stop'd and heard him tell that he had just parted with Billy Lewis who told him that Andrew Roberson was come from Lancaster this Morning, and assures him that our dear Friends were actualy discharg'd—I have heard the same report several times since Morning and I know not what ails me that I cannot believe such good news—so much has however laid hold on me that I shall be grievously disoponined if it should fall through, a Letter from my dearest confirming it would rejoyce my Heart. . . .

19   This Morning our officer mov'd his lodgings from the bleu Chamber to the little front parlor, so that he has the two front Parlors, a Chamber up two pair of stairs for his bagage, and the Stable wholly to himself, besides the use of the Kitchen, his Camp Bed is put up. . . .

[Feb.] 3   . . . I took a walk this Morning to see Hannah Pemberton; stay'd till near dinner time mett Sucky Jones in my return who told me her mammy wanted to speak with me; she intends to go before long to G. Washington, on account of her Son; she hinted as if she would like me to go with her,—which I think will not suit me; tho' my Heart is full of some such thing, but I dont see the way clear yet. . . .

5 . . . our dear Friends are to be continu'd at Winchester 'till further orders, and that the Congress have again offred them their Liberty on taken a Test,[1] which is all sham, as they know they will not do it. . . .

7 . . . I have been much distress'd at times, when I have thought of my being still here, when prehaps it might be in my power to do something for my dear Husband; which uneasyness I communicated to MP. who then show'd me a Letter from her Father; intimating something of the kind to her Mother and herself—I hope it will please the Lord to direct us to do that which is right. it would be a tryal on us to leave our Young Familys at this time, but that I belive, if we could conclude on the matter we should leave, and trust in kind providence—it is now between 11 and 12 o'clock, and our Officer has company at Supper with him; the late hours he keeps is the greatest inconvenienc we have as yet suffer'd by having him in the House.

11 dull rainy weather and a great thaw, very foggy—several in our Family and in many other Families have got Colds—Robt. Waln and J. Drinker call'd—J.C—drank Tea with us—5 month this day since my dear Henry left me.

17 . . . our major had 8 or 10 to dine with him, they broke up in good time, but he's gone of with them and when he'l return I know not, I gave him some hints 2 or 3 days ago, and he has behav'd better since. . . .

27 . . . going into the Kitchen to night, I met Heritta the Hession Stable—Boy, in the dark, I ran against him and hurt my Eye, my Cheek is much swell'd and painful. . . .

28th. Rain and Snow all day, clear to night the Blood has settled round my eye, and it looks very ugly, my Cheek much swell'd. Capt. Harper Son from Alexandria call'd this Morning said that he was at Lancaster 3 Week ago, and heard then that the Friends at Winchester were well—Becky Jones call'd this Evening—a Number of the Troops are gone in to the Jersys, tis said that the Rebels there, are burning and destroying all before them.

1. On Jan. 29 the Continental Congress ordered the release of the prisoners on condition that they take an oath or affirmation to the state of Pennsylvania whereby each man agreed to be "a good and faithful subject" (Gilpin, *Exiles in Virginia*, 188–93, 198–200; see also *Col. Recs. Pa.*, 11:395; *JCC*, 10:85, 98; Jonathan Bayard Smith to Timothy Matlack, Jan. 19, 1778, in P. H. Smith, *Letters of the Delegates*, 8:615, n.3).

March 1st.   First Day: Sally and Billy went to meeting this morning—Nancy still unwell with a cough and pain in her side, little Henrys face swell'd with the Tooth Ach—Abey Parish, S. Swett, Jos. Scott, Danl. Drinker, Anthony Benezet and the Major drank tea with us—Sarah Fisher and her Son James here this Evening—a fine clear day, Moonlight evening a Snow Storm Since night—a number of prisoners brought from the Jersys to day, 18 or 20 they say.

14   I took a walk to H Pembertons before dinner, Our Major din'd with us to day, for the first time; Saml. Emlen, Chackly James, call'd—Molly Pleasants junr. spent this Afternoon with our Children—I call'd while I was out this Morning at O. Jones, Susy full of the notion of going to Congress, gave me several broad hints, which I could not give into. . . .

25th.   Dr. Parke call'd this Morning he seems to think it somthing strange that we have no letters—Caty Howel here after dinner—Phebe Pemberton, M Pleasants, R. Drinker, Hannah Drinker, Polly Drinker and Sally Pleasants, drank tea with us—PP. and MP. came to consult me about drawing up somthing to present to those who shall acknowledge our dear Friends as their prisoners; I had sometime ago mentiond JD. as a sutiable person to assist us in such an undertaking—We went in the Evening to JDs.—he appeard rather reluctant, but tis likely he will think of it—our intention is, tho we do not yet say so, to take it ourselves, 2 or 4 of us—when we can hear how, matters stand with our dear absent Friends . . . our Hay is out, and I beleive I must sell our poor Cow. . . .

28   . . . Mary Eddy and her Son George came this Evening to consult about sending provisions &c to our Friends John Drinker went to O Joness to consult him on the matter—Our Children are all through Mercy in good Health at present—but little Henry swallow'd a pin Yesterday which adds something to my uneasyness.

31   . . . M. Pleasants sent for me before dinner, I went, she showd me a paper drawn up to send or take to Congress, she had drawn it up, and her Mammy had added somthing to it, Nics. Waln had also made out one for us, which was not approv'd—in the Afternoon O. Jones came to desire I would meet the rest of the Women concern'd at 5 o'clock at M. Pembertons, which I did, they were all there except R. Hunt, Hetty Fisher and T. Afflicks wife—Josa. Fisher O. Jones, A. Benezet, J Drinker and Nichs. Waln, were also there—Nicholas read the Address, and the Women all sign'd it—it is partly concluded that Sush. Jones, P. Pemberton M. Pleasants and E. Drinker is to take it—I wish I felt better both in Body and mind for such an under-taking. . . .

April 1st. . . . I sent Billy for John Burket, who came, I demanded the Money which has been so long owing, he promis'd to pay it next seventh Day—I took a walk to look for Shoes, but did not succeed—Sally Logan drank Tea with us, I step'd down to Abels to ask for J. Burkets account he say'd it was not in the Company Books—Sally Zane Becky Jones call'd—I had promisd to meet R Pemberton and M. Pleasants at H. Pembertons this Afternoon, but Sister declin'd taking the weight of the Family on her during my absence, which prevented my meeting them according to Promise, and distresses me much. . . .

2d. . . . I went to Rachl. Hunts who I found writeing to her Husband, she had flattred herself from some of the letters that he was getting better and that his disorder had terminated in a Rumitisam. when I came from their door, Patty Hudson call'd me, and told me, that John Hunt was no more—that the Account of his death was just come to Town, I then went to M. Pleasants, who had sent for me, to meet at O. Jones, to settle matters for our journey; I had reason to think that it would be no easy matter to get of, therefore say'd but little about it, but concluded in my mind, that to the care of kind providence, and my dear Sister I must leave my dear little ones, and the Family generaly— it will be a great care on Sister, as we have an Officer and his Servants in the House, but I hope she will be strengthen'd. . . .

3 . . . O. Jones call'd to tell me, that Isreal Morris had been to offer himself to accompany us on our journey, Owen seems inclin'd to favour his applyca- tion, for my part I do not approve of it, however we are to meet at 3 o'clock at O Jones to consider of it. Johnny Drinker call'd—and Josey Fox—I went accordingly after dinner to O. Jones mett the other women there—it was agreed to except of Isreal if he would come into our terms, he was sent for, and came, said that he had had a concern for some time to go to Congress on account of our dear Friends and that he look'd upon this as the proper time, we told him that, we could not agree to unite with him in the busyness, we spoke very freely to him, that is MP and myself—that if he could be willing to escort us, and advise when we ask'd it, we should be oblig'd to him for his company, to which he consented—but hinted that he thought it necessary that he should appear with us before Congress, which we by no means consented to—and he acques'd—I hope that his going with us, may turn out more satisfactory then it at present appears to me. . . .

5 . . . I left home after dinner went to M. Pleasants where were a great Number of our Friends mett to take leave of us, We took Coach at about 2 o'clock, S. Jones, Phebe Pemberton, M. Pleasants and Myself—with 4 Horses, and two Negros who rode Postilion. . . .

6 left J. Roberts after Breakfast, and proceeded on to the American Picket

guard, who upon hearing that we were going to head-quarters, sent 2 or 3 to guard us further on to another guard where Colll. Smith gave us a pass for Head Quarters where we arriv'd at about ½ past one;[2] requested an audience with the General—set with his Wife, (a sociable pretty kind of Woman) untill he came in; a number of Officers there, who were very complient, Tench Tillman, among the rest, it was not long before GW. came and discoarsd with us freely, but not so long as we could have wish'd, as dinner was serv'd in, to which he had invited us, there was 15 of the Officers besides the General and his Wife, Gen. Green, and G. Lee we had an eligant dinner, which was soon over; when we went out with the General Wife up to her Chamber, and saw no more of him,—he told us, he could do nothing in our busyness further than granting us a pass to Lancaster, which he did. . . .

9 . . . We set of after on our journey till we arrived at James Gibbons, where we din'd, his Wife is lyeing in, while we were at Dinner JG. and several other Friends came there from meeting . . . here we understood that our Friends were by an order of Council to be brought to Shipensburgh, and there discharged. . . .

10 we arose by times this Morning dress'd ourselves, and after Breakfast, went to Lancaster, several Friends went with us, I. Morris also . . . we were this day waited upon by T Matlack, who undertook to advise us, and prehaps with sincerety—we paid a visit to 3 of the Councilors . . . after the council had set some time, T.M. came for our address, which was sign'd by all the Women concern'd, he say'd he would come for us, when it was proper, but after above an hour waiting, he inform'd us, that our presence was not necessary, and put us of in that way. We sent for Capt Lang who is one of the Guards that is to conduct our Friends to Lancaster, or any place nearer home, that we shall chuse, Shippensburg was to have been the place, but to oblidge us it was chang'd. . . .

14 went to Town before Breakfast, to look for Jos. Reed, who we mett with at one Attleys, with Thos. McClane and 2 others,—he conferm'd the account of the death of J Hunt &c—we discourc'd with 'em for some time, they appeard kind, but I fear tis from teeth outwards . . . in our journey to day we found the roads so bad, that we walk'd part of the way, and clim'd 3 fences, to get clear of the mud, Isreal has enough to do with us.

19 First Day: . . . We went to Lampater meeting and return'd to A Gibbons to Dinner, after which set of for James Webbs. . . .

2. General Washington and the American forces spent the winter of 1777–78 and the spring of 1778 at Valley Forge, Pa. (Boatner, *American Revolution*, 1136–37).

20 fine clear windy weather such as will dry the roads,—Billy Lewis, Owen Biddle, T. Afflick, and Danl. la Fever came this Morning to JWs After dinner John Musser return'd from Winchester with Letters from our Husbands, giving us expectation that they would be with us, here, the latter end of this Week. . . .

21st. . . . we took a walk to Thos. Whartons, had a conference with him, not altogeather agreeable . . . din'd at Danl. Whitelocks . . . while we were at Whitelocks, T. Matlack came with our dear Friends sham release, and said that was the conclusion Council had come to, (of this order we each took a Copy).

24 James Gibbon call'd this Morning—we went to Town after Breakfast, drove directly to the Coart-House, where we mett with George Brion and Tim Matlack, going up to Council, we presented our second address, (requesting a pass for our Friends) as the first was not answ'd to our minds, GB. said that all was granted that could be, he would not feed us up with false Hopes, we desir'd they would reconcider the matter, which he did not refuse. . . . TM came from Council, saying he was sorry to tell us, that nothing further could be done, towards granting our request. . . .

25 I can recollect nothing of the occurances of this Morning—about one o'clock my Henry arrived at J Webbs, just time enough to dine with us; all the rest of our Friends came this day to Lancaster; HD. much hartier than I expected, he look fat and well.

27 . . . our Friends apply'd to Counsil this Morning for a proper discharge, which was not comply'd with, but a permission to pass to Potts-Grove, in the County of Philada. was all they would grant. . . .

30 After Breakfast we had a setting at John Robertss John Pemberton, speak to the Family, we set of after 8 o'clock, and traveled on without interuption, were wellcom'd by many before, and on our entrence into the City—where we arrived about 11 o'clock, and found our dear Families all well, for which favour and Blessing and the restoration of my dear Husband, may I ever be thankful—We have had such a number of our Friends to see us this day, that it is not in my power to enumerate them.

[May] 4 Went to Quarterly Meeting, call'd at Uncle Jerviss and at several Shops,—went out again after dinner to Shops, bought merceals Quilting[3] for Peticoats for the Girls—Campany here this Afternoon.

3. Cloth associated with Marseilles, France, a center for fine quilted petticoats and coverlets consisting of two layers of cloth, with backing in between for the raised pattern on the quilt or petticoat. Similar cloth, known as Marseilles, Marcella, or Marsella, was also imported from England in the eighteenth century (Montgomery, *Textiles*, 289–92).

23   little Molly sick and feverish, her Mouth sore this evening I am fearful of an Aptha Fever which she was bad with while I was absent last Month at Lancaster—the Army tis thought are going in reality to leave us—to evacuate the City[4]—some hope tis not the case, tho' things look like it—many of the Inhabitants are preparing to go with them,—Robt. Waln, Reba. Waln, Richd. Waln, Abel James, Saml. Emlen, Reba. Jones, Molly Pleasants, Sucky Jones, here to day—fine weather.

30   Henry better, Molly still poorly—tis reported that the British Army are giving the remainder of their Stores of Wood and Hay, to the poor, which seems to prove they intend 'eer long to leave us. . . .

[June] 9   The Major left us at a little past one, this Morning, was very dull at takeing leave,—Sister and self stay'd at the Door untill the two Regiments, (which quarter'd up Town) had past—J.C. bid us adieu as they went by—and we saw no more of them, a fine moon-light Morning. . . .

14   First Day: . . . I wrote a few lines to J.C— in order to send by Christopher, who expects to go early in the Morning. . . .

18   last night it was said there was 9000 of the British Troops left in Town 11,000 in the Jersyes: this Morning when we arose, there was not one Red-Coat to be seen in Town; and the encampment, in the Jersys vanish'd[5]—Colll. Gordon and some others, had not been gone a quarter of an hour before the American Light-Horse enter'd the City, not many of them, they were in and out all day A Bell-Man went about this evening by order of one Coll. Morgan, to desire the Inhabatants, to stay within doors after Night, that if any were found in the street by the Partrole, they should be punish'd—the few that came in today, had drawn Swords in their Hands, Gallop'd about the Streets in a great hurry, many were much frightn'd at their appearance. . . .

22   dull rainy weather an account of a Battle in the Jersyes, the perticulars not known, no great one—the Store and Shop-keepers, orderd to shut up, and render an account of their goods[6]—Reb Waln and John Drinker call'd.

4. After negotiations with colonial forces, the British army, under the command of General Clinton, agreed to turn control of the city over to General Washington and withdraw their troops on June 18 (George M. Wrong, *Washington and His Comrades in Arms* [New Haven, Conn.: Yale University Press, 1921], 196).
5. After withdrawing from Philadelphia on June 18, Clinton began to move his troops through New Jersey toward New York. Washington broke camp at Valley Forge on June 19 and pursued the British forces (William B. Willcox, "British Strategy in America, 1778," *Journal of Modern History* 19 [1947]: 110).
6. On June 4 Washington had ordered that once Philadelphia was occupied by American troops, measures should be taken to prevent the removal, transfer, and sale of all British goods and merchandise in the possession of the inhabitants. Gen. Benedict Arnold, who became the city's military governor following the American reentry on June 18, issued these orders as a proclamation on June 19, in effect closing all private shops until individual owners could make lists of their goods. The shops reopened a week later (*JCC*, 11:571; *Pa. Archives*, ser. 1, 6:606; Scharf and Westcott, *Philadelphia*, 1:385–86).

30 very warm, Robt. Valentine, Becky Jones, Sus. Lightfoot, Saml. Trimble, Sam Emlen, here before meeting. I went to meeting—SL—and S Emlen appeard in testimony, James Bringhurst and Hannah Peters were married—Lawrance and Dolly Salter din'd with us—Nany Oat here this Evening—gave her part of her Cloths—she is to call again for the rest,—Reba. Waln, and Capt. Spains widdow call'd—it is said that there has been a great Battle on First day last,[7] that great numbers of the British Troops were slain and taken, a young Solider that is disorderd in his senses, went up our Stairs this Afternoon, we had no man, in the House: Isaac Catheral came in and went up after him, found him in the entry up two pair Stairs, saying his prayers—he readly came down with him. Jenny up stairs all day, unwel with the Collick.

[July] 2 The Congress came in to day: fireing of Cannon on the Occasion—rain and thunder this Afternoon. . . .

4 . . . A great fuss this evening it being the Annaversary of Independance, fireing of Guns, Sky Rockets &c—Candles were too scarce and dear, for Alluminations, which prehaps sav'd some of our Windows—A very high Head dress was exhibited thro the Streets, this Afternoon on a very dirty Woman with a mob after her, with Drums &c. by way of rediculing that very foolish fashon—a Number of Prisoners brought in to day: moderate weather.

8 very warm to day: Sally very ill, with the vomitting and Flux, above 30 stools to day, she took a vomitt this Morning and I gave her a Clyster this Evening she has a great deal of fever. . . .

10 exceeding Hott my poor Child very ill, continues sick at her Stomach, and frequently vomitts quantities of dark green Boile, which as the Weather is so warm, gives me great uneasyness, she took to day 3 Spoonfulls of Castor-Oyl—one of which she vomitted up, it work'd her twice, she is very low this evening—I have not had my cloaths of since 3d. day Night, and tis now sixth day: little Henry and Billy are both unwell,—Lidia Stretch was bury'd Yesterday, she dy'd of the Flux. . . .

15 Sally took a dose of Rheubarb to day she is still very bad. . . .

20 Sally more unwel to day, with greater pain in her Bowels, and vomitting—many call'd to day.

24 Sally more unwell than Yesterday—John Drinker, E. Clever, Saml.

7. The Battle of Monmouth, N.J., June 28, in which each side lost approximately three hundred men. More than six hundred British soldiers deserted and made their way to Philadelphia (Boatner, *American Revolution*, 716–25).

Esborn, Docr, Nancy Waln, Nics. Waln, C. West and Wife, Peggy Hart, call'd—Robt Willis din'd—John Balderston call'd—HD. went to the Burial of the Widdow Gordon, who dyed of the Flux, we did not hear of her sickness or death, untill invited to the Funeral—warmer to day, our little Molly went to meeting for the first time, with her Sister Nancy, to the Childrens meeting, which is held at the Bank.[8]

27   Sallys disorder continues bad, tho' something abated. . . .

Augt. the 1st.   The weather very warm,—our Neighbor Abraham Carlile was yesterday taken up, and put into Jail,[9]—several here to day—Sally, not much change in her.

3d.   Sally much better, she eat her Breakfast down Stairs . . . Ann Carlile call'd, she had been to the Old Prison to visit her Husband.

5   HD. at meeting most of the day: Thos. Watson Breakfasted with us—Jas. Logan at Tea—Wm. Smith, Warner Mifflin, John Drinker call'd—weather more moderate—Sally very weak, her Bowels still disordred—S Swett and Doctor call'd—tis a month tomorrow since Sally was taken ill.

19   many Showers to day with Sun-shine—HD. went over the river, with T. Masterman and I. Catheral this Morning—I spent the Afternoon at Neigr. Walns—Parson Murry, Wm. Smith, Polly Gordon, Lawrence Salter &c call'd—Sister went down to Abels, for a peice Linnen and some Tea—Janney Boon left us this Evening and went to stay a week with her Cozin Jacob James's wife, and then to go to her aunts at Willmington who has wrote for her—she has been with us, 3 years and near nine months—Molly Lahew came to day in her place—a great noise last night or the night before at the Bakers, William crying Murder, while the Baker beat him.

21st.   . . . Billy help'd to carry Wm. Norton junrs. Child to the Grave this

8. The Bank Meeting, established in 1685, held meetings at a building on Front Street between Arch and Race streets that had been constructed in 1702. This building stood until 1790, when the Philadelphia Northern District built a new meetinghouse at Keys Alley (Edwin B. Bronner, "The Center Square Meetinghouse and other Meetinghouses of Early Philadelphia," *Bulletin of the Friends Historical Associaiton* 44 [1955]: 67–74).

9. Abraham Carlisle, a Philadelphia Quaker, was first named as a traitor in May 1778, along with more than fifty other Pennsylvanians. Against the advice of Friends, he had accepted a post from the British to grant passes in and out of the city (see above, Nov. 24, 1777; *Col. Recs. Pa.*, 11:481–86, 603–605; Mekeel, *Relation of the Quakers*, 193; notes on Carlisle's trial and petitions on his behalf are in *Pa. Archives*, ser. 1, 7:44–52 and 53–58, respectively).

Afternoon, Becky Shoemaker was again ordred out of her House last night.[10] . . .

25 . . . Joseph Yerkes was had up yesterday before a Magistrate for keeping School;[11] his School is stop'd, and our Son Billy is at a loss for employment, as well as many others, in consiquence of it; sad doings. . . .

[Sept.] 7 . . . Reba. Waln, myself, my two Sons, Bob Waln, Neddy Howell and Anna Waln, took a walk this Afternoon to Springsbury to see the Aloes Tree[12]—stop'd in our return at Bush-Hill and walk'd in the Garden,—came home after Sun Set, very much tired. . . .

10 I spent this Afternoon at Sarah Lewiss Sally Logan drank tea with Sister,—we are reduc'd from 5 Servants to one, which wont do long, if we can help ourselves, it is the case with many at present, good Servants are hard to be had, such a time was never known here I beleive in that respect. . . .

23 Stay'd within all day—cloudy with rain—Robt. and Reba. Waln, Wm. Smith, call'd—HDs allmost all night awake with the toothach—which he had had greatest part of the day.

24th HD. sent for Fredrick this Morning and had a tooth drawn which requir'd a strong pull; Neigr. Waln spent this Afternoon helping me to cut out a Satten Cloak for Nancy. . . .

25 Abraham Carliles tryal came on to day and is not yet concluded, are at a loss to judge how it will go with him. . . . James and Joseph Stear, from Virginia, came this evening to stay with us during the Meeting—HD. at home all day, a pain in his Face. . . .

10. Charles Willson Peale and other confiscation agents took possession of the Shoemaker home on Arch Street and ordered Rebecca Shoemaker out. Many years later, Peale recalled that the confiscation agents began with the property of those "who were of most consideration among those named in the Proclamation" and so accordingly they went first to the Joseph Galloway and Samuel Shoemaker homes (Coleman, "Joseph Galloway," 288, 289 n. 51; "Memoirs of Charles Willson Peale: From his Original Ms. with Notes by Horace Wells Sellers" [1896], typescript, Peale-Sellers Papers, APS, Philadelphia, 67).

11. Joseph Yerkes was called before a magistrate because he did not conform to legislation passed in April requiring all schoolmasters to take an oath or affirmation of allegiance. Those who failed to do so by June 1 could be removed from their positions and subject to a penalty of five hundred pounds plus costs. Yerkes was not the only Quaker schoolmaster who ran afoul of this legislation: some Quaker schoolmasters were imprisoned (*Laws Enacted in the Second Sitting*, 127–30; Mekeel, *Relation of the Quakers*, 189–90, 180, 187 n. 40).

12. Springettsbury Manor, a tract of land along the Schuylkill River in Philadelphia County, held two large country homes: Bush Hill, built by James Logan, and Springettsbury, built by Thomas Penn in the 1730s. A popular place to visit, Springettsbury was noted for its flowers, formal gardens, and greenhouse where the great American aloe tree was nurtured (J. F. Watson, *Annals*, 2:478–79).

26 . . . I went in this Afternoon to visit our depress'd Neigr Carlile, whose Husband they have brought in gilty of High treason, tho' it is hop'd by many that he will not suffer what some others fear he will. . . .

28 . . . we have nine with us this Night a great number in and out to day—I went to meeting Morning and Afternoon. . . .

[Oct.] 2. . . . John Roberts is brought in gilty at which some are surpris'd as they did not expect it, who had attended the court. . . .

3 . . . the womans meeting is concluded,[13] the Men have adjornd till second day—which I never rembember to have been the case before. . . .

6. . . . HD gone to Meeting, he is with Robt. Waln, to attend the marriage of Dl. Mifflin and Debby Howel, Sally Zane, and 5 or 6 of the wedding Guest came here after meeting,—we were just inform'd that our poor neighbor Abram. Carlile, has received sentence of Death. . . .

7 . . . fine weather, [sev]eral Friends went today to visit Neigr. Carlile in the Dungon.

1778 Octor. 17. . . . John Robarts Miller condem'd to die,[14] Shocking doings!—I spent this Afternoon with R Waln &c at Neigr. Howels, on a visit to Debbe Mifflin.

Novr. 3 This afternoon I spent at Catre. Greenleafs, the Evening at S. Pleasants, where I was inform'd that preparations were making this evening for

13. The Society of Friends, believing strongly that women's faith and gifts in the service of the church were as valuable as men's, set up parallel women's meetings to the men's monthly, quarterly, and yearly meetings. The difference in these meetings supposedly related to function rather than status, but in practice, women's meetings, at least in Philadelphia, had less power over discipline than the men's meetings. They were required to obtain the approval of the men's meetings before disowning women for marrying out or accepting their statements of apology before readmitting them to full standing. In neighboring Bucks County, the women's monthly meetings appear to have exercised full disciplinary functions without the approval of the men's meetings (L. Hugh Doncaster, *Quaker Organization and Business Meetings* [London: Friends Home Service Committee, 1952], 17–18; Frost, *Quaker Family*, 55–57; on Bucks County see Jack D. Marietta, *The Reformation of American Quakerism 1748–1783* [Philadelphia: University of Pennsylvania Press, 1984], 28–29).

14. John Roberts, a Quaker miller from Merion who had originally sought the intervention of the British because of his distress over the banishment of the Quaker exiles, had been forced to act as a guide and informer for the British, then advancing on Philadelphia. Roberts was tried with Abraham Carlisle at the Philadelphia Court of Oyer and Terminer on Sept. 27, 1778; both men were found guilty of treason and executed on Nov. 4 (*Col. Recs. Pa.*, 11:481–86, 600–605; petitions for Roberts in *Pa. Archives*, ser. 1, 7:21–43; Mekeel, *Relation of the Quakers*, 193; Judge Thomas McKean's pronouncement of the death sentence despite the jury recommendation for mercy is in *Pa. Packet*, Nov. 7, 1778).

the Execution of our poor Friends tomorrow Morning—Notwithstanding the many pertitions that have been sent in, and the Personal appearance of the Destress'd wives and Children; before the Council,—much Compy. here. I am still of the mind, that they will not be permitted, to carry this matter to the last extremity. . . .

Novr. 4.   they have actually put to Death; Hang'd on the Commons, John Robarts and Am. Carlisle this moring or about noon[15]—an awful Solemn day it has been—I went this evening with my HD. to Neigr. Carliles, the Body is brought home, and laid out—looks placid & Serene—no marks of agony or distortion, the poor afflicted widdows, are wonderfully upheld and suported, under their very great tryal—they have many simpathizing Friends.

19th.   . . . I had a fainty fitt this morning which lasted 10 or 15 minits, and continued poorly afterwards.

Novr. 25.   . . . I have been all day very ill with the sick headach. . . .

26.   . . . Sister has been very busy all day in the Kitchen with Isaac Catheral and Molly, cutting up and salting a Beef—rendring the Tallow, [&c.]

29   First Day: . . . our maid Molly went out last night, and has not return'd yet, so that we have had none other than little John Pope, to assist us this day; we were never so situate before; tis the case with many others. . . .

Dec. 18   Josa. and Caty Howel and their Daughr. Caty spent the Afternoon with us—HD—received a Letter from J. Cramound—our new Maid has had a visitor all day and has invited hir to lodge with her, without asking leave, times are much changed, and Maids are become mistresses.

Decr. 19.   P. Pemberton and M. Pleasants sent Molly this Morning to ask my Company with them, to see G. Washingtons Wife:[16] which visit I declin'd.

15. *Pa. Ev. Post,* Nov. 6, 1778.
16. The word "the" crossed out.

1779

1779. Janry. 4—S Swett and Abel James din'd with us—Several Young Folke here this Afternoon and Evening with our Girls—a young man came this evening from Atsion with a Waggon, for HD. and J.D—he lodg'd here.

6.   stay'd within all day, nobody here; the calf kill'd this morning in full view of the Cow, which I think a cruel way of manageing—little Molly unwell in her Bowels, as she has been great part of this Winter, she is often up these cold nights. . . .

[Feb.] 19   . . . R Waln here this evening she propos'd my being an Overseer with her at C. Howel approaching Nuptals,[1] she is to pass meeting on third day next, with Johns Hopkins from Maryland. . . .

23.   went to meeting monthly this Morning with Johns Hopkins and Caty Howel, Reba. Waln is my partner on the occasion, felt a little comical on going into the mens meeting.[2]. . .

26   dull weather stay'd all day at home—Reba. Waln and her Daughters, Sucky and Beckey, and P. Hartshorn drank tea with us—our great men, or the Men in Power, are quarreling very much among themselves.

March 4   . . . Billy began his first quarter yesterday with John Tomson to learn Latin—took a walk this Afternoon.

March 15th.   little Henry went to School to Jos Yerkes, the first of his going to a mans School.

---

1. To ensure that marriages between Friends were conducted in good order, a monthly meeting would appoint two male and two female overseers to attend the marriage and the festivities that followed. The overseers were responsible for seeing that everyone behaved properly and went home at a respectable hour. They were then obliged to make a report in person at the next monthly meeting and to make sure that the marriage certificate was recorded (Philadelphia Yearly Meeting, *Rules of Discipline* [1797], 67).

2. Overseers for weddings made their reports to both the men's and women's meetings. ED reported to the Philadelphia Northern District Men's Monthly Meeting that Caty Howell and Johns Hopkins were being married according to proper Quaker procedure (Philadelphia Yearly Meeting, *Rules of Discipline* [1797], 67; Philadelphia Northern District Monthly Meeting, Men's Minutes, 1772–78, p. 351, microfilm, Friends Historical Library, Swarthmore College).

30 . . . little Becky Follwell, who was yesterday at play with our Molly and several other Children, at Neigr. Howels door, fell of the Poarch and broke her Arm, very moderate weather—Billy went to Day a foot to Frankford, with Tommy James, [J.] Gilpen Isey and John Pleasants, came home in the Evening.

[Apr.] 5 Susy Jones and her daughter Sucky, Docr. Redman, John Drinker, Danl. Drinker, &c call'd—set up till after 12 making Candles. very fine weather E [J.] here.

[May] 4 . . . Docr. Redman here this morning consulting about Innoculating our dear little Molly—he has sent three pills for her to take preparati[ve] theretoo—one of which she took this evening. . . .

9 First Day: gave my little Molly a purdge of Rheubarb.—before 11 this Morning she was innoculated by Docr. Redman in her Arm. . . .

13 rain all day—little Molly[3] unwell in the night—bravely to day—MM, with us all day—Isaac Catherals wife here this evening—a bad night for our poor Cow, who is missing.

15 . . . little Molly full of a rash again this Morning—feverish tho' chearfull all day; the Doctor thinks her Fever yesterday, was not of the small-Pox—I am of a different oppinion as her arm run, and her breath was very offencive, she is gone to Bed with much fever; after having been very cold. . . .

16 . . . found the Cow.

20 Molly continues bravely—upwards of an hundred small pox made their appearance but not above 6 or 8 have come to perfection. . . .

28 Doctor call'd this morning discover'd a swelling under our dear childs Arm, which he has ordre'd to be bath'd with vinager, and talks of more purdgeing—George [Shloser] and a young man with him, came to inquire what stores we have; look'd into the middle Room and Seller, behav'd compl[as]ant[4]—their Athority the Populace . . . I call'd at Wm. Fishers, S. Fisher unwell in her Chamber—the Inspectors I find have been at most Houses to day: taking account of Stores and provision. . . .

[June] 6 First Day: the swelling under the Childs arm does not appear to be near ripe, tho I have by the Doctors order chang'd the Poltice, she is often in

3. The word "very" crossed out.
4. Words crossed out.

much pain. . . . John Drinker, yesterday had before the committe, for refusing to show what provision he had.

15 . . . George Pickering came this Afternoon for the Nonassosiation fine,[5] which came to 13 pounds, which is 13/- as the Money now is exchang'd 20 for one—he took a Looking-Glass worth between 40 and 50/- 6 new Fashion'd Pewter Plates and a 3 qt. pewter Bason, little or nothing the worse for the ware. . . .

26—the Bell-man went about the City at near ten this night—desireing the people to arm themselves with guns or Clubs, and make a sarch for such as had sent any Flour, Gun Powder &c out of town, with great threats to the Torys; said it was by order of a Committe.[6]

[July] 19 on sixth day last the Well in our Yard was open'd in order to repair the Pump, which has been long out of order, and this day a new tree put down, and the well closed again which gives me satisfaction; as I always look'd upon open wells of any kind very dangerous whe[re] there is young Children. . . .

23 . . . little Henry has giving me great uneasyness lately, by several times going into the river and attempting to Swim, which he knows nothing of:— living so near the river, the example of other little Boys, joyn'd to his own inclination, makes it hard to restrain him—he brus'd his fore-Finger of his right Hand badly this Afternoon between two Boats—Billy carried at a Bury-ing. Sammy Fisher was this day try'd at Coart, and brought in giltey of mispresion of Treason,[7] for which they say he is to forfit half his Estate and suffer imprisonment during the war—the Jury brought in verdicts to clear him twice, but being sent out a third time, they return'd with an opposet Verdict— fine Liberty.

5. Nonassociation fines were paid by those who refused to serve in the Pennsylvania militia. The people who first established the militia were known until 1777 as the Associators, or the Association. On Apr. 5, 1779, the Pennsylvania Assembly increased the fines for failure to serve in the militia from £40 in paper currency (about £2.5 in hard coin) to £100 in paper currency (approximately £6 in hard coin) (Rosswurm, *Arms, Country, and Class*, 46, 49, 163–64).

6. This call, one of several issued by the price-fixing committee urging direct action against those who evaded price control regulation, received little public response (Rosswurm, *Arms, Country, and Class*, 186–87).

7. *Misprision of treason* was defined as speaking or writing in opposition to the public defense; attempting to carry information to the enemy; advocating resistance to the govern-ment or a return to British rule; discouraging enlistment; inciting disorder; propagandizing for the enemy; and opposing or trying to inhibit Revolutionary measures. The jurors failed twice to convict Fisher, but the state prosecutor sent them back until they returned with a verdict that pronounced him guilty of holding correspondence inimical to the United States (Thomas R. Meehan, "Courts, Cases, and Counselors in Revolutionary and Post-Revolutionary Pennsylvania," *PMHB* 91 (1967): 29; S. R. Fisher, "Fisher Journal," 164–65).

[Aug.] 9   Thos. Say, one Barns with a Letter call'd I spent this Afternoon with M Pleasants at C. Logans—Furniture taken this afternoon from S. Pleasants for a Tax—we have had no Maid Servant for some weeks past but Molly Brookhouse who comes before dinner and goes away in the afternoon, so that now HD. and Sally are absent, we have but 7 in Family, Billy and little John are our Men, which makes it rather lonesome of Nights, in this great House. . . .

[Sept.] 25   Sarah Carry and Rachel Watson from Bucks Cy—Sammy Trimble from Concord—John Willis, James Mott and Elias Hicks from Long-Island came this morning to take up their aboad during the meeting.

30   went twice to meeting, 10 or 12 din'd with us, many at Breakfast—a great number of people ill of a Fever—many taken off—B. Woodcock went home this afternoon very unwell, scarcely a House but some one or more are indespos'd.

[Oct.] 30   Sally recover'd a gold-chain which she lost 4 or 5 weeks ago; Hannah Drinker Joseys wife, found it in the Street.

[Dec.] 28   third day a violent East'rly Storm, our House, as was most others, very much try'd by it, most of the front Rooms very wett—our maid abroad since seventh day last—Caty Hopkins brought to Bed yesterday morning—with her son Joshua—Josey James lodg'd &c here for near a week past he writes at the Store.

1780

1780 Janry. 2   Richd. Penns large House up Market Street took fire last night, and this Morning is consum'd all but the lower Story,[1] a most violent Snow Storm this Afternoon, and all night—a very foul Chimney in Water-Street opposite the Bank Meeting House—took fire this evening—and occasion'd a great Hubbub—First Day—on sixth day last Decr. the 31—Sam. Lewis a little Boy from Sleepy-Creek—came to live with us—he has the Itch; for which I basted him on seventh day night with Brimstone.[2]

[Feb.] 10   . . . I dismiss my maid Caty Paterson this afternoon, on her return home after 2 or 3 days frolicking, our old maid Molly Hensel is to Supply her place tomorrow.

11th   sixth Day HD. left home this Morning for Havourford Meeting, he returnd the 12th.

April 24   Billy went to School to Robt. Proud to learn Latten.

[May] 18th.   HD. sister and Sally come home before dinner—I have been unwell for many weeks past,—in great pain all night.

20   . . . myself in my chamber, where I have expected for some time to be confin'd—am thankful it is so far over, as it is what I had reason to expect.

May 22   began to Shingle the House, the Kitchen first.

June 10   James Pickering a Capt. at the Corner of race street—and 6 or 8 others with Bayonets fixt—came and demanded our Horses—after some talk they went and broke open the Stable took a fine Horse bought some time ago of Wm. Smith for 16 half Joes—and a Mare belonging to J Drinker—they

---

1. The house was occupied by Jean Holker, the French consul to the United States (*Pa. Packet*, Jan. 4, 6, 1780).
2. A combination of sulfur and rum used in treating skin diseases (Lois K. Stabler, ed., *"Very Poor and of a Lo Make": The Journal of Abner Sanger* [Portsmouth, N.H.: Peter E. Randall for the Historical Society of Cheshire County, 1986], 560).

---

took Horses from many others.—they now act under a Martial Law—lately proclaim'd.[3] . . .

1779 Molly went to School Octor 4.

June 27, 1780 . . . Salter and wife left us, after spending [ ] of yesterday and this day with us—[ ] Dolly seems in a bad way, and it is to [ ]ear'd she has neglected the complaint of her [br]east too long to be now effectually help'd [ ] Docr. Jones who has been consulted—[ ] feel much for her.

[Aug.] 25. . . . Rachel Drinker intends going with Dolly to Kingwood Lawrence with 'em, to ask the oppinion of a certain Docr. Willson, who 'its said has knowledge in Cansers. . . .

30 little Henry fell into the River this Afternoon, and after a quarter of an hour remaining in his wet cloaths, came home very cold and coughing, we strip'd him, and after rubing him well with a coarse towel, put on warm dry cloaths, gave him some Rum and water to drink, and made him jump a rope till he sweated—he is bravely this evening.

[Oct.] 2 went to Bed last night between 10 and 11, arose at 7 this morning without having slept one moment, 'tho as well as usual—it is what I have often done in the course of my Life.

10 . . . Nancy had a Blister laid last night behind her Ear, for the Toothach and pain in her face, with which she has been troubled for 2 or 3 month past at times. . . .

18. HD. and Josey James left us this Morning after Breakfast for Atsion— Nancy is still up stairs with pain in her Face and Tooth-ach, Docr. Baker, the famous Dentist, lanced her Gum this morning—he thinks she ought to loose a tooth, but leaves it at present.

21 I set up 'till after 3 this morning HD ill most of the night. he is better to day.

Novr. 12 First Day: a little before 12 o'clock this night, we were alarm'd by a hard knocking at the front Door,—while we were preparing to go down stairs; Josey James (who happned to lodge here with his Brother Chalkley in the front

3. Joseph Reed declared martial law on June 9, acting on a resolution passed unanimously that allowed the president or vice president of the Supreme Executive Council to declare martial law, if necessary, while the assembly was not in session (*Col. Recs. Pa.*, 12:383–84; *Pa. Packet*, June 10, 1780).

Room) came to our Chamber door and inform'd us, that Thos. Lawrencess
Negro-Man was waiting at the Door, he say'd that Several Men had broke open
the store on the Warfe; belonging to J & Dr. Chalkley and Josey went quickly
down but the thieves were gone off; they had broke the Lock and Door, and
opend the Windows,—but not any thing missing that they could then discover; as there was nothing but Iron in our Store, it is supos'd that their
design was to have rob'd the Store over ours, in which Math[w] Clarkson had a
large quantity of Prize-goods.

[Dec.] 31st.   First day: went this afternoon to S Emlen's came home after
Night, little Molly with me, several guns fired off very near us—the Bells
ringing according to the old foolish custom of ringing out the old year.

1781

[Jan.] 12   Nancy had a tooth drawn this Afternoon by Fredrick, it had been painfull for months. . . .

Febry. 1st.   Charles Mifflin and his Pupils mett in our little Front Room; he has lately undertaking to improve a few young Girls in writeing: teaching 'em Grammar &c—Hanh. Redwood, Sally Fisher, Caty Haines and Sister, Betsy Howel, Sally and Nancy Drinker, are his scholars at present—are to take turns at the different Houses; they began at Ruban Haines, the 8th. Ultimo when Sally first attended—Nancy being unwell, did not go 'till the 18th.

[Apr.] 5   I was very poorly in the night, sick at Stomach, vomitted much, eat no Breakfast or Dinner; took magnezar and Rheubarb, took a walk with HD to the furnace—saw DSs Breast dress'd, an affecting sight. . . .

6   very sick again last Night, fasted most of this day—spent great part of it with poor Dolly—she takes annodines twice in the 24 hours, which much relieves her pain, tho' at times she is in great distress; and at other times sets up and talks very chearfully—she is favour'd with one of the kindest of Husbands, in this her great affliction.

27   Polly Newgent was this afternoon Bound to[1] us by her mother, she has been with us a week, and appears cleaver, brought the Itch with her, which I hope we have nearly cur'd—received a Letter this evening from J. Crammond New York—and another from L. Salter, informing of the Death of his Wife. . . .

[May] 16   ED. was let Blood, had not been bleed for seven years and upwards.[2]

26   three Men were this Morning hang'd on the Commons for theaft &c[3]—J

1. The word "searve" crossed out.
2. ED, pregnant at this time, had not been subject to a long-term pregnancy since 1774.
3. John Dobbins and James Byner ("Byrnes" in Fisher's journal) were hanged for burglary, and Thomas McGee for robbery (*Col. Recs. Pa.*, 12:730, 735; S. R. Fisher, "Fisher Journal," 426–27, 428).

Scott din'd here.—a cool spring so far with much rain—Billy went home this afternoon with Jos[h] and Tommy James in their Waggon.

29   Joseph Scott took leave of us this Morning—he is going to New York to look after his Grand-Children, who have lately lost their Mother. . . .

June 1   many Dogs said to be mad in Town; Robt. Wharton lately bit by one supos'd to be mad.

July 1   First day: Jenney and her Child went away this Morning—I stay'd at home all day, which seems likely will be the case for many weeks to come (should I be spar'd) being unwell, and not in fitt trim to go abroad.—, Joshua Howel and Family have yesterday left our Neighbourhood; intending to reside for the Present, at their Place on Schuylkill,—a Deligate in Congress is to take their place next Door, I dont know his name; am not pleas'd with the change of Neighbours. . . .

[Aug.] 14   HD was let Blood—myself greatly distress'd, Mind and Body for several days past.

First Day Octor. 28—two days after the last memorandum my dear little Charles was born, on the 16th. Augt. towards evening; was favour'd myself beyond expectation, but my poor Baby was alive and that was all—did not expect he would survive many days; but he is now between 10 and 11 weeks old, and appears to be thriving, which is wonderful, considering how unwell I was for near a Month before his birth, and much falling away; the Child little more than Skin and Bone—Occasion'd prehaps by a cold I caught,—the first 7 or 8 months of my time, I was heartier and better than ever I had been in like situation—and am at present through mercy favourbly recover'd, so as to be able with the help of feeding to Nurse my little one—Nurse Molly Morris was with me near 2 weeks, her Sister Sally Stanberry near 4 weeks. . . . heard from New York of the Death of our old acquaintance and near Friend Nelly Moode; also of the Death of Js. Crammond a young Officer who had liv'd 6 months with us, while the British Troops were in this City, and Behav'd so in our Family as to gain our esteem, he dy'd after 8 days illness. . . .

the 17th. of this month Octor. Genl Cornwallace was taken; for which we grievously suffer'd on the 24th. by way of rejoyceing[4]—a mobb assembled

4. News of the British surrender at Yorktown on Oct. 19, which effectively ended most of the military operations of the Revolutionary War, reached Philadelphia on Oct. 22, and on Oct. 24 Philadelphians celebrated the surrender and illuminated the city. Once again Quakers were singled out by mobs for refusing to participate in the celebrations. Many Quaker residences were damaged (Boatner, *American Revolution*, 1230–50; Mekeel, *Relation of the Quakers*, 199).

about 7 o'clock or before, and continud their insults untill near 10; to those whose Houses were not illuminated scarcely one Friends House escaped we had near 70 panes of Glass broken the sash lights and two panels of the front parlor broke in pieces—the Door crack'd and Violently burst open, when they threw Stones into the House for some time but did not enter—some fard better and some worse—some Houses after braking the door they enterd, and distroy'd the furniture &c—many women and Children were frightned into fitts, and 'tis a mercy no lives were lost.

[Nov.] 17   Gave Sally Smith warning: dont like hir Conduct towards Henry Briggs, she left us this Morning.

Novr. 24   Sally Smith went away—Polly Moore from Atsion came.

Decr. 30, Polly Moore Shew'd Sister several things, such as, Handkerchiefs, Ribbons, Buckles, Pad-locks &c &c—giving her by our little Sam Lewis, to keep for him, 'till he had an oppertunity to sent 'em to his Parants, pretending he had bought them with his own Money—but upon being examin'd by his Master, own'd that he had taken 9 pieces of silver out of the Desk-drawer—by the account he gave of the things he had bought, they amounted to near £5—, so that he made a false confesion—HD. talks of sending him home to his Parants.

1782

1782 Janry. 1st.—Isey Pleasants came this morning to acquaint us, that his mamy was brought to Bed, at 6 this morning of a Son—who they call James.— their 10th Child; all living.

[May] 23   Our wicked Neighr. Pantlif in the Alley beat and brus'd Black Tom Thos. Shamefully, (a negro man we have lately hir'd) his Wife set their Dog at him, who bit his Thigh in 2 or 3 places, because he had throne a stone at the Dog, who had run at him some hours before.

24   Black Toms lame with the wound and under the Doctors care, he had Pantlif up, before Wm. Rush, who bound him over, 'till next Coart, but by no means humbld him—this Man and his Wife are two of the most Wicked Spiteful revengfull persons I think I ever knew they are dutch Foulk.

June 15.   our Son Henry with Sam Parish and 2 other little Boys, went to our place at Frankford, seventh day—when they clim'd on the limb of an old Chery-Tree, which gave way. Henry being badly hurt was taken to James Streets our Tenant,—Tom Kite being there, went quickly home and informd Becky James junr. who went directly to him and did what she could for him— [Sam] Parish came to Town to let HD know, who went immediately with the Chaise for him, he mett T Kite bringing him home, I knew nothing of the matter 'till I saw him with his Daddy enter the Parlor; Docr. Redman was sent for, who upon examineation found his collar bone was broke, and his sholder brus'd. I assisted the Doctor to set it, (which as I was favour'd with resolution) was no hard matter—he was much better after it was over then I could have expected, considering how much hed suffer'd from the first.

[July] 11   Pantlifs Dog Bit [I.] Hazelhursts Negro Boy in the thigh, worse then he had some time ago bit our Tom. Hazelhurst had the Dog shot.[1]

Sepr. 8.   HD. was let Blood having been unwell for some time past, which is generaly the case with him, Spring & Fall.

20   . . . Lawrence Salter was Married to Sally Howard the 22 Ultimo.

---

1. The words "and threatend the master and mistress" crossed out.

[Oct.] 7   Lisey Plumer from Mt. Holly came this morning with intent to suckle my Baby, but not having Milk sufficient, not so much as myself—she undertook to tend him &c at 10/– p week.

23   . . . My little Charles, who was all Summer very unwell, and at times ill, has since the cool weather altred much for the better; am in hopes from the present prospect, I shall be abel to suckle him myself this winter—he eats and sleeps well.

Novr. 1.   Billy came home about dinner time, his Face much Brus'd, had been Boxing with one of the Lattin School Boys,—an exercise that by no means suits him.

Novr. 4.   Nancy, Billy and Tommy James, began to learn French, they are taught by one Bartholemew at 4[½] Dollars each p month, and 6 Dollars each for entrance money—they occupy our smallest front Parlor, on second-day fourth day and sixth day evenings, from 6 o'clock, 'till ½ past 7. AD. received a B——l d——x from [JJ].

14   J Drinker came from Willmington to Day, brought a Letter from Sally to Nancy, She and her Daddy, lodges at Bancroft Woodcocks.

[Dec.] 8   First day: an old Stable took fire this Afternoon, at the back of B Shoemakers House at the upper end of Market Street, and was burnt down, our Polly Nugent who went out after dinner intending as she said, to go to Chapple, went to see the fire, near which place she was thrown down, and run over by a Man on Horse-back and badly hurt. . . .

1783

March 10 . . . Sally Drinker, Hannah Redwood Thos. Wistar and Benny Morris sat up with the Corps of Catey Greenleaf, second daughter of Catherine Greenleaf, she died of a Consumption—the first time Sally set up all Night.

[Apr.] 6 . . . HD. and his Son Henry left home, after an early Breakfast intending to morrow for King-Wood—HD in the Sulkey little Henry on Horse-back, his Daddy bought a Horse for him Yesterday.

[July] 22, 23 and 24 the weather was extremely warm, many dyd drinking cold water.

[Aug.] 11 Molly went first to writeing School, to Becky Jones.

[Sept.] 7 First-day: L. Saltar Buried from John Howards this Morning before meeting Sally Drinker came from the Funeral very poorly with the Head-Ach and fiveres Nancy still very ill a high fever, Sick Stomach and pain in her Bones—Billy came from evening Meeting, where he had a smart Chill, which was follow'd in the night by a high fever.

11 . . . Sister was taken ill; a violent fitt of the Chill and Fever, having been much fatigued and taking a nap on the foot of the Bed, with her Head towards the Chimney; she Had almost lost her hearing—the fever went of with a great sweat—she took the Bark,[1] had no other regular fitt but continu'd very weak for upwards of a week then recover'd her hearing and health. . . .

Our dear Friend and old acquaintance Hannah Stevenson departed this life, Sep. the 19 1783 in Child-Bed, in the 51st. year of her Age—the child a Daughter who they call Susanna.

Octor. 1 call'd up in the Night to S. Hartshorn; the child was born just before I entred the room a Daughter, nam'd Rebecca—it dyed in less then 2 Days.

1. The word "she" crossed out.

25[2]   seventh day morning WP.[3] spake to HD. on account of Nancy.

Novr. 6   . . . Abel James and Son Chalkley dined with us—and little Susan Edward they lodg'd at Frankford at AJs are on their way from N York to N. Carolinia, Sally and Nancy went with them to Several places, Chalkley also—to Simiters, to see Peels paintings to view the Wax Works &c.[4] . . .

Novr. 24   Sally Emlen spent this Afternoon, discorse conserning pouver WP.

1783 Decr. 2   third-day Morning—had Conversation with WP. . . .

2. The word "sixth" crossed out.
3. Probably Walter Payne.
4. Pierre Eugène du Simitière was a Swiss-born collector of American and West Indian historical materials and natural curiosities who also painted portraits. In May 1782 he opened his American Museum, located on Arch Street near Fourth Street, to display his collection. Six months later, Charles Willson Peale opened a skylighted gallery at his house on Third and Lombard streets to display his paintings of Revolutionary War heroes. The waxworks display the young Drinkers and their company viewed has not been determined (Paul G. Sifton, "A Disordered Life: The American Career of Pierre Eugène du Simitière," *Manuscripts* 25 (1973): 235–53; William John Potts, "Du Simitière, Artist, Antiquary and Naturalist, Projector of the First American Museum, with some Extracts from his Notebooks," *PMHB* 13 (1889): 341–75; *Pa. Packet,* Nov. 14, 1782, Nov. 6, 1783; Sellers, *Charles Willson Peale,* 1:219–22).

1784

1784. Jenry. 2. . . . the Committee of Friends oppointed to visit Families mett here this Afternoon. S Emlen, S Hopkins, Billy Savery, C. West, and Caleb Cresson, Magry. Norton, [Merry] Smith, H. Catheral, and R Jones.

18 . . . Josey Fox went out this Morning for Frankford on a Skitish Horse, who threw him over his Head against a Post at the upper end of third Street, his Body voilently brused, he was taken home on a Couch, sufferd great pain 'till some time in the Afternoon when he dyed.

Feby. 18, 1783 my little Charles cut his first Tooth, being 18 months and 2 days old.

Octr. 23 began to wean him at upwards of 2 years and 2 months old.

[Mar.] 13 HD. was let Blood—it has been a very cold unsittled winter—our dear little one after dilegint nursing had out grown most of his weekness and promissed fair to be a fine Boy, became much oppress'd with phlegm, insomuch that Docr. Redmans oppinion was that unless we could promote some evacuation he could not live, he ordred what he thought might prove a gentle vomitt, agatated him much, but did not work, and in little more then 20 minits from the time he took it, he expired aged 2 years 7 months and one day—about a week before he was fat, fresh and hearty—he cut a tooth a day before he dyed—thus was I suddenly depried of my dear little Companion over whome, I had almost constantly watchd, from the time of his birth, and his late thriving state seem'd to promise a [reward] to all my pains—he dy'd the 17 march, fourth day.

[May] 3 Molly began a quarter at A Marshs School—first of her going there.

May 4. between 3 and 4 o'clock this Morning—Sally, Nancy and Billy were all awakned ('tho in different Chambers) by the light of a Pot-House on fier in Elfriths Alley, our Familey were all soon up, a lane was made to our Pump—Gardners, Pantlifs and other fences were pull'd down—the Pot-House is burnt, several others Houses damaged—our much valued Friend and School-master Anthony Benezet departed this Life yesterday afternoon, after a short illness.

5 Billy went to the Funeral of AB it was very large, a great number of Blacks attended[1]—WP. came from Virginia.

7. Sister mett the Committee of 12,[2] this Afternoon for the first time.—she went to the Burial of Widow [Laniar], Aunt to Sarah Lewis.

23 Billy help'd to carry little Hannah Howel to her grave.

[July] 17 two Men were Executed for Robing and wounding Cap. Hustons wife, at Night in the Street—an Air Balloon was this Afternoon sent up from the new Jail Yard. it took fire, (when it was thought by some to be near a mile high) and consumed—the first sight of the kind that I have seen.[3]

20 . . . several alterations in our alley within the 2 or 3 last months, the House wherein Becky Jones and H Catheral liv'd, is now occupi'd by one Dows a Sailmaker,—A large quantity of stoleing good were found in Pantlifs house, for which he was taken up and put in Jail. E. Stiles bail'd him out, and he has run off—his Wife and Children gone I Know not where we are at last reliev'd from a very troublesom Neighbor—Strangers occupy that house—and this month our Neigr. Gardner has finish'd a large Soap House; directly opposite us—a disagreeable surcumstance.

Augt. 14 Cry of fier this morning Bells rang. Apothycarys Shop, in market street—our Polly Nugent unwell, sick Stomach and fever—gave her a puke this evening.

23 . . . a little before 7 this morning before I was up, S Heartshorn sent for me;—she was deliver'd about 8 of a fine Girl,—who they call Susanna; I breakfasted there, came home about 9—second day.

[Sept.] 26 First day: Hannah Hopkins and her Brother John came to lodge here.

1. Anthony Benezet had been a prominent abolitionist.
2. The Committee of Twelve was made up of four representatives from each of the three Quaker monthly meetings in Philadelphia (the Northern District, the Philadelphia Monthly Meeting, and the Southern District). It administered the common property of the meetings and joint accounts for taking care of the poor, and provided other services to the Philadelphia Quaker community as well as to non-Quakers (Philadelphia Northern District Men's Monthly Meeting Minutes, 1771–78, microfilm, Friends Historical Library, Swarthmore College, 131–32 and passim).
3. The Montgolfier brothers had built the first practicable hot-air balloon in France in 1783. In 1784 a Mr. Carnes demonstrated his American aerostatic balloon in cities in the United States. He scheduled his flight in Philadelphia for the late afternoon of July 17, taking off near the new workhouse. While in flight the balloon caught fire from its heating apparatus and descended near the new playhouse. Mr. Carnes was not seriously hurt (*Pa. Packet*, July 15, 17, 20, 1784).

27 John Hopkins went away—John Balderston came.—this Meeting I constantly attended which I have not done for several years before.

Octor 2 seventh day Thos. Watson here this morning had some discoarse with him conserning my Breast which I brus'd between 4 and 5 years ago—he alarm'd me much—began to diet myself—this day several of our Company left us.

27 fourth day Henry began a quarter at Josh. Sharplesss Night School, writeing &c.

30 the Girles went to Molly Newports feast Seventh day evening—little Henry went to Frankford this Afternoon.

[Nov.] 22 little Ned. Fifer came upon tryal; his mother is desirous of binding him to us 'till he is 16 Years of Age, he is now[4] between 8 & 9. . . .

Decr. 7: Peter Wallover came to us—a dutch Boy about 12 years of Age, purchased from on board a Ship.

10 Ned. Fife went home to his parants being to small for our busyness.

26 First day: this evening Waltar Payne took leave of us, intending to set of early to morrow morning for Virginia, and in a few weeks to embark there for Great Britain.

4. The word "about" crossed out.

1785

[Jan.] 18   third-day: HD. went into the Cold-Bath for the first time; after having ommitted it upwards of 15 years.

[Feb.] 3   Docr. Jones paid me a visit; gave me little or no, encouragement, respecting the disorder in my Breast—I think I never saw the Trees look[1] prittyer; not even in the Summer Season, then they do this day, so beautifully bespangled with frost—were I in perfect health I should enjoy it much.

[Mar.] 5   . . . a Docr. Henry Moyes, who has been blind since he was 16 or 18 months old, is now in this City exhibiting Lectures &c on natural Philosophy &c—Sally, Nancy and Billy attends them.

July 25,   second day visit from Dr. Jones; as usual very discouraging, advis'd me to go Shrewsbery and bath in the Salt water.

26[2]   third day sent for Dr. Kuhn, told him my trouble, he was much more encourageing then Jones, tho' I fear it proceeded more from his humanity then his better Judgment.—Nancy Thomas was this afternoon buryed from Neigr. Walns she has been a long time very ill, and suffer'd more than any one that has come within my knowledge, of a disorder of the nature hers was.—about this time one Francis Courtney was executed, for using a young woman very ill,[3] near Frankford.

30th.   Betsy Waln and her daughter Polly set of with us after dinner for Shrewsbury—HD. EW, HD junr and ED—in RWs Waggon, Nancy Drinker and Polly Waln in our Chaise. . . .

Augt. 1:   EW. myself and our daughters went into the Bath this morning. . . .

4   went to Bath this morning—Bose Reeds wife &c there before us, as they generly are—they lodge at Wardals—We set of after Breakfast for long branch on the Sea Shore—HD. EW. and ED. went round in the waggon—George

1. Word crossed out.
2. The word "fourth" crossed out.
3. Francis Courtney was executed for rape on July 22 (*Pa. Gaz.*, July 26, 1785).

Eddy and wife, Nancy, Henry and Polly Waln and John Fry, went in a Boat, we mett at one Brindleys to dinner—many others din'd there also; Jacob Morris and wife, Isaac Wicoff and wife, and Daughter—Saml. Ferman &c &c—took a walk to the Sea Shore which was very near the House—came back to Corlass to Tea before Sun Set.

[Oct.] 7 Nancy had her Teeth clean'd by Docr. Baker—by the desire of Docr. Kuhn—Sally Ashbridge at work here.

8 . . . Jenny Sibold or Sivile, formerly our Jenny Boon, came to stay a few days, with us—she has her sucking Daughter Anne with her—they live at East-Town, and is on her way to New-port—on Busyness for her Husband.

19th. fourth day evening JD. spake to HD—on account of Sally.

Novr. 3 fifth day: eat a small peice of meat at my dinner, the first I have tasted for upwards of 13 months.

1786

[Feb.] 11 seventh day: Sally, Nancy, Billy, Henry and Molly—Capt. Robinson John Hopkins Nancy and Hannah Waln went this evening to see Peals Exibetion and Paintings.[1] John Hopkins lodg'd here.

1. An exhibition, "Perspective Views with Changeable Effects; or, Nature Delineated in Motion," opened in Charles Willson Peale's gallery at his home on Third and Lombard streets in May 1785 and continued through 1786. The series of painted transparencies, displayed twice weekly on an illuminated stage, included views of Philadelphia, Revolutionary War battles, and a scene from *Paradise Lost* (*Freeman's Journal*, Feb. 15, 1786; Peale, *Selected Papers*, 1:428–37; Sellers, *Charles Willson Peale*, 1:242–49).

1789

July 3. ... Billy has been very busily engag'd, preparatory to a short voiage in the Ship Mary[1] Japhat Fletcher Comander, getting the Sailors togeather &c—which this day was partly accomplish'd—the Captain, Ben Wilson and himself—din'd early here, they then bid us adieu and went on board with the wind against them, weather very hot, which may probably bring about a gust)—they intend for Baltimore. ...

> With wind ahead, and threat'ning Storm
> We part,—to meet we know not when,
> My heart at times with anguish torn,
> For dearest Bill, and Cousin Ben.

Jacob and Sally Downing drank tea here.[2] ...

4 ... it began to thunder and lightning about 7 this Evening we went up stairs about 11, still contin[us] lightning very much.

> Tho' the voiage my seem short, and the danger not seen
> yet the heart of a parent bodes ill.
> with the thoughts of what possibly may intervene,
> Keeps my mind from being tranquil and still.

7 ... J Skirin came home with the Girles.

10 ... we are now but 5 in family, much reduc'd.

11 ... Dr. Kuhn, J Skirin here this evening Sarah Fisher dangerously ill.

> I'm tired and weak, and to Bed will repair,
> For 'tis now past eleven at night,
> Prehaps not to sleep, but to think when I'm there
> just at present no more can I write.

1. The *Mary*, owned by Robinson, Sandwith & Co. of Dublin, arrived from Cadiz in early July. HD, as the Philadelphia agent for the ship, contracted for a cargo of Maryland tobacco and lumber products for the return trip to Europe, where delivery would be made to a consignee in Amsterdam (Henry Drinker to Robinson, Sandwith & Co., July 11, 1789, and Henry Drinker to Thomas & Saml Hollingsworth, July 24, 1789, Henry Drinker Letterbook, 1786–90, HSP).

2. Sally Drinker married Jacob Downing on May 15, 1787 (Diary of Ann Warder, vol, 9, HSP).

12 First day: Jacob and Sally Downing—Nancy and Molly Drinker, in the new carriage with BO to drive them—set of this Morning for Downings Town. . . .

14th. . . . I wish much to hear from Baltimore and from Downings-town . . . 'tis not pleasant to have our Children scattred about the world, this very unsettled gusty Season. . . .

19 First Day: Sister, Henry, and Josey Downing gone to meeting, myself according to custom at home alone. . . .

21 [ ] Henry set of this Morning early for Atsion, so that our family at present consists of daddy Aunty and myself—no of our Children at home I took a ride this morning with HP. . . .

1790

1790—14th: Sept. third day John Hillborn and Wm. Drinker, left us this morning after breakfast, about 8 o'clock—intending for the beach woods—I went to Sallys and from thence to meeting. . . .

16 . . . This book was intended for memorandans of what occur'd during my Sons absence, for his information, not a diary of my own proceedings—but as it is the method in which I have been accostomed to write, and know my own movements better then any others—it must serve for an apology. . . .

17 S Fisher and Taby here, I went with them to visit H Baker.

21 Went to meeting this morning—Seamor Hearts daughter[1] hansel'd the new House, she past with one [Shupherd] Sally Downing, Molly and self drank tea at S Emlen's.

[Oct.] 6 . . . Sally Downing and her little chattering lively baby here in the morning.[2]

1. The word "past" crossed out.
2. Elizabeth Downing, born in 1789, was ED's first surviving grandchild.

1791

1791 June 17   sixth day fore-noon our [dear] Son William left us for German-town, where his Sisters now reside—he intends for bucks county &c,—in search of the greatest blessing that mankind can enjoy in this world, next to a good conscience—the latter I hope he in good measure possesses, the former may it please the Lord to grant, is my dayly prayer. . . . John and Nancy[1] their maid Polly went on fifth day their going to spend the hot weather out of the City is on little Eliza[s] account who has been for several weeks disordred in her bowels—and Nancy having been unwell for some time past, it was thought it might be of servece to her.

[July] 11   . . . left home after 6 this evening HD. ED. JD. JS—in the waggon, came to germantown. . . .

12   HD. JD. JS. and P Hartshorn left us this morning about 6 o'clock—so here am I with my 2 daughters, sewing this morning—lay down before dinner, Nancy was taken suddenly with the nettle rash or hives—very poorly for near an hour, then got better—took a walk this evening Sally, Nancy, Peggy and Eliza, and Self—came back to late Tea—HD. JD. and P. Hartshorn came up in the waggon. A Letter from our Son of the 4 Instant from Kingwood. . . .

15   JD. JS. went to town—Polly Wheeling din'd and spent the day with us—Sally Parker, Molly Newport and her niece Lisey drank tea with us, Jery. Warder call'd—John and Jacob, came up in the evening as usual, brought Caty, Elizas Nurse with them—the actual heat very great, tho' there is a fine air—

> Could I write, instead of Trifles;
> That which most employs my mind:
> All thats here would be ommitted,
> Nor should I mark, how blew the wind?

I have heard of people who have had so much work to do, that they knew not what to do first and so did nothing there is such a weight such a complicated weight upon my [Spirits] that words cannot express.

1. John Skyrin and Nancy Drinker were married sometime earlier in 1791.

20   our Husbands left us early this Morning—busy ironing before dinner—
Nancy & myself[2] drank tea at Jessy Walns, he came home with us in the
evening—Jacob and John came up later then common—Jerry Warder and Billy
Parker with them—the weather is uncommonly pleasent for the Season.—the
wife of one Miers a baker in Philada: fell into a Necessary on seventh day last,
and continu'd there for ¾ of an hour before she was found: they got her out
with great difficulty, and it was thought, when R Waln came up here, that she
could not live long—she was sunk up to her Shoulders, and had not the flore,
which went down with her) suported her, she would in all probability have
been dead when they found her—how careful should every family be, frequently to examine those places, that they are secure—to prevent these very
terable accidents which too often happen.

21   this is a delightful morning for WD—to travil, our men gone as usual—
we busy at work. . . .

22.   Nancy went to town this Morning in their Chaise with her Husband—
Jacob went earlyer—Sally and myself went to preparative meeting,[3] 16 women
and about the same number of men. . . .

sixth day night, 11 o'clock, here am I tout[4] suel,[5] sitting in M. Clarksons
parlour Germantown, all in the house (for aught I know) sleeping, but myself,
and I here of choice busy thinking, and mending Stockings for my Son Henry,
who has not thought it worth his while to come to see me, 'tho I have been
here near two weeks.

23   . . . our dear William came to Philada. last evening, not much better I
fear, tho' no worse through mercy then when he left us—expect to see him
tomorrow.

29   All the men left us but WD—he stays with us—No Company this day—
William and myself walk this evening an hour in the garden, I step'd over to
Justice Foxs—J Skyrin came up this evening—we have had a long spell of dry
weather, otherwise very pleasent.

30   JS. went to town—JD. there last night—WD. here no Company,[6]—Billy

2. The word "spent" crossed out.
3. Preparative meetings, initiated in the Philadelphia area at the beginning of the eighteenth
century, dealt with disciplinary problems on a more local and informal level than the monthly
meetings, in hope of resolving disputes without recourse to formal proceedings (Rufus Jones,
Isaac Sharpless, and Amelia M. Gummere, The Quakers in the American Colonies [1911;
reprint, New York: Norton, 1966], 251, 534–35).
4. Word crossed out.
5. All alone.
6. Two lines crossed out.

and self took a walk this evening—Jacob and John came up this evening—in the Waggon.

[Sept.] 14   Abraham came up with a large waggon to take the Furniture to town Jacob in a Chaise—I came away with WD. in our Chaise before dinner as it look'd likely for rain. it rain'd a little most of the way but did not wet us— Jacob and Molly came to late dinner, we have bid adieu to Germantown, for the present, I have been 2 months and 3 days there, never so long from home before since I was married, nor in all my life.

1791 Sepr. 20.   third-day: our dear William left us again this morning—to take a journey in search of health, the weather fine tho' rather too warm, as he is on Horse back, Jacob Downing and Ben. Wilson accompany'd him in our Chaise, intending as far as Trent-town, they to return tomorrow, it is uncertain how far WD will go towards the Eastward—may he return in peace.[7] . . .

21   Henry lodg'd last night at Sallys, Jacob being absent—Molly and self busy all the morning putting up Curtins—Docr. Rush, and one of the Pragers here towards evening—Nancy Skyrin drank tea—John Cannon, J. Drinker call'd—J Downing and B Wilson return'd this evening left Billy about 2 o'Clock on this side trenton ferry—he intends lodging this night at Prince-town—the Insurrection of the negroes in Cape-Francoies,[8] has occasion'd the rise of many articles here, such as Sugar, Coffee &c—cloudy this evening.

29   by deviating from the path of rectitude and eating super 4 nights successively, which is what I very rearly do—and last night after super I drank a small draught of New table beer and eat some grapes after it. about 3 this morning I was seiz'd with a sevear fitt of the colic, which lasted for an hour or 2—I am much better this morning thro' mercy, 'tho unsetled & weak. . . .

[Oct.] 4.   . . . This Afternoon R Waln and self went to visit A Skyrin.— Nancy upstairs she had heard of letters from R Bowne of New York, giving an account of WDs being ill at H Haydocks, he had ruptur'd a blood vesel in his lungs and was thought to be in danger—I went directly home, found several young girls with Molly who soon went away,—I set about preparing for a journey, had a sleepless night, and next morning the 5 set out for New York[9] fourth day.

7. Two lines crossed out.
8. On the night of Aug. 22, 1791, black slaves in the French colony of Hispaniola besieged the city of Le Cap François, killing many whites who had taken refuge there. The insurrection spread throughout the country and culminated in the Republic of Haiti's independence in 1804 (Ott, *Haitian Revolution*, 3–65).
9. The words "fifth day" crossed out.

1792

March 4. 92 first Day—we mov'd into the front parlor, intending to stay'd there a week or two, as our dear William has been confind all this Winter and thee last also, thought it would be more lively to be near the street &c. . . .

7 WC. breakfasted with us—he went away after an early dinner at 11 o'clock.—Jacob and Sally Downing din'd with us, Sally and her two Daughters spent the Day, the first time of little Marys being here, she is now turn'd of 5 weeks old, a very fine child—Molly gone visiting with Betsy Emlen.

14 Billy and Sally and little Eliza took a ride this fore-noon. . . .

15 My throat still sore; Sister mett with Doctor Kuhn at J Downings, and desir'd him to call on me.—our dear little Eliza on seventh day night last, put a peice of a nutt shell up her Nose, which continues there yet—the Doctor has made an attempt to take it out, with an instrument but without success, they bound her eyes, and held her fast down, she cry'd so, that nothing could be done. . . .

18 First Day: All gone to meeting myself and Billy excepted—Docr. Shippen who Kuhn call'd in, try'd with an instrument to take the nut shell out of the poor dear childs nose, but could not effect it—S Swett din'd here—rain this eving.

22. . . . our little Eliza here this morning I could plainly discover when she kiss'd me, that her nose was offencive—I went home with her before dinner, stay'd dinner there—after dinner her Father made an attempt with the silver hook, to no purpose but to make her Nose bleed, she screaming violently all the time, it being a case of so much consiquence he was loath to give out, and with three to hold her fast down, try'd again and was favour'd to releive the dear child—he brought away with the hook half of a ground ground nut shell—which has been there near two weeks,—it has taken one burden off my mind, had it continu'd, the consiquence might have been distressing indeed.

29.30.31, Very much oppress'd with the cough the 31 seventh day I was let blood fine weather.

May 25—Nancy Skyrin is now I hope getting better, she has been for upwards of 2 weeks very unwell in her Chamber—Dr. Kuhn attended her—a voilent sickness and pain in her Stomach—very little appetite and very frequent [ ]achings, I have been every day more or less there and stay several Nights with her—perhaps it may end in what is call'd a natural cause—'tho she has been worse then that generaly comes too in the begening—we are busy white-washing and cleaning house, have had a dry spell of weather after a long wett one—very dusty.

29   I went to meeting this morning where I have not been before, since the 12 mo Decr. last—took a walk after to Sallys and Nancys. . . .

30.   . . . Jo. Gibbs a negro man came. . . .

1792 Augt. 25.   seventh Day. after an early dinner, HD. set off for Atsion—Jacob Downing din'd with us—Sister is at his house seeing it clean'd, as his wife and Children are to return home from Downingstown next week, they have been there between two and three months. Nancy Skyrin has been at Haddonfield two weeks this day—John Skyrin removed from Ann Vaux's house in arch street, to a house at the corner of Water and chestnut Streets, beloning to James Pemberton the last day of last month. Our Son Henry is I hope recovering from a cold and fever, which has confin'd him for 4 or 5 days past—William continues bet weekly—'tho I trust not much worse then usual—Docr. Rush has visited HD. for some time past on account of a disorder in his left eye, which there is reason to fear is a fixt *Fistula lachrymalo*[1] [I] William and Henry took a ride in the Chaise—Sammy Emlen and J. Logan call'd—fine moon light evening.

1. Fistula lachrymalis is a hole or ulceration in the lachrymal sac causing a continuous discharge of fluid (tears). The term, however, was widely used to cover many diseases involving the lachrymal passage (Bailey, *Universal Etymological Dictionary;* Gardner, *New Medical Dictionary*).

1793

Feby. 3   first day Nancy Skyrin with her little daughter Elizabeth and Nurse Wilson din'd here the first time of her coming out since the birth of her Child who was four weeks old last night. . . .

[Apr.] 2   Nancy here this morning making a Hat for her little Elizah. . . .

[May] 13   Molly Drinker sits up to night with Nancys baby, it has the Hooping Cough and as it is but 4 months old they are fearful of its strangling if neglected,—Eliza and Mary Downing also have it, Eliza getting better, Mary poorly. . . .

17   sixth day Nancy with her baby and her Maid Hope [Sharp] and Sister went to   beyond Germantown where they have taken lodgings.

1793, July 8, second day: . . . came after tea to[1] George Hessers, near 8 miles from Philada. where Nancy Skyrin has taken up her abode with her Daughter for the Summer, mett Sally Emlen and her Daughter with Huldah Mott there, they reside at one Sniders half mile from Nancy, nearer the City—they left us towards evening HD. stay'd all night.

13   took a walk with molly as far as the 8th mile stone and back, is ½ mile, came back to breakfast—eat hearty—set down to dinner with little appetite, taken very sick while eating, was in measure reliev'd by vomitting—have been unwell ever since. . . . the weather cool, which after the reverse suddenly closes the pores, occasion'd myself, and prehaps many others being unwell.

16   . . . a Man went through Germantown this Afternoon with something in a barrel to Show which he said was half man, half beast, and call'd it a Man[de], we paid 5½ for seeing it I believe it was a young Baboon, it look'd sorrowful, I pity'd the poor thing, and wished it in its own Country. . . .

22   Molly Drinker went home this morning with John Skyrin, she has been here 7 or 8 weeks, two since my arrival.—HD. came up this evening himself Nancy and [I]. took a walk this evening to S Emlens, a delightful full-moon

1. The word "John" crossed out.

light night, stop'd at Lebarts and bought a bottle Oyl, to make oyl of St. Johnsworte,[2] this being the proper time[3] to make it.

29   John Skyrin and Molly Drinker left us this morning—Sally Wharton, M Sandwith, W Drinker, came up in the waggon. Jo. Gibbs drove them—rain came on in the afternoon which oblig'd them to stay all night, Billy lodg'd in the front parlor by himself. SW. with me in the Trundle bed, Sister with Nancy, little Elizath. in her cribb, all in the back room we had rather a restless night, the Child fretful, the flies very troublesome.

[Aug.] 16   . . . 'tis a sickly time now in philada. and there has been an unusual number of funerals lately here.

19   . . . 'tis seldom any one of the Family comes to stay a night with us, but[4] they bring an account of the death of one or more of our Citeicnes. . . .

20   . . . I dont know that I ever saw a more beautiful Evening, the House we are at lays open in front to the Westward, the Sun set without an interweneing cloud, the Sky remain'd red for near an hour afterwards, the full Moon riseing towards the back of the house, added Charmes to the scene, the weather very temperate. I did little else for near an hour, but walk up and down the Entry making frequent stops at the front door to see if one of our family were coming up, but in that am dissapointed; were all well, that I call mine, I think I should feel this evening, a little as formerly.

23   . . . a fever prevails in the City, perticularly in water-street, between race and arch streets of the malignant kind, numbers have died of it, some say it was occasion'd by damag'd Coffee, and fish, which was stor'd[5] at Wm. Smith, others say it was imported in a Vessel from Cape-Francoies which lay at our warfe, or at the warfe back of our Store; Docr. Hutchinson was ordred by the Governor or employd to enquire into the report, he found as 'tis said upwards of 70 persons sick in that square, of different disorders; several of this putried[6]

2. Saint-John's-wort (*Hypericum*) was long considered a remedy in the treatment of bruises and wounds. Its preparation included stamping the leaves, flowers, and seeds and placing the pulp in a glass with olive oil. The mixture was removed to the hot sun for several weeks before being strained, renewed with fresh ingredients, and sunned again. The resulting oil took on a bloodlike color, which according to Paracelsus's theory was a sign that the plant was efficacious in closing wounds (Millspaugh, *Medicinal Plants*, 114; Gifford, "Botanic Remedies," 265, 267).
3. The words "of year" crossed out.
4. The word "that" crossed out.
5. The word "by" crossed out.
6. Putrid fever, associated with pestilence, plague, and highly infectious epidemics, was thought to occur in large towns and cities, particularly in the poorer sections, because of a lack of cleanliness. General symptoms included sudden weakness, nausea, sometimes vomiting of bile, labored breathing, and stomach pains. Specific symptoms of putrid fever were a low pulse, dejected state of mind, dissolved state of blood, the presence of purple spots known as *petechiae*, and the putrid smell of excrement. In this instance, the putrid fever was later identified as yellow fever (Buchan, *Domestic Medicine* [1793], 132–39).

or billous fever,—some are ill in water street between arch and market streets, and some in race street—'tis realy an alarming and sereous time. . . .

27 . . . the yallow-Fever spreads in the City, many are taken of with it and many with other disorders. . . . they have burnd Tar in the Streets and taken many other precautions,[7] many families have left the City. . . .

28. HSD. left us at about 6 this morning I gave him a small spoonfull of Duffys Ellixr and Vinager in a spunge, and a sprig of wormwood[8]—JS. went after breakfast, useing the same precautions—this has been a serious thoughtful day to us. We have some reason to hope that HD. and Sister will leave home & come up to us, if they do not I must go to Town, as HD. does not seem quite free to do so—This Afternoon our Carriage, drove by a white man, a stranger, came up, with Mattrasses &c Blankets &c—and Sally Brant behind,—poor black Joseph gone away sick to some Negro House, where they have promis'd to take care of him, and Dr. Foulk is desir'd to attend him—we have hopes it is not the contagous fever that he has; Sister and HD. came up in the evening Docrs. Kuhn and Rush both advis'd it—as there is a man next door but one to us, who Docr. Kuhn says will quickly die of this terriable disorder—Caty Prusia over against us is very ill, and a man at the Shoemakers next door to Neigr. Waln's, some sick in our ally, we know not what ails them. . . .

30. . . . our House is left, fill'd with valuables, no body to take care of it— the Grapevines hanging in clusters, and some of the fruit Trees loaded— but those are matters of little consequence. . . .

31. . . . some naughty person or persons have broke into our yard, and stole the grapes & magnumbonums,[9] and broke the limbs off that beautiful tree—if they do not get into the house we will forgive them. . . .

[Sept.] 2d. . . . Neighr. Waln and Nancy Morgan came to visit us this forenoon RW. stays with her Son Robt. they inform'd us of the death of our poor Neighbors Caty Prusia and her Husband, Christian the biscuit baker, both nearly opposite our house, Christopher the Barber near the corner, and a fringemaker, on this side him. . . . we have heard this day of the death of a

---

7. Tar was thought to prevent yellow fever. Many Philadelphians carried tarred ropes on their persons in an attempt to ward off the disease or lit bonfires in front of their houses to purify the air during the epidemic (Powell, *Bring Out Your Dead*, 22–24).

8. Daffy's Elixir, a popular patent medicine concocted around 1650 by a British clergyman, was a tincture of senna leaves, jalap root, coriander seeds, and alcohol. It was a favorite tonic during the yellow fever epidemic, but was more commonly used to relieve colic and flatulence. Wormwood, also a tonic, was thought useful in preventing yellow fever as well (W. Lewis, *New Dispensatory*, 318; Powell, *Bring Out Your Dead*, 51, 23; *OED*, s.v. "wormwood").

9. The magnum bonum is a large yellow cooking plum (*OED*).

poor intemperate woman of the name of Clarey, who sold Oysters last winter in a Seller in front street a little below Elfriths Alley—she was taken out of her sences and went out of town, was found dead on the rode. . . .

4 . . . it is said that many are bury'd after night, and taken in carts to their graves—tis thought by some that the present tremendeous disorder is a degree of the pestelance, may we be humble, and thankful for favours received—We were told a Sad Story indeed, to day, if it be true, it was repeated by different persons and every thing considred it seems not unlikely, of a young woman who had nurs'd one or more in water street, who dy'd of the disease, she being unwel, the Neighbours advis'd her to go somewhere else as none of them chose to take her in, she went out somewhere, I did not hear in what part of the Town it was, and lay down ill at a door, a majastrate in the ward, had her sent in a cart to the Hospital, where she was refused admitance, and was near that place found dead in the cart next morning.

5 Our little Elizabeth Skyrin has been lately poorly, we last night discover'd her first tooth. . . .

6 . . . 'tis said that the Schools are all broke up,[10] . . . Caleb Hopkinson T Scattergoods brother in Law, died this morning of this raging fever, Docr. Hutchinson is also gone, 'tis said he got the disorder by putting a young woman in her Coffin who dy'd at his house, not being able readly to procure any one to do that office—the ringing of Bells for the dead is forbid for several days past.—John Cannon, one of the counsel drank tea with us, as he had business with my husband, he took this in his way home, as the Counsel and Assembly have broke up, on account of this very affecting Dispensation,[11] the officies are almost all shut up—and little business done,—the doors of the Houses where the infection is, are ordrr'd to be mark'd, to prevent any but those that are absolutely necessary from entering—such is the Melancholy and distresing state of our poor City.

8 . . . 'tis remarkable [that] not one Negro has yet taken the infection. they[12] have offered to as Nurses to the sick.[13]

10. The words "that many [are carried] to their graves in carts after night" crossed out.
11. The Pennsylvania House of Representatives adjourned on Sept. 4 (*Dunlap's American Daily Advertiser*, Sept. 4, 1793).
12. The words "are appointed" crossed out.
13. ED apparently saw the announcement placed by Mayor Matthew Clarkson in newspapers on Sept. 7 that the African Society would furnish nurses to the sick. John Lining, a Charleston physician, had first noted in the 1750s that blacks did not seem to contract yellow fever. In Philadelphia the leading exponent of this view, widespread throughout the Americas, was Benjamin Rush, who was proved wrong, however, when blacks in that city started contracting and dying of the disease. Figures from the black community indicate a mortality rate of 13 percent during the 1793 epidemic, not drastically different from the 18 percent

9 . . . JS. went this evening to S Emlens for MD. who has been there this Afternoon, she concluded to stay there all Night, as they had heard of a Man who came from the City, who lay ill in a field near the 8 Mile stone, that the Overseers would not go near him—We have also heard this account but 'tis not known whether the poor Man is sick or in liquor; such are the fears of the people—weather warm.

10 . . . it was thought on first day last from 50 to 100 had die'd, the disorder having greatly increas'd . . . we have also heard to day that the dead are put in their Coffins just as they die without changing their cloths or laying out, are buried in an hour or two after their disease—that way is made to enter freinds burying-ground with the Herse to the grave; that graves are dug before they are spoke for, to be ready. . . .

12 . . . we were inform'd 2 or 3 day past that two or three dead bodys were thrown into friends burying ground over the wall. . . .

16 . . . G Hesser told a sad story, of Robt. Ross Broker that he died in the night of the Yellow fever, no Body with him but his wife who was taken in labour while he was dying, she opend the window and call'd for help, but obtain'd none, in the morning some one went in to see how they fair'd, found the man and his wife both dead, and a new born infant alive, further I heard not. . . .

24 . . . the New York stage past this door to day—they are endeavouring to stop the communication between us and N–Y–. . . .

27 . . . I heard yesterday that Coffins were keept ready made in piles, near

mortality rate for the white population unable to leave the city. Still, the experience of some southern U.S. cities in the nineteenth century lends support to a theory of a greater tolerance of yellow fever among blacks. In the Memphis epidemic of 1878, for instance, over two-thirds of the whites who remained in the city died, while the black mortality rate was less than 7 percent. Historians and epidemiologists have advanced various explanations, none conclusive, ranging from genetic predisposition to early childhood exposure among African-born blacks (C. K. Drinker, *Not So Long Ago*, 119; *Federal Gazette* and *Dunlap's American Daily Advertiser*, Sept. 7, 1793; Powell, *Bring Out Your Dead*, 95–100, 254; Carey, *Short Account*, 62–63; Nash, *Forging Freedom*, 121–24; Richard Taylor, "Epidemiology," in *Yellow Fever*, ed. George K. Strode [New York: McGraw-Hill, 1951], 427–538; Todd L. Savitt, *Medicine and Slavery* [Urbana: University of Illinois Press, 1978], 240–46; John H. Ellis, "Disease and the Destiny of a City: The 1878 Yellow Fever Epidemic in Memphis," *The West Tennessee Historical Society Papers* 28 (1974): 87; Kenneth F. Kiple and Virginia Himmelsteib King, *Another Dimension to the Black Diaspora: Diet, Disease, and Racism* [Cambridge: Cambridge University Press, 1981], 31; Kenneth F. Kiple and Virginia H. Kiple, "Black Yellow Fever Immunities, Innate and Acquired, as Revealed in the American South," *Social Science History* 1 (1977):419–36).

the State-house for poor people . . . J Perott heard that they dig trenches in the poters-field, to bury the dead. . . .

29   . . . Eliston Perott bury'd his youngest Child a Son, this morning in the Germantown burying-groung, it was not suppos'd that it dy'd of the yallow fever—his family are at Sansoms place call'd parlaVille.—this is the fourth Child out of five that they have lost within 3 years, 2 Sons of the putrid sore throught, a little Daughter was over lay'd by her Nurse, they have one Daughter remaining. . . .

[Oct.] 4   . . . Nancy Skyrin came home very ill, Head-ach and sick stomach, she broke out with the Netle rash, occasion'd in measure by putting a small peice of Camphire in her mouth,[14] it happn'd so once before—she was better before Bed-time,—Saml. Macey and Jacob Wilson dead, The Accounts from the City this day, seem to be worse than has yet been, We were inform'd that dead Bodies have been found in some houses, in the City, who have been forsaken in their illness, and not discover'd for some days after death.

5.   Nancy 'tho better, is far from well, HSD—took a walk this morning with a Segar in his mouth, which he smoak'd out, and soon after found himself very sick and in a sweat, he made shift to get into G Hessers Orchard, where he discharg'd his Stomach, he was fearfull of doing so on the road, least he should be suspected of having the prevailing disorder, he came home sick and pale, and after it had opperated both as an emetic and a cathartic, he was better. . . . It is told to day that the day before—yesterday 40 persons were sent to the Hospital and a vast number bury'd, yesterday not so many laid in the Earth, but many sick—to day 'tis said that there is an alteration for the better, this has been a fine clear cool day. I have remark'd that 2 or 3 times when we have heard of an abatement of the disease, that the weather was cool. . . .

9.   William walk'd a mile down town to Hubbss Store, to purchase , Cassamer. . . . the Gloom continues in our City, The Awful disease by no means lessen'd—may we endeavour for preparation and resignation. . . . taking a walk this evening with HD. towards the meadow, by a cornfield that had been lately plough'd, the narrow road fill'd in places with stubble that had been thrown out of the field, my foot turn'd under me when I fell down, and was so strain'd and brused that I could scarcely step with help—my husband and G Hesser made a Chair with their hands, and brought me home on it, with my Arms round their Necks, as I have seen Children carry one another— I had it bath'd with Opodeldock[15] and wrap'd up in flannel. . . .

14. The word "as" crossed out.
15. Paracelsus, the famous sixteenth-century chemist and physician, coined the word *opodeldoc* to describe various medical plasters. By the 1720s the term had come to mean soap liniment (Griffenhagen and Young, "Patent Medicines," 161).

10 the pain in my foot keep'd me all night awake, dosed a little after day, 'tis much swel'd and painful. . . . we have heard of more deaths this day, than any day yet, and 'tis said that 150 were bury'd in the City yesterday—Betsy Howel told after meeting that Docr. Rush has wrote to Willm. Lewis "that the disorder was now past the Art of man or medicine to cure, that nothing but the power of the Almighty could stop it." or to this effect. . . .

11 I show'd my foot this morning to Docr. Lusby who desir'd me to chang my method of heating it, which was vinager and opodeldoc, and afterwards I bath'd it with Oyl of St. Johns-Wort, but he orders lead water alone,[16] twice a day. . . .

12 . . . On fifth day last 40 were sent to the Hospital, which with those there before amounted to 302 persons, 'tis now so full, that another is said to be preparing—17 graves 'tis said were dug in friends buring ground yesterday, 'tis very afflicting to walk through the Streets of our once flourishing and happy City, the Houses shut up from one corner to another, the Inhabitance that remain keeping shut up, very few seen walking about—The disorder now 'tis said rages much in the South part of the City, that great numbers dye in that part call'd Irish-town. . . .

16 . . . 'Tis a week this afternoon since my foot has touch'd the floor, unless by accident when geting of the Bed on a chair to have the Bed made, I set all day on it, working, or reading when able—the swelling is abaited but the foot very black. To sit so long in one possition is very tiresome, but patience alleviates most afflictions.

17 . . . Samuel Shoemaker Son of Benjamin of Abington who dyed some time ago of the Melignant fever, was thought dead by the attendant, who went out for his Coffin, and on his return into the Room where the Corps lay, found him sitting on the side of the Bed endeavouring to put on his Shoes, he ask'd him where he was going; was answer'd to take walk, but being desired to lay down and rest himself he comply'd, and dyed in reality about an hour after. had he remain'd as he was first found a quarter of an hour longer, A Livesley, who told the Story, think he would have been screw'd in his Coffen—Peter Browns Clark told my husband to day as he was returning home, of the death of three young women, Daughters of a Man in Kingsington who went home to their parants one after the other sick of the fever, from the City—some time

16. The external use of lead-based preparations for such injuries was urged by Thomas Goulard, a French surgeon (W. Lewis, *New Dispensatory*, 204–5; Mr. [Thomas] Goulard, *A Treatise on the Effects and Various Preparations of Lead, Particularly of the Extract of Saturn, for Different Chirurgical Disorders* [London: P. Elmsley, 1773], 201–3, passim).

after their deaths the Father and Mother, were so thoughtless as to lay in the Bed wherein they dy'd, and both were taken with the fever and died also. . . .

21st. . . . A Flag fixt on the Hospital, but 3 persons buryed from thence yesterday and one 'tis said this day.

24 . . . we are inform'd that the Malignancy of the disorder is much lessn'd, 'tho many are still ill. . . .

26 . . . 'tis remarkable, that no one has been known to take the infection in the Country of those who came out of the City disorder'd and die—I have not heard of an instance where it has spread. . . .

29 . . . The fever appears to be nearly at an end, for which we cannot be too thankful, the newspaper says that the 11th. of this month 2730 odd had dyed of the Yellow fever, on that day dy'd more than any preceeding day, and great numbers since[17]—very cold—The last 24 hours have been to me rather distressing.

30 MS. came home before dinner—J. and H Pemberton here this morning— I cant say that I walk'd, but that I got along to the fire-side with the help of two of my Children, it is three weeks this afternoon since I saw the Sunset, which I was gazing at, when I made a false steap and hurt my foot. . . .

[Nov.] 2d. . . . I had the agreeable intiligence from my Children, that the Waggons were taking the people and goods back to the City—it is clear'd up this morning with a fine frost—what a favourable reverse, which calls for humility and thanks. . . .

6 . . . HD. and HSD. gone down town to the Washington tavern on busyness—myself unwell—The inhabitants of Philada. were fast moving into the City before this storm, 'tis said there were upwards of 20,000 had left their dwellings, and retired into the Country. . . . The widdow Durdan din'd and drank tea with us, HSD. waited on her to the Inn where she lodges to night, HD. has purchased upwards of 200 acres of Land of her, part of Pennsbury Manor, for a farm for Henry. . . .

8 . . . I have walk'd across the room yesterday and to day, without Shoes,

17. The beginning of October saw the highest mortality of the yellow fever epidemic, with 119 deaths recorded on the peak day, Oct. 11. Mathew Carey, using cemetery records, recorded a total of 4,044 dead out of a total population of roughly 40,000, of whom 17,000 fled during the epidemic. Powell considers Carey's figure to be an undercount (Carey, *Short Account*, 65 and passim; Powell, *Bring Out Your Dead*, 281 and passim).

and with Sisters help—if nothing more than the disorder in my foot aild me, I beleive I should now soon get bravely.

11 . . . I can scarcely make shift to step on my foot without a Shoe,—'tho it is getting better.

16 very busy preparing for our departure, J Pemberton call'd.—after one o'clock Noke came with their Carriage, William and myself left Germantown with some of our lugage—the roads but middling—we arriv'd at home between 2 and 3—found things in Statu-[quo]. . . .

17 . . . How thankfull we ought to be, that we are return'd in safety to our own Habitation, If Jacob Sally and their dear little ones, were likewise well fixt at home, it would add to my Satisfaction, I trust 'eer long 'twill be so.

19 . . . Caty Mullen here to day, in great trouble; she came over from Irland a poor widdow, when her 2 Sons were small, she work'd industreously for their and her own maintannance, put them apprentice, took great care of them during that term, they have been some years free, and have work'd at their trades with reputation; she hop'd that they would be her support in the decline of Life, but how uncertain are all human prospects? they were both taken this fall with the prevailing desease, and died, one the day after the other, the poor mother 'tho very ill at the same time surviv'd them, and may be truly call'd a 'lone woman.—After her came poor Crissy Lambsback widdow of John who work'd for us—she says he did not die of the Yallow fever, as was reported, but of the pleurisy, he had a violent pain in his side, she could not prevail on the Doctor to bleed him, but he gave him wine, which he said he was sure hurt him,—after his death she went with her Children into the Jersyes, and on her return to the City, found the house where they had liv'd open, and most of her small property stolen, she is near lyeing-in, and has four small Children—how many are the instances of deep distress, that have this fall occur'd? . . .

23. . . . Crissey Lambsback was here, HD. gave her an order to receive share of monys subscrib'd for poor widdows, renderd so by the late Sickness. . . .

25 . . . I this fore-noon put on Williams Sliper: next day after tomorrow will be 7 weeks, since I hurt my foot, it continues to be much swell'd, the blackness not quite gone, it continus to mend 'tho slowly—I have been in my Chamber ever since I came home untill this morning after breakfast, went down stairs and spent the day. . . .

28 . . . so soon after very many of our old friends and Neighbours are laid in the dust, to see our own family all mett togeather, is cause of great thankfull-

ness and humiliation, after spending some hours in Company, I have laterly retired to my Chamber much fatigu'd, being inwardly week, I feel then, from under a restraint, can set and think, and bath my foot, and conceit I can do as I please. . . .

Decbr. 1. First Day. In my Chamber most of this day, which was very unusual for me, before my present indispossion, it is many years since I have spent a day in my Chamber, on my own account, 'tho often sufficiently unwell but but I lik'd it not, and to me it was formerly very disagreeable, but at present I have no objection to retirement, when necessary, 'tis rather pleasing. . . .

2 . . . made a pair Shoes for my grand Daughters ES. . . .

5 . . . Sally Dawson came upon trial, her Father intends binding her to us, she is 9 years and ½ old—a pritty looking Child—her mother dead, not long since.

15 . . . Eliza. Downing came this day to spend a week with us, if it should so happen. . . .

20 . . . Sally Dawson was this day bound to us, by her Father Thos. Dawson, for the term of Eight years from this day. . . .

25 Christsmass, so call'd, keep't by some pious well minded people religiously, by some others as a time of Frolicking—Thos. Stewardson din'd with us—rain and cloudy all day; clear'd towards evening.

28. Sally and Nancy here to day. S Swett spent the day with us—Ben Wilson, Jacob Downing here this evening—Nancy Rice formerly Corry call'd on Sister—to excuse herself from paying her ground rent, she has lost her Son, an only child aged 15 years, and Nursed her husbands brother and his wife, who both also died of the late fever.—Docr. Redman here at noon—HD. went this morning with those friends who were at the Indian treaty,[18] to wait on the President,[19] to have some talk with him, touching the Indian War &c.

18. Six Quakers—Joseph Moore, William Savery, John Parish, John Elliott, Jacob Lindley, and William Hartshorne—had attended a conference in July between U.S. commissioners and representatives of the Western Confederation of Indian tribes, held at present-day Sandusky, Ohio. The conference failed to resolve the two governments' differences, and no treaty resulted. (J. Moore, "Moore's Journal," 632–71, esp. 664; Reginald Horsman, *Expansion and American Indian Policy, 1783–1812* [East Lansing: Michigan State University Press, 1967], 96–98). Moore, who died Oct. 7, could not have attended this later meeting.
19. The word "dinner" crossed out.

31   They are now practizeing the foolish custom of fireing out the old year, may the next be spent to good purpose, by those who are spair'd to see the end of it. . . . HD. is at present favour'd with as good a share of health as I ever knew him—the Lachrymal Fistula which took place in his left Eye, in May ninety two, continues as it was when the swelling first subsided, neither better nor worse—MS. highly favour'd with a continued state of good health, much better than some years past. ED. far from enjoying a state of bodily health, Jacob Sally and their little ones much favour'd. Nancy at present but poorly, JS. and the little Elizabeth, well, she is a very promiseing Child. Our dear William, who has been in a low state of health for upwards of four years, is at present as well as could be expected considering what he has past through, it is four years this last fall since he had the Epidimic cold, call'd the Influensia, . . . he had another attack the spring following—was poorly all summer. . . . on the 9th. of Novemr. was taken with a sore throat, . . . the next day we sent for Dr. Kuhn, who said he had a touch of the Quinsey, but it turn'd out much worse than the Doctor expected, he was many days that he could not speak,— and when the disorder in his throat was better he lost the use of his limbs, so as not to be able to walk alone, or to button his Jacket, he was four months confin'd to his Chamber,—in the spring he rode out in a Close Carriage, seem'd to geather strength in the Summer. in the fall 91, he went on Horse-back towards new England—but was stop'd at a place call'd Rye 30 miles beyond New York, with a fever and spitting of blood—hir'd a Chaise and Man to bring him back to N-Y—where he was ill at Henry Haydocks. . . . We left H Haydocks on the third of Decemr. and arriv'd at our own dwelling on the 6th. after dinner, I believe I may say with thankful hearts. he was confin'd to the house most of the winter, very poorly in the spring, . . . he is now, the many pullbacks consider'd, as well as might be expected. the Doctors encour-ages us to hope, that if he can survive his Eight or nine and twentieth year, he may still become a healthy Man;—Our Son HSD. just turn'd of 23, is at present very well and hearty, it is remarkable in him that he looses flesh considerably in the Summer season, grows fatt and hearty in the winter—his chief complaints are a sick stomach at times, and two or 3 times in the coarse of his life a stitch in his side, a small obstruction in his liver, he is on the whole favour'd with good health & spirits. He is employ'd improving his farm which his father lately purchas'd and gave him, part of the Manor of Pennsbury, where he expects to spent his days as a farmer. May it please kind Providence to direct his steps—in that, and another undertaking of greater consiquence, which 'tis likely he will 'eer long be thinking, off—our Daughter Molly was born the finest and healthyest of 9 Children, she has been for several years at times complaining, 'tho far from sickly, and if she manages herself with care, may make a fine healthy Woman.

4. Grandmother and Grand Mother, 1794–1807

Although the last section of the diary spans only fourteen years, it represents fully three-quarters of the journal's entire contents. Drinker's prolific output during this period was a measure of available time, as was her voluminous reading, judging by the lists appended to the end of every year between 1799 and 1806. As her physical pace slowed down perceptibly, her intellectual activity sped up just as appreciably.

Advancing age did not mitigate her cares. Elizabeth's younger son, Henry, married Hannah Smith in 1794, and the fruitful couple proceeded to multiply at a rate that astonished even his mother. Molly, the most independent of the Drinker children, shocked her parents by eloping with Samuel Rhoads in 1796. Only Elizabeth's older son, William, whose precarious health was a source of constant concern, remained unmarried and at home.

Health—or the lack thereof—was always a central issue in Drinker's own life. As early as 1760 she claimed to be "frequently" unwell, and throughout the diary her various disorders and attempted cures are thoroughly documented. As she aged, she referred to herself more often as an invalid, and no doubt her stomach and bowel disorders were increasingly disabling. She complained more frequently of pain.

Elizabeth Drinker loved to be surrounded by her children and grandchildren, although toward the end of her life they were more likely to visit her than she them, and she was less likely to exert herself by flying to their side, as she once did in time of illness. By 1804 she no longer attended the birth of her daughters' children. Moreover, for most of her life Elizabeth Drinker had been a caregiver: a wife, mother, and grandmother whose advice was sought and accepted. During Drinker's last year, however, her family began to make decisions for

---

her. *They* summoned her doctor; *they* refused to let her walk any distance. By mutual consent, albeit with some regret on Elizabeth's part, she remained at home most of the time, although she was not bedridden.

Home was not a refuge from a "world of trouble," however. Drinker watched with sorrow as her daughter Nancy's marriage deteriorated and her son Henry left his wife and brood in Burlington while he embarked on an extended voyage to India. In this last stage of her life, she began to read old letters and occasionally spoke of her impending death. With each funeral she lamented the passing of a friend, almost surprised that she had outlived so many of her contemporaries. Her attitude toward life changed: "the older I grow, the less I think of triffles."

The lingering illness and painful death of her beloved daughter Sally in September 1807 probably hastened her own demise. In the last full month of her own life, she appeared to have little incentive to follow her doctor's advice, and she penned her last entry on November 18, 1807. She died a week later of "lethargy," leaving a husband, sister, five children, and nineteen grandchildren.

1794

Janry. 30.   A Snow storm last night, when we retired—this morning clear and cold, snow 9 or 10 inches deep—Sleighs flying about in great numbers with Bells at the Horses [e]ars a measure which took place last winter on account of the danger of a Sleigh coming unawares, and not being heard—when the pavements are slip'ry the people walk in the streets. . . .

31   . . . after an early dinner HD. JD. JS. and Eliza went in the Sligh to Gilbort Prichards, where they left Eliza, while they went to the farm which HD has had thoughts of purchasing. . . .

[Feb.] 10   E. Pound went away after breakfast, E Emlen spent the After-noon—A Committee this evening in front room, they concluded to purchase Langhorn-Park for a publick School.[1]

18   Anna Wells, James Logan, Nancy Skyrin here this morning Esther Trim-ble and her daughter Peggy with Jenny Richards here also—spar'd Peggy 11 yards Lutstring for a wedding Garment, Anna Wells, A Skyrin, Patr. Hart-shorn, En. Evans, here this evening—A shop burnt, in 3d. Street last evening heard nothing of it 'till this day—S Preston &c call'd.

25   HD. MS. HSD. gone to monthly Meeting John Pemberton call'd, S Preston drank tea, Jacob Downing took Eliza to visit her sister who is weaning at two years and one month old. Billy Salter left us after breakfast—the Dam at the Works has given way—and the Furnace stop'd.

[Mar.] 12   It seems as if most of our world, is in comotion, wars and rumors of wars.—a very fine day, Nancy and her Child, William and Henry, took a ride to the middle ferry, AS. din'd with us—Sally, Nancy and Molly, visited this Afternoon for the first time at Jos. Smiths, Elizabeth Dawson and Joseph Richardsons wife call'd—M. Pleasants and her Daughter Molly drank tea with us—J Skyrin, J Downing call'd—HD. agree'd this evening, with Daniel King

---

1. HD and several other Friends purchased Langhorne Park, a tract of 450 acres of land on Neshaminy Creek near Bristol, in Bucks County, Pa., in expectation that the Philadelphia Yearly Meeting would establish a Quaker boarding school there. The purchase took place before the 1794 meeting in order to forestall an exorbitant selling price should the site be selected (Dewees and Dewees, *Centennial of Westtown*, 1–29; Hole, *Westtown*, 20–28).

for his plantation on the old York road for which he is to pay him £3146—it is between 5 and 6 miles from the City.

17 Sally Smith, S Downing, A Skyrin calld—sent for Docr. Kuhn, he order'd William to loose 6 oz Blood, as he continues spitting phlegm of a sanguinary appearence, Michel perform'd the opperation at four o'clock in the Afternoon—the blood a little inflam'd. Molly Drinker with many others gone this Afternoon to visit Betsy Fisher—Nicholas Waln call'd.

18th. March. Docr. Kuhn call'd. examin'd Williams blood; approv'd of his having lost it. . . .

26th. HD. and MS. went after[2] breakfast to the place lately purchas'd, examin'd, and approv'd it.—came back to dinner:—My old friend Sally Moores black woman Ruth, call'd to see us. . . .

30. First Day: SD. m s——d yesterday, she seems pretty well to day considering—S Swett din'd here, I went after dinner to see Sally, the first time that I have been out of our front Door since my return from Germantown. . . .

[Apr.] 2. Jacob Downing awaken'd us this morning at two o'clock by knocking at the Gate, Sally was ill, and what we thought was settled on first day last happend this morning: Sister arose and went with Jacob, she stay'd there 'till I went before dinner and releas'd her, I came home toward evening—Sally is at present as well as may be, after being so ill last night and this morning. . . . Sister lodges this night with Sally. . . .

17. . . . Sally Downing call'd—MS. and MD. out this Afternoon, our front Room being the Coumpting room, takes off a number of transient visitors.

First day. 20. William and self at home, the rest of the family at meeting, Mary Savery din'd here S Swett also—I am generaly employ'd on a first day morning busyly, my Son and self both being unwell—in the Afternoon I can retire if I choose it.—Sally and Nancy drank tea with us, the Children here— Jacob and John call'd—Hannah Thomas and her two Sons calld our Daughter Nancy is complaining, and looks unwell, she is troubled with the sick head Ache.

26. fine clear weather—HD. and MS. went to the farm this Afternoon, bought a new black Horse try'd him and lik'd him—J Logan call'd—Betsy Fordham left us this afternoon, she has been near 2 weeks at work for us, Sally and Nancy hear—our dear Billy very poorly.

2. The word "noon" crossed out.

[May] 3.   Jacob and Sally went this Afternoon to the Farm in the Chaise to try a Horse which Jacob—has lately purchas'd—Molly spent the day with Nancy who is very poorly—Dr. Redman, Sally Downing, Dr. Foulk, Jacob Downing call'd—HSD. and his intended[3] went on Horseback to J Smiths place—fine weather—took [Medicine].

5.   . . . There was a rumpus at the wharf with a small Vessel, which 'twas said was going to take provisions or to carry intelligence or some thing else to the English fleet, I could not rightly understand the tale, but they took out her Main-Mast, and drag'd it with ropes up the bank, a mob collected, when J Dallis and others appear'd to put a stop to their proceedings.—I was really distress'd and have been at other times when at J Skyrins, to see the cruelty of the Dray-Men to their Horses, in forceing them to drag loads to heavy for them up the Hill—they whip them unmercyfully and are frequently after many vain exertions oblidg'd to unload.—I have long look'd on the treatment of Carters and Draymen &c to their poor dumb servants, a crying Sin that ought to be perticularly noticed.—came home after night; Huldah Mott, Betsy Saltar, Sally Saltar, John Adlum and Billy Ellis drank tea here—Polly Pleasants call'd—Molly was cup'd[4] in the back this evening on account of a small inflamation in her Eyes—cloudy, raw Easterly wind.

May 13.   . . . Sally, Nancy their Children and Hannah Smith drank tea here, the first time of Hannah's being here since Henry paid his court to her. . . .

15.   . . . little Eliza very poorly with a fever and violent cough—sent for Dr. Kuhn who order'd her a anodyne to night and gentle purge in the morning—HD. returnd this evening, and retired early to rest, having travel'd 80 miles this day, he found our friends in N York generaly in good health. . . .

May:16.   MS. Sally Brant, and Sam Sprigs went to the Farm, spent the day there, we sent up two Chimney Sweeps, they also had white washing done, a day or two more will 'tis suppos'd finish cleaning the house from top to bottom.—Dr. Kuhn call'd this morning he order'd the Child a purge which was given, of peach blossom suryp, it work'd kindly—but this evening 'tho she had seem'd better to day than for 2 or 3 days past, after a spell of Coughing she brought up some blood, which to us is very alarming, 'tho I hope it proceeds from the soreness of her breast rather than any thing fixt. . . .

17 May: . . . Henry brought home three Strawberries and 6 or 8 ripe Cheries

---

3. Hannah Smith, daughter of James Smith and Esther Hewlings Smith.
4. I.e., bled. In cases of inflammation of the eyes, William Buchan recommended that the bleeding be done as close as possible to the eyes. If the jugular vein was not convenient, then the arm or another part of the body was suitable for the task (Buchan, *Domestic Medicine* [1799], 194–96).

from the Farm, it proves this to be a very early spring, as I do not recolect seeing any before the Spring Fair, and I dont remember but once their failing at that time. half a Dozen ty'd to a stick for a penny.

24. HD. MS. and Sally Brant went to Clearfield. the name which HD. has given to the Farm, as James Fisher has a place that has been call'd Newington for many years past, 'twas thought best to change the name.—HD &c came home to tea they brought some green peas, and some Strawberries.

26. . . . I lodg'd last night in Williams Room, where Sister or myself, generly does when Henry is absent, . . .

27 May: . . . Sam came after dinner for to desire Molly to come set with his mistress as she is unwel and little Elizath. got the nettle-rash—rain all the afternoon and evening—Sally Rhoads spent the Afternoon and evening with us, Saml. Rhoads here this evening—Sam came for Mollys night-cloaths, as she doth not chuse to come home in the rain—so that we shall be 4 out of family this night—HD. HSD. MD. and Joe Gibbs.

[June] 6. . . . Jacob call'd—he paid a Boat-man[5] 1200 Dollars which were in a Bag, and going on board his foot slip'd, or by some other means he fell into the river, where he left the Money, but saved himself, it happend in the fore-noon, they have been most of the day endeavouring to recover it but in vain. . . .

7. sometime during last night, Emanuel a Negro man, whom J Downing had employ'd with his man Anthony, to watch on the wharf, that no one might take the advantage of night and obtain the Cash,—drew it up with a Hook and brought it home, for which he receiv'd 100 Dollars reward, the Sum stipulated, and indeed, sufficient. . . .

12 . . . Eliza to spend the day at home, where she has not been for upwards of three weeks. . . .

14. Sally Downing call'd this morning, our dear little Eliza left us after dinner and went home, she has been with us 6 months one day lacking—Ben Wilson Breakfasted, John the Gardner came this afternoon with the Cart and old Sorrel, took up a load of Necessaries, HD. and ED, in the Chaise, with our good old mare, Billy, Molly, and Sally Brant in the Coachee, Joe drove them. We arived at Clearfield before 6 o'clock, a very beautiful and pleasent place it is—how delighted and pleas'd would many women be, with such a retreat—and I hope a good degree of thankfullness is not wanting in me

5. The word "with" crossed out.

for the many favours we are bless'd with—should our dear William be restor'd to a comfortable state of health by our removal into the Country, the end would be abundantly answer'd in my view—Molly, Sall and self have been very busy this evening in arrainging matters here, we have left our dear Sister and Aunt to the care of seeing a large house clean'd in the City—but as she is not very fond of leaving home, she is more in her element.

As I am but weak and poorly and very sildom ride out, the coming up here and the bustle since has fatigu'd me, and as all of our little family Sall and self excepted have retir'd, I think 'tis time we should do so too—moon light.

15. . . . after dinner HD. and ED. walk'd into the garden, found a land Tortoise in a Straw-berry bed—which one of us brought into the house— William cut the Initials of his name and the date of the year, on the under shell WD. 1794—I have read some where of some one doing the like, and the Tortoise being found 50 years or upwards afterwards. . . .

17 June. . . . J. Courtney brought in a land Tortoise this fore-noon, with William [T]—June 18, 1789, carved on his undershell, the surname not intillagble, we replac'd him, as that of yesterday, near the spot from whence he was taken. . . . we went on the top of our house this afternoon, the top is almost flat and rail'd in, the prospect from it is beautiful, . . . yesterday I visited poor John Courtney Wife, she expects some time this summer to lay in with her seventh child, has had but one that was born alive, a fine little girl, now between 3 and 4 years of age, whom they have with them, by her own account, poor woman, she has suffer'd greatly, I feel much for her,—to be sick and poor is hard indeed.

21. . . . Jacob Downing Sally and Children, Caty and Anna breakfasted this morning at our house in Town, set off after for Downingstown, where they expect to spend the Summer, Jacob excepted. . . .

22. . . . My husband and Son William took a ride of 8 or 9 miles before tea. . . .

25. We are not very regular in riseing in the Morning or retireing at night, 6 or 7, 10 or 11. this morning between 6 and 7, busy after breakfast making Curant Jelly.—John brought in a Mole he found in a potatoe patch that he was laying out. A mole is, on examination a curious creature, but what shall we call it? it is nither Man nor Beast, Fish or Fowl, Insect or Reptile, prehaps it is of the[6] class of Vermin, 'tho I hardly think that proper. . . .

26. . . . Tis now near 11 o'clock, Nancy has been an hour asleep, after

6. The word "race" crossed out.

having been very ill—I intend seting up 'till she awakes, our little family consist this night of 3 Women and 3 Children it rains at present, very hard, Polly is up stairs setting by her mistress, the little one asleep in the Cradle. Sally Brant and Betsy Dawson are also fast, they are in the Old parlor with me. how many soleumn hours of watching, have I had in the course of my life?—I have been endeavouring to amuse myself by reading Moors Journal while in Paris,[7] if it can be an amusement to read of so many absurd and unheard of cruelities as have been practis'd there.

July 1st.   No Company the fore part of this day—took a walk this Afternoon with William he is better than for several days past,—Nancy and Molly went towards evening to Saml. Fishers, return'd to tea, HSD. came up to tea with us, says that his father has been blooded this morning on account of some blood that he observed in his spittle, the weather is I think much too warm for such an opperation, he intends being up hear tomorrow morning with some others to have this place survay'd &c.—poor H——y. C——p——r, put an end to his life, this morning with a pistole, I know not why—A French Man, has been exhibiting fire-works this evening in the City, we saw the Sky-Rockets here.—[S] Fisher here this evening—busy this day making Current Jelly &c.—warm.

7.   . . . Our people here have been busy to day, washing, we hir'd a dutch woman nam'd Rosanna, to assist—washing at home is a new business to me, having been in the practice ever since we were married to put out our washing—a fine clear day—D King call'd this morning—his wife in the Afternoon.

8.   . . . Nancy has begun to day to wean her dear little Girl, she is very good natur'd 'tho full of trouble. . . .

11.   HD. went to town before breakfast, early—a cloudy day with some rain—geather'd baum—and Hypericon,[8] rain this evening.

16.   HD. and JS. left Clearfield early this morning rain most of the day, no one here—HSD. came after 10 at night from Summer Ville to lodge here. Nancy and Molly were up stairs retireing when he came, he soon brought 'em down child and all; by the sound of an instrument he had with him, the dear little one was so delighted, 'tho in trouble, that she keep'd time with her

---

7. John Moore, M.D., *A Journal, during a Residence in France, from the Beginning of August, to the Middle of December, 1792 . . . in 2 volumes* (Philadelphia: Rice, 1793 [Evans, *Am. Bibliography*]).

8. Baum tea or balm tea, prepared from fragrant garden herbs, is used as a diaphoretic, to reduce fever, and for internal disorders. *Hypericum* is Saint-John's-wort (*OED*; see above, July 22, 1793).

legs head and feet for a considerable time and went to bed in a good humour, she finds it hard to be deprived of that nourishment, which has so long been her chief support.

20. First day. last night or this morning between 2 and three, William came into my Chamber, he was[9] disordered at Stomach and bowels, occasion'd I expect by the heat of the weather, I stay'd with him an hour, left him somthing better, he has been poorly all this day—little or no appitite, chearful this evening—John Thomas and wife, their two Sons, Arthur and John and HSD. came up in our carriage,—JS. AS. MD. and one of the little boys went to meeting. Henry drove his brother out in the Chaise. . . .

29. Arose this morning nearly, with the Sun, Gillbert mowing again to day, diets with us—heat'd our oven this morning for the first time—baked, Bread, Pies, rice pudden & custards. . . .

Augt. 1. rumpus.—JS. left us about ten this forenoon—H Pemberton and M. Pleasants paid us a morning visit—it is very warm to day, and WD. in town—a peice of nice corn'd Beef which we intended for part of our dinner, stole out of the Spring-house. . . .

Augt. 2. Jacob and John left us early, William and Henry stay'd breakfast, then set off—fine air this morning or 'twould be very warm—Pattison and Suckey Hartshorn, their 4 Children and M.A. Warder, paid us a morning visit.—Je suis bien Malade aujour'd'huy;[10] my health very precarious, and has been for a long time past, 'tho I keep about and appear tolerable.—H Smith sent us a basket of large ripe apples, fitt for dumplings, they came very opportunely, as we have no pies made, and only Chicken and Bacon for dinner having lost our peice beef. . . .

4. . . . this has been a very warm day—WD. and self took a walk towards even'g ½ mile out.—AS. underwent, and went under, a shower bath this evening she fixt herself in a large tub, the girles pour'd water thro' a[11] Cullender on her head—she has felt very pleasant since. . . .

8. . . . I have been for a week past under great anxiety of mind on account of our poor little and I fear miserable SB—'tis *possible* I may be mistaken, 'tho I greatly fear the reverse.[12]

9. The word "much" crossed out.
10. I am very sick today.
11. The word "large" crossed out.
12. ED was not mistaken. The young servant, Sally Brant, was pregnant.

11. The full moon arose last night very red, which I look'd upon as a mark of dry weather, it occur'd to me while looking at it, that it was to be eclipsed this morning totally for about two hours,—it was late when I retir'd to my Chamber, and later when I went to sleep—the thoughts of the unhappy Child that lay on a matrass at the foot of my bed, who does not appear to feel half so much for herself, as I do for her, keep't me wakeing. . . . Sun shone this morning through flying clouds, weather warm. . . . H. and ED. had a trying Conversation, if a conversation it could be call'd, with SB—poor poor Girl, who could have thought it? . . .

14. . . . finish'd reading, Youngs Centaur.[13]

18. . . . H. Mott and Betsy Emlen came this morning for Nancy, Molly and little Elizath. who went with 'em to spend the day—so that I am alone, as an Irishman would say, with Sally and Betsy—din'd by myself, Nancys maid Polly return'd this Afternoon—the same company that our girls went with this fore-noon, came back with them this evening,—Molly return'd with them again to Germantown, where she intends spending a day or two, with S Emlen &c. at Sniders—HD. and William came up this evening Billy continues poorly, bowels disorder'd.

19. . . . Joe Gibbs, was yesterday morning dismiss'd from our service, we suppose he is gone towards New-England, he has left, if we mistake not, a Memorial behind him. . . . Henry came home at 10 minuets after 10 o'clock, his father and brother had been in bed ½ hour, I waiting for him, and not a little uneasy; when young men go a Courting so far from home, they should make their visits shorter, and not walk two miles in a dark night alone; the resk of meeting with mischevous persons, or of taken cold this season of the Year, should have some weight with 'em.—I have my Husband and both my Sons with me this night, which is not common.

22. . . . HD. prevail'd on me, much against my feelings to take a ride of two or 3 miles,—(Rosanna hear to day weeding the Strawberries) I mett with so many frights in my younger days with my Children when they were little ones, that I cannot get over and I may say that I am a compleat Coward, it has been a great inconvenience and dissapointment in many ways to me. . . .

23. . . . a Jonathan Carmalt, grand Son of Thos. Say, was lately grievously abus'd on the Frankford road, who the person was that beat him I have not heard, his wife and Children were with him in a Carriage, he was pull'd out of

13. Edward Young, *The Centaur Not Fabulous: In Six Letters to a Friend, on the Life in Vogue* . . . (London: A. Millar and J. Dodsley, 1755 [*NUC*]).

the Carriage and beat with a horse whip 'till he was, as related, in a gore,[14] one of his eyes beat out, and hung on his Cheek, and otherways much injur'd, he put his eye in the socket with his own hand, but turn'd the pupil inwards, the Offence was, entering a gate by mistake—belonging to a person who was a stranger to him, he is since taken up and put in prison—I dont know JC. but feel much for his old grandfather, in whose house my Sister and self boarded 14 months after the death of our dear parants,—he is near 85 years old, and has lately mett with several tryals. . . .

26. . . . we may in measure become innured to bodily pain, 'tis rarely I pass an hour, without uneasy sensations.—This time twelve month our fellow Citizens were dyeing in numbers, with the malignant fever—not soon, I trust, to be forgoten, but remember'd by survivors with humble thankfullness—and amendment of Life.

Augt. 27. . . . this has been a fine day. I have felt rather better than usual— Different persons have different tasts, their likes and dislikes vary, to me the noise of insects is amuseing, the locust, the Cricket, the Cateydid, as it is call'd, and even the croaking of Frogs.—'tho their notes are inferior, they are pleasing.

28. Sam, came up this morning busy Ironing, Sam cook'd dinner, Rosanna here weeding. . . .

29 . . . HP. prevail'd on me to go to town with them, we arriv'd at our house just as HD. and MS—were going to dinner, the first time of my going to town, since I left it on the 14th. June, home and all things there, looks agreeable— we din'd early, set off soon after HD. ED. MS. WD. for Clearfield, where Sister had appointed to meet me, and our unhappy girls mother; she came at 3 o'clock, and was much affected at the sight of her Daughter Docr. Logan his Wife and Son Algernon, drank tea with us, I did not see S Johnson when she went away, having company with me. G. and DL,—HD. and MS. left us after tea, Billy stays with us to night. I have been very poorly this day, especialy in the fore-noon—donnez cet matin[15]—Sister has engag'd OG. for SD. begining April next.

[Sept.] 2. . . . Our girls saw, or conceited they saw a man passing more then once by our Spring-house, which is opposite the parlor window, where they could easily descern that we have no man with us,—we sent for J Courtney, who with a stick in his hand, and Sall with a Candle, (a fine way to take a thief) went in search of the man, but found him not, but as some of us feel a

14. The words "of blood" crossed out.
15. Gave this morning.

little cowardly, John has offer'd to sleep on the carpet in the Kitchen, which is agreed to.

4. . . . John Courtney went to town this fore noon for a load of dung, with a Cart and two horses, he took a note and some things from me,—[Sa]my. Fisher call'd after moon light, to inform us, that poor John had mett with a sad accident, the Horses had run away with him, and that one or two of his ribbs and Collar bone were broken. . . . We are worse of this night than ever, having no man with us, nor John to call upon in case of any emergancy—I thought it best to make the matter as light as possible to Mary Courtney, who is near lying in—I told her the Horses had run away and John had hurt his knee or thigh, that my husband thought it would not be proper for him to return to night, she made very little enquiry and appear'd less alarm'd than I expected—Our dear little one is much disordred in her bowels.—This is a world of trouble; 'tho much at same time to be thankful for, many mercies.

9. I lodg'd last night in Nancy's room, Arose early this morning spent the fore noon reading and mending the old Carpet.—just as Ann & myself wear seated at dinner, B Wilson made his appearance, he din'd with us, spent the day and lodges here to night—After dinner Sister and William came up, they stay'd but an hour or two, went home to tea—Huldah Mott and Betsy Emlen came, Nancy and Child took a ride with them, she came home to tea—while they were absent BW. and ED. took a walk—we amus'd ourselves this evening moon and Stars gazeing with a spyglass—this night is very like the last, most beautiful—we have had the advantage of two full moon light nights—which does not often occur, the Moon full'd this morning about 8 or 10 o'clock, and 'rose this evening near the same hour, so that it was last night, and this, equaly near the full.—HSD. went off this morning early, for Downingstown.

10. BW. left us early this morning—Rossanna here washing. Sam Sprigs came up fore noon with the new Chaise, brought with him a young woman, recommended as a Nurse for Mary Courtney by Js. Kenni[ns] wife—we are furnish'd as usual, with provision fruit &c from home. . . .

11 Sepr. went to bed last night in the room over the Kitchen, next to Nancys room, but was disturb'd by a noise could not account for, went to Nancys bed, and spent the remainder of the night with her and Elizah. we are easily[16] frighted I think—busy Ironing this forenoon, donz. our dear William came up with sam about 11—din'd with us, the phlegm he raises is a little discolor'd, redish, he left us between 5 and 6.—after they were gone, B Dawson with the Child, little Nelly, Romeo, Prince and myself, took a walk to our Lands end

16. The word "soon" crossed out.

and return'd by sunset. a fine clear moon light night.—finish'd reading a large
Volume pamphlets, on different Subjects—not very instructive or entertaining.

Sepr 17. HD. left us this morning after breakfast.—John came in for liquid
ladanem[17] for his wife twenty five drops he ask'd, which I concluded would do
no harm, if it did no good, as she had been us'd to take it, I went in some time
after to see her and gave her, by her own urgent desire 50 drops more in about
an hour after the 25—I then left her, in hopes it would still those useless
pains that she suffer'd—it appear'd to have little or no effect; the wid-wife
inform'd me that le enfant est fort grand, et la[18] mere bien pitit,[19] it was her
oppinion que l'enfant [sont] mort,[20] that she wish'd I would send for a Doctor.
. . . the Doctor confirm'd what the mid wife had said, et avec ses instruments
et beaucoup deficility, ill la delivera d'enfant mort,[21] the first male child of
seven, a very fine lusty baby—6 of the 7 dead born. . . .

Sepr. 23. . . . I visited poor Mary Courtney this forenoon, found her as well
as could be,—loosen'd Johns bandages, which were so tight, as to occasion
sores under his Arm, the broken bones I expect, by this time, are knitt, but
his sight is not yet restor'd, 'tho much better.—I beleive there are few, so low,
who do not at times feel satisfaction and comfort, and none so high, as not to
experience[22] anxiety, trouble, and distress.—yet I am of oppinion that a
tranquil mind is attainable, if rightly sought after. . . . the Army, rais'd to go

17. Laudanum, the liquid form of opium, was made by dissolving opium in a combination
of water and alcohol. The mixture was then filtered through paper. The strength of the
laudanum was determined by the ratio of opium to water and alcohol. ED could have
purchased the opium as well as the filtering equipment from any druggist. In the eighteenth
and early nineteenth centuries there were no legal restrictions on the importation or growth of
opium poppies or on the sale or use of opium. Before the Revolutionary War opium would
have been imported exclusively from England; after the war Americans diversified the trade,
although extensive connections continued between British Quaker pharmaceutical exporters
and their Philadelphia counterparts. The two major exporters of opium poppies were India
and Turkey; the latter provided most of the opium used medicinally in England and the U.S.,
although both countries attempted to grow poppies domestically. Opium was a main ingredient
in many of the popular medications of the day, and many handbooks advised consumers how
to prepare their own medications (Gould, *Dictionary of Medicine*; W. Lewis, *New Dispensatory*
315–16, 618–19; Virginia Berridge and Griffith Edwards, *Opium and the People: Opiate Use in
Nineteenth-Century England* [London and New York: Allen Lane/St. Martin's Press, 1981], 3–
13; H. Wayne Morgan, *Drugs in America: A Social History, 1800–1980* [Syracuse, N.Y.:
Syracuse University Press, 1981], 2–3; Dean Latimer and Jeff Goldberg, *Flowers in the Blood:
The Story of Opium* [New York: Franklin Watts, 1981], 61, 162, 51–53; S. Stander, "Transat-
lantic Trade in Pharmaceuticals during the Industrial Revolution," *Bull. Hist. Med.* 43 (1969):
326–43; see also Roy Porter and Dorothy Porter, "The Rise of the English Drug Industry:
The Role of Thomas Corbyn," *Medical History* 33 (1989): 277–95; see above, June 25, 1769).
    18. The word "mear" crossed out.
    19. The child is very large and the mother very small.
    20. The infant was dead.
    21. And with his instruments and much difficulty, he delivered her of the dead infant.
    22. The words "at times" crossed out.

against the Insergents to the westward,[23] left the City yesterday, many mothers wives and Sisters &c. are left with aching hearts. . . .

24. . . . The nights grow long, and when all our Men are in town, it seems rather lonely. . . .

25. Nancy and her little one, and SB. lodg'd in my chamber last night. Betts in the little front room, to be as much togeather as possible—Nancy had a trying contest with Elizath. to oblige her to lay down, she held out for a long time, but the mother at last conquer'd. . . .

Octr 1. . . . BW. inform'd us of a considerable loss we have mett with lately at Atsion by the distruction of the Forge House and its contents, by fire. . . .

Octor. 2. . . . BW. was mistaken in his account of the fire at Atsion, it was the Furnice, not the Forge, that was burnt, all the wood work, and the Bellows &c—the loss, HD. thinks, including repairs and loss of time, will amount to, one thousand pounds and more money. . . .

6. . . . We were early up, Rossanna here washing . . . Nancy and self, sat down to Iron our small cloaths. . . .

7. Isaac Howel here this morning to take my acknowledgment of a Deed,— HD. MS. HSD. MD. gone to meeting this morning William walk'd out, myself at home alone as usual on meeting days. . . .

8 Octor. Cloudy, and rain, most of this day—I paid Mary Courtney a visit this forenoon, no one up, our men all in town, we staid all day in the house, no one call'd on us, but in truth, a Sturdy beggar, who enquir'd if he was in the way to New York, being answer'd in the Negative, said he had lost his way, wish'd for something to eat, and a draught of Cider, which having obtain'd, walk'd off. we were carefull to see him fairly out of the gate. . . .

9. last night we set our watch by guess, and this morning found by its variation from Bickleys clock, that it was near one o'clock when we retir'd, we were busy'd making habilliment pour la noir au jaun illigetemate.[24] . . .

12. First day: came down stairs last night between eleven and 12. with Sally, in my dishabille, to call up John Courtny, whose cow was in the meadow

23. After fifty-two hundred militiamen had departed for western Pennsylvania on Sept. 9 to suppress the Whiskey Rebellion, volunteers were still being mustered in the following week to form additional companies should they be needed (Baldwin, *Whiskey Rebels*, 185–222; Kohn, *Eagle and Sword*, 157–70).
24. Clothing for the black or yellow illegitimate.

eating of a heap Apples, laid there ready for grinding, I fear'd she would injure herself if she continu'd all night at that business. . . .

Octor. 14.   One third of a year, since we came here,—George and John, Betsy Dawson and two or three other little foulk, busy to day, bringing in potatoes. . . .

Octor. 16.   . . . Nancy and self set off about 10. to go to Jacob Bekeys, a Shoemaker at Miles town, the fineness of the day induced us to take the walk, it is about a mile and quarter from our house. I stop'd short of the intended rout by ⅛ of a mile, and Nancy went on, the place I stop'd at belongs to one John Shields, who does not live there, there was no body but an old Dutch woman, name'd Nany White, she was busy spining tow, about three score and ten years old. I ask'd her if she was spining to make cloath for her own ware, oh no! I take it in, at a 1½ d a cut, how many cuts dost thou spin in a day? she was not willing to tell, can thee spin twelve? oh no! six? No. 3 then? maybe so, then thee earns 4½ d a day? yes some times;—I had but a nine penny peice in my pocket which I gave her, and say'd if she would except of it, she might venture to take a days rest, as that was two days earning, she was much pleas'd and gave me many thanks. Well, thought I, to use the words of an Old Author, This is one of the *commoditys that comes of infelicity*, to be delighted with so trifling an acquisition. . . .

Octor. 17.   Nancy and self busy sewing this morning. . . .

18 Octor.   Danl. Trimble, Jacob Downing breakfasted with us. My Sister kindly took my place in the Carriage and set off with my husband and Son William after 10 this fore-noon for Downingstown. . . .

20 Octobr.   . . . John Skyrin came from Clearfield forenoon, he gives but a sorrowful account of Nancys health, . . . I am the only one of the family, servants excepted, at present at home, or would go immediately to Nancy. . . . S Swett fitted a mantua gown on me, which I had provided in the Summer, she is so kind as to do what little I want in that way for me, I beleive I never had a gown better made in my life, and she is now within about seven weeks of 73 years of age, to work so neatly at such an age is the cause of my making the memorandum.

21st. Octor.   Sister gone to meeting this morning HD. stays at home being disorder'd in his bowels, and somewhat oppress'd by a cold—J Skyrin came to town forenoon, says Nancy continues very poorly, I sent for Docr. Kuhn, advis'd with him on her complaint, he orders her loosing 10 oz blood, as soon as may be. . . .

Octor. 22.   John Skyrin came up this[25] morning with the Carriage to take Nancy to Town if she was able to go—Dr. Kuhn could not come this fore noon, but would try, if she was realy ill, to see her here, Afternoon, I sent word back that we must see him if possiable—Nancy continues very sick, can take no sustinance, and is very Yallow. I think 'tis the Jaundice she has taken. . . .

Octor. 24.   . . . Nancy appears better this morning not so sick but very Yallow, eat a little breakfast—After dinner Dr. Kuhn came, he order'd pills, Calomel[26] &c to be given every two hours 'till they opperated. . . .

Octor. 25.   between midnight and 3 in the morning my poor dear Child was extremly ill, with excessive hard reachings and pains about her, an uncommon tast and sensation in her mouth and stomach. . . .

Octor 26.   First day: one of the most stormy days I ever knew, and a trying day it has been.—Nancy much against taking medicine, and hard to [me] to urge it, but as her case was desperate, thought it best to persist,—she had less reaching this morning but a constant sickness, said her Stomach and throat felt as if she had been eating Allum, we were much at a loss what to do. . . .

28.   JS. went to town before breakfast; my poor Child, is to day much better, 'tho very Yallow, she has taken nourishment several times to day, and set up. . . . Molly went home with her father and Aunt, to prepare to attend on her intended Sister on sixth day next. . . .

29.   Nancy 'tho much better, is far from well. . . .

31.   I seem'd lost yesterday afternoon and this morning after a time of steady nurseing, felt as 'tho I had nothing to do, nor could I, for some time set about any thing, should I, by rest and retirement, recurit a little health, it will be cause of thankfullness. Sally Johnson and her daughter Franks came here before dinner, on a visit to her daughter SB. they stay'd an hour or two, eat dinner, then went to Germantown, she left herbs to make tea for SB. said it was good to procure an easy ——. . . .

[Nov.] 5.   . . . A very pretty female Cat, intruded herself on us this evening we did not make her welcome at first, but she seem'd to insist on staying, Sall then gave her milk, and very soon after, she caught a poor little mouse, and

25. The word "evening" crossed out.
26. Also called mercurous chloride, calomel was a common treatment for jaundice (Buchan, *Domestic Medicine* [1793], 254; C. K. Drinker, *Not So Long Ago*, 122–27).

is now laying on the corner of my Apron by the fireside as familiarly as if she had liv'd with us seven years. William reading, Sall asleep on couch, Sip in kitchen. . . .

7. . . . I settled matters with Mary, concerning our poor Sall, who I intend leaving with her, 'till her grevious business is settld, I look on Mary as a well minded and well disposed woman, and who, with our help, will take the proper care of her. . . .

Novr. 8. . . . being left *tout sule*;[27] about noon I took a pleasent 'tho solitary walk, din'd comfortably by myself, 'tho agreeable company would have been more pleasing. . . .

9. First day. morning and a Charming morning it is. 'Tho all days are alike[28] with the Lord: yet I have thought that there was a solemnity in this day, somewhat different from others, and when I was young, I have thought, that if I had been asleep for weeks, and awakend on this day, that I should know it was first day, by the shineing of the Sun. . . .

11. . . . A Mary Baley, a poor Woman, spent an hour in the kitchen, she has been here once or twice before, says she has a daughter, a criple, which perhaps is true, but she told two or three fibs, as I beleive, for which I like her none the better, William out most of this morning in the Garden with George.—was walking out with Billy before dinner when we saw a neighbour-ing taylor, whom I had sent for, going to our house, we turn'd homewards and had Sip measur'd for a new Coatee, I have been busy this forenoon mending his overalls, and underments, to make him fitt to appear when we go to the City, for he looks now like a compleat Ragamuffin. . . .

13. . . . after dinner, I disclosed to our Sarah my intentions of leaving her with Mary for some time, she wep't and appear'd in trouble[29] but before we left her seem'd reconciled, about four we bid adieu to Clearfield and arriv'd at home to tea. . . .

21. . . . HSD. went to Clearfield this afternoon, to see a load of new furniture put into the house, prepatory to his and Hannahs going there.

22. . . . little Peter, a negro boy, aged 7 years, came to us to day, from Virginia he has not had the small pox, and appears weakly, otherwise well disposed, we are to give, if we keep him, fifteen pound for his time—wash'd

27. All alone.
28. The word "to" crossed out.
29. The words "for some time" crossed out.

him this Afternoon in a tub of warm soap suds, his head with lark spur and rum, and changed his apparel. . . .

28. . . . Molly Lippencot call'd after dinner for Molly to go to J Smiths to tea with the Bride, may not a young woman be call'd a Bride after she has declar'd her intentions of marriage publickly? I think she may with propriety. . . .

Decr. 2. . . . J.C. came this forenoon to inform us, that S.B—was this morning about 6 o'clock deliver'd of a daughter, the mother and Child both well. . . .

6. . . . Sister and William went this fore noon to Clearfield—they found S.B. and her bantling well, Sally weep'd when she saw MS—and cover'd her head with the bed-cloaths—The Child is very Yallow for one so young . . . A Negro boy of the name of Peter Woodard, came this Afternoon to us, from one of the lower Counties, Kent I believe it was, sent here by Warner Mifflin, he was raged and lousey, having been for upwards of a week on board the Vessel, and in poor trim before, fifteen pounds is said to be the price for him, WM. writes that he is 11 or 12 years of age, he says his aunt told him he was going in 14. . . .

10. . . . Anthony Woodard, Father of black Peter, came this morning to see his Son, whom he had not seen for eight years before—he took him home with him to see his Mother, has not return'd since. . . .

Decr. 11. A delightful moderate Morning, Azure Sky, favourable for my Sons marriage, and to enable me, who have not been to meeting for a long time, to attend it,—

> If the Lord, in condescension,
>   Deigns to hear a Mothers prayer,
> He will attend this mornings Meeting,
>   And be with my Harry there;
> Great indeed's the undertaking!
>   When we give our selves away,
> But if he approve the action,
>   Blessed is the Nuptial day.

Hetty Smith being too unwell to accompany her daughter, I went with my husband, from our house to the Market-Street Meeting House, Henry and Hannah &c. were but just seated when we enter'd, the meeting was large, and agree'd by every one, that I heard speak of it, that it was a favour'd time, Nichs. Waln and Samuel Emlen, were the only Ministers who had any thing to communicate—Henry and Hannah spoke very distinctly and in a proper key—were much commended for their conduct and beheaviour.—Robt. Coe read the Certificate.—Henry and Hannah went to, and from Meeting in a Carriage, and the Brides Maids in an other, the rest of the company walk'd, there was about 50 persons at the Wedding—our dear William came about 11 o'clock to meeting, being desirous to be a witness to his brothers marriage, the day was spent agreeably, nothing occur'd to cause displeasure or uneasiness, that I heard of, as sometimes does in large companys—A very plentifull and elegant dinner well serv'd after three o'clock, Supper at nine, tea omitted, indeed there was no time for it the days being so short—My Sister and William left us towards evening, the latter much fatigued.—the company broke up about 10. James and Phebe Pemberton, William Lippencot and wife were overseers. . . .

13. . . . As our Son Henry was desireous of having the young people invited here after his marriage, this Afternoon was appointed, 'tho we are not fond of such parties, yet could not deny so innocent a request. . . . they had Cakes, Wine, Coffee, tea, Almonds, Reasons, Nuts, pears, Apples &c—they spent the evening very inoffensively, I beleive, in our front parlor, but made rather too much noise. . . .

14. . . . My Husband was very unwell indeed this morning chilly and sick, Jammy Smith, HSD. call'd before meeting.—sent for Dr. Rush, who order'd bleeding. . . . I sent James with the bowl to empty in the river, in preference to the necessary, I do so generaly when convenient, not that I have and fixt, or good reason for doing so, but having heard M. Penry say, that they, at Bethlehem were in the practice of throwing [their] blood into the Lehigh. . . .

23 Decr. HD. MS. gone to monthly meeting. Hetty Smith sent to know if I would go with her to Clearfield to see our Children. 'tho unfitt, and not altogeather willing, I wish'd to go, as the day was remarkably fine. . . . They appear to be agreeably settled, and very happy. I left them, well pleas'd and satisfied—call'd at John Courtneys just before we came away. S.B. is very well, and in rather too good spirits, everything considered, she had nam'd the Jaune pettet,[30] Hannah G——bs, I disaprovd it, and chang'd it to Catharine Clearfield, with which she appear'd displeas'd. . . .

24. . . . I have been led to think, I may say to conclude, on reading Docr. Rush's account of the Yallow fever,[31] that my daughter Nancy had it towards the later end of October last, at Clearfield—and do suppose that Docr. Kuhn, who attended her, knowing that we would steadily attend her, be it what it would, kindly endeavourd to conceal it from us. . . .

30. The little yellow one.
31. Benjamin Rush, *An Account of the Bilious Remitting Yellow Fever, as It Appeared in the City of Philadelphia, in the Year 1793*, vol. 3 of *Inquiries and Observations*, 2d ed. (Philadelphia: Thomas Dobson, 1794 [*Brit. Mus. Cat.*]).

26. . . . I have been for some weeks past busy every night bathing my little maid Sally Dawsons, face for a swelling, and dressing her knee for a sore, I have had much to do for the little black boys also, those small foulk ought to be of service when they grow bigger, for they are very troublesome when young, to those who have their good at heart. . . .

29. . . . I took a walk this forenoon to visit my old friends Beulah Burge and Hannah Shoemaker, at their present dwelling in Arch street above fifth street,—came home to dinner, I have not takeing such a walk in the City for a long time past. . . . Sammy Rhodds here this evening.

31. Another year past over, and our family mercifully keep't togeather—How many calamities have we escaped? and how much to be thankful for;—. . . Molly Drinker, Sally Smith and John Smith went to Clearfield, they dined there, Henry and Hannah came back with them, they spent the evening at Edwd. Shoemakers, with near 30 young people—'tis not the way I could wish my Children to conclude the year, in parties—but 'we cant put old heads on young shoulders'. . . .

1795

[Jan.] 2d.   Snow in the Night, wind N.E. in the morning N.W. this evening fine clear moon light. I spent this day at my Daughters Sallys, 'tis I beleive upwards of two years since I have so done. . . .

4.   First Day: . . . No person, our family excepted, has been here this day that I recolect, which is rather an uncommon circumstance.

6.   HD. MS. MD. at meeting this forenoon—Saml. Parker brass founder, and Sally Howel, were married at meeting, he is so deaf, that he uses a machine, call'd by some a Trumpet, when any one preaches, but to day he omitted it. . . .

9.   cloudy all day. 39. years since the loss of my dearest and nearest female friend, and the same day of the week. . . .

11.   First Day: . . . Joseph Merrifield drank tea and spent the evening he and Thos. Stewardson sup'd—This day has been rather tedious and painful to me, being unwell, and confin'd, without anything to do, but sat with Company.

14.   We removed this morning into our front parlor, as the back is more expos'd to the North west wind, and otherwise not so warm a room, in the depth of winter the Sun is excluded by neighbouring back buildings—the front more lively. . . .

21st.   . . . Caty Dennis here to day makeing a collico gown for Molly, J Logan call'd—Peggy and Hannah Saltar, Maria Saltar and Molly Clarkson, call'd on Molly this fore noon—I made an assent before dinner into our Cock loft, to take a view of the river, which is broken up, before the City, large cakes of ice floating, Boys were yesterday Skaiting on them. . . .

25.   First day: began to snow in the night, has continu'd all day, is now prehaps 12 or 14 inches deep. . . .

26.   A most beautifull day. temperate, clear sky.—upwards of forty Sleighs past our door, between breakfast and dinner. . . .

29.   This has been a *proper* Stormy day, wind at S.E., The word proper has been much in vogue, and very improperly us'd for a few years past, in the country, and in most kitchens in the City, is has crep't also into the houses among the Children, Some say, I am proper sick, others have purchas'd something that was proper dear &c. . . .

Febry. 3.   . . . We heard to day of the death of Jonathan Evans Senr. said to be in his 81st. year, When my sister and self were Children we call'd him and Wife, Uncle and Aunt Evans, she being Sister to our Uncle Jervis's wife— There is a french man some where in our Neighbourhood, that serenades us frequently in an evening by a hand Organ, 'tho for a very short time—I beleive it is a very good instrument, and he a good hand on it, as it is very Agreeable, and I will own, that I am fond of hearing what is call'd good musick. . . .

14.   . . . intercepted a letter to day, from J.G. to our S.B.—, John Saltar din'd here, Molly went this Afternoon with Sally Smith, Betsy Emlen, G. Benson, R. Smith, and T. Tylee, to J. Saltars, they did not return 'till after nine at night, very dark, wrong doings. . . .

16.   . . . Joseph Kite invited yesterday to the burial of one Elliots wife, who was lately deliver'd of twins and died soon after, Sister desired him to miss Jacob Downings House, as our dear Sally reckons in about a month or 6 weeks, she is very lusty, and generally at that time of distress, is peculiarly tried, she has hitherto been favour'd with good Spirits, 'tho by no means void of apprehension. . . .

19.   . . . This day is sett apart by the President, for prayer and thanksgiving for the blessing of peace &c &c.[1] 'Tho an Ordinance of Man, yet I beleive there are many pious persons who have past the day, measurably as they ought, or as they thought it their duty to do—many others, as is too common, on what they call Holy-days, spend it in dissipation;—I was pleas'd to see many of what is call'd the establish'd Church, and presbyterians, going in a solid manner to their respective places of worship—it had the appearance at least, of their unity with good government, and I hope more. . . .

20.   . . . Alice, a yallow woman, who has taking our cloaths in to wash for some time past, came here before dinner, in great distress, her Child in her Arms, her husband John Wright, a negro Man, and a white Girl, attended by a Constable, who was taking them all to Jail, for keeping, as he said, a disor-

---

1. On Jan. 1, in thankfulness for the restoration of domestic tranquillity following the suppression of the Whiskey Rebellion and General Wayne's victory over the Indians, President Washington had set aside Feb. 19 as a day for public celebration of peace (Carroll and Ashworth, *George Washington*, 226–29, 235; the text of the declaration is in J. D. Richardson, *Messages and Papers of the Presidents*, 179–80).

derly or riotous House—As we knew nothing of the business and but little of Alice, could say no more in her favour but that we hop'd she was honest,—he took them off, I expected we should loose our Linnen &c that was in her Custody, a dozen quite new Shirts and Aprons and many other things, as they had left their house open and nobody in it—in about an hour after she return'd in good Spirits, informing that her Husband and self had procur'd bail, but the white Girl was put in Jail—soon after she brought our Linnen home, nothing missing. . . .

25. . . . many Men in the Office this forenoon as is common, of whom I take no account. . . . Molly and Sally Downing gone this afternoon to visit Nancy Skyrin, where they expect to meet Nancy Morgan, Anna Wells, Dolly Large &c &c, I think such a very cold day, home might be the most proper place for most women, SD. especially, unless they had some very urgent affairs to call them fourth, Yet, doubtless, there are many other Gossips going too and fro like themselves. . . .

27. Clear and very cold, as yesterday, wind N. West—Thermometer at 9 or 10.—mon jour natal[2]—

> May I, each Year, that it occurs, be thankfull for the past,
> And spend my time, as tho' assur'd, that it would be the last.

[Mar.] 2. . . . I have been unwell all day, which is often the case, 'tho sometimes favour'd to be better than at other times. William, Mary and self spent the evening ensemble[3]—Molly reading some elegant poetical quotations, she reads well, 'tho not perfectly well.

March 4. . . . Polly Noble, formerly Nugent call'd Afternoon with two of her Children, she has had four, all Daughters, I am pleas'd to see her look so fat and fair, hearty and reputably—she served her time with us, four years, has, as she says, and I believe, an industrious husband.—About a mile on this side Clearfield my husband and Sister mett Joe, he had the impudence, as M Courtney told MS. to come up into her room, she ask'd him what he wanted, he reply'd, to see something you have got here, and then look'd into the Cradle—she ask'd him if he own'd it, he say'd No, and further this deponent sayeth not.—If he had not seen the Child, he had all reason to belive it was his, but the colour was convincing, he had frequently boasted of it, but was fearful of the expences that might accrue. . . .

11. . . . HD. James Pemberton, David Bacon, Jonathan Evans &c. had a conference this Afternoon in our back parlor, with Hannah Burrows a Mulatto

2. My birthday.
3. Together.

Woman who has, for some time past, made her appearance frequently in our meetings as a preacher or teacher. . . .

15. . . . Betsy Emlen and her brother Saml., Sally Smith and her brother John Sally Large and brother John, My daughter and her two Brothers, here this evening—What a favour it is, to a young woman to have a good Brother, or brothers—S. Preston call'd—H.S.D. lodges here to night, cold this evening— It has been remarked that a greater number have died and been ill of the pleurisy this winter than, some say, any other since thier rememberance—I ask'd Docr. K—the other day, if it was not the Yellow fever that Nancy had last fall, he answer'd in the negative. Notwithstanding all my conjectures.

17. . . . about noon, William concluded to loose blood, as he feels an uneasiness at his breast, and continues to bring up bloody phegm, Dr. Kuhn desir'd him, if those indications took place, not to omitt it, 'tis now near six months since he had a vain open'd. About one o'clock Frederick took 7 ounces, he feels weak since, yet I trust it was right. . . .

28th. . . . HSD. came to town forenoon, yesterday he left N. Bank and came to Clearfield,—Henry is not one of the invulnerables, nor is he, in a general way, rash or imprudent, yet he is venturous and resolute. . . .

30. . . . read a romance or novel, which I have not done for a long time before—it was a business I followd in my younger days, not so much as many others, 'tho more than some others, it was intitled Interisting Memoirs, said to be writen by a Lady[4]—it is no very great affair, 'tho there are some good sentiments, and many moral reflections, some of them very good. . . .

[Apr.] 6. There was a time, that if either of my beloved Children were in the Situation that my dear Sally is at present, I could not have found in my heart to have made a memorandum; is it that as we grow in years our feelings become blunted & Callous? or does pain and experience cause resignation? 'tis now past 11 at night my dear afflicted child has just taken anodoyne from Dr. Shippen, she has been all this evening in afflictive pain 'tho unprofitable, I came here yesterday afternoon, went to bed at 11 o'clock Jacob call'd me up after two this morning when I had just fallen asleep, Sally being rather worse, before four o'clock Jacob went for Hannah Yerkes, After breakfast we sent for Dr. Shippen, he felt her pulse, said he hoped she was in a good way—he din'd with us, and as Sally did not wish his stay, he left us, saying he would return in the evening she continu'd in pain at times, all day, was worse towards evening, Neighr. Waln, H. Yerkes and Sister with us—sent for the Doctor who

4. A Lady [Susanna Harvey Keir], *Interesting Memoirs*, 2 vols. (London: A. Strahan and T. Cadell, 1785 [*NUC*]).

soon came, towards night we precieved that all things were not right, I did not venture to question the Doctor, but poor Sally was not sparing in that perticular.—she suffer'd much to little purpose,—when the Anodoyne was given, two Opium pills, the Doctor went to lay down, when all was quiet for a short time, but poor Sally who instead of being compos'd grew worse, the Doctor was call'd, when he came I quited the room, knowing that matters must 'eer long come to a crisis. I was down stairs in back parlor by myself an hour and half as near as I can judge, when observing that my dear Child ceas'd her lementation and a bustle ensu'd—with a fluttering heart I went up stairs, in a state of suspence, not knowing if the child was born, or Sally in a fitt, as I heard no crying of a Child.—It was mercy fully born, the Doctor blowing in its mouth and slapping it, it came too and cry'd—The Doctor then told us, that a wrong presentation had taken place; which with poor Sallys usual difficulties call'd for his skill more perticularly; by good management he brought on a footling labour, which 'tho severe, has terminated by divine favour, I trust, safely. . . .

7.   heavy rain in the night with some thunder and lightning—wind N.E— Henry Downing, the second of the Name, was born the seventh of the fourth month, between one and two in the morning, on the third day of the week— Sally is this morning as well as can be, all things consider'd—the effects of the anodoyne not gone off. Neighr. Waln, Hannah Yerkes and Dr. Shippen left us after breakfast—no Nurse as yet obtain'd to our mind. The little one seems hart whole, 'tho the blood is much settled in his legs feet &c. his feet almost as blue as indigo—Sally sleeps sweetly this Afternoon, her cough very hard when she awoke, the child put to the breast this evening he is, as the Nurses say, very handy at the buseness—Patty Mullen came this evening very oppertunly, she nurs'd Sally with her two first Children—I left Jacobs this evening about nine o'clock came home in a mist, I have been absent 50 hours, and sleep'd but two in that time, I feel at this present time much fatigued, bones ach, flesh sore, Head giddy &c. but have at same time much to be thankfull for. . . .

8.   . . . It was late last night when Sister and self retir'd, having had a conversation with S Dawson, relating to S.B. who has form'd an acquaintance with one of Gardners workmen, I fear we shall have more trouble with the bold Hussey. . . .

11.   . . . John Courtney and family mov'd from Clearfield to Philadelphia. Mary left Sall's Child, with Geo[ ] Frys wife. . . . How many vicissitudes do I pass through, in the small sphere in which I daily move,—declineing health and strength has been my lott for a long time past, I yet have abundant cause of thankfullness—If life is a blessing, and it is generally thought so to be,—I have been much favour'd, as I am now near four years older than my dear father was when remov'd hence, and near 14 more than my beloved Mother.—

May I be thankfull for the time past, and endeavour to be resigned to what may occur in the little, that in all probability, remains. . . .

13. . . . 'tis about a week since we mov'd into back parlor—we avoid the morning Sun, and have the pleasure of seeing the trees put fourth, and the Garden in bloom. . . .

April 17. . . . HD. gone to C. Wests funeral—Jos Sansom call'd—Molly England and Leonard Snowdens wife waited here to join the procession as it past our door,—I counted upwards of 300 persons, his wife was not there—How solemn and affecting must be the parting of Man and wife, after living 40 years together, was an observation of WDs and a very just one, To be seperated from a near friend and companion and father of her Children must be one of the greatest tryals in this life, to an affectionate wife. . . .

19. . . . Sally Johnson here this Afternoon, ask'd if SB could spend a day with her this week, to which I consented, told her of her daughters late conduct wish'd she would take her and Child of our hands, that she had a year to serve from this month, which would have been of more worth to us, had she been a virtuous girl, than any other two years of her time, a girl in her place would cost us 8 or 9/P week, that she is as capable, or perhaps more so, then any one we could hire; I was afraid of her bad example to our other little girl &c—she appeard more angry than griv'd, said she should not care if the childs brains were beat out &c—she would never have anything to do with it—I told her we would make no account of the expences we had already been at of Sallys laying in and board, the childs nursing since &c. she said she would take her daughter provided they, nither of 'em, should ever have any thing to do with the Child—she went away rather out of humor—when HD. come home we related the above to him, concluded were we to turn her off, upon her mothers terms, she would be in the high road to further ruin—he call'd her into the parlor this evening and talk'd closely to her, told her he had a right to send her to the work house and sell her for a servent, that it was in pity to her, and in hopes of her reformation that he did not send Joe to prision, she had always had a good example in our house, if she did not mend her conduct she should not stay much longer in it &c. she cry'd but said nothing—How it will end, or what we shall do with her, I know not,—set aside this vile propensity, she is one of the most handy and best servants we have ever had—and a girl of very pritty manners.

28th. . . . A black woman, named Reba. Gibbs, and her daughter Patience, a girl of 12 years old. came from the lower Counties, from Warner Mifflin, the girl sent up for John Skyrin, we gave them their dinner, then sent them there. . . .

May 1st. . . . Nancy Skyrin call'd after dinner, then went to pay S Downing a visit, it being visiting time, as 'tis calld.

4. . . . S. Emlen call'd, he paid 50 Dollars which he had borrow'd some days ago, he desires it may be expunged from the book of memory—I assur'd him it should be as much as was necessary. . . .

5. . . . Molly Drinker, Betsy Emlen, Sally Smith, Sally Large, George Benson, Richd. Smith, Richd. Morris and Jonan. Hervey, were all at Grays Ferry this Afternoon, as Molly this evening informs me—which I, by no means approve,—Friends Children going in companyes to public houses, is quite out of Character. . . .

6. . . . Jacob and Sally here this Afternoon, the first of Sallys being out, since the birth of her Son. . . . John and Nancy, has had a rumpus, this evening with Thos. Dawson, on account of Betts—There is great trouble with Servants sometimes, more especially with some, when we are thoughtful for their wellfare.

11. . . . I did wonders this Afternoon in the visiting way—my first induce-ment was to go see my friend H. Pemberton . . . P.P. and H.Y. there &c—took tea there, went from thence to J Smiths a long walk, stay'd but a short time, then went, Jonney Smith with me, to J Skyrins. . . .

15. . . . George Fry's wife parted with the poor little yallow one, to a Negro woman in the Neighbourhood 'till we can otherwise dispose of it. . . .

20. . . . S. Dawsons Step-Mother here this morning says Sall is at their house, they found her when they came home, in bed with her little Sister, it was near eleven when they came home, would have brought her, but thought it too late, she had complain'd that Billy struck her.—he told her it was very true, but it was a week ago, he gave her a blow, the only time he ever touch'd her,[5] that she deserv'd much more then he gave her—It was a new thing to Sall, for him to strike her, she has never been beat since she liv'd with us, more than a light slap on her cheek—'tho she has often deserv'd it. . . .

22. . . . It looks as if I spent most of my time reading, which is by no means the case, a book is soon run over, and 'tho I seldom make mention of any other employment, yet I believe I may say, without vanity, that I was never an indolent person, or remarkably Bookish, tho more so for 5 or 6 years past, than at any other period since I was married,—haveing more leisure—when

5. The words "in his life" crossed out.

my Children were young I seldom read a volume; but was I at present favour'd with health, I should delight in it. As it is I often find it a consolation.

30. . . . An account in this mornings paper of three Men who lost their lives fighting, yesterday in Southwark[6]—Had such an affair happen'd 30 or 40 years ago, the whole town would have been in an uproar, but we heard nothing of it 'till we saw the account in the News-paper. Jacob, Sally and their Daughters were here this afternoon, they wish'd me to go with them to the Statehouse Yard, and to Peels Museaum[7] which is keep't in the State house,—I declin'd the motion, but Molly excepted it, and went with them. . . .

June 7. First day: . . . I have all my grand-Children with me this Afternoon, few as they are, 'tis but seldom that I see them all togeather. . . .

8. . . . H.D. received a Letter from John W. DeBrahm, Georgia, with a phial of Elemental Condensation,[8] for Williams use, 20 drops to be taken at a time—early in the morning—when he has taken sufficient, we are to return what remains in the vial.

14. . . . S.B.s Sister Letty came for her to go see her Sister Betsy whom she reported was dieing, Sally went, but on her return inform'd otherwise.

19. . . . I went with Nancy this evening to Jacob Downings, they are getting ready to set off tomorrow morning for Downingstown with their family— Jacob and Sally came home with me, It has been a very warm day, We must think of going, also, in the country, on Williams account, or this separation of families is very disagreeable to me. . . .

20. . . . Betsy Fordham sewing for us for the present—I have been busy with her for near three weeks, and am almost tir'd of confindment—not that I shall go, much, or any more, abroad—Molly has been for some days past, at times reading while we work'd, three romantic Volls. intitled The Mysteries of

6. On May 29 a fight broke out between some French crewmen of the privateer brig *Brutus* and workers at a Southwark ropewalk. Two crewmen and one worker were killed. The fight and subsequent rioting necessitated calling out troops to patrol the area (*Gazette of the United States and Daily Evening Advertiser*, May 30, 1795; *The Philadelphia Gazette and Universal Daily Advertiser*, May 30, 1795).

7. Charles Willson Peale's museum, located in Philosophical Hall, housed both works of art and natural history. Portraits of Revolutionary War heroes were displayed along with exotic stuffed birds, animals, and artifacts from the world over. The museum also sponsored lectures, exhibitions, and concerts (Sellers, *Mr. Peale's Museum*).

8. Most likely a vial of water from deep in Indian territory. DeBrahm, the Drinkers' friend and neighbor at Clearfield, was a mystic who considered water, particularly water from before the Biblical flood or water on the American continent that was unspoiled by Europeans, to be the "unblended element" (John Gerar William DeBrahm, *VII. Arm of the Tree of Knowledge* [Philadelphia: Zachariah Poulson, 1791], 55–57).

Udolphia[9]—A tremendious tale—but not quite like the old fashon Gothick stories that I was fond of when young, 'tis seldom I listen to a romance, nor would I encourage my Children doing much of that business. . . .

21. . . . Molly and self went towards evening to Hannah Pembertons, found her alone—HD. came to us—we came home by moon light—walk'd through the Market place, which has been for some years past, illuminated by Lamps,—I saw, for the first time, Cooks grand Edifice,[10] at corner of market and third streets, where Charles Jones's old house stood—it cuts a dash—indeed—and the New Presbyterian Meeting house, I belive they now call it Church—built within a year or two, the Appearance is something grand, tho the situation not so—the four pillers, the largest I have seen[11]—We call'd at J Skyrins, Nancy had been documenting her Daughter and was in trouble for[12] having done her Duty. . . .

22. . . . Jacob Downing return'd this evening he makes his home with us, dureing the absence of his family. . . .

23. . . . gave S. Dawson a dose of Castor Oyl, by direction Dr. Rush—black Cato came this Afternoon to white wash. . . .

25. . . . A Man call'd with two Books of paper hangings for us to chuse, they were all too gay, save one, which was not quite to our minds. . . .

June 29. . . . HSD. came to town, he informs us, that little Caty Clearfield is very unwell, her bowels much disordred, I suppose she is teething. . . .

[July] 2. . . . received a note from Henry, telling us, that his fever went off with a copeous sweat, that poor little Caty was dead—Jacob Morris, a black boy, whose Mother had her to nurse brought the note, and came for a— Shroud to bury her in. . . .

July 4. Clear. 'tho the wind continues at N.E—Anniversary of Indepen-

9. Ann [Ward] Radcliffe, *The Mysteries of Udolpho,* 3 vols. (Dublin: 1794 [Averley, *18th-Cen. Brit. Books,* 3:3303]).

10. Joseph Cooke, a jeweler, erected a four-story block of buildings on the southeast corner of Market and Third in 1794 in the hope that the "magnetism of its magnificence" would attract both commercial and residential customers (Joseph Jackson, *Market Street Philadelphia* [Philadelphia: Patterson & White Co., 1918], 36).

11. The new First Presbyterian Church, built in 1794 at the corner of Market and Bank streets, was one of the first churches in Philadelphia based on Greek motifs. Four pillars with Corinthian capitals supported a pediment, and eighty marble steps led up to the main floor. It replaced the former meetinghouse, known as Old Buttonwood (Scharf and Westcott, *Philadelphia,* 2:1270).

12. The word "doing" crossed out.

dence, 19 Years.—General Orders in News-paper this forenoon, for a fuss and to do,—I think, orders for peace and quietness, would be more commendable and consistant, in a well regulated Government or State,—those days seldom pass over without some melancholy accident occuring from riotous doings. . . . Billy set off after dinner in Chaise, HD. and self in the Carriage, we arrived at Clearfield between three and four, I was taken very sick, soon after I came, drank near a pint of warm water. . . .

5.   . . . I told SB. yesterday, a little while before I left home, of the death of her Child, and took that oppertunity to talk to her on that and some other Subjects, she shed a few tears, but all, appeard to be got over in a little time after. . . .

9.   . . . It is a very fine day. I am here by myself—Mary and Sip in the Kitchen, am rather better than yesterday, 'tho far from well, Billy poorly, I din'd by myself, on cold leg lamb, bacon, eggs and beans, 'tis not the first time that I have din'd Sola.—to me 'tis not, at times disagreeable, there are some things that we may easily reconcile, and by so doing they become pleasent—I have been very busy all this day, reading, mending Stockings & taking extracts. . . .

10.   . . . William and self had an Affecting conversation, touchant mon fils et son frere[13]—a worthy fellow. My heart was much softened and melted:—Afterward, reading in the pleasures of memory, I shed more tears, than I have done for Years, at one time, 'tho I have often been sufficiently distress'd, had they been ready . . . Our little family, which consists of 8 persons, besides 4 grand Children, are divided at present, in five different parts of the State, HD. MS. and MD. at home in the City, S.D. in the Vally. A.S. at Bristol, H.S.D. I expect is at North bank, WD. and ED. here at Clearfield. grand Children with their mothers.

14.   . . . I feel more happy this evening than for some days past, having heard of the well fair of our family, and having both my Sons with me. I paid the black woman, Sally Morris 2"1"3" for nursing little Caty near 7 weeks at 6/- p week— Henry paid Betsy Fry, some time ago, the same sum, for the same service, for between 5 and 6. weeks at 7/6 p.—many are, the number of poor little Infants that go out of the world, for want of perticular care, 'tho I have no reason to suppose this child was neglected, I paid Mary Courtney, between 8 and 9 pounds for nursing it &c, she did her duty by it, I doubt not, and Betsy Fry appear'd to take good care of it—And Sally Morris, I do believe did her best, she has had several Children of her own, her family were very fond of it and I was told they weep'd much when it died—I should have taken it home,[14] it suited, and brought it up, or had it brought up in our family, but a fear of bringing the parrents togeather, or

13. Concerning my son and his brother.
14. Words crossed out.

reviveing the former likeing to the sire, as the mother is still in our house, but tis gone, and no doubt but all's for the best.

July 15. . . . I came up here without work, intending to assist HD. to make her petites choses,[15] but they were not here, so I am left at leisure to read, or do any thing I please. . . .

July 25. . . . Nancy and her Child &c. have been 4 weeks at Bristol, she thought that the loss of a few ounces of blood might be of service to her, as she is unwell and feels heavy, as she spends this day with us, I have sent for Docr. Kuhn to ask his opinion. . . .

Augt. 1. rainey morning wind N.E—last night, or rather one this morning I was awakened by a great noise, and a hard blow on my head, when lo! the cord that held up the cornice, had given way, and down it came upon us. The hurt I received is triffling, my husband none, this shall never be put up again says he;— so farewell to raised Teasters.—I believe there are very few of them now in use, this is near 49 years old, made for my dear mother before the birth of her last Child. Post bedsteads, which are a very old fashon, are now in general use. . . .

Aug't. 23. . . . William was in considerable pain in the night, Sister and self were up with him—at four in the morning gave him 10 drops more Laudunum—he sleep'd a little in the morning Doctor here after breakfast, order'd a decoction of bark to be given every hour, and an injection to be administred. . . .

26th. . . . William has been, mercyfully, easier most of this day—last night 'twas not easy to say, which way the Scale would turn, had it been the other way, what a different situation should we have been in this night—Having been lately up in the night for hours together, I have observed a Solatery tree-frog, who has taken up his aboad in one of the trees in our yard, who begins to croke or chip, (his noise being more like an inseect than a common frog) at the close of day, and leaves off, a little after the dawn, his noat becomes weaker and weaker as the day advances, as tho he was singing himself to sleep. . . .

27. . . . we were up again in the night with William, he went to bed clear of pain, and we omited the Anodyne &c. about one o'clock Sister call'd me up, the pain &c had return'd.—We then gave him laudanum and Antimonial wine[16] and &c. . . .

15. Little things.
16. Antimony is a native metal widely used in the eighteenth century, primarily as an emetic. Tasteless when combined with other ingredients, it was commonly given to children instead of preparations calling for quinine or bark, which were difficult to administer. Antimonial wine (tartrate of antimony dissolved in distilled water and combined with sherry) was often given in doses of one or two ounces (Estes, "Therapeutic Practice," 368, 381; Haller, "Tartar Emetic," 236, 238, n.5).

30.   . . . My dear William is, I trust on the recovery—two or three days in last week I was in much distress, on his Account more than I own'd at the time, may I be sufficiently thankful if he is spared us.

[Sept.] 11.   . . . Nancy was very unwell all the afternoon and evening we sent for Hannah Yerkes, her pains were frequent, but not of the right kind, at about 11 o'clock they prevailed on me to go to bed in the front room. Nancy undressed and went also to her bed—I lay all night in a degree of pain my ear throbbed much and I felt weak 'tho feverish. sleep'd very little during the night, a little after day I arose, and dressed myself, but finding all quiet lay down in my cloaths, waiting to hear some stiring in next Room, but being very much tired I fell asleep, a little after seven, Molly came into my room, and inform'd me, that Nancy was delivered just before, that they had sent out in the night, as quietly as possibly, for M. Aimes, and Hetty Smith, Nancy was very ill, a hard tedious time is agreed on all hands—I look on it now, when all is over, a favour to me that I did not know of her great distress at the time,— I had not an idea that she would be so soon deliver'd, tho she had been so long very unwell, being used to lingering tedious times—I was so weak and poorly when I came into Nancys room, I could hardly stand, and quite deaf of my right ear, but truly rejoiced and I trust thankful, that all was well over.

12.   Eleanor Skyrin, was born September the 12, 1795. a little before 7 o'clock in the morning, on the seventh day of the week. An old saying of the Nurses, "No Moon, No Man."[17] our dear little one was born 18 hours before the moon changed—there is, I believe, but little in the saying—HSD. called this morning Hy. Smith went away with him, Hannah Yerkes stay'd dinner, then went home—Patty Jones, who was to have nursed Nancy, when we sent for her let us know that her Eyes were so sore that she could not attend— We have been all day at times, looking out for a Nurse but have not yet succeeded. Molly Drinker was up all night, and is tired and poorly this morning A new scene to Molly, she is gone home, Sister is out looking for a Nurse. . . . Sister came in the afternoon with Nurse Howel, who appears to be agreeable—I left Nancy about nine o'clock to the care of her Nurse. . . . John R. Alsop lodges here to night, as HD. JD. and our man John are absent.

Sepr. 24.   . . . finished reading a Romance or Novel, entitled, The Banished Man, in two Volums, By Charlotte Smith;[18] A string of probibilities, part

17. "No moon, no man" was a popular maxim of English folklore referring to the sex of the child. It was even believed in certain parts of England that a child born between the interval of the old moon and the appearance of the new moon would not reach puberty (G. L. Apperson, *English Proverbs and Proverbial Phrases: A Historical Dictionary* [London, 1929; reprint, Detroit: Gale Research Co., 1967]).
18. Charlotte [Turner] Smith, *The Banished Man: A Novel*, 2 vols. (London: T. Caddel, Jun., and W. Davies, 1791 [*NUC*]).

truth, part fiction, wherein some scetches of the authors life is set fourth.—'tis said that she suported herself and three of four Children by this sort of writeing.—Sam Sprig came between 9 and 10. to inform us that Nancys Nurse was sent for to Capt. Strongs Daughter to whom she is engaged, Sister went late as it is, to Nurse Fisher up Chesnut street, who had promised to come to Nancy when her Nurse was called, but found her ill of a fever; so that I was under the Necessity of going to spend the night with my daughter, who has lain in 12 days, she and her babe are, through mercy, as well as can be expected, the baby lay with its Mother for the first time, Myself on the trundle Bed with Hope Sharp, we past the night quite as well as we expected: the Child is a quiet one, but Nancy has caught cold, has the head-ach and Coughs.

28th. ... S. Brant sent for, her Sister said to be dieing. ... SBs Sister dead, she went there after dinner, her mother brought her home in the Chaise, she asked my husband for an order to bury her in friends burying ground, it was granted, tho they have no claim to such indulgence. ...

30. ... Nancy sent Oliver to request the Carriage to take her out—she has lain in but 18 days, has had a cold, and this day, in my oppinion, unfitt to go out for the first time, I therefore refused. ...

[Oct.] 11. ... Jacob came home to supper, he thought he saw Henrys Chaise with two men in it a little before dusk driving down second street, 'tis not unlikely that he is come for Doctor &c as the moon changes tomorrow and Hannah at her full time—I told him if the weather was unfair, or if they sent towards, or in the night, not to come for me, as it would be very improper for me to go in such case. ...

14. ... The Doctor, SL, HSD, and myself left our door at eight o'clock, arrived at Clearfield before 9—found poor Hannah complaining in the Easy-Chair[19]— The Germantown Midwife, Englee there—Hannah was delivered about one o'clock, after being between two and three hours ill, the Doctor said it was a severe

19. Easy chairs were originally designed to be used by sick or aged persons. By the late eighteenth century the term was used to denote both the ornate lounge chairs found in affluent homes and the more specialized chairs used for lying-in women, the sick, and the aged. The chair noted by ED may have been similar to one illustrated in Charles White's *Treatise on the Management of Pregnant and Lying-in Women* (1773; first American edition, 1793). It shows a wheeled chair similar to a present-day recliner, with a frame on the back, possibly to support a chamber pot. White recommended it for fatigued women so they could rest during labor without having to be put to bed. Some Anglo-American women of this period did give birth in special chairs, but the more common position was reclining in bed (Patricia F. Kane, *300 Years of American Seating Furniture: Chairs and Beds from the Mabel Brady Garvan and Other Collections at Yale University* [Boston: New York Graphic Society, 1976], 227; White, *Management of Pregnant and Lying-in Women*, 108–10 and plate 1; Claire Elizabeth Fox, "Pregnancy, Childbirth, and Early Infancy in Anglo-American Culture, 1675–1830" [Ph.D. diss., University of Pennsylvania, 1966], 137–44).

labour, but not more so than was common with a first child, dear girl, I felt much for her, but I have been accostomed to severer labours.—William Drinker, Son of Henry and Hannah Drinker was born the 14 day October at about one o'clock P.M. on the fourth day of the week 1795. at Clearfield—a fine strong boy, as far as one can judge. My husband and Son William came up about and hour before the child was born, they stayed dinner. . . .

19. . . . Nancy left her daughter here, and came herself again after dinner, she and self went to Shops, a business that I have not been in for several years before—I purchased three painted glass muggs, one for each of my daughters. . . .

31. . . . Sister spent this day up stairs, her cough not left her, nor is it likely it will sudenly, the way she manages herself.

Novr. 4. . . . SR. knock'd at the door this evening HD. went to the door! . . .

5. . . . Sammy Rhoads here this evening Molly just going out, he went with her.

8. . . . Hannah S Drinker came down to dinner today, the first of her leaving her Chamber. . . .

10. . . . Sammy Rhoads called in meeting time to enquire how Molly was,— she was at meeting, if it should be an adieu I should not wonder at it. . . .

13. . . . Betsy Howel and Hannah Hopkins called on Sister and self while I was out, for a subscription for the relief of the poor this winter, 18 young women have embarked in this business,[20] HD. ordred Molly to put down 20 dollars in her own name, which she had rather been excuse'd from.

15. . . . S.R. called this forenoon in meeting time, parler avac moy,[21] he had done the same with HD. on sixth day last, of which I was entirely ignorent. matters are, I expect, concluded—I sincerely wish we may do better. . . .

16. . . . *A dull day*, tout a fait[22]—I spent it cutting out underments for our blacks and whites, in the kitchen. . . .

20. This was probably the Female Society for the Relief and Employment of the Poor, founded in 1795 by Anne Parish. Margaret Haviland, " 'Inasmuch as ye have done it unto me': Quaker Women and Benevolence in Philadelphia, 1790–1820," paper presented at the College of Physicians, Philadelphia, Mar. 30, 1990.
21. To speak with me.
22. Entirely.

25. . . . Molly Kelly put up three suits Curtains for us, one of them a new white suit in our Chamber, she dined here; We sent S Swett her dinner as usual, she says she is better, but Sister thinks her very poorly. . . .

27. . . . As Peter complained this morning of the pain in his side, 'tho he eat an hearty breakfast, we sent for Lewis Guilliams, Fredrick out of town, to bleed him, he took 8 or 10 ounces—said Fredrick was married last night to a widdow in the Country, aged fifty years, with seven Children, he has Courage. . . .

[Dec.] 2. . . . Were I to make a memorandum when ever I felt my self indisposed, I should daily say I was unwell, but when more than commonly so, I may of a truth say, very poorly, which is the case at present,—'tho at same time I might be much worse, therefore ought to be thankfull. . . .

3. . . . We had the satisfaction to day of the company of all our Children to dine with us, which in the whole amounted to no more than 14 Grand children included. . . .

7. . . . Henry, has sold Scipio to George Emlen, and we have given him our little Peter Savage, I hope he will be a good boy, 'tho he is but little worth at present. . . .

12. . . . a little relaxation from business may be useful to HD—I am not acquainted with the extent of my husbands great variety of engagements, but this I know, that he is perpetualy and almost ever employed; the Affairs of Society and the public, and private, out of his own family, or his own concerns, I believe takes up ten twelfths of his time, if benevolence and beneficence will take a man to Heaven, and no doubt it goes a great way towards it, HD. stands as good, indeed a better, chance than any I know off. . . .

13. First Day. . . .

> I stay much at home, and my business I mind,
> Take note of the weather, and how blows the wind,
> The changes of Seasons, The Sun, Moon and Stars,
> The Setting of Venus, and riseing of Mars.
> Birds, Beasts and Insects, and more I cold mention,
> That pleases my leisure, and draws my attention.
> But respecting my Neighbours, their egress, and Regress,
> Their Coaches and Horses, their dress and their Address,
> What matches are making, whos plain, or Whos gay,
> I leave to their parents, or Guardians to Say:

For most of those things, are out of my *Way*.
But to those, where my love and my duty doth bind
More than most other Subjects, engages my Mind.

16.   . . . Molly gone with Sally Smith and Sally Large to sup at Gedian Wellss with a large Company. . . . Molly came home about mid-night, never so late out before, they walk'd home, as did many others, Richd. Morris waited on Molly home—there was upwards of thirty in company—she is not displeased that she went, but wishes not to go again to such late entertainment knowing it is disagreeable to her parents.

Decr. 17.   . . . Setting up late last night for my Daughter, I finish'd knitting a third pair of coarse large cotton Stockings for self—it is an employment I once was very fond of, when my boys were little, but having a pain in my breast the Doctor advised against it, as affecting the Nerves, 'tis many years since I have done much in that way till lately, the relish returnd. . . .

Decr. 19.   . . . Peter took S. Swett her dinner, she told him she was now bravely, that there was no longer occasion of bringing it, as her Neice, and Neices daughter were come to live with her—I was pleased when I first heard of her intention to have company, it is several years she has lived quite alone day and night, we have long thought, that for a person of her age it was very improper, and have more than once mentioned it to her, which always seemed to displease her—I have often observed that old Women who have been accustomed to live alone, very much dislike the thoughts of a companion in the house with them, 'tis strange it should be so, but they do not like to be, in the least, put out of their usual way. . . .

25.   Called Christmass day: many attend religeously to this day, others spend it in riot and dissipation, We, as a people, make no more account of it than another day. . . .

27:    . . . I read to day, a large Pamphlet, entitled A Vindication of Mr. Randolphs Resignation.[23] some say it does not make good the Title. for my part I look not on myself as a competent Judge. . . .

23. Edmund Randolph, *A Vindication of Mr. Randolph's Resignation* (Philadelphia: Samuel H. Smith, 1795 [Evans, *Am. Bibliography*]). On Aug. 19, 1795, President Washington had forced Edmund Randolph to resign his position as secretary of state after the British turned over confiscated correspondence from Joseph Fauchet, the French ambassador to the U.S., that appeared to implicate Randolph in treasonable activities. The day after Randolph's resignation, Timothy Pickering had stepped in as acting secretary of state; he accepted the permanent appointment on Dec. 10 (Henry J. Ford, "Timothy Pickering, Secretary of State," in *The American Secretaries of State and Their Diplomacy*, vol. 2, ed. Samuel Flagg Bemis [New York: Pageant Book Co., 1958], 160–93; Irving Brant, "Edmund Randolph, Not Guilty!" *WMQ*, 3d ser., vol. 7 (1950): 179–98; John J. Reardon, *Edmund Randolph: A Biography* [New York: Macmillan, 1974], 284–334; Clarfield, *Timothy Pickering*, 157–64).

1796

Janry. 1. 1796. . . . Nancy Skyrin and her eldest Daughter dined here, they had been to Childrens meeting, the first time of Elizabeths appearence at a meeting, which notwithstanding previous orders and explinations, was not fully understood by her, so that her Mother was constrained to send her out before the conclusion. . . .

Janry. 2d.   Another very fine day. wind S.W.—Dr. Kuhn called—Betsy Devenshire called—Sister out, myself, as usual, very unwell. . . .

7.   . . . I have read two Vollums intitled The Victim of Magical Illusions, or the Mistery of the Revolution of P——L —A Magico-Political Tale. founded on Historical Facts: Translated from the German of Cajetan Tschink, By P. Will.[1]—It may appear strange to some that an infirm old woman should begin the year reading romances—'tis a practice I by no means highly approve, yet I trust I have not sined—As I read a little of most things.

19.   . . . Jery. Warder sent for the Key of Clearfield house, it is but three days since I knew it was sold or selling. . . .

21.   . . . I read a peice of twelve pages, published by Rebecca Griscomb, on the propriety of taking people of colour into society. Sally Johnson here this evening—I made a Cloak for S. Dawson, the first I ever made unless for a Doll.

22.   . . . I have been but twice to my Daughter Sallys since her return from the Country, and not once to Nancys in that time—I frequently see and hear from them.

23.   . . . Sally Brant went this Afternoon with her Mother in a Sleigh—Saml. Emlen called.

---

1. Cajetan Tschink, *The Victim of Magical Delusion; or, The Mystery of the Revolution of P——l: A Magico-Political Tale, Founded on Historical Facts,* trans. P. Will (London: G. G. and J. Robinson, 1795 [*Brit. Mus. Cat.*]).

24.   First Day: . . . Thos. Dawson came home with his daughter Sally, she had been to visit him near the Hospital.

Janry. 25.   Clear, wind N.E. . . . We received a letter from Henry, Hetty Smith one from Hannah, they are bravely, little William groes like a sucking pig. . . .

26.   . . . Black Hannah, a girl whom my husband bought of[2] Charles Logan, between seven and nine years ago, she lived with us upwards of a year, was then about 10 years old, but so very naught that we parted with her to James Jess, and never received a penny for her, he sold her to a very severe master, with whom I suppose she served her time out—she is lately free, and married, came this morning to pay us a visit, and make a Collection against her laying in—she favours us with her company to lodge to night.

30.   . . . while Sister was out yesterday, she saw a croud in Arch Street surrounding a Woman who was laying on a cellar-door, enquired what was the matter with her, one said she was dead, another said otherwise, she told them as she passed along, that there was two or three Doctors lived near, and advised sending for one, she then went to Jacob Downings and saw no more of it—Sally's Catty sent us word to day—that it was poor Molly Hensel, who three hours before was setting in our Kitchen eating bread and Cheese, and drank a tumbler of table-beer, Sister had laid out two Dollars of John Joness legacy for her, and by adding to it, had got for her a flannel peticoat, a Shift, an Apron, a Neckerchief and a cap, she was rejoyced and thankful for them, as Molly Drinker had made them all up for her, and went away in high good humour, 'tho feeble. I had given her a little money, and fear she made a bad use of it, tho perhaps that was not the case—she lived at service with us many years ago, was an industrous ignorant poor woman, lately married to a drunken old man, and was I fear addicted to the same failing—I look'd upon her with pity and compassion, as I believed her, one of the many beings from whom much was not required. . . .

Febry. 1st.   . . . Our three little Downing grand Children was here with Caty, this Afternoon. I have not seen them before, for several weeks past. . . .

2d.   . . . A large Committee in front parlor this forenoon on Indian Affairs,[3] I understand they are to meet here once a month. . . .

2. The name "James [Jess]" crossed out.
3. HD was one of the original fourteen members of the Committee for the Civilization and Welfare of the Indian Natives, created in 1795 by the Quaker Yearly Meeting of Philadelphia. The committee lent money and farm implements to various Indian tribes, helped them in their negotiations with the federal government, sent missionaries to Indian encampments, and took some Indian children into Quaker homes to educate them (Philadelphia Yearly Meeting, Minutes of the Indian Committee, microfilm, Friends Historical Library, Swarthmore College, 3, 47–50, 69, 73, 78; for a general discussion of the subject, see Kelsey, *Friends and the Indians*, 89–110).

Febry. 6. . . . Nancy Skyrin and her eldest child, and Sally Downing called here in thir way to visit Rachel Drinker—S. Downing has not been here for near seven weeks. . . .

14. First Day: . . . Betsy Fisher was deliver'd this morning of a Daughter, her fourth Child, the other three boys, the eldest not 4 years old 'till next May, she is ill at present, in a very low way.

22. . . . I went to the front door this evening to see if the moon was rising when R Jones was passing by, she stoped to inform me, that she had been to Sammy Fishers, that Betsy Fisher was, as she thought dyeing, she had been talking in a very affecting manner to her Brother Sammy &c.

23. . . . Our agreeable young Neighbour Betsy Fisher, departed this life about 12 o'clock last night—aged about 26. years—she has left four small Children—her poor Afflicted mother Sarah Rhoads, I feel much for. . . . John Bowing or Boadwin our coachman was dismist to day, and a Negro Man, named Jacob Turner hiered in his place—Johns conduct respecting our Sall, and other things were offensive to us, for some time past.

29. . . . finished reading a foolish Romance entitled The Haunted Priory: or the Fortunes of the House of Rayo.⁴—read also, Mrs. Barbalds hymns for Children in prose,⁵ very beautiful in my oppinion—finished knitting a pair large cotton Stockings, bound a peticoat, and mad a batch of Gingerbread—this I mention, to shew, that I have not spent the day reading. . . .

[Mar.] 3. . . . Sally Dawson began a quarters Schooling with Rebecca Price this Afternoon.

5. . . . for two nights past, I have had little or no sleep, oweing to the tooth ach or rather stump ach—one of my Eye theeth very sore, my face much swelled and painful. . . .

March 6. First day: . . . sent to desire Dr. Kuhn to come in Afternoon time, he came, said my pulse were more tense than he had known them before, ordered me to loose ten or twelve ounces blood, and to have it done this Afternoon. Fredrick accordingly came and preformed the Opperation, S. Swett, Hannah Yerkes, &c. here at the time,—My blood very much enflamed and a thick coat of tough buff on it. . . .

4. [Stephen Cullen], *The Haunted Priory; or, The Fortunes of the House of Rayo: A Romance, Founded Partly on Historical Facts* (Dublin: William Jones, 1794 [*Brit. Mus. Cat.*]).
5. Anna Laetitia Barbauld, *Hymns in Prose for Children: By the Author of Lessons for Children* (London: J. Johnson, 1781 [*Brit. Mus. Cat.*]).

March 9. . . . a quarter of a Century, this day, since we came to this House, a very short time it appears to me, on a retrospect. I had little reason at that time, to expect I should live to see this day!

11. . . . went this morning to J Skyrins, found Nancy busy with her little ones, all well, called in my return at Jacob Downings, Sally and her three togeather, and, apparently, in health—I have not been out since the beginning of November excepting twice to visit little Henry in the small pox, once over to Neighr. Hartshorns, and once besides Yesterday at Hannah Pembertons. . . .

23. . . . Elisha Perkens or Docr. Perkens was here this Afternoon, he operated on HD—with his Metalic instruments for the rheumatism:[6] if my faith is necessary to the cure, I fear 'tis not compleat. . . .

27. . . . Sally Downing came in evening meeting time.[7] . . .

30. . . . Anthony and Alice Woodard bound their Son Peter Woodward to HD. this morning before Hillary Baker, Alderman, he was 12 years old the 17th this month, is to serve till 21. . . .

April 5. . . . I went down to Nancys after dinner, Betsy still very unwell. Dr. Kuhn twice there to day—he ordred her bleed again, and a blister laid on her side, which I assisted Nancys Maid Hannah, to lay on, she has not appear'd very ill to me, her blood looks very good, I believe she will soon be better. . . .

10. First Day: . . . Our Yard and Garden looks most beautifull, the Trees in full Bloom, the red, and white blossoms intermixt'd with the green leaves, which are just putting out, flowers of several sorts blown in our little Garden— what a favour it is, to have room enough in the City, and such elegant room,— many worthy persons are pent up in small houses with little or no lotts, which is very trying in hott weather. . . .

12. . . . I received a note from Nancy Skyrin informing that her little Eleanor was poorly, she wished I would come down to see her,[8] after S Swett had fitteed a gown on me, and we had done tea I went, found the child poorly but not ill . . . Sally Johnson came to day, she very willingly agree'd to Sallys

---

6. Elisha Perkins, formally trained in medicine, devised in 1795 an instrument he called a metallic tractor, which resembled a modern horseshoe nail. Perkins claimed that when the tractor was stroked over an afflicted body part it provided a relief for such ailments as rheumatism. Finding no acceptance in his native Connecticut, Perkins moved in 1796 to Philadelphia, where he and his tractor were a great success (C. K. Drinker, *Not So Long Ago,* 44–45; *DAB,* s.v. "Perkins, Elisha").

7. The words "elle parlez beaucoup" (she talks a lot) crossed out.

8. The word "which" crossed out.

staying with us two months longer as we shall be cleaning house &c—she is, I expect, sensible, that we might, if inclined so to do, oblidge her to serve us near a year longer for the expences we have been at on her and Childs account, instead of giving her freedom Cloaths &c—I wish the poor girl may do well when she leaves us. she has behaved herself better for a month or two past than for a long time before, whether it is to get the more from us, or whether she is actualy better I know not, but must hope the best.

16. . . . John Skyrin came with disagreeable intelligence, his little Eleanor was ill all last night with a Cough, fever and great oppression. Dr. Kuhn ordered her blooded, and a dose of Castor Oyl.—two and half ounces blood— 'tis a trying circumstance, to a tender Mother, to have a vain opened in an Infant Child.—The opperator found it very difficult to find a vain, and did it partly by guess—Nancy was not present. . . .

18. . . . Received a letter this evening from HD. dated at Joseph Pottss giving an account of Thomass drunken conduct &c. as they got safe there, and he is a very good driver when sober, 'tis to be hoped they will keep him so. . . .

19. . . . Our valued friend and old acquaintance Robert Stevenson senr. departed this life this morning about eight o'clock aged 74 years, his disorder apoplectic—When I think, which I often do, how few of our old friends and intimate acquaintance are left, and how many are gone, I am surprised that I am, at past 60 years of age, still here. . . .

April 22. . . . I have read a large Octava volume, intitled The Rights of Woman, By Mary Wolstonecroft.[9] in very many of her sentiments, she, as some of our friends say, *speaks my mind*, in some others, I do not, altogether coincide with her—I am not for quite so much independance.

April 30. . . . Sally Dawson appears to have the measles coming out on her. I sent for Dr. Kuhn, he order'd her a dose Castor-Oyl, which operated en haut et en bas,[10] he says she has the Measles in a favourable way. . . .

[May] 12. . . . WD. received a letter from Henry dated the 9th. instant desiring us to send the Carriage for himself Hannah and the Child, as yester-day, but as we received his letter not till this day, and our Carriage &c not in order, he will be disapointed. . . .

14. . . . We have three young Men at present in our Compting house, Thos.

9. Mary Wollstonecraft, *A Vindication of the Rights of Woman, with Strictures on Political and Moral Subjects* (Boston: Peter Edes for Thomas and Andrews, 1792 [*NUC*]).
10. Above and below.

Potts, Gers. Johnson and Peter Widdows, prehaps one good one would be worth them all. . . .

May 18. . . . William Nice from the neighbourhood of Shiholoc called for mony due him from John Ry[r]eson, he entered into conversation relative to Children, let me know, in the course of talk, that he had twelve, the three last at a birth, who were now 13 years old, two Sons and a daughter, fine hearty Children &c.—'tis very uncommon that three at one birth live—R Waln sent Peggy over to inform us of the death of Rachel Wells Senr. she died last night of an Apoplexy,—she was one of my juvenile acquaintance and about my age, an agreeable woman, she has left one of her daughters in a very low state of health—It frequently occurs to me—on hearing of the departure of my coevals, and at other times, that my turn must be eer long; May I be prepared for it! . . .

May 20: . . . H Pemberton sent Noke, I rode with her two hours, came home to dinner, S Swett dined here—HD. and Nancy Skyrin went to the funeral of Rachel Wells—I went to Jacob Downings—Betsy Watson and MD. there—Nancy came there after the burial, she and self took a walk up town, came home to tea, John Skyrin and S.S. took tea here—Nancy went home with sick head ach, sent Sam for Elizath.—I went this evening to Jacobs, he, Sally, Molly and self went to J Smiths, a number of young people there—Jacob and Sally came home with us, sup'd here—HD. took tea at H. Pembertons—My many excursions this day have been uncommon.

31. . . . John DeBrahm here this evening he appears earnest to purchase Clearfield.—could my husband, like some other Men attend to and enjoy that pretty and healthful place, I would not wish it sold, for twice as much as we shall get for it, if it is parted with.

June 1. . . . our dear little William was sent to take leave of us, there is something in him peculiarly engaging, not that he is my child, for I think I can see with impartial eyes. . . .

2d. . . . S. Johnson here forenoon asked for Sally to go home with her, two weeks before the time proposed and by her agreed too—we are busy cleaning house—I would not agree to it, she was rather impertinent—and all things considered very thoughtless and ungreatful, as she knows if we were to try titles we might keep her near a twelve month to pay expences.[11] . . .

11. Sally Brant owed the Drinkers extra time on her indenture due to her pregnancy and the subsequent death of her child. In eighteenth-century Pennsylvania a pregnant servant was indebted to her mistress or master for the cost of a nurse to attend her, legal fees, and the rearing or burying of her child. Since most servants could not pay these debts, they usually worked an extra eighteen months or two years. Time lost during lying-in was not held against a servant, but was considered time lost to illness (Mary M. Schweitzer, *Custom and Contract: Household, Government, and the Economy in Colonial Pennsylvania* [New York: Columbia University Press, 1987], 43–44).

June 4. . . . HD. struck the bargin this morning with John DeBrahm, and has actualy sold Clearfield, it is two years this Summer that I had many pleasing serious hours with my dear William, we were both invalides, and continue so still, 'tho I trust rather better than worse. . . .

8. . . . Polly Noble called to scilicet our business for her husband, who is a blacksmith. . . .

10. . . . white washer came again, 'tis a great work to clean this house throughly from the cock loft to the Cellars especialy when damp or rainey weather intervene. . . .

12. . . . Sally Dawson had behaved amiss yesterday, by her mischievious sisters advice—I gave her a whiping last night or rather endeavour'd so to do, it was the first time I ever whip'd her, I wish that, or anything else may mend her. . . .

15. . . . Betsy Franks our Salls Sister came here this Afternoon to wait on Salley to her house, she left us before tea 'tis Eight years this month that she has been with us, a little smart lively creature she was, I wish I may be disopointed for I fear much for her conduct.

24. . . . great numbers of people have been lately taken with vomitting & lax. . . .

27. . . . R Waln sent over for me in a hurry, the girl said she was very unwell, I went directly, she was much alarm'd by a sudden swelling on her tongue which much affected her voice, she was apprehensive it was paralytic, I comforted her as well as I could, not viewing it in the same light, and advised her to send for a Physician—Isaac Catheral was accordingly sent for. . . . I left her seemingly better. . . .

July 9. . . . Our Sall Dawson a deceitful naughty girl—I fear we shall have some trouble with her dispossion. . . .

11. . . . Js. Gardette Dentest was here forenoon cleaning Williams teeth— they were not foul, he extracted one, and scraped the others, then rub'd them with dentifrice, for which he was paid 5 Dollars—if what he does will tend to preserve the teeth, 'tis a trifle well laid out.

15. . . . R. Walns Peggy came to tell me that little Becky Waln, Roberts daughter, died last night—she was a beautiful little girl about 4 years old. . . .

19. . . . MD. at dinner parle trop a son Pere![12] . . .

12. Spoke too much to her father.

---

20. . . . I spent last evening and this morning looking over, prehap, 50 religious ballads, or pieces entitled Cheap Repossatory, wrote, as I suppose, for the use of the Sunday Schools in London.[13] they were lately sent over, and are well calculated for the use of those called the lower class of people, and may be very usefull. . . .

July 29. . . . Jacob went with Molly this afternoon beyond ninth street in market street, to see an Elephant lately arrived, the first, I believe, that ever was in this part of the world. . . .

[Aug.] 4. . . . HD. came to a sudden conclusion this forenoon to set off for Downingtown after an early dinner, which put us into a little hurry not uncommon to us—they set off a little before one o'clock; My husband, Sister, Son William and E. Skyrin in our Waggon, black Jacob Drove—so that we are 5 less in family than common, I shall seem lonely, having only my Daughter Molly with me, besides 3 Servants, and Molly most of her time, laterly, upstairs. . . .

6. . . . A Man called this Afternoon to know if HD. would subscribe for a portrait of David Rittenhouse, I told him that my husband was abroad, and if at home, I believed it would not suit, as he was one that did not deal in pictures, he said that several genteel Quakers had subscribed—I was desirous of saving my husband the trouble of refusing, or the Man of calling again. . . .

Augt. 10. . . . After Candle light a young Man whom I had no knowledge of, William told me afterwards it was Richd. Jones, came into the back parlor, and gave a small unsealed letter into Williams hands then went out as my husband and Robina Miller came back into the parlor,—it was directed to Henry and Elizah. Drinker, William handed it to me, I wondered from whom it came, directed to us both and by that mesenger, but upon opening it and reading the address on the top "My dear Parients." I cast my Eyes down, and to my unspeakable astonishment saw it signed Mary Rhoads—I exclamed something—and no doubt my Countenance showed my inward feelings in measure—what is that said my husband! Our visitant said I see you have mett with something afflicting—and bid us good night—William told me since— that seeing who brought the letter, and knowing his Sisters hand observing it was unsealed—that if he had been told that Molly Drinker was dead, he should not have been more shocked, but the Subscription of Rhoads—took a greater burden from his mind, not that he had any other particular person

13. Hannah More, *The Cheap Repository* (London, 1795–98). This influential collection of moral tales and tracts for children was later published in the U.S., where it also had wide circulation (G. Watson, *New Cambridge Bibliography*, 2:1599; Rosenbach, *Early American Children's Books*, 105–6; Weiss, "More's Cheap Repository Tracts," 539–49, 634–39).

in his thoughts, but we did not know that she had seen or spoken to S.R—for 6 months past, we had not the least suspicion of any thing of the kind occuring—My husband was much displeased and angry, and when I wished to know where she was at present, he charged me not to stir in the affair by any means—Molly has looked very unwell for 2 or 3 weeks past, has lost no small quantity of flesh, and has had little or no appetite—not suspecting any thing, I could not account for it.—HD. retired at the usual hour—Sister, William and myself set up 'till after one o'clock, when MS. went to her bed—I went into Billys room knowing I could not sleep, and unwilling to disturbe my Husband I stay'd all night in WD. Chamber, he went to bed but did not sleep above ¼ hour all night, I lay by him in my cloaths, up and down all night, without sleep—The next day, which was yesterday the 9th. William and myself stay'd up stairs, both of us very unwell—Sister went over to R Waln to enquire if she had heard where Molly was—She informed her that Patterson Hartshorn had been told in the morning by Sally Large that they would have trouble in their Neighbourhood to day—that Molly Drinker was married last night to S.R— at the widdow Pembertons house in Chestnut street, the family[14] were all, her Son Joe excepted, out of town—Robt. Wharton being a magistrate had married them, according to friendly order—that immediately after the Ceremony they with several others, we know not yet who, sett off for Newington James Fishers place, about two miles from the City, and where Sam Fishers Children and indeed himself at present reside—this was some little alleviation of the matter, as we did not know before, where she was, or how she had been married, wether by a Priest, or what Priest.—little did I think that a Daughter of mine would or could have taken such a step, and she always appeard to be one of the last girls that would have acted such a part—to leave her fathers house, and go among strangers to be *married!* James Pemberton came here in the Afternoon had a talk with my husband[15]—he sayd that Sammy was a Lad of a very good Moral Characture, and that those who he had heard speak of the matter, made light of it,—so do not I, said HD . . . J Logan said he thought it was a very sutiable match, Sam being a worthy young fellow—and that they thought HD. would never consent, was the reason they took the way they had. . . .

Augt. 13. . . . I have heard nothing to day of my poor run-away Child. what will her absent Sisters and brothers think, and how surprised will they be to see the first account of their Sisters Marriage in the Newspaper. . . .

14. The word "was" crossed out.
15. Many of the key players in the marriage of Sammy Rhoads to Molly Drinker were maternal relations of Sammy's: James Pemberton, who had been an exile in Virginia with HD, was his great uncle; Samuel (W.) Fisher, his brother-in-law; and Nancy Pemberton, his aunt (Thomas Alan Glenn, *Genealogical Notes: Lloyd, Pemberton, Hutchinson, Hudson, and Parke* [Philadelphia: 1898], 46–47, 54).

14.   First Day: . . . Tabby and Becky Fisher here this evening—they tell us that S. Rhoads and Molly are to come tomorrow to town, to Sally Rhoadess—I am pleased to hear it. . . .

16.   . . . Hannah S Drinker came again after dinner, she had been to Sally Rhoads to visit our daughter Molly she told WD. that she, Molly, was in much trouble and looked very poorly. . . .

18th.   . . . S. Swett allez cet matin chez un person a mon desire[16] . . . SS. says that MD. is not so unwell as represented.

Augt. 21st.   First day: . . . A Note or small Letter came this forenoon in meeting time by Sally Rhoadss little girl signed by Mary Rhoads and Saml. Rhoads, directed to Henry and Elizabeth Drinker, expressive of their uneasiness at the pain they had caused us, and wishes to be taken into favour &c.—I have undergone a *pretty* large share of uneasyness. . . .

Augt. 25.   . . . Jacob Downing came home after night. he has received a letter from Sally—informing of the indispossion of our dear Nancy, she was taken on second day with a chill and pain in her limbs and breast. . . .

26 Augt.   . . . I awoke after a very poor night with a great weight on my Spirits—Nancys illness and Mollys absence &c &c. lays heavy at my heart—Sally Dawson came up to inform me, that our milk woman told her, that our poor Sally Brant was dead—that she went last first day to Burness (a tavern) was taken with a Chill on second day, became delirous and died yesterday, to be buried this morning. . . . poor young Creature, it may be she is taken in mercy from the evil to come, and that appear'd to await her, having some wrong propensities in herself, and no extrodinary example of good, in her near relatives. . . . Sister called this morning at S.Rs from which visit I from which visit I have received no consolation.—The report of S. Brants death is false with all the circumstances, as her Sister informed MS—what a pity 'tis that the lower class of people, as they are too justly called, are so prone to lieing. . . . On questioning our Milk Woman, the truth comes out, She told our Children, that is Sally and Peter, that Sally who had lived with us was dead, and all the rest—It proves to be Sally Evans who lived a month with us after S. Brant left us—I had need to ask, in my mind, our poor Milk Womans excuse, for accusing the lower class of people of telling fibbs—she may be clear, 'tho many are not.

29.   . . . Un parlez avac HD. pas fort agreeable—comme quelque autres.[17]

16. Went this morning to the home of a person at my request.
17. A talk with HD not very agreeable—like some others.

30. . . . One trouble, sometimes, lessens another, for as we cannot bare but to a certain point, 'tis a favour when one gives way as another comes on—when Nancys breast was bad I fear'd for her, when she was better, Henry was ill, and trouble for my poor little runaway seemed to lie dormant for a time, but not long, that, and its possible consequences hurts me much—and other troubles—may I be enabled to bare all that kind providence thinks proper to suffer or permit. . . .

[Sept.] 10. . . . Sister out this evening maid hunting. . . .

12. . . . WD went cet matin[18] to S.Rs and this evening he went to the State-house Yard and eat ice'd cream[19]—for which I give him no credit. . . .

17. . . . WD. went to S.Rs his Sister Molly has had the tooth-ach, and the Dentest had just gone away, he had endeavour'd to draw two stumps, that were troublesome, but in vain, he could not extract them. . . .

18. First day: . . . sent Peter Afternoon in meeting time to S.Rs to enquire how Molly was, and to take some of her flannel garments. . . .

[Oct.] 9. First Day: . . . Our Daughter Mary came in meeting time to see me, this Afternoon 'tis nine weeks tomorrow, since she left us I was pleased to see her, and heartily wish an Amicable meeting would take place between her father and her. . . .

11. . . . this is our Election day:[20] WD. gave in his vote. Elizath. Skyrin spent this day here with her Cousins Eleanor was also here, the four dear little Girls look finely—burnfires and Noise this evening—HD. MS. were to meeting forenoon—I have not been over our door sill for upwards of nine weeks—and but twice this four months. . . .

12. . . . I put a Burgandy pitch plaster on WDs back. Buchan recommends it, and I believe it to be good for a Cough.[21]

13. . . . Dr. Kuhn called, he has not yet lost a patient for upwards of 17—

18. This morning.
19. See below, Jan. 30, 1797.
20. City, county, state, and congressional elections took place this date. The Jeffersonians, or Democratic-Republicans, won the congressional seats, but the Federalists won the city council and state assembly seats (Scharf and Westcott, *Philadelphia*, 1:485; R. G. Miller, *Federalist City*, 79–86).
21. Burgandy pitch came mainly from trees grown in Saxony. A soft reddish brown color, hence its name, it was made from resin, turpentine, and distilled oil and used in plasters in which the pitch was mixed with beeswax (W. Lewis, *New Dispensatory*, 203; Buchan, *Domestic Medicine* [1793], 193).

weeks, which I think is wonderful—a proof of the health[22]ness of the City . . .
Molly Taylor and Elizath. Bartram called afternoon for MSs and my
subscription[23] to monthly meeting, not yet due, and for a Donation for the
poor—I gave, what I afterwards thought, too little, but HD. in giving, will no
doubt, do enough—which often has some weight with me, as I have no
independent fortune, nor do I wish for one, unless it was in case of necessity,
which I trust is not like to be the case. . . .

15. . . . Well I have been this Afternoon to SRs without leave, and no reason
giving why, I should not—William went with me, we stay'd 'till night, moon
shine—no body there but the family, I feel best pleased that I went. . . .

17. . . . Sally, Nancy, Molly and the three little Girls, came here in select
meeting time—I was much pleased to see them all together—Sister ask'd
Molly to stay dinner with us, but she was affraid to see her father. . . .

22. . . . busily employed most of this day as usual.

26. . . . Tom Batts wife came to solicite HD. to assist her to get her husband
out of Jail, where she had been the means of putting him the night before, he
being then very drunk and threatning to kill her &c. she now wished him
out that he might go to her mothers funeral, who died since his confindment—
HD. called on the Magristrate who committed him, and they concluded it
best to let him stay where he was some days longer. Thos. Morris came this
evening for HD. to sign an order for the interrment of Sally Emlen, who
departed this life about three o'clock this Afternoon. She is, at last, gone out
of a world of trouble! Aged about 52. years. . . .

28. . . . Betsy Emlen returned from New-York with her Aunt this morning in
the Mail-Stage, they rode all night, but, she, did not know for certain that her
Mother was deceased 'till she came into the house—her Affliction must be very
great indeed.

Octor. 30. . . . I sent Peter to enquire how Molly was, received for answer
that her cough is very bad, she has cough'd all night for several nights past—I
am at a loss how to act on her account she being from me, and things so out of
joint: I am really distressed.

Novr. 1. . . . this morning a little before the dawn of day, we were awakened
by the ringing of bells and cry of fire at a distance, it was soon over after we
heard it. How different, I thought at the time, are we circumstanced from

22. The letters "y" and "ful" crossed out.
23. The word "for" crossed out.

what we were some years heretofore: when our family were all together, and my husband, one of the first at a fire, our two Sons also—at present, he thinks he has done his duty in that department, William not in health for that business, and Henry gone.—when I hear the cry, my daughters come first in my mind, as is natural, and 'till I know where it is, I am uneasy. . . . S. Downing here after dinner[24] Molly came in while she was here—Sally went to Nancys, Molly stay'd untill her Father came in, he came out of the fourth street meeting, being disordred in his bowels, and had taken a dose Rhubarb this morning he mett Molly here unexpectedly to them both—the first time they have seen each other since her marriage—He talked to her plainly, and at the same time kindly, she wiped her eyes and made a speech, that I did not attend too, having feelings of my own at the time—he promised to call and see her mother Rhoads whom he said he valued.—I hope matters are getting in a fair train, which I think will be a great favour. . . .

4. . . . HD. paid his first visit at S.Rs glad am I that he has been there—he desired SR. to keep an account of what she laid out for S. and M. and he would repay her. . . .

12. . . . between 3 and 4. I set off for Hannah Pembertons WD. with me—I have not seen HP. for 3 months past, as she never, it may almost be said, goes out, but to take the air in her Carriage, and home again without stoping at any place,—We walked under the covered market to avoid the wet pavements, and when in the middle of the third and last, WD. pointed to an Alley, there said he, is kep't the Elephant, which is returned to the City for a Shew—I immediately concluded to see it, and we went back into a small and ordinry room, where was tag. rag &c. No body that I knew but Abil. Griffits with two of her grand Children, she was in the same predicament with myself, and we were pleased to see each other—The innocent, good natured ugly Beast was there . . . I could not help pitying the poor Creature, whom they keep in constant agitation, and often give it rum or brandy to drink—I think they will finish it 'eer long. . . .

19. . . . Catty Decon and the three little Downings came this Afternoon to see us—I had not seen the dear little Creatures for a long time past—Molly Rhoads took tea Samuel came in the evening they suped here—for the first time.

29. . . . Parkers man came this morning to set our clock agoing. it has been dumb for several weeks past, I, who stay much at home, am pleased to hear its sound—and in the night, to know how the time passes. a time-piece is a monitor, which if properly attended too, gives usefull hints. . . .

24. The words "much out of [her   ]" crossed out.

[Dec.] 3d. . . . Hannah Catheral sent a note to HD. and called herself some time after, for an old coat, for a poor relation—sent Peter with one &c. this evening. . . .

15. . . . black Peter came in before nine this evening to desire me to come and look at two stars, that he thought made an uncommon appearence—I did so, A Planet with a large star very close by it—the planet white and brilient, the other red and not so clear—they appeard nearly to touch each other. . . .

19. . . . sent for Docr. Kuhn as Williams Throat continues sore, he came and ordered 8 ounces blood to be taken from him. . . .

20. . . . the thoughts of my Sons indispossion, the high wind, and other things keep't me awake untill near morning, I arose as usual at 8 o'clock. . . . HD. went this evening to see Nancy Skyrin, John gone to New-York, she tells him that Sally Downing has a very bad cold, but will not consent to be blooded—I am much uneasy—and know not what to do, advice will go but little way—she has always been very fearful of having a vein opened.

Decemr. 24. . . . We are preparing to remove into the front parlor tomorrow, it being much the warmest room. . . . HD. took tea at H. Pembertons and visited his three daughters.

31st. and last of the year. . . .
    EDs bodely health as good as for many years past, and till within 2 or 3 months, it was better for near six months—an infirmity under which she lives, and renders it rather improper for her to spend 24 hours out of her own house, is not yet worse, through mercy; than for many years past, tho very trouble-some at times, and almost a continual uneasiness—appitite good, tho not craving, little sleep, almost always at home—uses but little boddly exercise 'tho not indolent, and seldom idle. she has many things to trouble her, and many to be thankful for. . . .
    S.D. and M.R. are both in the *Way* as some call it—a way, that was always attended with great difficulty to me and mine—should it please kind provi-dence to suffer or permit me to see my dear family around me, the latter end of next 6th. month, I shall have abundent cause of thankfullness—but his will must be done—my anxiety is great on account of my dear Children—they are, and always were, very near my heart, their real good, both soul and body— Decr. 31. 1796.

1797

[Jan.] 13. . . . 36. years married. . . . HD. out this evening Wm. Cooper called to know if he would go with him tomorrow to North bank[1] to visit HSD. . . .

14. . . . Wm. Cooper came according to agreement for HD. who went with him . . . they sett off in Coopers Carriage and four horses, between 12 and one, for HSD. N. Bank . . . No one here since HD. left us. P. Widdows lodges here durring his absence.

Janry. 15. . . . Jacob Downings Dan came near 10 at night to borrow Buchans family physician,[2] he says his mistresss cough is worse again—poor Sally. . . .

16. . . . HD. returned home before dinner, he left our Son &c. pretty well: the Doctor has order'd a Blister behind each of little Williams Ears for the benefit of his Eye—John Balderstone was here forenoon—he seems very full of his intended spouse—I have been often surprised in observing how much more light, and delighted, some old men are, after loosing one, two or three wives with the thought of getting another, and less seriously thoughtfull than Young Men generally are on the same occasion—'tis very disgusting—John is not quite so much so, as many others that I taken notice of in the[3] like circumstance. . . .

19. . . . Betts Dawson has burnt Elizabeths Leg badly with the warming-pan, which may be without great care an ugly circumstance this cold weather.

23. . . . Molly Rhoads came forenoon she stay'd dinner, she went home in our Sleigh soon after dinner. . . . Our Jacob went after taking Molly home on towards North-Bank to take the old Sleigh to Henry, as we have purchas'd a

---

1. HSD's farm in Pennsbury, Bucks County, Pa.
2. William Buchan, *Domestic Medicine; or, The Family Physician: Being an Attempt to Render the Medical Art More Generally Useful, by Shewing People What Is in Their Own Power Both with Respect to the Prevention and Cure of Diseases: Chiefly Calculated to Recommend a Proper Attention to Regimen and Simple Medicines* (Edinburgh: Balfour, Auld, and Smellie, 1769). The first American edition of Buchan, one of the most popular medical books of its time, was published in 1771; by 1797 it had gone through at least fifteen editions (*DNB*; *NUC*).
3. The words "same occasion" crossed out.

new one. HSD. has also a new one making, yet that may be of use to him—
Sammy and Molly talk of going to house keeping the first of next month. . . .

24. . . . HD. MS. gone to monthly meeting—Mollys case was mention'd
there—Hannah West and Sarah Tomkins were appointed to visit her.[4] . . . We
sent Jacob with a Sleigh loaded for Molly to their house, Chairs, Potts, End-
irons, &c.—We received a letter from Henry, the blisters on little Williams
Ears have been very sore—the blister plasters were removed in the night and
the flies[5] that were on them scatter'd over his ears, that the poor Child must be
in a sore condition. the grissel of the Ear to be strip'd of its skin is very hard to
bare. . . .

30. . . . WD. out twice to day, he mett M. Malerive in the street who insisted
on his going home with him, which he complyed with to see his Sister, in
ninth street, up 3 pair of stairs, they treated him with iced cream which they
make and sell for a livelyhood[6]—poor things.

Febry. 1. . . . I wish I knew how all my Children were at this minuit—I am
far from well myself.

2d. . . . Sammy Rhoads called, he informs us that they go to their new
habitation to day. I am not capasitated to be with them. . . .

3d. . . . I have just cut the fourth finger of my left hand, by cutting a peice of
Whalebone, the knife which is rather dull slip'd and went with force against
the knuckel, and took off a piece of the flesh, I have lap'd it up in the blood,
hoping that may heal it—I can now, neither sew nor knit, but read and scrible
I may. . . .

4. Overseers of the women's Philadelphia Monthly Meeting of the Northern District had
reported that Molly Rhoads had married "contrary to the good order establish'd amongst us
as a religious society." Following the ordinary procedure of the Society of Friends, a
committee (Tomkins and West) was appointed to determine whether she wished to acknowledge her misconduct, write an "offering" publicly stating her sentiments, and be re-accepted
into the meeting. A similar procedure was being followed in the Men's Meeting with regard to
Sammy Rhoads (Philadelphia Northern District Monthly Meeting, Women's Minutes, 1796–
1811, 17, Men's Minutes, 1795–1804, 116, Friends Historical Library, Swarthmore College;
Frost, *Quaker Family*, 55–57).
5. The blisters were apparently made from dried beetles or Spanish flies (*OED*, s.v. "fly-
blister" and "cantharides").
6. Ice cream, developed in Europe in the sixteenth and seventeenth centuries, became well
known in New York in the 1780s. It was a popular dessert among the elite as well as President
Washington and members of his administration. The arrival of French refugees in Philadelphia
in the 1790s further spread its popularity, since many of the refugees, like Malerive, sold ice
cream and other special foods (Paul Dickson, *The Great American Ice Cream Book* [New York:
Atheneum, 1972], 20–24; Catherine A. Herbert, "The French Element in Pennsylvania in the
1790s: The Francophone Immigrant's Impact," *PMHB* 108 (1984): 461).

5. . . . HD. went after evening meeting to Sammy Rhoadss he suped with him and Molly the first visit, no communication from him relative to them.

8. . . . William and self went down about 12 o'clock to Saml Rhoadss, the first time of my being there, and the first time that I have been out since B. Oliver took me to see Molly when she was unwell. . . . Hannah S. Drinker, her maid and Son dined here. Henry took his Son home in his Arms.

21st. . . . Molly called, she is going to attend our monthly meeting with a paper of condemnation for her outgoing in marriage.[7] . . .

26. First Day: . . . HD. MS. gone to meeting. they invited this morning at the three meeting houses to the burial of Rebecca Trotter on third day next— she has left 7 Children, was in the 42 year of her age—probably, had it pleased providence to have spared her, she might never have had another—I have often thought that women who live to get over the time of Child-bareing, if other things are favourable to them, experience more comfort and satisfaction than at any other period of their lives—'tho 'tis sometimes otherwise; want of health, mistaken conduct, and what is called misfortunes.

March 4. . . . HDs. birth day—sixty three years of age, has past through the Grand Clymatric.[8] . . .

5. First Day: . . . HD. as is usual for him to bleed in the spring,[9] and having

7. Though Molly Rhoads acknowledged "accomplishing her Marriage contrary to the good order established among friends, and in disobedience to her parents," the committee that had visited her told the meeting that they "did not think her at that time in a suitable disposition to make satisfaction to the meeting." When a written apology or acknowledgment was not explicit or contrite enough, the meeting could insist upon changes and clarifications, which it apparently did here. Since Molly and her offering could not "pass" the meeting, her case would be continued and a new committee appointed to visit her (Philadelphia Northern District Monthly Meeting, Women's Minutes, 1796–1811, 18–19, Friends Historical Library, Swarthmore College; Barbour and Frost, *Quakers*, 110).

8. It was widely believed that climactics or climacterics, critical stages in human life when a person was especially susceptible to changes in health and fortune, occurred in the years that were multiples of seven or nine; hence the sixty-third birthday was considered the "grand climactic" (*OED*, s.v. "climacteric").

9. HD believed in being bled twice a year, around the time of the vernal and autumnal equinoxes. This belief was held by many scientifically trained doctors of the eighteenth century, who also thought that the new moon similarly promoted discharges of blood. The power of the heavenly bodies to influence bodily health was commonly acknowledged in the eighteenth-century English-speaking world. A Philadelphia physician writing in 1795 reported that in the lower counties of Delaware people believed that blood had to be drawn within two days before or after the full or change of the moon; drawing blood at other times would be fatal (C. K. Drinker, *Not So Long Ago*, 9; Richard Mead, *A Treatise Concerning the Influence of the Sun and Moon upon Human Bodies, and the Diseases Thereby Produced* [London: J. Brindley, 1748], 1–35, 53–57; *Observations on the Influence of the Moon on Climate, and the Animal Economy: With a Proper Method of Treating Diseases, When under the Power of That Luminary* [Philadelphia: Richard Folwell, 1798], 13 and passim; see also Thomas, *Religion and the Decline of Magic, 353*).

a cold sent for Fredrick who open'd a vein, he made too small an Orifice, the blood run slowly, stop't of itself, about eight ounces was taken—it looks good, no ways inflamed. . . .

11. . . . B. Oliver took me in his carriage to my daughter Mollys. Dr. Way came there by appointment, he had a conversation avac moy solas[10]—ordered MR. to loose 6 or 7 ounces blood. . . . Molly always beheaves with steady resolution on those occasions, she eat no dinner having breakfasted late and not proper so soon after bleeding, her blood inflamed and sizey.[11]. . .

13. . . . Betty Borrage left us this afternoon. she has a disagreeable temper and was no good example to our little folks in the Kitchen,—her absence not to be regretted.

24. . . . Mart. Hart, M Smith and S. Scatergood visited our Child yesterday forenoon—her outgoing in Marriage ought to have been the subject in question—but M.H took upon her to talk of things wide of the mark—and I believe intend to lengthen out the business as long as they can—MS. beheaved more like a Woman of sense than the other two—If innocent young women are so treated, I fear it will drive them further from the Society, instead of bringing them nearer. . . .

[Apr.] 5. . . . Molly Rhoads came forenoon, she went into race street to buy a baby Basket. . . .

6 . . . HD. our black Jacob and Peter are putting up the Grapevines &c. in the garden this Afternoon, it being high time, and John the Gardener does not make his appearance according to promise. . . . Sister S.R—sent in the accounts to day of articles purchas'd for S. and M. Rhoads—They were upwards of 5 months at her house after they were married—and she had undertaken to bespeak some things for their going to housekeeping before we had visited or seen our daughter—the hearing of which, perhaps, expidated our visiting there,—I thought after we had made matters up with the young foulks that it was rather a dilicate matter to take the business out of her hands, suffer'd her therefore to have the trouble of buying and collecting—they have, except such things as I sent and gave besides, she shew'd her taste and judgement in furnishing a house &c.

10. With me alone.
11. Molly Rhoads was seven months pregnant at the time Dr. Nicholas Way was having her bled. It was widely held that pregnant women had a superfluity of blood from lack of menstruation. Sisey, or sizy, blood, according to Benjamin Rush, was blood that when drawn had a buffy coat indicating some sort of inflammation (C. K. Drinker, *Not So Long Ago*, 61, 41; Rush, *Inquiries and Observations*, 3d ed., 4:344).

April 11. . . . the full Moon rising more like Copper than Silver, indication I believe of dry weather—I love the Moon. . . .

12. . . . I arose as usual this morning found Wm. Ashby here when I came down stairs waiting to try on HD a suit cloaths—I had some talk with him, as he is one of those appointed to treat with Sammy Rhoads,[12] he is, or appears to be an innocent well minded man, if they were all so, men and women, the affair would not be so long in hand—he said there was a great deel of out of doors talk, which he disapproved. . . .

20. . . . Saml. and Molly Rhoads came forenoon—Sammy went home and left Molly here, she went to dine with her Mother Rhoads. she expects another visit tomorrow from the curious impertinants under a shew of religious duty. . . .

25. . . . Polly Smith here this evening—'tis plain she disapproves of the many impertinant questions ask'd MR—she is one of the Committee appointed to treat with her on account of her outgoing in marriage—'tis well they have no thing worse against her, 'tho it is bad enough. but there are some who have endeavour'd to make more of it than it comes too. . . .

26. . . . My poor Daughters SD. and M.R—near the time of destress. could I be favour'd to see my dear family once more in good health and spirits—how rejoyced should I be. . . .

[May] 2d. . . . a letter from HSD. to WD. desiring him to send a pound of good pale bark, as he has had a severe fitt of the Ague; dear Henry, I wish he was here, that I might nurse him. . . .

3. . . . Molly went to dine with her Mother Rhoads she has a bad cold leaving off a flannel under Jacket, how shall we teach young people wisdom or prudence? . . .

8. . . . finish'd reading nine volumes of ten. the 3d. lost from the Library, of Letters from the Merchioness De Sévigné, To her Daughter the Countess De Grignan, translated from the french:[13] wrote in the last century—They are wrote in an easy free stile, the Affectionate and maternal regard she so very often expresses for her daughter is natural: but I think, in the first volume

---

12. See above, Feb. 21; Philadelphia Northern District Monthly Meeting, Men's Minutes, 1795–1804, 116, 124, 131, Friends Historical Library, Swarthmore College.

13. Marie [de Rabutin-Chantal], marquise de Sévigné, *Letters from the Marchioness de Sévigné to Her Daughter the Countess de Grignan*, 10 vols., 2d ed. (London: J. Coote, 1763–68 [*NUC*]).

rather overdone—but when we consider that they were private letters, not intended for public inspection, renders them execusable. . . .

10. . . . I went down to Saml. Rhoads about 11 o'clock—dined and spent the day there, 'tis a long time since I have seen such a concourse of people as past by their house, in second street, and Penn street, going and returning to and from the Friget which was lanched about one o'clock a little below the Sweeds Church,[14] The first vessel that ever was built here, and I wish I could say it was the last that ever would be. . . .

17. . . . My Eldest and Youngest Daughters are near a very trying time, and my poor dear Nancy! 'tho not in their situation, is, I fear, far from well.

18. . . . I have done a good deal of work lately in the baby cloaths line, finish'd knitting a pair of cotton stockings for E. Downing. . . .

May 22. . . . WD. out this evening till 11 o'clock, he loves to strole about after night, we have the satisfaction of knowing he is not in mischief, yet I do not feel easy least he should meet with some drunken fellows in the street—or take cold from the night air.

23d. . . . S. Swett dined here she inform'd us, that Mollys paper was received without one desenting voice.[15] . . .

24. . . . Sally Downing and Son were here this Afternoon, she, poor thing, is just in Mollys predicament, expects just at the same time.

25. . . . I know not which of my daughters will call first, the Moon changes

14. Congressional legislation of Mar. 27, 1794, and Apr. 20, 1796, authorized the construction of three frigates for the infant American navy. Joshua Humphrey designed all three and built the frigate *United States* at Philadelphia, where he was superintendent of the navy yard. The *United States*, the first of the vessels to be completed, was launched amid much hoopla on this date (Gardner W. Allen, *Our Naval War with France* [1909; reprint, Archon Books, 1967], 42–48; Scharf and Westcott, *Philadelphia*, 1:490).

15. Molly Rhoads's offering was accepted by the women's monthly meeting and reported to the men's meeting, which directed its committee to meet with the couple once more. Sammy's and Molly's offerings would finally be accepted in their respective monthly meetings in August and September 1797, and the couple would be reinstated in November 1797 following a public reading of their statements (Philadelphia Northern District Monthly Meeting, Men's Minutes, 1795–1804, 131, 151, 164, Women's Minutes, 1796–1811, 32, Friends Historical Library, Swarthmore College).

the coming morning at half past 3 o'clock, but as they both seem so well this evening I hardly think they will alter much before morning.[16]. . .

26. . . . Sammy and Molly Rhoads came to tea, they had a very pleasent ride, our horses at present behave well, having been used often lately. . . . 'tho I am pleased that my Children should go sometimes abroad and take the air and use exercise, yet I am so great a Coward, that when ever they ride out, I am under more or less anxiety least they should meet with some accident. . . .

27. . . . finished reading a small Folio Volume: The life of Pope Sixtus the 5th.[17]. . . The translator who was a Roman Catholic, speaks of Sixtus as a just and good Man. I think he was a brutal hypocrite—he did evil that good might come of it: punished triffling crimes with severity by way of example; over strain'd justice, and by his severities caused terror; and restored order to the Papal Dominions.—The misuse, or abuse of Power, does much mischief in Church or state, in public or private, in republicks or families, and is I think, the greatest calamity that the world labours under. . . .

[June] 4. . . . for near a week past I have been in hourly expectation of being called to Sally and Molly—it is a time of suspence and anxitity. . . .

9. . . . A Woman was here yesterday dress'd very fine in but a middleing way, gold ear-bobs, white french dress and a vail on, she had a young girl with her who made, partly, the same appearence, she show'd me a paper directed to

16. Folk beliefs and superstitions relating childbirth to phases of the moon date back to classical mythology's identification of Lucina, the goddess of light and childbirth, with Diana, goddess of the moon. ED's more specific belief that her daughters were likely to give birth during a full or new moon or a lunar eclipse (see below, Sept. 21, 1801) was derived not from folklore but from contemporary medical theory. Just as full and new moons increased tides, it was held, so they increased blood pressure, thus bringing on birth. While astrologically based systems of medical belief waned in the eighteenth century, many doctors in England and the U.S. still thought that the moon played a role in fevers. Benjamin Rush believed that yellow fever attacked more people three days before and after the "full and change of moon," with more deaths occurring during these periods than at other times (Thomas Rogers Forbes, *The Midwife and the Witch* [New Haven, Conn.: Yale University Press, 1966], 61; E. Radford and M. A. Radford, *Encyclopedia of Superstitions* [1948; rev. ed. by Christina Hole, Chester Springs, Pa.: Dufour Editions, 1969], 53, 239; Carl J. Pfeiffer, *The Art and Practice of Western Medicine in the Early Nineteenth Century* [Jefferson, N.C.: McFarland, 1985], 155, 163–67; Thomas, *Religion and Decline of Magic*, 354–55; Benjamin Rush, *An Account of the Bilious Remitting Yellow Fever, as It Appeared in Philadelphia, in the Year 1793*, 2d ed. [Philadelphia: Thomas Dobson, 1794], 27).

17. Gregorio Leti, *The Life of Pope Sixtus the Fifth (One of the Most Remarkable and Entertaining Lives That Is to Be Met with in Ancient or Modern History); In Which Is Included the State of England, France, Spain, Italy, the Swiss Cantons, Germany, Poland, Russia, Sweden and the Low Countries, at That Time; With an Account of St. Peter's, the Conclave, and Manner of Chusing a Pope; the Vatican Library . . . and Other Noble Edifices, Begun or Finish'd by Him . . . Translated from the Italian . . . by Ellis Farneworth* (London: W. Bowyer and C. Bathurst, 1754 [*NUC*]).

charitable Ladys, setting fourth, that a woman of good characture was in distress, and had been very sick, wanted a sum of money to pay her rent &c. with a line or two at bottom in her favour signed A. W. Bingham, I ask'd her if she had been long sick, she said it was not for herself, but for a person whose name was not to be told. It was prehaps, some one who had not been used to ask Charity: many of that class, I do believe suffer deeply. . . .

June 12. . . . I have evry night for a long time past expected to be called up in the night, as I cannot with propriety stay with either of my daughters not knowing which will call me first. . . .

13. . . . HD. has informed me, that he was at J Skyrins this Afternoon, and that little Eleanor had got a dry pea up her nose, Dr. Kuhn had been sent for, but could not get at it. . . .

14. . . . after 3 o'clock Sammy Rhoads, knock'd at the Door, Sister answer'd him, and desired him to go immeadeately home to Molly who was taken in pain and sick stomach—I arose and dress'd as quick as possiable, it being a summond I have been long wishing for 'tho at the same time dreading. Our black Jacob went with me, it was still and beautiful weather, I was well illuminated on the way, the Moon shone bright, the lamps were burning—and day dawning before I got to SRs did not meet with any living Creature save one dog, who hearing us pass came barking out of an Alley—I found my poor Child very unwell a foreruning and certain symptom, which I could have wished had not occur'd so soon unless she had been sooner releived, made me think it necessary to send out for more assistance which after settleing some preliminaries I did, my self nor Daughters were never quick in this business lingering tedious, destressing times have always been our lots.—Jacob went with the Carriage for Hanh. Yerkes, afterwards for Sister Rhoads and M— Pleasants, Sammy went for Dr. Way, my Sister came after breakfast—after all were arrived nothing could be done to purpose—My dear Child was all day, at times in great pain, HY &c. doing all they could for her—All night the same, HY. went to bed, MP. and MS. all night with her—the Doctor frequently with her to little purpose—it was a trying night to me.

15. fifth day: the same scean continued—we were frequently encouraged by the Doctor to hope all would be soon well over, My poor dear girl with apparent calmness and risignation bore all—at dinner the Doctor was Chearfull, and 'tho I dreaded how things might end, yet I did not suspect how it was with her at that time but judg'd it to be a long and lingering labour[18]—in the Afternoon Sally Lampley came, who is to nurse Molly, her pains 'tho not much stronger were improved by her own efforts: from many things that

18. The word "towards" crossed out.

occur'd I was led to conclude that all was not right, by the difficuelty and tediousness &c. and so it proved, the birth presented, and the Child came into the world for some time double, wedged as it were and the poor Mother benum'd, no regular labour pains—the Doctor got down the feet and legs, it was long afterward that it was wholly deliver'd—I did not know her situation 'till after all was over—It had frequently evacuated before birth, being as I afterwards supposed in the agony of death at that time, it was still born between 5 and 6 o'clock, a very pretty well made boy, resembling both father & mother a middle sized child, rather tall; the loss gives me great concern, not only being deprived of a sweet, little grandson, but the suffering of my poor Child, who lost, what may be called the reward of her labour, and promissing a good breast of milk, may pass through, if she lives, the same excruciateing trouble a year the sooner for this loss. . . .

16.   found Molly when I arose which was early—Awake and feverish—she lay very still most of this day, but very sore, and complain'd of her left side being brused by lieing so long on it, and straining so hard—the blood was settled in the ends of her fingers, by hard pulling, and her nails[19] blue. . . .

17.   in the morning she sleep't two hours, occasion'd as I afterwards under-stood by her taking Ladanum which I knew not of—The Nurse had proposed giving it, I told her I rather not—she did not tell me that the Doctor had order'd it, but had a mind to be consequential—I dont approve of Nurses or any other but a regular Physician, ordering Anodynes to Woman in Child bed—so lately deliver'd and so ill—had I known it had been by the Doctors orders I should not have objected to it—I received a note this morning from my Husband informing, to my great surprise and joy that Sally Downing was deliver'd this morning between 2 and 3 o'clock of a Daughter. . . . went to see my poor Sally; where I was informed that she had a very sharp labour and rather difficult.—as soon as the Child was born she fainted away and lay a long time in that state, Dr. Shippen was oblig'd to force her mouth open to give some thing with a view of reviving her—Dr. Kuhn was sent for, he came before she had recover'd and gave her Ether[20] which was serviceable—she had

    19. The word "black" crossed out.
    20. Ether was first synthesized from sulfuric acid and alcohol early in the sixteenth century and was so named in 1730. Its properties as a gas, however, were not known until the early nineteenth century; in the eighteenth century ether seems to have been used in liquid form, combined with alcohol. Its ability to lessen pain and promote sleep was poorly understood. The most common preparation using liquid ether was Hoffman's Anodyne (see below, Mar. 2, 1805). It was also recommended as an antispasmodic drug, and since some writers thought that fainting or syncope was accompanied by spasms, Kuhn may have given Sally ether to revive her gently. Most writers on childbirth recognized that fainting after childbirth was not rare and recommended that the woman be left undisturbed until she revived (Victor Robinson, *Victory over Pain: A History of Anesthesia* [New York: Henry Schuman, 1946], 34–35; W. Lewis, *New Dispensatory*, 454–55; William Cullen, *A Treatise of the Materia Medica*, 2 vols. [Edinburgh; reprint, Philadelphia: J. Crukshank and R. Campbell, 1789], 2:256–57; William

a numbness in her limbs, and pain in her breast, a very great discharge—
Hannah Yerkes who had been at S.Rs in the forenoon with her daughter
Tomkins while I was there, had inform'd me that Sally was fainty after
delivery, but was then bravely—and so I found her, all things considered—but
her natural dispossition is, to be easy and Chearful when ever it is possiable for
her to be so—a little pritty plump babe whom they call Sarah, after her
Mother and mine—I came home after 10. and lodged at home with my mind
greatly releived to what it was some time past, 'tho not at ease, as I think both
my lieing-in Children in rather a ticklish[21] situation—They inherit, I believe
their difficulty in this respect from their Mother, 'tho all but Nancy have been
worse than myself, and she has very labourous times. . . .

June 18.   First day: . . . On sixth day last, the day after it was born, while I
was there, Mollys baby was buryed: Sally Rhoads and the Nurse, Sammy
Rhoads & William Drinker went to the funeral in our Carriage about 8 o'clock
in the evening. it was laid by Jacob Downings first Child.[22] . . . Sally Downing
told me an Anecdote of what had occur'd to her, a day or two before she was
confine'd—setting alone in the parlor, a Man, who was a stranger to her came
in to enquire if J. Downing had not a good Chair horse to sell, she told him he
had and she believed he was now at the stable where the horse was—he went
out, but soon returned and set down to wait for Jacob, some common place
discourse follow'd, when Fennos paper was deliver'd to her, Sally took it up
and made some remarks on [Gallatin] and others, she being a free spoken
body—amongst other things, she said she had read Harpers speech and
thought it very good, but she supposed Cobbett had dressed it up, Indeed
Maddam, said the Stranger, I have not altred a word of it—'twas well it was no
worse!—I did not know thee said Sally, and then, I doubt not, she talked as
freely as before, for more so she could not well have done, 'twas just like her.
while she was telling me the above, I realy thought Gallatin was the person
present.[23]

19.   . . . Molly rather better she was taken up, and had her bed made for the

---

Cullen, *First Lines of the Practice of Physic*, rev. ed. in 2 vols. with supplementary notes by
Peter Reid [Edinburgh, 1802], 2:118; Thomas Denman, *An Introduction to the Practice of
Midwifery*, 4th ed. [London: J. Johnson, 1805], 2:353–541; correspondence with Prof. Bert
Hansen, New York University, Aug. 23, Sept. 3, 1987; see also the advertisement of druggists
Maclean and Stuart, who sold "nitrous and vitriolic ether," in *Pa. Journal*, June 17, 1762,
which states that ether was used externally to suppress pain and internally to relieve nervous
disorders).
    21. The word "way" crossed out.
    22. Henry Downing, Jacob and Sally's first child, who was born in Philadelphia Mar. 14,
1788, and died there nine days later (Cope, *Smedley Family*, 183).
    23. John Fenno was the editor of the *Gazette of the United States*, William Cobbett a
Federalist journalist and pamphleteer who wrote under the name of Peter Porcupine. Albert
Gallatin was, at this time, a Republican member of the House of Representatives and Robert
Goodloe Harper a Federalist leader in the same legislative body.

first time, continues feverish, milk in her breasts which the Nurse sucks, but very little, hoping to backen it.[24]. . .

21. . . . I left home at 9 o'clock and went down to Mollys, where I spent the rest of the day—she is rather better, sat up this evening half an hour and walk'd round the bed holding by the Nurse. . . .

22. . . . I went before dinner to visit Nancy Skyrin, found her on the bed— Betsy Jervis with her, very unwell she is hysterical in some degree, weak and low. . . .

23. . . . I went down to Nancys, found her better. . . .

June 24. . . . Nancy continues better 'tho far from well—she is preparing to remove from their present dwelling, which is rendred very dissagreeable by the porters with their Drays, who are in crowds before their door; to the house lately occupied by Joshua Howel in Arch-street for which they are to give 150 pounds p Ann, and the taxes, it is but a small house, but the situation so much preferable to that they are in, that I am pleased with the change—from thence I went to see my poor dear Molly, who is at present in the most dissagreeable and threatening situation of either of my dear Children and not one of them, unless Henry is favourd with health, is well at present. . . .

27. . . . little Mary Marott a french Child, daughter of a french Man and Woman who live in one of Stiles houses in our Alley—was this morning buried. she died of the small-pox about 7 years old, a little pretty chattering girl, was often in our yard and spoke English much better than either of her parents, she was their only Child—the father appears to be in much trouble. . . .

30. . . . Molly looks languid and cannot yet walk across the room without pain. . . .

24. It was necessary for Molly to express milk to prevent engorgement, but at the same time to minimize stimulation in order to stop her supply. Her nurse may have applied a plaster, a resinous cream, neat's-foot oil, or goose grease, or used a breast pump. The latter method was similar to one employed in cupping blood: small glass cups with fluted edges made to accommodate the nipple had the air withdrawn from them and were then placed over the breast to perform by suction (A. Davis and Appel, *Bloodletting Instruments*, 34–35; William Moss, *An Essay on the Management, Nursing and Diseases of Children from the Birth, and on the Treatment and Diseases of Pregnant and Lying-in Women, with Remarks on the Domestic Practice of Medicine*, 2d ed. [Egham: C. Boult and T. Longman, 1794], 435–37; Jane Sharp, *The Midwives Book* [London, 1671; reprint, New York: Garland, 1980], 338–39; see also Valerie A. Fildes, *Breasts, Bottles and Babies: A History of Infant Feeding* [Edinburgh: Edinburgh University Press, 1986], 137–38).

[July] 4. . . . Annaversary of Independance—May this day pass without the Commission of any enormity, by those who pride themselves in their independence, but know not how to prize or use it. . . . Well! I have been to Meeting this morning—It is 5 years this month since I have been to the North meeting house,[25] and very rarely at any other. . . .

5. . . . Nancy has, by Dr. Kuhns advice diped her daughters in cold water this morning[26] 'tho I generaly revere the Doctors oppinion, in this I must be excused, a poor little creature, whose bowels have been for a long time much disorder'd by cutting teeth, which are now all through, and might get better without so severe an opperation.—I dont like this kill or cure work. . . .

6. . . . this day I lay'd down after dinner for a short time and sleep'd a little—a practice very unusual with me—head ach'd and unwell afterwards it does not suit me, perhap 'tis for want of use, but I believe not to be desired—I never was a sleepey body, nor unless by chance never fond of bed. . . .

12. . . . sent Jacob with the Carriage for Molly Rhoads. she came before noon. Nurse Lamplugh with her, they dined and spent the day, Sammy Rhoads also dined here went away about dusk WD. with them. poor dear Molly! her late sufferings will I fear, leave something destressing for a length of time. . . .

July 16. . . . A letter received this evening from Henry, informs that his Hannah was brought to bed, at 11 o'clock last night, and that she and her Son were bravely—but no further perticulars except that Dr. Belville was there this morning and Hannah not quite as well as last night—I suppose he deliver'd her—poor girl to have none of her friends with her at so trying a time— perhaps 'tis sooner than she expected—I have been quite mistaken and Dr. Shippen's rule has in this instance failed, as according to it this Child of Hannahs should have been a Daughter.[27]

18. . . . Js Smith called, inform'd that Hannah was deliver'd without help,— two Neighbours, the Doctors wife and Joseph Buntings wife being there accidently and their Maid who is a handy woman Molly Weazle. . . .

25. A Quaker meeting had been established in 1791 at the northern edge of Philadelphia in Keys Alley, which ran from Front Street to Second Street between Sassafras (Race) and Vine streets (Bronner, "Quaker Landmarks," 212; *Philadelphia City Directory, 1791*, xvii).
26. Dipping children in cold water, a popular practice in eighteenth-century America, was based on John Locke's recommendation of such baths in his *Thoughts on Education*, published in 1690 (Linda Grant DePauw and Conover Hunt, *Remember the Ladies: Women in America, 1750–1815* [New York: Viking Press in association with the Pilgrim Society, 1976], 27).
27. See below, Oct. 7, 1801.

20 . . . WD. called on Dr. Kuhn who encouraged him to go to a bathing house in Race Street,[28] to wash him self, rather than in the river. . . .

26. . . . read the Contrast[29] a small rediculous Novel, S Kidds brother brings them to her, he lives, I believe at a book shop, 'tho I have read some of them myself, I have been talking to her against the practice.[30] . . .

[Aug.] 4. . . . Oliver was here this evening to borrow Buchans family Physician for Nancy, as she thinks Eleanor has worms—a poor little weakly thing—her mother has much trouble with her.

12. . . . T. Stewardson here fore-noon he says that the people down town are alarmed on account of the fever. . . . the Physicians have had a meeting, and 'tho they do not, quite, agree in oppinion of the sort of fever, yet all conclude it is of an infectious kind. . . .

Augt. 14. . . . The Alarm rather increases, on account of the fever—some are going out of the City—Many have taken places in the country—Germantown, it is said is all taken up.

Augt. 21. . . . My husband has concluded that WD. and myself go tomorrow to North-bank, as it is thought advisable to leave the City—The Committee of health have concluded with the Governors concurrance that if any person is taken ill, in any house, they shall immeadiately be removed out of town by their friends, or sent to the Hospital . . . I shall be seperated widely from all my dear daughters—My husband and Sister are to follow us, as soon as they think it expedient. . . .

23. . . . After 9 o'clock forenoon, William, Sally Dawson and self, left home, Jacob drove for North bank . . . We baited the horses at Shamany, arrived at Henrys between 3 and 4 Afternoon. . . . I have been feverish for some days past and feel a stagnation in my feet: shall take Lenitive Electuary[31] this evening to be from home illey suits me, but composure and risignation is best if attainable. . . .

24. . . . Sally Dawson sleeps for the present, at the foot of my bed, I was up

28. Either Wigwam Baths, founded in 1791 at the foot of Race Street and the Schuylkill River, which featured two shower baths, a plunging bath, a bowling green, a tea garden, and a tavern, or one of the baths established by the new French community (see below, Aug. 3, 1798; Scharf and Westcott, *Philadelphia*, 2:943).

29. Elizabeth Sarah Villa-Real Gooch, *The Contrast: A Novel*, 2 vols. (London: C. and G. Kearsley, 1794; 1st American edition, Wilmington, Del.: Joseph Johnson, 1796 [*NUC*]).

30. Sally Kidd was a servant.

31. A honey paste lozenge containing senna, coriander seeds, licorice, figs, prune pulp, tamarind pulp, and double refined sugar; a mild tonic (Estes, "Therapeutic Practice," 373).

a little after six desturb'd by what I had taken—'tho every thing here is as much to my mind as I could expect, yet to invalids home is home. . . .

25. . . . Henry, Hannah and the two Children were out in R. Croziers Waggon after dinner, the first of her being out since her lieing in, I wrote home Yesterday.

29. . . . We received this evening a letter from my husband, and several newspapers HD tells us that the disorder has not spread, and according to the Newspapers it looks like it—but he further adds that it is supposed that more have already left the City, than did in the Year 93. which was said to be 20,000 fright'ned out. . . .

31st. . . . Parker came home about two o'clock, he brought a letter from my husband to HS.D. Parker had behaved very much amiss, had got in licquor and left the horses in the road near Godfrey Haggers at some distance from town, A stranger took them back to our stable, with a letter from Godfry Hagger, informing that the Negro Man lay dead-drunk in the road.—Henry gave him a whiping, which he bore with patience and contrition, beg'ed to be forgiven and weap'd, signs of a very good dispossion. . . .

[Sept.] 2d. . . . little William had another fitt of fever this evening, 'tis no wonder he is ill, out, in almost all weathers, in the heat of the noon day sun, without any covering on his head and bare-footed—Dr. Jardine told me, that he found him lately, fast asleep on the earth near the Gate, no hat on his head, he wak'd him and took him in—he is a lively boy, of an extrodinary constitution and his fathers darling. . . .

4. . . . Our dear little William is very poorly indeed, he has had a fever for 5 days past, physicking and starving—I think him in rather a ticklish way, the little maid Nancy, is in bed all this Afternoon with a fever and cough, Nurse has enough to do—My poor Son Henry, I believe must be a Nurse, which his father never was. . . .

5. . . . HD. informs us that our Neighbourhood is almost deserted, and that 1300 houses are said to be shut up in the City. . . .

6. . . . My husband and Son Henry went into the river this morning a cool diping. said they felt better for it. . . .

11. . . . Hannah, WD. and self, in our Chaise, HSD. on horse back, we went to Isaac Barnss between 2 and 3 miles from hence, where we were entertain'd with the sight of several curiosities which he brought from Santacruce, particularly two little stone Images about as big as a mans Thumb, curiously

wrought., strang uncouth figurs, they were found in diging up the earth, and must have been there time out of mind—they are in form like the pictures I have seen of some of the heathen gods setting on their legs with their hands on their breasts. . . . We return'd home after sun-set—riding tries my back, makes my mouth dry and I feel weak after it—I cannot get over the fear of riding.

12. . . . HSD. brought a letter from his father: They have at last concluded to sett off for this place tomorrow, 'tis with great reluctance they leave home, on many accounts—patience and resignation, if to be acquired, are desireable favours.

26. . . . I have done more sewing since I came here than for a long time, in the same space; Molly, also, being very industrious is busyed in that way—'tis what what I much love making up new cloaths.

[Oct.] 12. . . . WD. and self took a walk before dinner—to the Bordington road upwards of a mile from home—I did not know that I could walk upwards of two miles without resting, and be so little tired. . . .

25. . . . We bid adieu to Henry, Hannah &c—and set off after 10 o'clock . . . We arrived at our habitation about 4 o'clock: found all things, as far as we have yet discover'd, in proper order. . . . The report of this day is, that there has not been any admissions or deaths at the Hospital in all the last twenty four hours.

[Nov.] 10. . . . John Adams President of the united states return'd from a visit to his Native place Boston about 3 o'clock, went by our door, attended by the light horse and a few others, 'tho I am not for parade of any sort, in the general way, yet on this occasion, every thing considered I should have been pleased to have seen a little more of it.[32]. . .

26. . . . Nancy Skyrin and her 2 daughters came after dinner, she intended to have gone to meeting, but Eleanor would not permitt her leave without much noise, and crying, she would not have giving into her humor, but as she was yesterday innoculated for the small pox she stay'd with her—Dr. Kuhn innoculated her, she is two years and two months old. . . .

30. . . . HD. and seven others went this forenoon to wait on Congress, with a

32. Adams, returning from his native Braintree, Mass., was greeted by a small military parade of about ninety soldiers. Customarily, much larger parades greeted presidents, but the newspapers had condemned Adams for leaving the city in August during the yellow fever epidemic, accusing him of "reveling and feasting in Boston and New York while our unhappy city was the prey of disease and death" (Scharf and Westcott, *Philadelphia*, 1:491).

petition for the poor blacks.[33] Our society has done much in this business with good effect—but not so much as could have been desired.

[Dec.] 7. . . . Saml Rhoads here this evening Molly, he says, has the tooth-ach, 'tis rare, but something, ailes some of them—WD. out this morning and Afternoon—he removed his lodging last night from the Yellow-room to the front S. East chamber, Peter in the room with him. Eliza and Mary Downing called after School—they have began schooling to day with Mrs. Price.

13. . . . WD. brulez son —— cett matin,[34] he took a walk out this morning so that it cant be very bad. . . .

27. . . . WDs burn is, I hope healing, he has been long confined.

33. The petition, presented by Rep. Albert Gallatin, requested cessation of the slave trade and reminded Congress of Quaker-manumitted slaves who were being reenslaved under North Carolina law (*Annals of Congress*, 5th Cong., 1st and 2d sess., 656–70, 945–46, 1032–33).
34. Burned his —— this morning.

1798

1798. Janry. 1st. . . . I never heard of so many Bankrupts and imprison-
ments, of those who call themselves Gentlemen[1]—What times are these?—bad
indeed.—Sister Rhoads moved the end of last week from Arch Street to
Spruce Street, in the house formerly Hannah Rhoadss much nearer to her
Son, which will suit her much better.

5. . . . Thos. Parke junr. brought a letter from our Son Henry, to Brother
James Smith, informing of the Death of his little Son Henry, who died on the
fourth day night. the 3d. instant and is to be buried this day, at the falls
meeting burying ground. Aged six months wanting 12 days. this account was a
shock to me, having understood that the dear infant was getting Stronger and
more healthy. My Son has his troubles! and who are without? that are of a
susceptiable nature—A Negro Man named Richd. Stevens came here forenoon: sent by Warner Mifflin to go to our Son at North Bank. . . .

6. Jacob set off forenoon, with the Negro Man, or lad, for North bank—HD.
wrote to our Son, a long letter. . . .

7. First Day: . . . Jacob return'd to dinner, brought a letter from Henry, he
says therein that their baby was taken with a lax which soon carried it off. . . .

10. . . . Nancy Skyrin and her Daughters came after dinner brought a little
book with 64. little stories, for the Children with a picture to each story, of
her writing and drawing. . . .

Janry. 14. First day: . . . S. Dawson went to her fathers,—were they what
they should be, she might go oftener than she does.

1. Economic hardships caused by English and French disruption of American shipping hit
Philadelphia mercantile firms heavily in 1797–98. Leading merchants found that their cargoes
were often tied up in port while creditors demanded payment. More than 150 Philadelphia
firms were ruined or financially crippled by the hard times, and such prestigious figures as
John Swanwick and Robert Morris had already gone bankrupt. Morris and several others were
also overextended because of land speculation (R. G. Miller, *Federalist City*, 93; Roland M.
Baumann, "John Swanwick: Spokesman for 'Merchant Republicanism' in Philadelphia, 1790–
1798," *PMHB* 97 (1973): 178–80; Oberholtzer, *Robert Morris*, 335–49; Allen C. Clark,
Greenleaf and Law in the Federal City [Washington, D.C.: W. F. Roberts, 1901], 170).

29. . . . Our Jacob and Sarah, with some other black gentry were out this evening with our horses and Sleigh, a fine clear evening many suffering horses.

[Feb.] 14. When I had been about an hour in bed last night, at ¼ past 12. fire was cryed—I arose and dress'd myself—went into WDs Chamber—could see no light—up or down town—was thoughtfull of my Children, Sally and Nancy is so near us that I knew it was not there—and William says there was 8000 chances against it being at Mollys. . . .

15. Sally Dawson came into my chamber at 8 o'clock, when I was about getting up, she informed me that Sammy Rhoads was down stairs, come to let me know that Molly had been ill all night, and wish'd to see me—I knew she must be ill, or she would not have sent for me, knowing how bad it is under foot for walking, and my unwillingness to riding—I went as soon as possiable with Sammy in our Sleigh, found my poor Child in bed, she was taken last night between 8 and 9 o'clock with a sick stomach and faintiness, which after fell on her bowels . . . Sammy went for Docr. Kuhn who soon attended, he said she had some fever, and it was absolutely necessary to check her present disorder, he ordered An Ounce of Gum-Arabec in a quart of flaxseed tea, to be given frequently in the coarse of the day—in small quantities. Sago and baum tea also at intervals—all which I prepared.[2] . . .

16. I arose at 8. Molly at 9. said she was free from pain, but felt sore, she is very carefull of her diet. . . .

19. . . . Read The Fille De Chambre A Novel. By Mrs. Rowson, of the New Theater Philadla.[3] An Actress and an Authoress.

21st. . . . Electionering going forward, at a great rate, violent party work—Benn. R. Morgan and Isreal Isreal candidates for Senators, tomorrow the day: I wish there may be no mobing.[4] . . .

2. Gum arabic, from the Egyptian acacia tree, and boiled flaxseed, both strong mucilages, were sometimes prescribed in situations where the "natural mucus of the intestines was abraded" and often used in combination with other ingredients. Sago, considered nutritious, came from the trunk of palm trees and cycads; Indians often beat it with water to make cakes, bread, and pudding. Balm was thought helpful for disorders of the stomach, head, and uterus; strong infusions were drunk to help "a weak, lax state of the viscera" (W. Lewis, *New Dispensatory*, 150, 170, 176, 216).

3. Susannah Haswell Rowson, *The Fille de Chambre, A Novel* (Philadelphia: H. & P. Rice, 1794 [Evans, *Am. Bibliography*]).

4. A special election would be held the next day for the state senate seat from Philadelphia. In the regularly scheduled election in 1797 the Democratic-Republican candidate, Israel Israel, had narrowly defeated Benjamin Morgan, the Federalist candidate; the Federalists charged that unqualified voters had participated, giving Israel the victory. The state assembly voided the result, and both parties began electioneering for the special election, the intensity of which created fears of riots (R. G. Miller, *Federalist City*, 95–102; *Gazette of the United States*, Feb. 19, 20, 1798).

23. . . . Robt. Hartshorn came over to inform us that Ben Morgans ticket had got the better of Isreal Isreals, by between 3⁵ or 400, I do not feel so much delighted by this party getting the better, as I should have felt depress'd had the other side gained the victory. . . .

Febry. 24. . . . William Fisher called to enquire for a kitten: Our Cats progeny are much in demand whether it is her real merit, or the value her mistress sits on her, that gives her such consequence I cant say. . . .

26. . . . Sent Jacob with the Carriage for Molly, she has not been here for many weeks. she came, Sally Downing with Eliza and little Henry were also here, and Caty with the little one, so that we had 5 of our grand children here, as HD. brought E. Skyrin. . . .

[Mar.] 8. . . . I made Tar water[6] to day for Nancy.

9. . . . John Watson and my husband has purchased or agree'd to purchase, 600 and odd acres of land of James Logan, the writings were sign'd and delivered this evening—The land is in Bucks County,—John Watson and HSD. are to have it between them, they intend to sell it out in parts, to pay JL—and devide the profits.

13. . . . After tireing my eyes, cutting out Shirts and drawing threads—I took up and read, The Address to the Inhabitants of Pennsylvania[7] by our Friends and others who were then prisoners in the Masons Lodge, 20 years ago. It revived old feelings. . . .

22d. . . . Nancy Skyrin called, she is going to look at Ed. Stiless house in our Neighbourhood, where John Fry lived—I expect they will take it, and shall be pleased to have my daughter so near us. . . .

23. . . . A Negro girl and Boy arrived here this Morning from below, sent by Warner Mifflin, the girl is to be purchased for Nancy Skyrin, her name Henny, she says she has no second name. aged twelve years. 6 days before Christmass, her own father is gone off, but she has a step father who lives with

5. The word "and" crossed out.
6. A combination of tar and water allowed to settle and carefully decanted. It was especially recommended for lung ailments after Bishop George Berkeley popularized its medicinal use in 1744 (C. K. Drinker, *Not So Long Ago*, 78).
7. Israel Pemberton et al., *An Address to the Inhabitants of Pennsylvania, By Those Freemen, of the City of Philadelphia, Who Are Now Confined in the Mason's Lodge, By the Virtue of a General Warrant, Signed in Council by the Vice President of the Council of Pennsylvania* (Philadelphia: Robert Bell, 1777 [Evans, *Am. Bibliography*]).

her mother, this is her account.—The boy named Samson Smith, has no parents, about 7 or 8. by his appearance. . . .

27. . . . Nancy Skyrin was here several times this day, they are getting the house cleaned—in our Neighbourhood, expecting to move some time in next week—Sallys four Children, and Nancys two were here this Afternoon. . . .

30 . . . WD. received a letter from his Brother, which tells us that dear little William has burnt his hands with a hot warming-pan, that one has the worst burn that he ever saw, extending over the whole palm of his hand and fingers—but he appears not to mind it: poor child! tis pity where there is but one, it cant be taken[8] better care of. . . .

[Apr.] 5. . . . A well duped Woman of the Name of Mary Scott, with a little tidy girl between 2 and 3 years old, and a little boy of 7 months in her arms, came to desire I would take her Child 'till she was 18 years of age, that she might go out to service with her other Child—I told her I had several grand Children and was in years myself, it did not suit me to take so young a Child. . . .

9. . . . I went, for the first time, to our Neighbour Skyrins, found Nancy very busy, the House is handsom, and in most respects convenient: brought the Children home with me—as I saw they were much in the way. . . .

10. . . . Sister and self went to meeting this morning I have been, but one before, to morning meeting in this City for 5 years past. . . . I have done wonders to day—been to meeting, and took so long a walk—I ought to be humbly thankfull that it is in my power, as it is far from what I had any reason to expect some years ago; 'tho infirmity is still with me. . . .

19. . . . We have lost our Neighbour Waln, she died this forenoon between nine and ten o'clock. . . . I went over and stay'd with the afflected children 'till their other friends and relations arrived—Molly Humphriss who lays her out, was also come, I then came away before that awful bussiness commenced. We have lost in R.W. an old friend and acquaintance with whom we have spent many agreeable hours. . . .

20. . . . Sally Downing spent this Afternoon here, I assisted her to cut out a piece of linnen, in Shirts for Jacob. . . .

21. . . . I went over to the house of mourning to take the last look at my old friend—We prepared two Rooms for Company at the funeral. . . . This has

8. Word crossed out.

appeard to me one of the longest days I have known, I cant, altogether account for it—being spent in a different manner, than costomarry, perhaps.

23. . . . Nancy sent for me this evening Elizabeth being unwell, found her in a fever rather high, with a sick stomach—made baum tea and barly-water— put her to bed a little better as I thought. . . .

27. . . . M. Rhoads came here after dinner, she went with me to Saml. Shoemakers up market street, she left me there and went next door to Saml Pleasants,—M. Pleasants abroad—she came back to SSs to me—where we spent the Afternoon with my old Acquaintances, Becky Shoemaker and Bulah Burge. . . .

[May] 3. . . . Richard Hartshorn and Caty Hains were married this forenoon at the Middle meeting—she is his third wife.

4. . . . 41. years this day since HDs first marriage.[9]

10. . . . Betty Newton came to fitt Sister for a gown, she is one of the most talkitive women that I know, and no scandle to say so. . . .

May 12. . . . Sally Downing came after dinner to finish cutting out Shifts for Mary—she has 30 shirts and Shifts, now ready to work on. . . .

May: 15. . . . John Collins came this evening I thought he had something on his mind to communicate to HD. therefore left them together—it seems, he inclines to be taken as a member amongst friends—I hope he is sober and well inclined. . . .

16. . . . Patience brought Eliza Skyrin here after School, she is to stay with me till her mothers return. . . .

17. . . . I sent my little bedfellow to school with two young girls that called for her. . . . WD. out this evening black visitors in the kitchen as usual.

21. . . . Sally Downing is sending part of their furniture to be left with us, dureing their residence in the Country, as they intend giving up the house that they now occupy, and where they have dwelt for Eight years, at their departure, intending to move into their New house in fourth street, which they

9. Henry Drinker's first wife was ED's friend Ann Swett. ED had been a witness to their marriage on May 4, 1757. Ann died at age 22 on May 23, 1758 (Drinker-Sandwith Papers, HSP).

expect will be compleatly finished and ready for them on their return from the country in the fall. . . .

22. . . . Elizabeth something—came to slack her lime, she is to whitewash here tomorrow—a very nice hand at the business, but very cross and huffy, as we are told. . . .

24. . . . Molly Rhoads was here before dinner, she is bravely. an attempt was made to break into their kitchen window, on first day night last—several Hogsheads and barrels lay before the door of their tenent who lives under their kitchen and keeps a grociers Shop—about 2 in the morning their Neighbour Latimers Man heard a noise and got up, to the window, saw a man mounted on the barrels, which he had put on a Hogshead, and was trying to open SRs kitchen window, he called to him to know what he was about, he then jumpt off and run away. . . .

29. . . . Susan and Becky Hartshorn came over, sent by their mother to inform me that Nancy Morgan was brought to bed last night of another Son, she has now 4 Sons and 2 daughters—In all her former confindments she experienced the anxious care of a good and kind mother, which now she will feel the loss of.[10]—little Henry Downing is sent here to spend the day, with us, as they are very busy moveing—he is a troublesome bargin. . . .

June 1st. . . . I went over, this forenoon to Charles Pleasants, they are moving to market street—Our Neighbourhood will appear deserted, Pratts are gone out of town—Neighbour Waln gone forever! Hartshorn are going into the country—If our City is favoured with health we shall remain at home I expect.

4. . . . A Skyrin here fore-noon assisting me to make Gingerbread. . . .

15. . . . a woman of the name of Lloyd was here yesterday to enquire the Charecture of Betsy Dawson our Sallys Sister, I was sorry I could not give her a good one; poor thoughtless young creature, she is now left to herself, with few, or none to care for her. . . .

20. . . . Anna Webb came this morning to sew for me. . . .

23. . . . I gave Jacob 3 Dollars last night, to buy meat this morning in market, he brought one home this morning which he said he could not pass, as it was lead—it look'd like lead indeed was lighter and thinner than a good

10. Nancy Waln Morgan was the daughter of Rebecca Coffin Waln, who had died April 19, 1798.

one[11]—I am realy afraid he did not get it from me, 'tho I am loath to suspect him. . . .

30. . . . My husband, Nancy Skyrin and little Elizabeth sett off in our Carriage between 12 and one for Downingtown, Jacob Downing went with Billy Sansom to same place—I expect they will return next second day—WD. MS. and self dined little Eleanor Skyrin with us, she is to stay here 'till the return of her Mother—Anna Webb told us to day of a young Man named Mark Miller, who lays dangerously ill of a billious fever, and black vomitting—Peter Widdows confirmed it—Eleanor Skyrin voided a worm this Afternoon the first. All Children, tis thought, have more or less of them. . . .

July 1st. . . . Molly says that Hetty Smith informed her, that Hannah S.D. expected to lay-in, in September next: quick-work. . . .

2d. . . . Sally Dawson empty'd the port wine decanter into a tumbler, perhaps a large wine glass and a half—with design to wash and fill the decanter, to give little Eleanor some with water, as her bowels are disorder'd, she took up the tumbler and drank all off that was in it thinking it was prepared for her, and being very dry had ask'd several times for drink, she soon after fell asleep, and when she awak'd seemed heavy, but got over it much sooner than I expected she could. . . .

July 3d. . . . Read, The Age of Reason, Unreasonable: or the Folly of Rejecting Revealed Religion. In a Series of Letters to a Friend, By G. W. Snyder, AM.[12] In answer to Tom Paine.—Much may be said in answer to his blasphemies, but the misfortune is, that all who read his poisoned discourses, do not take the pains to look for the antidote. . . .

4. . . . Annaversary of Independence, much fuss to day, the light horse and Vollentears are to pearade, and to have a dinner—My Daughter Ann, like many other Simpletons are gone to look, I expect many will be taken sick, overheated &c. . . .

5. . . . Nancy Skyrin was so unwell this forenoon, with a giddy head &c. that she sent for the bleeder and had 8 or 10 ounces blood taken. . . . I went this evening to Nancys to look at her blood, 'tis not good, nor very bad according to my idea. . . .

11. As a result of the Coinage Act of 1792, dollar coins issued by the U.S. mint in the 1790s were 89.24 percent fine silver and 10.76 percent copper (Mort Reed, *Cowles Complete Encyclopedia of U.S. Coins* [New York: Cowles Book Co., 1969], 17, 19, 182–84).

12. G. W. Snyder, *The Age of Reason Unreasonable* . . . (Philadelphia: William Cobbett, 1798 [Evans, *Am. Bibliography*]).

7. . . . S. Emlen here Afternoon, his finger sore, I dres't it. . . .

18. . . . HD. gone down to Sammy Rhoadss this evening he tells me that Molly has been blooded this forenoon by the advice of the Doctor and seems better, he did not ask what Doctor. I hope 'twas Shippen as he is to offici-ate.—It is very extrodinary I was not sent for. . . .

19. . . . I went down to visit Molly, found her at work, 'tho not a little indisposed, she had taken 25 drops Ladanum last night, says she is rather better, but still in a critical way, a great agitation at times continues, she bares up wonderfully, as is common with her. . . .

20. . . . Our Neighbour Henry Pratt, is pulling down and demolishing great part of the Old respectable House next door, that poarch where I have spent many hours of moon light night, enclosed and built back as it was, made it agreeable—Sister and self lived near four years, when girls, with Anna Warner;[13] boarded with her, she was then the Owner of it—it is to be renovated, enlarged, and beautified, as our Neighr. Pratt intends.—but in my view, it was better as it was,—had he sold that, and built another else where in the Modern stile or tast, 'twould have been more consistent—but every one knows their own business best, or ought to do—for my part, I am, and always was, attached to old fashons, and old things, which is no reason others should be so. . . .

24. . . . Molly is not as well as yesterday, she has taken pills composed of Assafatida[14] and Opium, which I had advised against, as the Doctor has not seen her, Sister Rhoads undertook to inform him how she was, and I expect she told him she was hystiracal, which is not the case, she has been a little uneasy at her situation, and no wonder, all things consider'd, but by no means so as to amount to what is called low-spirits, having always been favour'd with a good degree of Fortitude—Sally Rhoads had procribed Assifatida, I dis-proved it, as it is of a forceing nature, and Molly in a ticklish situation, and the Doctor has not seen her. . . .

28th. Clear and very hot wind S.W—we lay last night with our door and one window open, an unusal thing with us, after one o'clock I had not sleep'd, arose and shut the window. . . .

13. The word "who" crossed out.
14. The gum resin of *Ferula asafetida,* a plant native to Asia Minor. Because it was used as an emmenagogue as well as an antispasmodic, ED advised against its prescription to her pregnant daughter (Estes, "Therapeutic Practice," 369, 365; *The Merck Index,* 5th ed. [Rahway, N.J.: Merck & Co., 1940], 58; W. Lewis, *New Dispensatory,* 568, 95; Bard, *Compendium of Midwifery,* 227).

29. . . . HD. went under the Shower bath this morning for the first time, he and MS. went to meeting—I stay'd at home alone, took a large dose Castor Oyl, which makes me shake to think on. . . . Nancy Skyrin went this evening under the Shower bath, talks of repeating it. . . .

31st. . . . we have heard several accounts within these few days of deaths, said to be the billious fever. . . . Nancy pulled the string of the Shower bath again this evening she seems better reconsiled to it—the water has stood some hours in the Yard, which alters the property much, she goes under the bath in a single gown and an Oylcloath cap. . . .

[Aug.] 3d. . . . William took a walk this evening—he went this forenoon into the bath in Race Street—keeped by a french Man.[15]

6. . . . Hannah Evans called, it is said, and I fear with some reason, that the fever has spread in Water Street, between Walnut and Spruse—that many Stores are shut up. . . .

Augt 7. . . . sent Jacob for Molly, Sammy came with her, he left her here, and went directly to Germantown to look for a place to retire too, as there is a great alarm down town on account of the fever. . . . Nurse Cross called after dinner—she and Molly have settled matters as well as they can . . . Jacob is desireous, if we should leave home that we would come to Downingtown, where we might be well accomodated, and where I should like to go, if it was not on Mollys account—to go so far from her would not suit at this time—Our little Samson Smith went this[16] evening to Jacob Clarksons to whom he is to be bound—We having no employ[t] for him, as we have two young ones, beside two other Servants, which we find enough. . . .

8. . . . Sally Dawson gone to assist Molly in packing up her necessary garments to take to Germantown. . . . The disorder, I fear, increases rapidly, and is in many different parts of the City, and can be traced from several

15. Bathhouses came to Philadelphia in the 1790s with the arrival of French refugees in the city. In 1795 a M. Glaise installed seven bathtubs of sheet iron in his home at 120 S. Front Street and charged admission fees based on frequency of use. His establishment was popular with the French community. ED is probably referring to the bathhouse run by Jean Baptiste Massie, or Massieu, at 119 Race Street, in an area where many French refugees resided. In January 1801, after the municipal water system was turned on, another French émigré, Joseph Simon, opened a public bathhouse near Third and Arch streets where patrons could bathe in permanently fixed bathtubs equipped with running water. Simon ran his establishment for over twenty years; his customers included William and Henry Drinker (see above, July 20, 1797; Moreau de Saint-Méry, *Journey*, 324; *Philadelphia City Directory, 1798;* Ritter, *Moravian Church*, 259; Harold Donaldson Eberlein, "When Society Took a Bath," *PMHB* 67 (1943): 43).

16. The word "morning" crossed out.

different vessels that are infected—'tis a gloomy aweful season: I wish my husband could see it his place to go out of town. . . .

11. . . . Jacob Downing came here after dinner, he is very importunate for us to go to Downingtown, where he intends to go tomorrow morning early, I cannot think of going there at present, by myself, and leaving my family and my poor dear Molly in her present situation—My husband seems to desire I would, but is not explicet, I am always at a loss how to act, but hope I shall be directed for the best. . . .

14. . . . The Post office is removed[17]—The Library shut up—Many of our Neighbours round us are removed, things look sad. . . . HD. as usual writing in the Office, he is one of the greatest Slaves in Philadela.

15. . . . Our black Sarah told me this morning that she heard a man straining hard to vomitt in the Malatos chamber next door and that she had smelt sugar burning several times yesterday and to day—that a poor sick man boarded there—upon enquiring of Benn. Airs who lives in the house, we understood that it was a man who has a very hard cough but is no other way disorder'd, what the burnt sugar ment we know not, as they are not very nice or cleanly. . . . I think that, all who can afford to leave the City, would do well so to do, unless they stay as a duty to attend on the sick or to assist those that cannot go—by many going, those who stay behind stand a better chance. The number of flies increase, maybe for the best. . . .

16. . . . most of our Neighbours have gone, or are going, the Huxters & poorer sort of people excepted—We are still here, 'tho we have had importunate invitations from HSD. and JD—of sending each a Waggon and Man to take anything away that we would wish to send—Lord grant we may be rightly directed!—could I find in my heart to leave my poor Molly, I would go to Sally in the Valley, in hopes that HD. would follow. . . .

19. . . . John Skyrin in the Chaise, my poor Nancy, her 2 Children and two black girls in the Carriage, after breakfasting here, sett off for Downingtown. . . . it seems to me, my husband is turning his mind to leave the City.

20. . . . HD. has wrote to our Son Henry to send his waggon down to morrow—for such things as will be proper to send away, so that we are preparing for a solemn movement and seperation. . . .

17. During yellow fever epidemics the post office moved to locations beyond the more congested section of the city. On Aug. 13 it relocated from 34 South Front Street to Market Street, west of Eleventh Street (*Philadelphia City Directory, 1798*, 61; Scharf and Westcott, *Philadelphia*, 3:1810; *Porcupine's Gazette*, Aug. 11, 1798).

21. ... 45 admitted in the last 24 hours into the Hospital, a great increase. . . .

Augt. 22. ... Henrys Man and Waggon went away after breakfast loaded— My two dear Sons left us about 11 o'clock, Henry in his Chair, William in our Chaise with the old Mare, who is a little lame, A Chest of valuable papers, and a trunk of Plate is to be sent to the Bank of the United States, in third street, and also a trunk of valuable Cloathing[18]—the dread and apparent danger increases. . . . we have engaged Ben Oliver to take us this Afternoon to Germantown—my husband intends to go in our waggon to North-bank, Jacob and Peter with him. Sarah Needham our black girl is going to Burlington where she will continue till we may be likely to want her—We strip't our trees of all the fruit, and gave it away, the grapes excepted, great quantities are hanging on the vines, those that are near ripe we take with us—shut up the House between 4 and 5 o'clock and sett off—as we proposed—parted where the roads seperates, HD. &c towards North bank—Sister, Sall Dawson and self to Germantown where we arrived in due time. . . . After spending the evening at SRs we retired to the lodging room we have taken, at the Widdow Bensels. . . .

24. ... My husband came here from North bank towards evening he left all there well, it was pleasing to see him, spent the evening at S.Rs some who were ill in the City are better, HD. lodged with me at the Widdow Bensels, Sister at S. Rhoads. cool day, cloudy evening lightening.

25. ... I have been painfully disorderd with my old weakness for two[19] days past. . . . my situation at present, 'tho I never through favour, was dependant on any one, seems rather disagreeable to me, but for my Childs sake, I can let down, or lower my pride, 'twould be a pity, if at this time of life, it was not in my power. . . .

28. ... Richd. Allen a black man of consequence advertise's that he wishes those of the Citizens who have left Dogs and Cats shut up in their houses to starve, would employ some friend to let them out, as they disturb the Neighbours by their howlings &c. . . .

31. ... Thos. Fisher called forenoon, he related several distressing cases, and says that a person from the City told him, that it look'd awful and distressing a forsaken place or nearly so. . . .

18. Construction of a new vault in 1792 allowed persons to deposit trunks of valuables in the Bank of the United States (Bank of North America Papers, Vault Deposit Ledgers, vol. 1, HSP).
19. The words "or three" crossed out.

Sept. 3. . . . Molly was taken this evening in pain and great wail, she was too unwell to leave, we lodged there, as S. Rhoads is not yet return'd, she became more easy after some time, and I trust will keep up till the right time—I had before bed time asked M. Bensels Nurse who is still with her, if my Child should be suddenly taken in the night, if she would be with us, and dress the Child, as her nurse is some miles off, she readily consented.

6. . . . were I in tolerable health, I could accommodate myself better to occurances as they pass—but the want of that greatest of earthly blessings makes those things hard that otherwise would not be so much so could I ride about the Country like some women, I could do better being separated from my Children, some in one part of the country, and some in another, makes my difficulty, and Mollys present situation: The bodily infirmity which I labour under prevents my traveling, or I would strive to get over cowardice. . . .

Sepr. 8. . . . WD. not as well as when at North bank, Chilley and unwell, he is like the rest of us, out of his element, my husband excepted, who is always at home, and never at home.

10. . . . The Moon changed at two this morning and my daughter is quite as well as common, so that I shall endeavour to leave her with my mind as calm and serene as may be,—after breakfast pack'd up our matters and prepared to set off—bid farewel to our old Roomlady Bensel, and the Doctors family—it appears as tho I intend to return, but that I do not expect to do till our return to the City, if favour'd ever to arrive there—My Sister stays in Germantown, 'till after Mollys trial, which takes a burden off my mind. . . . Arrived at North-bank about 5 o'clock. . . .

16. . . . A Comparative Table of Deaths in Cobbetts paper of the 14th. instant From the 8th. Augt. to the 31. in 93 there were 264. deaths, from the same to the same in 98 621.—From the first to the 14 Sepr. in 93. there was 375 deaths. from the same to the same in 98. 858 deaths."—In Octor. 93. were the most deaths of any other time. . . .

17. . . . I trust my husband will not go into the City, if he does, 'tis very few he will meet with there, and probably run the risk of his life. . . . The mixing families and Servants is a trying thing to many at this time, where a proper disposs[t]ion does not prevail, it makes easy things hard.

18. . . . HD. left us between nine and ten for Burlington &c. . . .

20. . . . finished working a Queen-stitch[20] Matt work'd the fellow five years

20. Queen's stitch, an elaborate and complex needlework stitch, reached the height of its popularity between 1780 and 1810. Because of the intricacy of the needlework and the cost of the silk yarn generally used, queen's stitch was usually reserved for small items such as pincushions and purses (Swan, *Plain & Fancy*, 91, 98–99, 151–62, 231).

ago at George Hessers, as I set on the bed with a lame foot.—being from home & not employ'd in the usual way, I have amused myself in that way, having always loved work of that kind. . . .

22. . . . what a world of trouble is this: May we be fitted for a better, when it shall please the Lord to call us hence—public and private Calamities, the lott of human Nature, can be made easy by nothing but a dependance on, and risignation to the divine Will! . . .

24. . . . how often have I suffer'd Labour pains in my mind for my daughter, and it is all to do yet. . . .

25. . . . No husband this evening. . . . if there was no change in Molly, he wrote, it was his intintion to be here this evening poor Child, she may at this instant be in extremity, or it may be over, or not arrived—'tis much easier to be on the spot with any one we are anxious for, than in suspence at a distance. . . .

26. . . . My husband came before tea, after 8 days absence. . . .

29. . . . Our Son Henry sett off . . . for James Smiths. . . .

30. . . . continued suspence on account of Molly.

Octor. 2d. . . . an afflicting account of a bad hurt my poor dear Sally has received She went out accompany'd by Sammy and Jane Downing, in search of grapes, and was by the breaking of the Saddle girth thrown off one of the Coach horses, and received a very severe bruse on her Arm near the Elbow. . . .

3. . . . we talk of setting off tomorrow morning for Germantown, and next day to Downingtown. . . . Henry return'd home this evening I was afraid to see him! his accounts were that Sallys right Arm is miserably brused, and swelled as large as two Arms, her hand also swell'd and on a pillow, they told him it was vastly mended—which if he had not found her in very good spirits, he could hardly have thought the case: it looked so bad. . . .

Octor. 4. . . . got to Germantown about 4 o'clock. Molly appears bravely, Sister and all there well. . . .

5. . . . after H.D. had settled what he had to do in Germantown as well as he could, we sett off for Downings . . . came to Jacob Downings just at Candle light . . . Sally in very good Spirits, glad to see us. she was at Richd. Downings when we came, her fingers are black and green, and her fore-arm

---

likewise, the Swelling much gone down, but she cannot raise her Arm yet; there is a hard lump near the Elbow, which I dont understand. . . .

6. . . . We have heard of several deaths of those I do not personaly know, but upon the whole they deminish—40 odd in 24 hours, and but few new cases compared to what has been. . . .

7. First Day: rain this forenoon wind with it. it may bring about my poor Mollys storm, it is high time. . . .

8. . . . it is 10 months tomorrow or next day, the 10. Decemr. last since Molly—I am very uneasy on her account. . . .

9. . . . Dr. Todd called this morning before Sally came down, he continues to say, that her Arm will be as it should be, and by her renew'd desire to Gossip I am led to hope it is getting better. . . .

10. . . . HD. gone to school with his Granddaughters, beyond Hunt Downings, to Jonathan Mendenhall who is the master. . . . My Child is at last deliverd, on second day last—about two o'clock Nancy thinks, but dont appear to know much about it, she was not there at the time, she tells us that Dr. Shippen was sent for in the night, but nothing could be done, the reason why, I am not inform'd off, she is said to be bravely, the Child also—which is a girl,—a ten months Child. . . .

11. . . . Deaths in the City, by last Mail only 14 in twenty four hours, the new cases much lessen'd, my husband, Jacob, Sally, Nancy the Children and myself, dined comfortably together, they went out after dinner to catch fish, a mess of fish with tea, by way of supper. . . .

Octor. 16. . . . went after breakfast with Sally to take a ride, she has no use of her right Arm yet wish'd to take two or three Children with us, which I opposed, rather chosing to stay at home than go in any ways—we went near three miles out, Sally all the way endeavouring to convince me, there was no danger in rideing, but to little or no effect, we view things in a different point of light—Sally is her fathers own Child; Ann and William belong to me— Henry and Molly to us both, but reather incline to my side. . . .

Octor. 21. First day: . . . Sally in trouble on account of her Arm, she has descover'd since the Swelling is gone down, that the bone is not right, I think so too—She wishes to go to Germantown to consult Docr. Shippen, but as Jacob Downing is not here to go with her, and sucking Child to be taken, I find myself unequal to the undertaking. my situation, and my Sons at a distance.—I know not what to do, or how to advise. . . .

22. . . . My poor Sally had a very poor night, I did not sleep, I believe an hour, got up before Sun rise to endeavor to preswade Sally to send the Carriage for Dr. Shippen, and not to go to Germantown herself—but she had made up her mind to go, and had discover'd in the night that her Elbow was out of the socket or right place, which by its appearance is the case, 'tho not very far, it is 4 weeks tomorrow since the accident—She, John Skyrin, Caty and the Child, sett off at quarter past 9. o'clock, the latter part of the journey will be the worst, they should have sett off 2 hours sooner, but when servants do as they please, Masters and Mistresss must do as they can—Nancy or myself, should have gone with her, but here is five Children to look after and Caty gone—and I am not well enough for such an undertaking, the Carriage crouded, Germantown crouded, and the opperation if done, to be dreaded. . . . JD. lodged with my husband on fifth day night at Js. Smiths, he told him that WD. was quite well, pleasing intelligence.—a mixture of good with the bad, makes the pill of life go down. . . .

24. . . . Jacob and Sally return'd this evening Nothing done to her Arm: Dr. Shippen examined it, he said it had been too long out of joint to venture to reduce it. it should have been done at first. . . .

Novr. 1st. . . . My husband and myself on a average, are a couple of active, venterous, useful members of society:—Thos. Cope called, he has been to the City, says that Dr. Rush and other Physicians say, it is quite safe for the Citizens to return home. . . .

2d. . . . I received a letter dated last evening in Philada. from my husband, he was at Danl. Drinkers, intends writing to Sister to return with WD. and our Servants as soon as convenient—and wishes me to do the same as soon as may be. . . .

3d. . . . JD. received a letter from My husband, who says he has open'd our house, and has a fire made in the office and sent for Alice to clean house, which I had rather he had omitted, as he says she is scrubing it. . . .

5. busy getting ready for home. . . . Arrived at home between four and 5.— Sister and William had been in about an hour before us.—they left all well at HSDs—Hannah brought to bed on fifth day last Novr. 1. of a Daughter whom she calls Esther after her grand Mother Smith—a fine hearty Child. . . . Sammy Rhoadss Tom called this evening to tell me they were come home and that his Mistress was not well, and would be glad to see me as soon as I could come tomorrow.

6. . . . My husband went this evening to Saml Rhoadss—Molly up stairs, her Nurse was called away before her month was up: she poor thing knows little

how to manage a Child, never having lived where one was born or tended since she was 7 years old; 'tho she has some times helpd her Sisters. . . .

Novr. 7. . . . William went out this evening he return'd about 8 o'clock and inform'd me that Molly Rhoads had a swelling in her breast, by a cold she has taken—I am too unwell to go down, having took medicine, and a bad cold in my head. I sent her a note advising her to send for Dr. Kuhn, as I was not qualified to advise her, she sent word back that Sammy was gone to Nurse Cross, and what she advised, she would do: had I known that she would not send for the Doctor I should have undertaken to advised something. . . .

Novr. 16. . . . Dr. Shippen called here to look at Sallys Elbow . . . poor girl! I fear she will never be able to bring her wrist near her face, but she can sew well, and feed herself awkwardly, can write &c. . . . Sister called to see Becky Thomson, and Molly Cresson, they have each lost a Child in the fever. . . .

19. . . . Eliza Downing went to school this morning with her Sister and Cousin to Reca. Price. . . .

25. First Day: . . . finish'd reading Letters written during a short Residence in Sweden, Norway, and Denmark By Mary Wollstoncraft.[21] A well informed I was going to say, but rather an highly informed woman—I dont like her, or her principles, 'tho amused by her writings. . . .

Novr. 28. . . . Sally Sherer formerly Brant with her little Son John 6 months old, was here this Afternoon. . . .

[Dec.] 8. . . . Hope Sharp, a young woman who formerly tended E. Skyrin, has gone out in marriage with one Warren, an Old Man that has been disowned, he is supposed to be worth something. Hope has been remarkably plain and precise. . . .

15. . . . Yesterday or the day before Racl. Green, sister to Sally Brant; came to ask for an order to bury her Mother in friends Ground. HD. not being at home, we could not give her an answer. A young man came afterwards and procured one—for Sarah Johnson our Sally Brants Mother, not a friend, but as they said she was desirous of being buried there, it was granted—some are desereous I believe to save expenses. . . .

Decr. 20. . . . We have agreed to take Eliza Downing, who has been with us ever since we return'd from the Country, to live with us this Winter—I trust it

---

21. Mary Wollstonecraft, *Letters Written during a Short Residence in Sweden, Norway, and Denmark* (London: J. Johnson, 1796 [*Brit. Mus. Cat.*]).

will be for the Childs good, having no other little ones to attend too—Saml Emlen called after dinner, having some secret communication, as usual, to HD. . . .

23.   First Day: . . . spent this Afternoon reading, as I generly do on a first day.

31.   . . . Jacob Downing begining to move to his new house,[22] the last day of the Year. . . . WD. bought a flying Squirel in market, brought it home to please the Children. put it in a very convenient wire Cage with three appartments, where it may be as comfortable as a little prisoner out of its element can be by proper attention, I should have been better pleased it had remain'd in the woods. . . .

22. Downing and his family moved to N. Fourth Street, next door to the Academy (the University of Pennsylvania). Previously they had lived at 32 Arch Street (*Philadelphia City Directory, 1798, 1799*).

1799

1799. Janry. 1st. third day. Cloudy, wind N.E—snow'd most of the forenoon. . . . I have for a few years past keep't a sort of a diary, but intend to
discontinue it and make this a memorandum book, but seeing a fine snow
falling this morning and being used to make observations on the weather,
began this first day of the year in my accustomed manner.[1]

3. . . . Sally Downing her two yongest Children Caty and the Servant [left]
Nancy this Afternoon and went in our Sleigh to [their new] habitation, Mary is
yet with her Aunt, [dear Eliza is to spend the winter with us—Nancy spent
the evening here—Jacob Turner and Sarah Needham,] Negro and Negriss went
to a Wedding this evening Jacob dress in a light cloath coat, white casamer
vest and britches, white silk Stockens and New ha[t,] Sarah, the brides Maid,
in white muslin, dizen'd of with white ribbons from head to foot, Yallow
Morocco Shoes with white bows, &c. They went in Benjn. Oliver's Coachee,
drove by his white Man—'tis now near 11 o'clock and they are not yet
returned They are both honest servants but times is much altred with the
black folk. . . .

7. . . . river fast, boys skaiting on it—our three oldest little girls din'd and
spent the day: they love to be here, and we dont like to affront them by
sending them away, they went[2] Sleighing this Afternoon with their Grandfather. . . .

11. . . . Jacob Downing called Nancy Skyrin brought in after dinner three
naked Dolls for me to assist in dressing.[3] . . .

1. In fact, ED continues to begin most entries with weather notations, generally omitted in
this edition.
2. The word "Slaying" crossed out.
3. During the colonial and early Federal periods, American children were likely to have
enjoyed dolls of European origin. Although some were made exclusively for children, others
were dressed as models to acquaint adult Americans with the latest European fashions, and
only later passed on to children. Philadelphia, however, was an early American doll manufacturing center, with extensive commercial production by the 1820s. Thus it is hard to say where
or for what purpose the dolls mentioned here were made, although the other references to
dolls in the diary suggest that they belonged to one of Nancy's two daughters, aged three and
six at the time (see above, Jan. 21, 1796, and below, Sept. 4, 1800; Monica Kiefer, *American
Children through Their Books, 1700–1835* [Philadelphia: University of Pennsylvania Press,
1948], 214, 217–18, 219; Alice Morse Earle, *Child Life in Colonial Days* [New York: Macmillan,
1899], 362–65; Max Von Boehn, *Dolls and Puppets,* trans. Josephine Nicoll [New York: Cooper
Square, 1966], 127–28, 134–53; James Mackay, *An Encyclopedia of Small Antiques* [New York:
Harper and Row, 1975] 82–84).

Janry. 12. . . . 'tho Eliza is happy in being with us, it is a kind of weaning, as she had more of her own way at home, and was not quite so regular, there being other young Children—we must make it as easy to her as is consistant with prudence. . . .

15. . . . Jacob and Sally, very unadvisedly, sent Dan this morning for Eliza to spend 2 or 3 days with Phebe Downing who is at their house: if she goes, 'twill be disagreeable to have her back, she is happy here, but when she sees any of their people she wishes herself at home, where she can do more as she pleases—and just now, when she is weaning, to knock up all that has been done is foolishness—Nancy Skyrin called—Caty Decon with the three Children and Phebe Downing called while we were at dinner. I had wrote a Note to Sally, but she was out, and had not received it—they informd Eliza that her father and mother had sent for her, instead of going to school she cry'd to go with them, and I Suffer'd her to go—poor little girl, 9 years old, and cannot read—I pity her—too much under the care of delegated Authority. . . .

[Feb.] 7. . . . I have not been abroad for upwards of two months, I think 'till this Afternoon, when I went to Sarah Fishers whom I have not seen since our return from the country—then went to Jacob Downings to their new dwelling, which I have not seen before, It is a commodious handsom house. . . .

Febry. 13. . . . Nancy Skyrin here with her Daughter Eleanor who she left under my protection while she went gossiping to Sallys. . . .

15. . . . Nancy Skyrin here after breakfast, she, Sally, their husbands and John [Hod]gson an Englishman who lodges at John Skyrins and Nancys Children are going this forenoon to Peels Museum—on some accounts I do not like it, there are some queer sights there.[4] . . .

23d. . . . Henry and William in the Office, engag'd with a Man, I belive from Bucky County, selling a tract land . . . Jacob Dg. called, he took his Daughter Eliza home with him to spend the Afternoon there . . . HD. gone to JDs he took Elizath. Skyrin with him. . . .

Febry. 28. . . . Elizabeth and Eleanor were left with us, according to custom, little dears, they are sometimes a little troublesom. . . .

[Mar.] 5. . . . five Men with two Carts &c. are about a dirty Jobb in our Yard

4. In January and February Charles Willson Peale was advertising the museum's powerful electrical machine, which was "prepared to exhibit some interesting experiments" that might prove useful in medical cases, along with his newly patented fireplaces (*Claypoole's American Daily Advertiser*, Jan. 9, Feb. 5, 1799; see Sellers, *Mr. Peale's Museum*, 99–101, and Peale, *Selected Papers*, 2:234).

to night, they are removing the offerings from the temple of Cloacina,[5] which have been 44 years depositing. . . .

March 7. . . . The jobb in our Yard is finish'd, except what the Carpenters are to do—It has been nothing to what we expected—I dreaded it before commencement, and am pleased 'tis over—they were at work two night, from between 8 and nine at night till between 4 & 5 in the morning and were very industrious, I believe, it is now sunk near 16 feet from the seat; upwards of 13 from the top of the well, a dreadfull gulph it looks like—they would have dug, had HD. premited them, nearer to the Antipodes then they have, for the sake of 3 dollars a foot, and good living during the night, for they not only eat at their business, but it appears, have a good appetite! wonderful! If liberty and equality which some talk much about, could take place, who would they get for those, and many other hard and disagreeable[6] undertakings. . . .

13. . . . Sammy Rhoads was here after dinner to inform me that their baby was very ill last night they were up with her almost all night. . . . It is painful to me, not to be able to go to them on those occasons, but I have been much at home, this wenter, and farr from well, it is 6 long squars to their house. . . .

21. . . . nobody in the parlor this forenoon, but several in the Office, dined by ourselves—some would call this a gloomy day—to me it has been measureably so, being much more than usually unwell—or all days are much alike to me, as I go but little abroad—and enjoy myself as much as I can at home. . . .

26. . . . James and Esther Smith, Hannah S. Drinker and A Skyrin and HSD spent the afternoon or rather evening with us, 'tis the fashon and has been for some years past, to come to late tea, and stay in the evening in former days, it was the custom to go visiting at 3 o'clock and return home early in the evening. . . .

27. . . . Our black Jacob Turner informed Sister this morning that he was to be married to our Sarah next week, we have had a hint of the kind before— We may loose a good Servant by it, but if it is for her benefit, I shall be satisfied. . . .

31. . . . Sarah Needham left us, and went to her Mothers this evening I do not expect to see her again 'till after she is married, as our Jacob Turner and she are to be join'd in the bonds of matrimony on next 5th. day, nothing

5. I.e., privy contents; ED's elaborate euphemism is a play on *cloaca*, or sewer (*OED*, s.v. "cloaca").
6. The word "jobbs" crossed out.

preventing—she promises to return the later end next week, to stay with us 'till after the Yearly meeting, then they go to room keeping.

[Apr.] 4. . . . Jacob Turner and Sarah Needham were, I expect, join'd in the bonds of matrimony this evening By Parson Absalom Jones, they talk of coming home next first day We offer'd to give them a weding supper, if they would have it here in a sober way, they were much obliged, but had taken a room at his brothers &c—a wedding without a frolick would be no weding, I believe, in their view. . . .

April 17. . . . JS. sent in to ask what was good for a bruise, as Eleanor had hurt her forehead, and her mother gone to meeting—I went there, examined her forehed, where there was a contusion so deep as to bleed, she fell with her forehead against the corner of the steps at the front door.—John had apply'd brown paper diped in brandy, I laid a double rag, wett with warm vinager over the paper and bound it up.[7] . . .

May 9. . . . I went down, Eliza with me, to Mollys, called at Nancys: Molly was gone out, I spent an hour, to rest myself and play with the little one, then return'd home, a little tired to dinner. . . .

May 25. . . . I was taken, while at tea, with a sence of Soffacation which I have, some years past experienced—'tis very dreadfull while it lasts.—oweing, I believe to weakness. . . .

27. . . . My husband, Henry and Hannah dine to day at Jacob Downings—E. Skyrin dined here in her grandfathers place; The little dears are always glad to be with us. . . .

28. . . . I spent this Afternoon with Sarah Fisher and her daughters, they are going out of town soon to spend the Summer, as many are apprehensive of the Yallow fever visiting us again, Sarah Fisher is an old acquaintance, and is now very near 81. years of age. I thought it was very possiable I might not see her again which was my reason for paying the visit—but we are short sighted creatures. . . .

29. . . . went to Hannah Pembertons, she was out riding, I sat down by myself in her front parlor and employ'd myself knitting a silk garter which I brought in my pocket Hannah return'd home about noon, I dined with her and John Wilson, and spent the day there. . . .

7. The alcohol in the brandy acted as a disinfectant, while vinegar, an astringent widely used for many ailments, was esteemed for its prophylactic qualities (W. Lewis, *New Dispensatory*, 75, 292).

30. . . . Observing our Neighbours Hartshorn were preparing to go into the Country to spend the Summer, I went over, found Sucky busy'd making ready, with a heavy heart, was app[er]rent—After [wishing] her endeavouring for composure I bied her farewell, poor thing! the loss of her Son lays heavy on her heart—James Logan called, he is in very poor health—Dr. Redman called, he has a bad cold, and other complaints of old age—My dear Son William is unwell, he looks very pale and languid—Myself more unwell than usual. This is a world of trouble! May we deserve a better when time, in this, shall be no more. . . .

[June] 12. . . . Nancy Skyrin and self took a walk, calld at Polly Drinkers Shop,—went into the Presbyterian meeting house in market street,[8] it was open'd and the Candles burning, service time not quite arrived—one man was there, Brook Smith Urn which stands in the South end of the Church, A beautifull piece of Workmanship—the Marble highly polish'd, I could not see to read the incripttion 'tho it is in bl[a]ck letters. from thence we took a walk, up second street to dock Street, then to third street, to chestnut street and to front street to home—I was tired and heated, the weather very warm today. . . .

June 14. . . . Jacob and Sally Downing called in their Carriage for Eliza to ride with them—Sister is gone this evening to their house—poor Sally! is already so heavy, she finds it difficult to walk—Our black Sarah took tea with our quality in the kitchen. . . .

June 15. . . . H. Yerkes was here while HD. and self were at breakfast, to request leave for her Neice Betsy Grant, who is at work for us, to[9] go for a week to P Bunting whose Wife was delivered last night of a dead Child, and her Nurse not come—I could not deny in such a case. . . .

16. . . . I was up this morning about 6.—'tis now past 11. I feel very tired, pain in my knees &c. I am weaker than I was a year ago.

June 22. . . . I arose a little after six—was informed that a fire had occur'd at the corner of Callohill and Second streets, about 3 in the morning I heard nothing of it—seem'd pleased at first, that I had escaped the fright, but felt

---

8. Philadelphia's First Presbyterian Church stood on the southeast corner of Market Street and White Horse Alley (the alley was between Second and Third streets). Its new building, erected in 1793, featured a classical facade with four Corinthian columns fronting on Market Street. In the southern end of the church stood a memorial to Brooke Smith, a merchant who died in the 1780s (Alexander Mackie, "The Presbyterian Churches of Old Philadelphia," in *Historic Philadelphia*, 217–18; James L. Whitehead, ed., "The Autobiography of Peter Stephen Du Ponceau," *PMHB* 63 (1939): 436).

9. The word "leav" crossed out.

rather pain'd when I considered what a second death sleep appear'd like! I am generaly, the first in our family that hear the cry of fire, 'tis rare that I miss hearing it: I retire about 11 o'clock, and seldom or ever, I may almost say never, am asleep till after midnight, and not a heavy sleeper at any time. . . .

June 23. First Day: . . . Hannah Buckley formerly Gardner, call'd this evening Sally Gardner her daughter lived with us from the age of 14 to 18. without being bound, she was a girl of Spirit, but an affectionate and faithful little Nurse to my William when he was an infant. . . .

24. . . . A fear has laid hold on me that my husband and William may go in the river to wash—it is a business HD. is very fond of—it would be very dangerous for WD. to venter, I hope he will not attempt it. . . .

30. First Day: . . . Jacob Downing inform'd us that W. Sansom had heard a young man was dead of the Yallow fever in Penn Street. . . .

July 1. . . . the Neighbours are, some of them moving away . . . My husband invited Sammy and Molly with the rest of their family to come to us, they are to conclude by evening. there is a degree of perverseness in some dispossitions which occasions them much trouble, as well as those who have their good in view—They left Sally Rhoads would not come here, but went in the midst of danger—I am realy, distress'd for my daughter—I step'd into John Skyrins, Nancy at work she is rather better—I sent a note to Molly letting her know that I should not have one easy moment while she was in that infected Neighborhood, and that I would send Peter for the Child, he returnd with the account that they were gone to Sally Rhoadss—which was some ease to my mind 'tho I would rather they had come to us . . . Nancy came here this evening she and self went into the Shower bath. I bore it better than I expected, not having been wett all over at once, for 28 years past. . . .

7. First Day: . . . this has been one of the most pleasent days we have had this Summer, I was at home all day, which is mostly the case, having no heart or Spirits to go abroad, and 'thro favour I love home, better than any where else, I believe I may truely say 'tis not oweing to an indolent dispossion, but to other causes—Othniel Alsop took tea here—Nancy come in this evening to bath as usual—I sometimes think I shall be overwhelm'd, 'till I make comparrisons and then think I have cause of thankfullness. . . .

July 9. . . . I sent Peter to Sally Rhoads to enquire after my Child and her Child, she seems to be very much from under my jurisdiction, but very near my heart. . . .

21. First Day . . . John and Nancy Skyrin and their Children sett off about

6. this Morning for Downingtown. They were to have to gone Yesterday, but ASs indispossion put it off—HD. and MS. went to meeting—We have no little dears to run in and out, at present—all gone—May the Lord be with them!—I feel much for them.—for[10] some years past I have been favour'd with a Chearful serene mind, for which may I be thankfull—but laterly I have been more than usualy indisposed with a weight on my Spirits.—Nancys black girl Henny came here to stay till her mistress returns, as she is not to be trusted from under the care of some one. Patience stays at home. . . .

22. . . . Black Judey was here to day, she is now about 52 or 3 years old—My Sister and self sold her, when 9 years old into the Country, we did not think we were doing wrong, but did not know what to do with her, as our parents were dead and we going to board out—we loved the Child, and after a few week consideration took a ride to her mistresss habitation and offred her 40 pounds for the Child, they gave us 25. promising to use her very kindly; she said that she would not part with her for 100 pounds, she thought providence had directed her to the Child and she ment to treat her with great kindness— we came away disapointed, she was afterwards sold again, but has been many years free, and her Children are free when of age[11]—we had formerly some uneasy hours on her account. 'tho nothing to accuse ourselve of as a crime at that time, but parting with a little Child whom we lov'd, to be a slave, as we fear'd, for life.

23. . . . I miss WD. to night, he is so seldom from home. . . .

July 28. . . . I went this evening to see how Patience goes on, found the Door lock'd, rang the bell, but no answer—there is a risk in leaving a house &c to the care of Servants, young ones especially.

29. . . . Sarah Lewis widdow was here this morning at a loss how to make out a livelyhood.—with 3 young Sons, and little business, she came to advise with HD. . . .

31. . . . I have not heard from my Daughter Molly for several days past— Sammy Rhoads does not act well in not calling oftener, I have frequently desire'd that she would let us know when we should send Jacob for them to spend the day with us—but do not hear. . . .

10. The word "several" crossed out.
11. Under the provisions of Pennsylvania's Gradual Abolition Act of Mar. 1, 1780, no children born after that date could be slaves. Negro or mulatto children born of slave mothers were to be held as servants until age twenty-eight, at which time they would become free (*Statutes at Large*, 10:67–73; Stanley I. Kutner, "Pennsylvania Courts, the Abolition Act, and Negro Rights," *Pa. Hist.* 30 (1963): 14–28).

[Aug.] 10. . . . Oronoko is dead, our Jacob went to his funeral, many a pleasent ride have I taken with his Mistress under his care and protection, poor Noke. . . .

12. . . . Betsy Grant finish'd working for us this evening she has been 7 weeks. . . .

21. . . . I have often wish'd to know, what it is that makes so much noise in the trees, as soon as sun sett they begin—I knew it was not what is called tree frogs, nor Catydids, I once follow'd the noise before dark, 'till I was directly under it, and saw some little transparent matter move, which I endeavou'd to take, but it evaded my hand, sent Peter, who can see better, since, to catch one, he brought me a little insect or fly, not an inch long, of a light green, colour, and transparent wings, very slim body—but I could not think it possiable so small a creature could make so great a noise, 'till this evening, I hard one in our middle room, which Peter caugh, it proved to be the same little thing he shew'd me before.—I want to know what it is called.—'tis less than a Cricket, but makes a louder noice. . . .

Augt. 22. . . . we hear from all quarters that the fever is very bad in the lower part of the City—Dr. Kuhn says he knows it rages there, that he shall hold himself in readiness to go out of town if it should spread in the City. . . .

26. . . . Cadr. Evans was here this forenoon, he thinks things are in an alarming situation, very great numbers going out of City. . . .

28. . . . 'tis astonishing to hear of the many familys that are gone and going out of the City—for the last 24 hours 10 deaths reported—5 of them were Children—which is a great decrease—John Skyrin has taken Parkes new house in downingtown and has sent a waggon load of necessaries to day, their girl Henny is gone among the rest—Jacob and John dined here—My husband has concluded to go with Sister and self to the Vally—WD. intends going to his Brothers—so that we shall be in Chester or Lancaster county, and William in Bucks—60 miles apart, I dont like the seperation in his weak state of health. . . .

31. . . . we are preparing to be gone, as fast as we can . . . there are few left in the City to call or to visit. . . .

Sepr. 1. First Day: . . . I prepar'd to depart with J Dg. . . . we arrived safe at J. Downings dwelling about 4 o'clock. . . . Nancy Skyrin came over soon

---

after our arrival, and several other relations—I went home with Nancy to tea, it is a convenient handsome house they have taken. . . .

3. . . . Sally Downing is gone to Tommy Downings next door to a quilting match where I was invited, but did not suit me to go. . . .

4. . . . if my husband and Sister are detain'd in the City, by Sickness or any other cause, they will find it very inconvenient, everything there is deranged— the City is so deserted that it is not easy to get without some trouble, such things as were eaisily procured heretofore, the Water in the pumps[12] is bad for want of use—I hope our foulk are at Richd. Thomass may have arrived late, and this very dark evening[13] may have prevented our hearing from them. Black Charles has just arrived, with the Cart, my husband and family are at R.Ts, intend being here by and by—they arrived here before noon. . . .

8. First Day: . . . the giddiness in my head, occasion'd by the obstruction in my bowels is distressing, it does not go off at any time of the day: loosing blood might be a temporary relief, I am astonish'd at myself for being afraid of the opperation—but I have not good veins for bleeding. . . .

9. . . . I have been rather better to day then yesterday busy at work, makeing little Shoes for little S. Rhoads. My husband reading, Sister and Sally knit- ting—the Children playing and Noisey—confinement does not suit us [all].

Sepr. 11. . . . I have spent all the fore part of this day in suspence waiting for Dr. Todd to come and bleed me, 'tis now 3 o'clock Afternoon, I have given him over for this day. . . .

12. . . . Dr. Todd came at 11 o'clock, he bleed me with a thumb lancet in the same vain that was open'd last fall at Germantown but never before, tho I have been blooded above 40 times, he made a very large gash, said he could not see the vain, but opperated by feeling—he say'd my veins are not very good for bleeding, which I have always been consious of, and fearful of the opperation, 'tho I make the best of it.—I spent the day without work, and having no new book to read, made it rather tiresome, feel very languid and weak having lost, at least 12 ounces blood. . . .

19. . . . My poor Nancy has had a tooth drawn early this morning by Dr. Todd. she sleep't none all night Peter tells us.—he says it bleed very much, her gum, Sally has a Young Woman at work, a Betsy DeChamps, making a little man of Henry—he is very pleas'd. I went to see Nancy afternoon, she is in

12. The word "are" crossed out.
13. The word "has" crossed out.

a great measure releived by the loss of her tooth but her gum is sore and somewhat painfull, her face bound up. . . .

23. . . . little Henry was Yesterday put in Jacket and trowsers, one of the happiest days of his life. . . . Browns paper tells us that many of the inhabitants are return'd to the City, and things look lively there—this will encourage Sally to go home—and all of us, if she goes. My husband will have no objection.

24. . . . Nancy Skyrin spent the afternoon here, doing up Sallys little Caps which Sister iron'd this morning—Nancy and self took a walk to the bath house which has been built by a subscription in this Neighbourhood—there is a plunging and Shower bath, inclosed in a seemingly convenient house, it was locked, but I could descern through the keyhold, the bath, the pump &c—it is supply'd by a spring of clear water. . . .

Sepr. 27. . . . called at Dicky Downings the first time I have been there—his wife is better than could have been expected all things considered, but such a tiney infant, I think I but one saw—I have not been in the way of seeing new born children as much as most women, not being desireous of or laying out for the business. . . . My husband, Jacob Downing, Ben Wilson and Nancy Skyrin is gone to catch fish if they can. . . .

28. . . . Nancy Skyrin with her Elizabeth spent the evening she is busy makeing flannel underments for her Children. . . .

[Oct.] 8. . . . we were up 'till after midnight busy preparing to go homeward tomorrow if the weather will allow of it. . . .

10. . . . We observed as we rode how deserted our City appear'd, here and there a barbers Shop, some grocirs and a few other tradsmens were open, but the generality of the houses are still shut up, it has a sorrowful appearence.— So we are once more favour'd to enter our Dwelling, (where I would rather be than any where else at most times. . . . The Watchman is now crying the ninth hour which has something very awfull in it, not being accostom'd to[14] hear them before ten, it is the better to guard the City, in the absence of its inhabitants. . . . It is pleasing to me to see things round me that I am accustomed too, even the vane in the Cherry tree, 'tho the wind is easterly—I am one of those that deal in triffels, 'tho things of greater Consequence do not always escape me. . . .

23. My poor dear Sally was taken unwell last night. . . . Nancy Skyrin came

14. The word "it" crossed out.

---

in, she had been to see Sally. I believe she dont intend, if she can help it, to be with Sally at the extremity . . . I went—found Dr. Shippen half alseep in the back parlor by himself. . . . went into Sallys Chamber she is in pain at times, forerunning pains of a lingering labour, a little low Spirited, poor dear Child— This day is 38 years since I was in agonies bringing her into this world of trouble; she told me with tears that this was her birth day, I endeavour'd to talk her into better Spirits, told her that, the time of her birth was over by some hours, she was now in her 39th. year, and that this might possiably be the last trial of this sort, if she could suckle her baby for 2 years to come. . . . Sally in almost continual pain, I came home again in the evening. . . . Sally was all night in great distress, the pain never quite of, sometimes on the bed, but most of the night in the Easy chair; as it is called,—between two and 3 o'clock in the morning Dr. Shippen desired Jacob to call up a John Perry, who lives near them, to open a vain, 'tho it is a opperation she very much dreads, she gave up to it without saying a word. . . . Sally had two smart, or rather hard pains while the bleeder was there, he is a married man;[15] she has taken 80 or 90 drops liquid ladanum during the day and night, but has not had many minuits sleep for 48 hours. . . .

24th. . . . in the Afternoon the Doctor said, the Child must be brought forward—he went out, which he had not done before, that he was going for instruments[16] occur'd to me but I was afraid to ask him, least he should answer in the affirmative—towards evening I came home as usual, and after seeing all things in order, was getting ready to depart, when little Dan enter'd, the sight of him flutter'd me, yet I had a secret hope that it was over, when Dan told us, that his mistress had a fine boy and was as well as could be expected— Charles was to have come at 10 o'clock for me to spend the night like the last, as I thought probable, I had left Nancy there 'tho against her inclination she as well as myself, dreaded the finishing—but this joyfull intelligence quite changed my feelings, I was apprehensive that the Child would not be born

15. Perry's marital status may have mitigated this violation of a longstanding tradition that excluded men from the chamber of a woman in labor, with the exception of a male physician. Although women were frequently bled during pregnancy, bloodletting in cases of difficult labor did not become a common obstetrical practice in Philadelphia until the 1790s, when it was thought to ease the pains of parturition and help in dilating the uterus, thus speeding up delivery (Scholten, *Childbearing*, 29–38; C. K. Drinker, *Not So Long Ago*, 60; William P. Dewees, *An Essay on the Means of Lessening Pain and Facilitating Certain Cases of Difficult Parturition* [Philadelphia: Thomas Dobson and Son, 1819]; Rucker, "Pain Relief in Obstetrics," 101–5; Siddall, "Bloodletting," 101–10).

16. Probably forceps, first invented in England in the seventeenth century, but not widely known until Dr. William Smellie popularized their use in the mid-eighteenth century. Smellie's students included William Hunter and Colin Mackensie, who in turn trained Shippen (C. K. Drinker, *Not So Long Ago*, 121; Richard W. Wertz and Dorothy C. Wertz, *Lying-In: A History of Childbirth in America* [New York: Free Press, 1977], 35–45; Jane B. Donegan, *Women and Men Midwives: Medicine, Morality, and Misogyny in Early America* [Westport, Conn.: Greenwood Press, 1978], 49–79; Scholten, *Childbearing*, 30–37).

alive;—My husband went with me there, they were at supper, very Chearful, like Sailors after a storm—I went up to Sally, would not suffer her to talk.—I was thankful, that I happend to be absent at the time, tho' I intended otherwise. . . . My husband, Nancy and self came home about 11 o'clock—as I had not had my cloaths off for two days and one night, going backwards and forwards, with my mind disturbed, I felt exceedingly weary when I went to bed. . . .

26. . . . I went towards evening to J Downings. Sally was about suckling her infant—her milk is not yet come, she is quite as well as I expected, indeed much better. . . .

28. . . . Nancy Skyrin called, her daughter Elizath. was here for a book, she is a very bookish child, and reads extrodinary well for one of her age. . . . sent Peter to know how Sally is, she sent word, better, and that her milk is coming. . . .

29. . . . black Charles brought little Sally Downing here forenoon, Henry was here before her, so that we shall have them to amuse and disturb us to day . . . about 11 o'clock John Skyrin, who is return'd from Baltimore, since yesterday afternoon, sent for me, Elizabeth had just swallow'd a pin, and was lamenting sadly—I made her take a raw egg white and yolk, and recommend it to her father, to give her another in an hours time.—it is what frequently happens to Children, and is admirable that so few bad consequences follow—it slips down the common sewer, with other things, and kind nature often eludes calamity. . . .

[Nov.] 2d. . . . Old Betty Burrage called forenoon, she is, she says, indis-posed, and has received a hurt on her side by falling out of a waggon, she wishes my husband would give her a character to recommend her to the overseears of the poor,[17] I gave her victuals and some money, she is to call again, but I dont expect HD. will give her a good Character. . . .

5. . . . we called at a Saddlers shop for some soft leather to make soles of babys shoes. . . .

6. . . . Betty Burrage came again urging for a character. I gave her one, such as I could give with truth HD. wrote it, I sign'd it, saying that she was honest as far as I have heard or know, and at present is an object of Charity. the word honest is very extensive, but here it means, not a thief.

17. Needy Philadelphians who made application to the neighborhood Guardian of the Poor learned that it was advantageous first to obtain a character reference from respected citizens such as the Drinkers (Clement, *Welfare and the Poor*, 67–68).

9. . . . Sister went this forenoon to Mistress Bedfords school at the school house in fourth street, to engage her to take Eliza and Mary Downing, they are to go to her on second day next. . . . William has brought home his Brothers portrait,[18] which he claims as his property. . . .

11. . . . WD. went this evening to Js. Smiths, took HSDs portrait with him, which he left there, JS. not being at home, it is what may be called a good likeness, but I was astonish'd to observe how old my dear Henry look'd to what he did 5 years ago, the picture is very like him at present all but the eyes; his Eyes were the best feature in his face, but in the picture they are the worst, there is a queer black look in them that dont belong to him, and an odd look out which never was his—the Ear is much too large, and one eye seems higher than the other, a swelling under the right eye appears in the picture, which may be occasion'd by the constant use of spectacles, he has worn them for some years past being near sighted. . . .

Novr. 18. . . . A Negro woman named Mary, who was hear on & off, for a week or upwards, we dismist last seventh day, not for any fault, but she could not be here but when it suited herself, being a married woman, we have hired another who came this Afternoon, named Jane Gibbs, a black woman—Jacobs wife Sarah Turner, was here to day with her little black bantling, properly so called, I beleive,[19] HD. gave her an order on the Despensary on account of her Child, who is 7 weeks old, and by some wrong management sa Nombril[20] is not as it ought to be—Alice Wright has been at work for Nancy to day, washing, she wants her again tomorrow, it being a long way to her house, she lodges here to night with our new comer—so much for Negros, who are usefull to us, when they behave well. . . .

21st. . . . S Swett was bemoaning herself, yesterday on account of her lonely, and as she now thinks dangerous situation—being quite alone and near 78 years of age, she yet does all her household work, she grows infirm compar'd to some years ago. she is fearfull she may fall in the fire, or down her celler stairs bringing up wood &c and lay there without help, she is a little panic struck, and no wonder. . . .

18. A recently completed portrait of Henry Sandwith Drinker by James Sharples, a member of a family of British-born portrait painters active in the U.S. 1793–1801 and 1809–11, who worked primarily in pastels. The portrait remained in HSD's family and was reproduced in Henry S. Drinker's history of the Drinker family in 1961. HSD also sat for a portrait by Henry Elouis some years earlier, as did William Drinker (Kathleen McCook Knox, *The Sharples: Their Portraits of George Washington and His Contemporaries* [New Haven: Yale University Press, 1930], 1–17, 95; Stephen B. Jareckie, *The Early Republic: Consolidation of Revolutionary Goals* [Worcester, Mass.: Worcester Art Museum, 1976], 31; H. S. Drinker, *Drinker Family*, 51; see below, Nov. 11, 1799, and Jan. 6, 1801).
19. ED appears to be using the word *bantling* to mean "illegitimate child," since Sarah was already pregnant when she married Jacob in April (see above, Apr 4; *OED*, S.V. "bantling").
20. Her navel.

30. . . . MS. was again at S. Swetts, and at 2 or 3 places to look for boarding for her without success. she ask'd Sister if she could not come to our house, and be chiefly, in the room over the kitchin, where she would not be much trouble, Sister told her she would ask HD. and self—poor old woman, 'tis not easy to deny her, tho we should have been better pleased, if she could have been some where else, where she could be comfortably accomodated, but be she where she may, if sick, we must have to see that she is well taken care off, and for 2 or 3 winters past I have had many uneasy thoughts, on her account being quite alone. but we are growing old ourselves, and to have the care of one much older, is not desireable, but after all, how could we refuse her, she having no one besides that has any care for her, I for my part, making the case my own, freely consented. . . .

[Dec.] 2d. . . . HD. is not explicet on SSs coming here, but leaves it to us— he can have no objection, that would not be, also, mine, I can have no wish but for her sake, and believe if once settled here, she will be well and hearty. I have many and many times, experienced the great inconvenience of not understanding or fully knowing his mind. . . .

3d. . . . Sallys Nurse left her to day or yesterday.

8. . . . John and Nancy Skyrin and their Children here after meeting—I went with them to see Sally—saw, in the way, the burial of Aquila Joness daughter a young woman, a sight daily to be seen, burials, tis strange it makes so little impression on the living. . . .

Decr. 18. . . . our dear little Esther Drinker was innoculated about 8 or ten days ago, before she came to town, in four several parts[21] . . . I could have wished it had been done[22] sooner in the Season, and before she was wean'd, for a Child but a year old, or very little more, breeding teeth and without the breast to depend on, this cold season I fear is a resk. . . .

25. . . . There is to be great doings tomorrow, by way of respect to General Washingtons memory.[23] . . . I was sorry to hear of his death, and many others, who make no shew—those forms, to be sure, are out of our way—but many will join in the form that car'd little about him. . . .

30. . . . HD. went out after breakfast, and inform'd us when he return'd of the departure of Saml. Emlen Senr. he died about 4 o'clock this morning in the 70th. year of his age, an old friend and acquaintince, he was husband to my beloved friend E. Moode, between 5 and 6. years, and since to Sally

21. The words "of her body" crossed out.
22. Word crossed out.
23. George Washington had died on Dec. 14.

Mott 26 years,—I did not think last time he was here, that he was so near his end—'tho he was complaining. . . .

31. . . . Nancy Skyrin, very much tryed by the sick head-ach, and otherwise unwell, she is I think rather weakly, 'tho about, and keeps up her Spirits— my Sister and self were formerly much troubled with the sick head ach, but as we advanced in years, it left us.—S. Downing is better than formerly, on that account. . . .

With respect to keeping a Diary;—when I began this year, I intended the book for memorandams, nor is it any thing else, the habit of scribling some thing every night led me on,—as what I write answers no other purpose than to help the memory—I have seen Diarys of different complections, some were amuseing, other instructive, and others repleat with what might much better be totally let alone—my simple Diary comes under none of those descriptions—The first I never aim'd at, for the second I am not qualified, the 3d. may I ever avoid[24]—'tho I have had oppertunities and incitements, some times, to say severe things, and perhaps with strict justice—yet as I was never prone to speak my mind, much less to write or record any thing that might in a future day give pain to any one.—The Children or the Childrens Children of the present day, may be quite innocent of their parents duplicity, how wrong is it to put on record any thing[25] to wound the feelings of innocent persons, to gratify present resentment—I have seen frequent instancies of people, in the course of time, change their oppinions of Men and things, and some times be actuated by pique or prejudice: yet, perhaps, 'tho convinced that they have been wrong; unwilling to tear or spoil what they have wrote, leave it to do future mischief.—this ought to be avoided by every sensible or prudent person. . . .

24. The words "not, but" crossed out.
25. The words "that [mig]" crossed out.

1800

[Jan.] 2d. . . . William took a long walk, he has almost got the better of his cold, and seems bravely, has reduced his snuff taking to 4 pinches p day. . . . few days pass, without some occurance to put us in mind that we are poor frail creatures—I have frequent hints, that give me reason to think that I cannot be long here.

5. First Day: . . . Nancy sent word about noon that Mollys Child was ill of something like the Hives, I was too unwell just then to go to see her, my husband went after dinner, found little Sall very Chearfull. . . .

Janry 8. . . . We may now sett it down as winter, as water in a cup froze in the Chamber last night. . . . I went this evening to Nancys to be instructed in knitting gloves, found she had a Number of young Company with her, return'd home without going in. . . .

17. . . . Our watchman came, as he does every night, for fire in his bucket, poor Man, to be exposed such an night to the wind and rain, we gave him a good supply. . . .

21st. . . . WD. writeing in the Office, he has lately done more at that business than for a long time past—I am pleased he is able, but fearfull he may hurt his breast by it. . . .

30. . . . our Jacobs wifes mother came to tell us that their little one was very ill with an oppression like the hives, I gave her an onion and some deers suit, and desired her to go to the Doctor at the Despensary for advice. . . .

[Feb.] 4. . . . the last youths meeting was held this morning at the middle house market street, as usual, it is concluded to drop that meeting as deem'd rather unnessary as meetings now stand.[1] . . .

10. . . . Tho' I love society, yet having been laterly so little used to

1. The Philadelphia youth meeting was one of several such meetings, none well attended, that were discontinued at the end of the eighteenth century as Quaker schools came into prominence (James, *Quaker Benevolence*, 69–70, 272).

Company, it is at times burdensome to me, even tho' of the agreeable kind; as I have always something before me to do, in the sewing, reading way or &c— I spend my leisure hours when tolerably well, much to my mind at home.

11. . . . I have been as usual unwell to day, but through mercy, not in very great pain. . . .

Febry. 12. . . . I finish'd knitting a pair fine yarm gloves for my husband, the first Mens gloves I ever knitt . . . I seldom make a memorandum of my employments: 'tho generally busyed. . . .

23. First Day: . . . I have been busy this evening dressing and plastering burns & sores, ES. has a burn on her foot, and a Chilblain near her heel— Eleanor has a burn on her hand and 2 sore fingers, perhaps they are also burns, her lips are sore, they should take cooling physick. . . .

24. . . . Mary Courtney came this Afternoon, she wishes we would take her daughter Nelly to be bound to us, John is a Roman Catholic and has put the child to a family of his own sort on trial, Mary appears to be in trouble. I told her that if I took her Child, they must be, both of them, quite as free to bind her to us, as we to take her, and further I said not, 'tho she is about the age I should wish one, Sally Dawson being now fitt for kitchen business, we want a little one to fetch and carry any thing, and go about house on triffling errents. . . .

27. . . . last night when I retired, my thought were taken up thinking of my dear mothers situation on the eve of my birth, this morning when I awoke the same thoughts occur'd the time not being over, as I as born about 10 o'clock and this my birth day—I have never brought a child into the world without thinking how much my dear mother might have suffer'd with me. . . .

[Mar.] 4. HDs birth day. 66 . . . very busy all day which is not uncommon. . . .

14. . . . AS. had yesterday un Dent artificial, met dans sa bouche.[2] . . .

March 15. . . . Jacob and Sally Downing, John and Nancy Skyrin, Henry and Hannah Drinker, Molly Rhoads and Richard Thomas dined here—after Dinner our 10. grand-Children were brought here, vizt. Elizabeth, Mary, Henry, Sarah & Sandwith Downing. Elizabeth and Eleanor Skyrin—William and Esther Drinker and Sarah Rhoads. they and their attendence took tea

2. An artificial tooth put in her mouth.

here—it rain'd after dinner, our Jacob went for Hannah, MR came[3] after Sally Downing in their Carriage, they all went home in JDs Carriage, but Nancy and her Children who spent part of the evening—dear little Creatures, I fixt them in a roe according to their ages and called their parents in to see them in back parlor where we had dined—if it should please kind providence to give them grace, may they live to be a Comfort to all those that love them. Or may they be taken in a state of innocence from the evel to come!—Sammy Rhoads has hurt his legs by a fall, he did not dine with us. . . .

22. . . . little Wm. Drinker junr. dined and spent the day here, dear little fellow, he seem'd in trouble this evening Paul had been talking to him, of Heaven and Hell, and he ask'd many questions; when he came into the parlor, where he should go when he died, and if the Lord would make him over again after he was dead, and some others which I have heard Children ask, not easy to answer, as who made the Lord and so fourth. . . .

28. . . . HSD. and his Son William came after breakfast, they brought us unexpected intiligence, that Hannah was[4] this morn'g about 3 o'clock deliver'd of a fine Son, by the assistance of Dr. Jardine, his wife was the only gossip[5] sent for—Hannah dined yesterday at J Downings, and was as far as pine-street towards evening, she went to bed apparently well—said she did not reacon till the latter end next month, or begining of May, the Child is very lusty, and appears to be come to its full time. . . .

[Apr.] 3. . . . went to Nancys after dinner, and to 2 or 3 Shops—call'd at J Downings after meeting Sally at a Shop, little Sandwith has got a cold—Nancy Morgan was there, I came home to tea, Nancy and her Children took tea here. . . . I have frequently walk'd in our little garden lately, and am pleas'd to see the flowers &c coming forward.

April 4. . . . Polly Sharpless at work in S Swetts room makeing, for me, a dark green india Silk gown. . . .

April 9. . . . Jacob Turner left us last night, he has lived here near 5 years, My husband has hired a black man nam'd William Croaker, he is married, but is to lodge here mostly, we have no Character of him but one from the country

3. The word "with" crossed out.
4. The word "last" crossed out.
5. The term *gossip* derives from *god-sibling*, originally one who witnessed the birth and subsequent baptism of a child. By the seventeenth century *gossip* had come to mean a close female friend who attended a woman at childbirth (*OED*, s.v. "gossip"; Adrian Wilson, "Participant or Patient? Seventeenth-Century Childbirth from the Mother's Point of View," in Roy Porter, ed., *Patients and Practitioners: Lay Perceptions of Medicine in Pre-Industrial Society* [Cambridge: Cambridge University Press, 1985], 134).

where he says he lived two years ago.—and has been ever since in the City—I wish he may be any better than Jacob. . . .

10. . . . I thought from circumstances, that I had lost my Sleve buttom this evening in a certain place where I went in the dark, and seem'd sure it had decended—Sally brought a Candle to see if it could be discover'd shining at the bottom—but very unexpectedly found it between the bricks just out side of the door—they are locket buttons set in gold with my name inside—ES. HD. brought them from England the year before we were married, so that it will be 40 years next June that I have worn them in my sleves, and should have been loath to lose it. little William frighten'd us and himself this evening by almost swallowing a copper cent, he lay on his back on the Sofa with one in his mouth, we heard him choaking, as it were, and saw him rise up, by a great effort he got it up, before we knew what was the matter; he look'd pale for some time afterwards, when it was over, I endeavour'd to empress on his mind the danger of putting improper things in his mouth—he appear'd convinced.

15. . . . HD. MS. ED. went to meeting—Richd. Jordan, Danl. Dean and Danl. Havaland appear'd in testimony, the first is a great preacher, the seacond a good one, of the third I say not. . . .

22. . . . sent a note to Molly to enquire how her Child does. . . . Peter brought word that she was very poorly, but not dangerous. . . . I could not feel comfortable this evening without going to Saml Rhoads's—William went with me after night, and a trying walk it was—the wind very high and cold, I had not been out for a long time before—when we came there found Sammy and Molly in the parlor, the Child was with the girl in the kitchen, not very ill, thinks I, she brought her in, and the little hussy was laughing, I could have wiped both their bottoms, 'tho pleas'd, to find her no worse, came home very much tired. . . .

[May] 19. . . . a weight on my spirits or a heavy heart has lately been my portion, tho' some times for a length of time, I am favour'd with a tranquil mind—The first does not arise from a guilty consience, nor the latter from an unsteady disposistion of temper, which I esteem a great favour—but so it is—was "every ones faults written on their foreheads,"[6] we should see, as I think, crouded characters where they would not be expected, and clear smooth fronts where faults would be looked for: I hate the lieing Tongue. . . . Nancy and Molly were here this evening they were under some apprehension in passing the Streets after night on account of the following intelligence in this evenings paper Fennos: vizt.—"For some nights past the most horrid cruelty has been practised in this city, upon the persons of unprotected females, by

6. An English expression dating back to the 1660s (W. G. Smith, *English Proverbs*, 179).

some unknown villain who has attacked and stabbed them. The weapon used has been a Shoemaker's Awl, one having been extracted from the back of a Lady.—The attacks are confined to no particular quarter. it has been done in several streets and at various hours, after dark.—it is hoped the villain will not escape justice."—something of the same nature occur'd in this City many years ago. it was, then, cutting with a knife, instead of stabbing. . . .

21. . . . Nancy Skyrin and self, Eleanor with us, went this Afternoon to visit at Jacob Clarksons, I have not paid what is called a visit for a long time past. . . .

June 1.   Its First Day . . . Jacob Downing went this morning before 5 o'clock to T. Stewardsons to enter Eliza[   ]. name for a place at the boarding school,[7] 14 had been before hand with him. people are in a great hurry, I think, to get rid of their Children, 'tho I believe it to be the best thing many can do for their children, in some cases, but had I a dozen daughters and health to attend them, not one should go there, or any where else from me. . . .

June 7.   . . . I was at Nancys after dinner, John was about pulling out one of Elizabeths teeth with a double thread of silk, but after 2 trials did not succeed, after her trouble she came home with me—Children have their afflictions, and some times feel, very sensibaly, some much more susceptible than others—ES. is grived at heart, when any thing ails her mother or Sister.

19. . . . keep't the Children from School, keep't school myself—cut out work for them, and heard them read. . . .

June 20.   . . . black Mary who has been at work here some months, went home sick this morning she never lodges here having a husband. . . .

21. . . . Peter, Sally and self, busy above an hour striping our walnut tree of its bearings, the first year that it has yielded any fruit.—we obtain'd 116 fine nuts, which I propose pickeling. . . .

23. . . . Our dear William is poorly and low Spirited, he eats scacerly any thing, and takes a great quantity of snuff. . . .

25. . . . My dear Son William is very poorly, I intend lodging in his room to

7. Westtown had opened with forty students, twenty of each sex, in May 1799, and in the following three months had admitted approximately ten boys and ten girls each month. Thereafter, whenever a vacancy occurred, the school would admit the next applicant on its waiting list. Though Downing applied for his daughter in June 1800, she would not enroll in the school until April 1801 (Dewees and Dewees, *Centennial of Westtown*, 45; Hole, *Westtown*, 52; Smedley, *Catalog of Westtown*, 2, 3).

night. . . . black Mary is gone home again sick, she is breeding I believe. a world of trouble. . . .

July 1st. . . . it will be 7 years the 8th. this month, that I have made a daily memorandum, not omitting a single day, till the last 5 days, unless it was when my daughters were ill. . . .

5. . . . A Squabble in Elfriths Alley[8] between A Negro man and Nancys two black girls, he affronted Patience and Hen—they got a horse-whip &c and beat him, rais'd a sort of mobb in the Alley. . . .

8. . . . Nancy Skyrin with her little Eleanor went under the Shower bath— the Child stompt but could not cry, she fell down in the bath house, Nancy put her out, after a while she affected to laugh, and says, but with reluctance, she will go in again. . . .

9. . . . Jacob Downing tells us that on first day last as he and his Children were walking by the side of the Creek a water Snake of a yard in length, on which he supposed Eliza put her foot, wound its self round both her legs, she scream'd, and kicked till she got it off, it run into the water, there was a little mark on her leg which was bloody, that it must have bit her, but it has not swell'd, and they hope no bad consequences will occur, she was very much frighten'd. . . .

15. . . . I went this evening to see our Neighr. Pratt who lies-in of a Son, I have never been there before since they lived there.[9] . . .

18. . . . Elizath. had a stomach tooth drawn before dinner by the tooth drawer, it was fast in her head with a very long root, for a first tooth. . . .

21st. . . . my husband expected to have finish'd the arbitration this morning but was obliged to brake up on account of the disagreeable news of Brother John Drinker being struck with the palsey last evening at Fair-hill. . . .

July 22. . . . the Accounts from JD. are that he he lays more still, without the twitchings which he has had.—but Docr. Kuhn is desireous some other Physician should be called in—I fear he is in emminent danger. . . . How must J Drinkers poor Children feel to see their beloved Father blistred, shaved, and cup'd on his head, those are hard tryals, to Affectionate Children. . . .

8. Elfrith's Alley runs east-west from N. Front Street to N. Second Street, between Arch (or Mulberry) Street and Race (or Sassafras) Street (endpaper map, *Historic Philadelphia*).
9. The merchant Henry Pratt and his family had lived next door to the Drinkers nearly four years.

24. . . . Nancy Mifflin and A. Warder, came this Afternoon with a Subscription paper, to raise money for the building of an Infirmary at the Western School. their application is to Women only. . . .

July 27. . . . I received a few lines from My husband after 7 o'clock informing that "Our dear brother quietly breathed his last at about half after six o'clock." . . . Our brother J. Drinker in his 68th year. . . . they have concluded to bring the Body here to be buried from our house as their own is not prepared for such an occasion. . . .

28. . . . HD &c return'd forenoon they have concluded to invite, to meet here tomorrow morning at 8 o'clock—the Corps to be brought here early tomorrow morning—William Letchworth the inviter called for the list.[10] . . .

29. . . . My husband, myself and Sister, went to the funeral J Downing walked with Sister—a large or long prosession—W Savery spoke at the grave, in commendation of the deceased.—the grave was dug next to my dear fathers, the spot I expected to have occupied myself, I dont know how it happen'd—but I have no objection. . . .

July 30. . . . I went into J Skyrins, Nancy busy keeping School. Elizath. and Eleanor were heming handkerchiefs—little Beck saying her letters. . . .

Augt. 2. . . . After three years successively, being visited by what, I believe, may be called a pestilence, to escape it! . . .

Augt. 3. . . . I have remarked that we have had very few flies, or any other insects this year, Locust excepted, tho' this is the month for spiders, Musquitos &c to abound, fewer than common have as yet made their appearence. Nancys girl Patience brought in the other day, a new species of spider in a tumbler, it was about as large as my thumb nail, the legs were red, the back variegated with uniform figures. black and a yellow ground. . . .

Augt. 9. . . . Sammy Molly and Child lodges here to night, the first time since their marriage—Nancy and Elizath. took tea here—I sent Paul to the

10. Quakers participated in the early American custom of sending personal invitations, delivered by a paid inviter, to funerals, but also sought to limit the invitations to those who had a right to attend burials in Quaker grounds. The practice declined in the nineteenth century as families began sending printed invitations through the mail (Margaret M. Coffin, *Death in Early America: The History and Folklore of Customs and Superstitions of Early Medicine, Funerals, Burials, and Mourning* [New York: Elsevier/Nelson, 1976], 69–72; Philadelphia Yearly Meeting, *Rules of Discipline* (1797), 16–17).

Library for the works of Rabelais a french Author.[11] I expected some thing very sensible and cleaver—but on looking over the books, found them filled with such obscene dirty matter, that I was ashamed I had sent for them, it was late when I sent for them and the sun set soon after which time they do not give or receive book at the Library, or I should have sent them back. . . .

14.   . . . last night or this morning near one o'clock, John Skyrin knock'd at our door, Nancy was very ill . . . I found her cold, and without pulse, she had been near 3 hours vomitting at times, with violent headach, and spasms in her throat she had appeard near gone . . . John went for Docr. Kuhn, while he was gone I rub'd her with Lavender water, the coldness went off, and her pulse beat, but very low—Doctor order'd Eather to be given internally and her forehead rubd with it—pills given, which she had by her, of Rhubarb, castile soap and magnezer[12] . . . I sleep't by her, 'till 6 in the morning when she was much better. . . .

15.   . . . went to see Nancy who was at work—she feels weak. . . .

Sepr. 2.   . . . William and self took a walk this evening of 10 squares, stop'd at the Methodest Meeting in fourth street . . . The preacher was loud, but not immoderate, the Audience appear'd quiet and attentive. I have heard much of their manner of worship, but never saw any thing of it before.—they may have different modes at different times. . . .

3.   . . . William and self walk'd 14 squars this evening stop'd to look at the col[er]ed bottles in an Apothecarys shop in third street. . . .

Sepr. 4.   . . . Our dear little girls brought in their wax Doll, for me to fasten on its head, which has got loose, 'tis well if I dont make part of two heads of it. . . .

6.   . . . J. Downing came to a sudden conclusion to go to his family, he left us about 2 o'clock after dinner in Sulkey. I have been often pleas'd to see his fondness to be with his family. . . .

11. Francis [sic] Rabelais, *Works*, trans. M. Le du Chat et al., 4 vols. (London, 1794), listed in Library Company of Philadelphia, *Third Supplement to the Catalogue of Books Belonging to the Library Company of Philadelphia* (Philadelphia: Zachariah Poulson, Jr., 1796), 37; for HD's membership, see Library Company of Philadelphia, *A Catalogue of the Books Belonging to the Library Company of Philadelphia* (Philadelphia: Zachariah Poulson, 1789).
12. The words "which she had by" crossed out.

11. . . . J. Downing return'd from the Valey before dinner, he left Sally unwell with the head-ach. . . .

13. . . . SS. talks of leaving us, is rather dumpish about it. if she could be comfortably accomodated else where we should have no objection. . . . Our old Clock, which keeps time extrodinarily well, struck 10 with both the town clocks: such trifles pleases me. . . .

23. . . . I sent Peter to Sister Rhoadss with some grapes, and to enquire how Molly was, she said she was very well when Sammy return'd from German-town. It may seem strange that she knows so much more of my Daughter then I know myself, but the matter is, he lodges[13] at his mothers, and seldom waits on us; he requires more attention than he choses to pay, and it dont suit us to run after him, was my child sick I should not neglect her, if able to attend— she is to come home tomorrow or next day SR says. . . . I should have had a fire, but the thoughts that my husband and son were exposed to the wind and wether, hendred me. . . . sent Paul yesterday to the Library with a list, none were to be had but the last on the list, which was "Bolinbroke on the study and use of History."[14] Nancy put it down, and tho' I like'd not the Authors name, I had no objection to the title of the book, but found on looking it over, that it set at nought the Holy scriptures, it was the first volume, got out in my name, I sent it back unread, and did not let Nancy have it. how pernicious are such writings to young people.

24. . . . my husband is a Man of good judgment, but venterous, scacerly any wind or weather stops him. I am realy uneasy on account of my dear William, who has not been so exposed for 9 years past since he has been an invalid. . . .

[Oct.] 8. . . . little S. Rhoads is 2 years old this day, and not yet weaned.— Sandwith Downing went alone when he was between 10 and 11 months old.— clear.

Octor. 12, . . . My poor Nancy went home between 9 and 10. with a bad head-ach threatening worse,—I went about 10, with my night cloaths to stay all night with her, she had taken 28 drops liquid ladanum before I came, hoping to deaden the violent pain, I was not clear that she had done right.— but before 12 o'clock she was more easy and fell asleep, I lay down by her in my cloaths and sleep't. . . .

13. . . . this evening we fully expected Jacob Downing, as tomorrow is the Ellection. . . .

13. The word "with" crossed out.
14. Henry Saint-John, Viscount Bolingbroke, *Letters on the Study and Use of History* (1752; London: T. Caddell, 1792 [*Brit. Mus. Cat.*]).

Octor. 14. . . . we know not yet how the Election will go, but, I, for my part, have little doubts about it.[15]

23. . . . Molly Rhoads told Sister yesterday that her child bore weaning so far, better then she expected. . . .

[Nov.] 25. . . . Peter went this evening to know how Alice Wright was, and to take her several necessarys, she has been ill for 3 or 4 days past, her husband has been here, and Peter there every day since we knew of her illness, better this morning worse to night.

26. . . . Our little Skyrins took tea here, they received a present of pictured Cards from their Grandfather . . . HD. read to us, An Account of the Convincement and call to the Ministry of Margaret Lucas, late of Staffordshire.[16]

30. First Day: . . . My health is not so good as it has been for two or 3 years past, I feel disagreeable inward pains, owing to obstructions in my bowels. . . .

Decr. 11. . . . had an account this Afternoon that Sally Downing was unwell, took cold lately. My husband called there, she was up stairs, Nancy had the head ach this Afternoon, sent in this evening when she said she was better— those who have children whom they love, have fears and cares enough. . . .

25. Christsmass day: . . . Nancy went yesterday with Nancy Morgan and Anna Wells to visit Dr. Catherals wife, who lives directly opposite to J Skyrins in Stitess house, they mett our old Neighr. Catheral there, she told them that the Summer before last, when their family were at Germantown, from the Yellow fever, they lived in an old house, that was haunted, she, her husband and daughter, actuly saw an Apperition, a Spirit—A women with her gown Skirt over her head, walking in their bed Chamber, she spoke to it, but received no answer—saw it several times—I believe she thought so, but further, cannot say. . . .

28. First Day: . . . Nancy Skyrin and her Children spent the Afternoon and evening she continues unwell; I have made a sorrowfull discovery.

15. A small Federalist majority carried Philadelphia, though the state as a whole voted for the Jeffersonians (*Gazette of the United States*, Oct. 15, 1800).
16. *An Account of the Convincement and Call to the Ministry of Margaret Lucas, Late of Leek in Staffordshire* (Philadelphia: B. & J. Johnson, 1800 [Evans, *Am. Bibliography*]).

1801

[Jan.] 4. First Day: . . . I spent the Afternoon & evening with Nancy in her Chamber, she has agreed that I may speak to Dr. Kuhn on her account as I cannot order an Emetic or otherwise without his concurence—she is very unwell indeed, looses flesh and is almost constantly very sick. . . .

5. . . . I wrote this evening to Nurse Kimble on Nancys account, I wish she may have her, as I think her a very good Nurse. . . .

Janry. 6. . . . while I was with Nancy, Dan brought a picture of Sally Downing, drawn by Sharpless, a profile tis like her, 'Tho not exactly—WD,— ordered it done for him, as he has his brothers and wishes to have Nancys and Mollys in his possession.[1] . . .

8. . . . Eliza and Mary Downing and their brother Henry, and E and E. Skyrin did us the pleasure of taking tea with us—dear little creatures I love to have them here, but when many of them meet together, they are almost to much for us. . . .

Janry. 13. . . . It is 40 years this day since our marriage, and the same day of the week—third day. . . .

17. . . . I received a Letter this evening from Nurse Kimble: letting me know that she cannot think of coming into the City at that season of the year", August! so we are to look out for another. . . .

18. First Day: . . . Molly Rhoads and her daughter took tea here, she went after tea to Nancys—she suspects herself soon after Nancy; I like it not. . . .

22. . . . MS. out, morning and Afternoon looking for Nurses, Patty Jones, she has engaged for Molly in Sepr. next, Nancy has still to seek—it is trying to me to have two daughters in that way—may the Lord preserve them! . . .

1. The next day James Sharples would receive sixty-four dollars from Jacob Downing for three portraits. The receipt records payment for portraits of Mrs. H. Drinker, Mrs. Downing, and Mr. Downing (Drinker-Sandwith Collection, HSP, 4:120).

23. . . . MS. out again to day looking for a Nurse for Nancy, she engaged a Nurse Cooke, who bears a good name, I went to visit Nancy this evening she is very sick again. . . .

[Feb.] 10. . . . went to see Nancy before dinner, found her in the usual way—she has dismist her attendant Lydia—her Maid Patience Gibbs goes with her father tomorrow into the lower Counties, he has come for her, as she has been free for some time. . . .

11 . . . black Patience Gibbs came to bid us farewel—her father Absolem Gibbs a decent sensiable Negro man, has taken her home, highly pleased with her Education &c. . . .

19. . . . I went after dinner to Nancy, she had been here forenoon—she discoverd last night that some body was concealed in the Necessary sent for Neighr. Sleiseman, he and his Son opend the door and brought out a Negro Man, their impudent Hen was privey to his hideing there, she said it was Patience's sweet heart who had come to enquire after her—he appear'd to be very much frighten'd, and promised never to come there again, they let him go. . . .

Febry. 28. . . . I have filt frequent pain in my left breast lately—whatever bodily pain I may suffer on that account, I trust and hope I shall never suffer so much in my mind,[2] as I have formerly done, but as that dont altogether lay with myself my dependance must be on a supereor power on that account and all other.[3] . . .

[Mar.] 5. . . . Sally, Nancy and Molly were here before dinner, I am always pleased when I see them meet here together. . . .

March 16. . . . Elizath. and Eleanor went to School this morning the first of Eleanors going. . . .

[Apr.] 15th. . . . Sally Downing with her Daughter Eliza came this forenoon, the Child bid me farewell, expecting to go tomorrow to the boarding School. . . .

April 18. . . . Jacob Downing was here this morning he left his Daughter yesterday well at the boarding School and apparently well satisfied. . . .

[May] 7. . . . Wm. Garrigass daughter who lately came from the Westren

2. The words "on that account" crossed out.
3. The words "favours I meet with" crossed out.

School brought love from Eliza Downing to her Mother, Sally ask'd her if she was happy and contented, she said middleing, she had expected to have seen her father before this time. . . .

11. . . . Sally, Nancy, Molly, intends going this evening to see some waxwork in second street—John Skyrin has taken a house in Frankford for the Summer season, I did not know how to say anything for or against it—Nancys situation may occasion some difficulties, but it may be for the best. . . .

16. . . . Caty whitewashing here—Nancy came in before dinner—I went after dinner to the paper makers and engaged them to come next week to paper our entry[4]—called at Manleys in market street and bought a pair shoes for self.[5] . . .

17. . . . HD. MS. went to meeting, Jacob Downing called after, with a letter from Eliza to her Sister Mary, in which is shown improvment in writing &c . . . I went with HD. to afternoon meeting, John Webb spake twice, Reba. Price, Sally Catheral, Hezekiah Williams whom I have not heard for upwards of, I believe, 20 years before, I have not been to morning meeting but 2 or 3 times for many years past. . . .

19. . . . Nancy in bed most of this day, I brought the Children here—they wish'd to stay all night—Nancy is under a great weight of something more in mind than otherwise—I feel distress'd to leave her this night, she dont appear to wish it otherwise. . . .

27. . . . went in to Nancys, she, Molly, and their 3 little girls, left our door about three o'clock for Frankford, no other waite[r]ing Man but the driver; the horses Spirited, considering their situation, I shall be pleased to see them safe at home in the evening—they came here to tea WD. and self went with Molly, Pompy and the Child as far as Walnut Street, we went to Dr. Jardines, they were abroad, their daughter Mary play'd several tunes on the fortepoanio with her little fingers, and sung to it—from thence we came to J Downings, they were out also, Gossiping women. . . .

4. When the Drinkers had moved into their home in 1771, the American wallpaper industry was in its infancy. Few Americans used wallpaper in their entryways, and until 1801 the Drinkers appear to have been satisfied with the elegant architectural detail in their own foyer. By the 1790s, however, the industry was thriving and people were beginning to use wallpaper as a decorating device in entryways and halls (Survey for HD's home, Philadelphia Contributionship, Nov. 17, 1770, policy no. 1454–55, courtesy of archivist Carol Wojtowicz; Catherine Lynn, *Wallpaper in America: From the Seventeenth Century to World War I* [New York: Barra Foundation/Cooper-Hewitt Museum Book, W. W. Norton, 1980], 107–9, 154).
5. Henry Manly's shoe warehouse was located at 40 Market St. (*Philadelphia City Directory, 1801*).

May: 29. . . . Nancy Skyrin was putting up many woollen things in Chest in our cellar. MS and Nancy went to shops. . . .

[June] 8. . . . Sally Dawson began a quarters schooling at Peter Widdowss school, her last quarter. Bignal here, bottling Beer this forenoon.[6] . . .

22. . . . William and self took a long walk[7] by moonlight; went first down to visit Molly, found her alone, if a person with a [book in hand] can be called so—she says her Child is not in prime health, but not very unwell—after resting a while, we went by the way of dock street to Jacob Downings, Sally alone, Jacob gone to his bed—we came home by our open burying ground, we went in at the opening for a gate—next third street, a very little on this side where our family lays, the dirt was thrown over my grandfathers grave, but grandmothers, my dear fathers and mothers, are in Stato quo, as we have always taken care to keep them up and have them sodded . . . there is a serious satisfaction in looking round that solemn silent spot, with the moon shining on it. . . .

June 26. . . . Richd. Downings waggoner who was in town this Afternoon told Peter that Jacob and family got up safe to Downingstown. . . .

[July] 4. . . . there has been guns fireing, Drums beating from day break, rejoycing for Independance:[8] the most sensible part of the Community, have more reason to lament than rejoice—in my opinion. . . .

July 5. First day: . . . MS. and WD. went this evening to Nurse Cooks to let her know that our dear Nancy was out of town, not to neglect to hold herself in readiness when wanted . . . Peter went after meeting to visit his parents and to read to them in the Bible.

11. . . . John Skyrin called forenoon, says Nancy and Molly are both disordered in their bowels, Nancy sick at Stomach, when she was a few doors off, I could visit her every day—some may say, I could do so now, but they are mistaken. . . .

16. . . . Sally has been ill of a very sick head-ach—she has wean'd her little Sandwith. . . .

---

6. Peter Bicknell was a bottler who lived in Elfrith's Alley in 1801. Philadelphia had become a major center for the commercial production of beer in America in the eighteenth century, but the Drinkers, like many others, evidently brewed their own beer and arranged to have it bottled (*Philadelphia City Directory, 1801*; Stanley Baron, *Brewed in America: A History of Beer and Ale in the United States* [Boston: Little, Brown, 1962], 1–135, esp. 59–60).
7. The word "after" crossed out.
8. See military orders in *Poulson's American Daily Advertiser*, June 24–July 3, 1801.

23. . . . WD. does not appear well, it gives me pain when I see him dull or low Spirited—I have not heard from Nancy or Molly this day—Sally is to far off to hear. . . .

31. . . . the end of the month, and no Yellow fever, what a favour it will be if we escape it.

[Aug.] 4. . . . T. Cope's brother came to borrow our Carriage to take Tommys Child to the grave yard this evening—Polly was brought to bed this morning the child died in about an hour after his birth. . . . poor Polly, she must feel sad when she reflects on the contrasted situation of her babe, whom, she felt last night, alive and warm! now inanimate, and in its cold grave—My poor Nancy will pity her. . . .

5. . . . I have often reflected of late years, with astonishment, and I trust, with thankfulness, on the favour'd state of our family, with respect to sickness, 'tis true, bodily weakness or infirmity attends some of us; but how seldom are any of us laid up, or have had occasion to call in medical aid, compar'd to formerly when my Children were young, I was often ill myself, and they very frequently.

12. . . . between 4 & five o'clock I left home after bidding friend Swett farewell, as she expects to go to her new lodgings at the Widdow Boltons in Moravian Alley,—My Son William with me, my dislike to rideing will continue, I believe as long as I continue, which will not, probably be long.—we arrived safe at J Skyrins in due time, Nancy and the Children bravely. . . .

16. First Day: . . . Nancy is in pain almost constantly, the apprehension of her being suddenly taken, and the necessary help so far off, keeps my mind on the tenters. . . .

It is several days since I have made any memorandum, but will try to recolect circumstances as they occur'd—it has been a trying time to me, On first day night, Nancy walk'd as far as Ryans John Skyrin with her, it is but a little way off—she seem'd then as well as common, but going to bed complain'd, about an hour after I had retired she came in to my room, said she was in great pain . . . about 3 o'clock JS. went off in his Chair, he return'd about 7 o'clock second day morning the 17th. with M Scott, who after being with us some time said, Nancy might continue as she was for a week or ten days, I scrupled not to tell her, that she might for 2 or 3 days, but not for a week or 10 days, she order'd her blooded, a bleeder was sent for, he came and took 12 ounces blood. . . . My husband brought Nurse Cooke up in JSs chair after dinner. . . . M Scott left us towards evening. . . . Nancy was all night in pain at times . . . on the [18th.] in the morning she was so uneasy and in such frequent pain, that we thought it expedient to send black John to town with a note to Sister, desering her to send for M Scott. . . . between 8 and nine she grew worse, and between 10 and 11 she was deliver'd of a Daughter, after a very laborious time of upwards of 2 hours, she had been evidently all day in labour . . . Nancy appear'd as well after it was over as could possiably by expected M Scott went to bed at 12 o'clock as she said she should do, many hours before, Nurse and self stay'd in Nancys room, she sleep't but little but said she was bravely. . . .

August 21. . . . Nancy complains of the headach she thinks 'tis caused by taking Laudanum & spirits of nitre[9] last night, she tasted it, and told Nurse, who said a little was good for her, M Scott gave her ladunum when in labour, it may be right, but I should prefer the advice of Dr. Kuhn, rather than take a portian from a Nurse and not know what I take—this is one of the disadvantages of townswomen lying in in the Country. . . .

23. First Day: . . . had Nancy gone out her full time, this would have been the time of her reckoning; but I trust all is for the best. . . .

Augt. 30. First Day: . . . after dinner Nancy went in the waggon JS. with her, 3 miles, this is the 12th. day, she dined downstairs! Nothing like this was ever done by me; had she milk enough for the Child, I should think her bravely, tho' she has some complaints yet, and is very venterous. . . .

31. . . . E. Skyrin told me that her Uncle Jacob Downing had pulled out two sound large eye teeth from his daughter Eliza. . . .

Sepr. 1. . . . our Son Henry with his wife and Children came here in their way home; Henry looks and is very unwell, his bowels has been long disorderd it has become a tenesmus. . . . Henrys indispossion gives me uneasiness, as I have thought of several things since he is gone that I ought to have said to him on account of his disorder. . . .

2. . . . about 4 o'clock My husband, daughter Molly and her Sally came up, Nancy took a short ride with Nurse and the baby:—between five and six we left her, I wish she may continue as well as at present, she will be lonesome—We came home to tea, it is 3 weeks this day since I left home. . . .

9. A treatment for difficulty of urination. Spirit of nitre (or nitre drops) was saltpeter mixed with water and oil of vitriol; sweet (or dulcified) spirits of nitre consisted of a small amount of spirit of nitre, or nitrous acid, mixed with a larger amount of rectified spirit of wine (distilled wine or other fermented liquor) (W. Lewis, *New Dispensatory*, 455–56, 184, 446–47, 232–33; R. Thomas, *Modern Domestic Medicine*, 277–80).

3. . . . JD. gave me Eliza's teeth last night which I put with others in the desk. . . .

8. . . . Molly is complaining she felt unwell last night, better this morning, and not so well again this evening—I may expect now, every day, or perhaps every hour to be sent for. . . .

16. . . . I look upon this to be the Equinoxal Storm, it prevents me from seeing Molly at this critical time, as often as I could wish—sent to know how she is, bravely was the answer, and a desire, if I was willing to send the Carriage for her tomorrow to spend the day here.—it will be nine months and ten days tomorrow since!—but it was longer with both her other Children—I dont know what to say to sending for her. . . .

21. . . . we learn that our Son Henry was on fourth day last at J Sterlings store, so that we may hope he is in health—he is very remiss in not writing more frequently, but I forgive him. If Molly should send out to night, it will be, not very pleasent going there, but that is not the worst of the business, I fully expected that at the full of the moon she would call.

29. . . . S. Swett came from Meeting here, she spent the day with us, does not seem satisfied with her place of aboad, considering what she pays, which is three dollars p week. . . .

September 30. . . . sent Peter this evening to Molly, and strange to tell! she is yet about house & bravely—after 9 this evening who should come in but our Son Henry and his Son William, they drank tea at J. Smiths and lodge with us.—We have 9 besides our own proper family here this Night, tho' they are all of our family: JD. HSD. WD. junr. Nancy and her 3 Children, and 2 servants. . . .

Octr. 5 . . . heard that Nancys little one has been very ill of the colick so as to alarm her mother, she Nurs'd her so as to relieve her and fall to sleep. . . .

7. . . . Well! the great affair with my poor Molly is so far settl'd that she is deliver'd of a Son this evening between 6 and 7 o'clock—to my great relief. this morning about 6 o'clock, Pompey came for to let me know that his Mistress was *sick* and his master was gone for the Doctor—I immeadiately arose and went down. . . . "the Child was ready for the birth, but there was not strength to bring fourth," The doctor supply'd the place of Nature—I trust she is safely delivr'd Sally Rhoads, Hannah Yerkes, Nurse Patty, the Doctor and my self were the Company. . . . I intended to have stay'd all night, but after Molly had took 30 drops of Ladunam, as the Doctor order'd, and knowing she had a good Nurse, I came home. . . . was I to have a daughter in

this way every month for a Year, I believe it would put an end to my existance! but, we know not what we can pass through! . . . I never went, that I recollecd, on the buseness of this day, that I came home on the same day, before this time—The long time of suspence that I have been on Mollys account is for this time over—it is ten months this day since she was unwell as the women call it . . . Dr. Ss rule has fail'd in this instant, by it, Mollys Child was to have been a girl—I never knew it fail but once before, but I have taken notice only in my own family. If a Child is born in the old of the moon, the next will be of the same sex, if in the increase there will be a change of sex in the next.[10] . . .

Octor. 8. . . . about 10 at night Nancy came in with her babe, she was in trouble, the child had been very tedious all day, and while she was here at tea and at dinner, her bad girl Hen and new maid Fanny, and good for Nothing black John, drew off rum from one of the Hogsheads in their front Seller, which they can get at when they please, one of them was intoxicated when Nancy went home, John gone off, Hen in the Seller where her Mistress could not go to her, she felt cowardly and came here.—I went back with her and stay'd till JS. came home, when Hen and John were not to be found, he was much displeasd, and made a rumpus, Nancy came away again and brought the Child—after staying here 'till 12 we advis'd her to go back,—black John & Hen were gone to bed, JS. in a passion, she would not stay, which, all things consider'd I did not wonder at—came back again with me, having a violent head-ach, did not go to bed 'till near three o'clock, I went to bed with the Children, lay about half an hour without sleeping when Nancy told me her right Eye felt as if it would burst, I arose got vinager warm and rub'd her forehead and press'd it hard, before 5 she fell into a dose, but I went not to bed, or sleept any all night. . . .

Octor. 9. . . . when Man and Wife do not live in unison, what latitude it gives to servants! poor Nancy she has a crooked[11] [mate] to deal with—I have rearly seen a beautifull woman so altred as she is. . . .

Octor. 12. . . . Sally Downing was here this morning brought a silk pocket book a present from Eliza, of her own making at boarding School. . . .

14. . . . a Young woman from Downingtown named Mary Ann Witticer came

10. William Shippen's belief that the phase of the moon at the time of birth of a child determined the sex of the next child in that family was based on an astrological doctrine that postulated correspondences between the waxing and waning moon and growing and declining nature. These beliefs retained their hold on the popular imagination in England into the nineteenth century (T. F. Thiselton Dyer, *English Folk-Lore* [London: Hardwicke & Bogue, 1878], 41; see above, July 16, 1797).

11. The word "rib" crossed out.

to offer to Nancy as a Childs maid &c. if I can judge by appearences, she will not do—Wm. West was here before dinner, Silas Dinsmore took tea with us—I was just about sending Peter down when Pompey came here, for a breast plaster, he says they are all well, but his mistress's breasts are hard—I hope she has taken no cold. it may be her milk coming in abundance.

15. . . . the plasters Nurse wanted was for the Childs breasts, not for Mollys. . . .

17. . . . this evening Peter went to see the learned pig, Pompey went with him, the pig spelled one of their names, by taking out every letter one by one in his mouth, told the day of the month in the same manner. . . . Elizath. and Eleanor has been with us 2 months this day. . . .

19. . . . I am apprehensive that I shall not see Molly as often as I could wish this winter, if we both live, as she has a young child, which will confine her, and I find the walk rather more tiresome than formerly. . . .

20. . . . there is fine goings on at J.Ss the Negress who Nancy had dismist was at the door to Night with their bad boy John—with all the care that Nancy was capable off, she could not keep order in the house—far from it—such irregularity sildom is known—where heads of families are unsteady, servants take the advantage. . . .

22. . . . My husband found himself more then usualy unwell towards evening discoved that he discharged blood with his Urine we were much Alarmed, and advised him to send for Dr. Rush, he advised bathing his feet and legs, taking 30 drops Ladunun, and peper mint tea, with marsh mallows.[12] . . .

23. . . . One Britton from old England, a Shoemaker, or Shoe Seller was here, HD. bought several dozen Shoes of him. . . . Fredrick bleed my husband this forenoon—he is much better this Afternoon. . . .

October 24. . . . My husband continues better, the lax is not stop'd but the other complaint is check'd, Doctor order'd prepared Chalk[13] with 40 drops Laudanum in a six ounce Vial of peper mint tea & mallows. . . .

27. . . . A letter to day from JS. to AS. . . .

28. . . . JS. paid AS. a visit this morning . . . Mollys Child is 3 weeks old

12. The mucilagenous root of the marshmallow plant, considered to be an effective anti-inflammatory and diuretic, was commonly prescribed for kidney stones and inflammation of the bladder (W. Lewis, *New Dispensatory*, 446–47; Blackwell, *Curious Herbal*, vol. 1, pl. 90; Gifford, "Botanic Remedies," 267).

13. Carbonate of lime, used for diarrhea (Thacher, *New American Dispensatory*, 414–15).

to day and she has rode out 3 times with Sally Downing, new fashoned doings. . . .

29. . . . Alice came to tell Nancy that Hen threaten'd to go off with a married man. JS. was hear this evening said he would get a warrant and put her in Jail this evening but saying and doing are two things with him. . . .

Novr. 1st. First Day . . . Js. Smiths Nurse came to inform us that little Js. Drinker was very ill of the Hives,[14] that J and E— Smith were going directly to North-Bank expecting to find the dear little boy dead. . . .

3. . . . received a letter from my Son Henry with the account of the death of his little Son James, who departed on first day last about one o'clock, near twenty months old—his disorder was, or had been, the Hives. . . . there is consolation in the thought that he is out of all pain, in this world and that to which he is gone—yet it is very trying to part with a dear child, just beginning to know and love you.

5. . . . Jams. Smith was here this evening we were talking of our dear little deseased grandson, he was scarcely ever known to cry, or make any complaint, he was the same during his illness:—Our Son Henry sleept none for 3 Nights, attended him deligently: and he died in his Arms.—My Son feels much as a father. . . .

7. . . . Nancy had concluded to stay here 'till second day, but John Skyr. came in this morning and desired her to come home this forenoon, she is gone. . . . it is a month tomorrow since Nancy came here, Elizabeth is to stay with us, dear little girl it is what she earnestly desires. . . .

23. . . . Eleanor was here this evening dressed in Boys cloaths, she looked very hiddy hoddy, some of the maids tricks. . . .

Novr. 27. . . . Jacob Downing borrow'd our chaise to go to Weston school to visit his daughter. . . .

14. Hives could be any of three ailments: not only the skin disorder to which it refers today but also inflammation of the bowels (enteritis) and of the larynx (croup) (*OED*, s.v. "hives"; Estes, "Therapeutic Practice," 368, 381). In this instance it is likely that James Drinker suffered from a throat disorder more serious than croup or laryngitis, which were commonly labeled hives. Philadelphians also used the term to indicate cynanche trachealis, an acute disease probably equivalent to diphtheria or scarlet fever (for an instance of hives being used for cynanche trachealis, see obituary notice of Mrs. William Dewees in *Poulson's American Daily Advertiser*, Jan. 13, 1801; on cynanche trachealis as diphtheria, see Ernest Caulfield, "Some Common Diseases of Colonial Children," *Publications of the Colonial Society of Massachusetts* 35 (1951): 34; as scarlet fever, see Duffy, *Epidemics*, 114–15, 135).

[Dec.] 10. . . . Sally Dawson well again, she was very unwell on first day night last, headach, pain in her limbs &c—going out too thinly cloathed for fashions sack, no wonder they get sick. . . .

12. . . . Charles Smith brought me a Letter from our Son Henry, informing that Hannah was last night delivered of a daughter, whom they call Elizabeth, that both of them are as well as common in such cases. . . .

Decr. 20. First Day: . . . Our Sally Dawson is free to day, or rather her time is expired for which she was bound, her Father when he bound her, said she was not quite ten years old, but he would not bind her for more then Eight years, I have seen her Age, since in her fathers Bible, she was 17 years old last Octor. so that she wants ten months of being 18 years of age, poor Child, I wish she may be reasonable; she is very fond of dress and fashions, young girl like, I have heard nothing of an intent to leave us, when she does I shall be anxious for her: some giddy girls think they cant be free while they continue where they served their time, but we have heard nothing, as yet like it. . . .

Decr. 28. . . . Polly Sharpless finish'd this evening she has made a gown, mode cloak and a calliminco peticoat for S Dawson in two days—quick work, what I should have been a week about—but it would be differently done, yet not to be found fault with, if nicely done, so much would not be finish'd off— poor girls they earn their money. . . .

1802

Janry. 1st. 1802. . . . I never was fond of Idleness and as my Sister seems to choose looking after the family, I have the more leisure to amuse myself in reading and doing such work as I like best. My health &c. is such, that I cannot go much abroad, but can stay pleasently at home when my mind is at ease, and I never go out from my family to look for comfort. . . .

9. . . . It is 46 years this day since the departure of my dear mother. . . .

13. . . . it is 41 years this day since our marriage. . . .

18. . . . Thomas Reynolds brought his little daughter Rosetta, and left her here on tryal—Nancy Skyrin here this evening. Polly Noble here Afternoon, she complains that her husband, who is a black-Smith, can get no work. . . .

30. . . . My husband was too unwell this evening to go to the quarterly meeting committee, he has had very frequent calls to make water, has agreed that we shall send for the Doctor tomorrow—he took 10 drops more ladaman than common, 35 drops. . . .

[Feb.] 2. . . . Molly is unwell ever since her Son had the Measles, has had less milk and a pain in her back and breast, he is a very fatt hearty child and lives entirely on her, which will not do!—Thomas Reynolds came this evening he bound his daughter Rosetta to us, I believe he is well pleas'd in so doing. I hope she will be a good Child, nine years old next March. . . .

Febry. 20. . . . Nancy here forenoon, she went home to correct dear little Eleanor, who has been rather naughty, not doing as she was bid, it is hard work to whip such a child, but sometimes necessary. . . .

[Mar.] 5. . . . Mary Downing and little Sally came after school with a shift for me to slope.[1] . . .

March 11. . . . Elizth. went with her mother after dinner down to Mollys,

---

1. I.e., turn into an outer garment, such as a cassock, mantle, or gown (*OED*, s.v. "slop").

she was going on a *Party* to [T] Smiths daughter—HD. on a committee this evening at Ed. Tilghmans. . . .

March 22. . . . I have a cold on my breast, and pain in my side—feel rather dull this evening.

24. . . . A Negro man, named Peter, from Virginia, in a tatterd trim[2] called to ask for something to help him out of town—we had very little doubt of his being a run-away—I pittied him a young man. . . .

26 and 27. . . . the fever and Cough have not left me, the pain in my side is better . . . Dear little Mary Skyrin is very ill, Nancy Sent this morning for Dr. Kuhn he order'd two ounces of blood taken from her Arm and a blister apply'd to her breast, Nancy sent in for Sister who attended at those trying opperation[s] to blister and bleed a Child of 7 months old, is a great tryal to a mother. . . . I am not fond of Chambering, but here I am like to be, I know not how long—the nights are tedious, the days not comfortable, as my head is not well enough to allow me to work. . . .

30. . . . I have not yet had the least desire for any kind of food since I have been up stairs the cough continues very hard, I have still a pain in my side, and am oppressed—my head stop'd—I dread going to bed at night, tho' am obliged to lay down every day. . . .

[Apr.] 3. . . . after a poor night, I remain very unwell. . . .

8. . . . an ill taste continues in my mouth, and dislike to all kind of food.—It is two weeks this day since I came up stairs. . . .

11. First Day: . . . Sally Downing with her Daughter Eliza came this afternoon, she came with her father from Downingtown to day, has left the Westren School for a few weeks, to get new Cloathed and to return their after the Yearly Meeting. I am much pleased to see her look so hearty and well, and behave so prettyly. Nancy Skyrin, with the help of her father has got rid of her two hired maids, who had laid their heads together to be as saucy as they could be, or nearly so. . . .

14. . . . Nancy and her Children took tea here—her husband very seldom at home. . . .

21. . . . Jacob paid me a visit forenoon—while the family were at dinner I went up stairs, I did not know I was as weak as I am, my knees pain'd me so

2. I.e., in tattered clothing (*OED*, s.v. "trim").

that I held by the banisters—it is four weeks tomorrow since I have been Chamber'd. Nancy and Children here afternoon—Hannah sent her little Baby to see her Grandfather. . . .

22. . . . R Jones, who is down stairs has inform'd sister, that Mary Stille is dead, an uncommon fine child, few die at the age of 8 or 9 unless of epidemic disorders, she was at J Skyrins a few days past—I am since informed by Nancy who called as she came from meeting, that it was the Scarlet fever she died of. . . .

24. . . . I eat more at my dinner to day, than at any time since I was indisposed, and drank some beer after it for the first time, I have lived almost on renet whey. . . .

26. . . . I went down to dinner for the first time. . . . S. Stamper has lost her only grand Son, of whom she was speaking affectionately, to us the other day, by the Scarlet fever after 48 hours illness, her Daughter T. Moor's wife, and one grand daughter is all she has left—her grand Son was 16 years old. great, I doubt not, is her Affliction. . . .

28. . . . My husband was taken last night with his distressing complaint, a great difficulty of making water—what he did make was very Sanguinary, and the same this morning he sent afternoon for Dr. Rush, who came this evening he advised 35 drops laudanum to be taken at bed time. . . .

May 1st. . . . WD. went to Chrisr. Marshals apothacary to ask him to look over his old receipees, in order to discover what it was that Dr. Chovets pro[cor]ibed for Joseph Scott, who he cured of the disorder HD. now labours under.[3] . . . I walk'd in our yard a little while to day the first time since my Sickness, did not go into the garden.

May 3. . . . Poor Sally Stille, has lost her other dear little daughter Emma Stille, of the putrid sore thoroat and Scarlet fever—I sincerly pity and feel for her. . . .

7. . . . Nancy called after dinner—she had been this morning to visit Sally Stille in her Affliction, she came down stairs with a Note she had written in her hand, and a bundle, two of her dear Childrens Dresses which she wish'd Nancy would except of for her little girls, as they were, the only acquaintences of her Children &c. . . .

3. Dr. Abraham Chovet, who had practiced medicine in Philadelphia from 1774 to 1790, had introduced the policy of written prescriptions for patients (George W. Norris, *The Early History of Medicine in Philadelphia* [Philadelphia, 1886], 91–97; LaWall, *Pharmacy*, 404).

8. . . . little Mary Skyrins first tooth was discoverd this evening, one of the under fore teeth which generally comes first, but not allways—she wants 10 days of nine months. . . .

13. . . . Molly seems better of her cold, but her face is yet swell'd by the tooth ach—she was very much fright'ned yesterday they lost Sally for some time, look'd all over the Neighbourhood, Molly run out in the damp to enquire for her, sent all her people different ways.—found the little hussey under the back Chamber bed, where she had hid, and heard them looking for her—she should have been whiped. . . .

14. . . . Jacob and Sally Downing sett off about Noon with their Children, Eliza, Mary and Henry, on their way to the boarding-school, where Eliza and Mary are to be depossited, Henry to return with his parents on second day next. . . .

[June] 5. . . . Sally Downing here this evening she and Molly &c. have been to the place in Popular lane, that Saml Rhoads has taken for the season. . . .

7. . . . William and Esther appears to have got over the Measles—the little one has not yet taken it, that they know of. . . .

10. . . . My husband mett a committee at the fourth street meeting house, on the business of errecting a Meeting-house in the grave-Yard.[4] he and I, are of opposite oppinions relative to the propriety of such a step. . . . Nancy Skyrin who was here this evening with her Children talks of going to morrow to Frankford. . . .

19. . . . Caty Roberts finished whitewashing to day, she has been 4 days on and off—charges 9/4½ p day. . . .

21. . . . Alice Wright came to inform that she had a sister with 3 Children at her house, they came from Virginia, her sisters husband is a free man, the oldest child is left behind; their master was about sending them to Carrolina slaves for life! they contrived to make their escape, and are now with alice, she is in a qui endier a Je about it as the master has sent persons to hunt them

4. The committee, appointed by the Philadelphia Yearly Meeting, recommended building a new meetinghouse over the Quaker burial ground at Fourth Street to hold the yearly women's meeting (Philadelphia Yearly Meeting, Men's Minutes, 1799–1827, Friends Historical Library, Swarthmore College, 80–81).

up, the oldest of the 3 Children is 5 years old, the youngest a sucking infant.[5]
. . . I tried the experiment, this evening, of rubbing two peices of loaf sugar
together in the dark, and plainly saw a luminous appearance on rubbing. . . .

22. . . . we have parted with our dear Elizabeth, after being with us 10.
months and five days, she is very thin and rather pale, we all thought the
Country air may be useful to her. . . . we put two quarts of strawberries in two
bottles, filled them up with brandy, and added a quantity of pounded loaf-
sugar—HP. recommended it to HD. as a medicine—he takes it with water for
drink at meals. . . . It requiers fortitude, Patience and resignation to live in
this world as we ought to do; if we can be fitted for the next, all will end
well! . . .

26. . . . we sent this evening for Othniel to lodge here, but he is gone out of
town, so that we have no one to guard us but sleepy Peter, who is now fast in
the window—Sister, Sally, little Rose, Peter and self are all at present in the
house—if we lived in a little log house, with but one appartment, we should
seem a comfortable family—and why not as it is, or as we are—if happiness "is
but oppinion" why are we not generally free from care? . . .

29. . . . Sally Downing here forenoon, they are getting ready to go to their
Country residence. . . .

July 1st. . . . John Skyrin has moved his store into water street, is house is
now shut up; where our Daughter is next to go, we know not.

July 8. . . . WD. and self took a walk this evening of 16 squares, which
almost over sett me. . . .

11. First Day: . . . Peter went to Sl. Rhoad's to enquire how they are, and to
have a walk to visit Pompey, he brought us word that they are all well. . . .

14. . . . we have heard of several cases of fever up town, perhap there is not
half as many as is reported—still, it is awefully alarming! . . .

15. . . . great talk of the fever, many are moving out of the City. . . . My

5. Alice Wright's sister was one of many blacks during the early years of the republic who
followed the route to freedom via Pennsylvania, a free state bordering on three slave states.
Many free blacks and escaped slaves remained in and around Philadelphia, where the African-
American population increased twelvefold between the early 1770s and 1810 (Gary Nash,
"Forging Freedom: The Emancipation Experience in Northern Seaport Cities, 1775–1820,"
in *Slavery and Freedom in the Age of the American Revolution,* ed. Ira Berlin and Ronald
Hoffman [Charlottesville: University Press of Virginia for the United States Capitol Historical
Society, 1983], 4–12).

husband appears to have no idea of leaving the City, should things grow worse I hope he will alter his mind, tho' there are few to whom it would be more inconvenient than my self—on account of bodialy infirmity &c.

25. First Day: . . . Oh! my dear Children, how near are you to my heart; My 3 dear dear girls; and my beloved Henry, all of whom I seldom see; I think more off, in some respects, than my equally beloved William, he being, as it were, under the shadow of my wing; you are all entwin'd in my very heart-strings—I never was so much taken up with the pomps & vanities of this world as many others if I know myself, but since I have been a mother, my Children have been my chiefest care, both soul and body—May the Almighty in his fatherly kindness unite you one to another, so as to give you strength in your union, to be councellours and helps to each other, which may be, without any slight or neglect to your Husbands or Wife—That you may be dutiful and kind to your dear father, now in the decline of life, kind to your Aunt, and nearly united, kind and affectionate to one another, is the sencere desire and prayer of your very affetionate mother. . . .

[Aug.] 3. . . . My husband, this evening said, if we went out of town we should do so and so, I forget what, but it is the first hint we have had of the kind, which I think we must improve by preparing tomorrow; if we get away well, we may be thankfull, but how many of our fellow citizens will be left behind! . . .

6. . . . My husband wrote to Jacob, letting him know that we⁶ have con-cluded to go there as soon as convenient. . . .

9. . . . about 11 o'clock HD. WD. and myself sett off in J Downings Carriage, his black Harry drove. . . .

10. . . . There is no less than 8 servants in the Kitchen five of Jacobs and three of ours—which generally makes confused work, they are seldom [what] they ought to be—Our Sall is consumately impudent when she takes it in head, and Peter very fond of idleness and fun—the servants of this house are not what they ought to be by any means.

12. . . . The flies here are very troublesom, very unlike home.—Our house, I expect, remains as we left it in Statuquo, The 2 Clocks which were wound up when we left home, every hour give the time to the insects & mice if any there be: our Neighbourhood is almost deserted. . . .

[Sept.] 25. . . . When J Downing return'd from the City on fifth day last he

6. The word "were" crossed out.

brought to us, a small basket of grapes from our garden, he sent B. Wilson's Jeffory to John Webb, with an order from HD. for the key—J Webb told him that a Girl in the Alley had been in the Garden a strip'd the peach tree of two bushels or more of peaches—it was a young tree, bore but one peach last year, and that a very large and fine one, it was very full of fruit when we left home, the limbs were prop't up there was grapes and figs &c. which 'tis likely were, many of them, also stolen—which is treffling, I mean the loss,—compared to what might have happened—if they dont get into the house, 'twil be well.

Sepr. 29. . . . Dr. Parke has wrote to his Son here, to day, that the disorder in the City is much increased and is of a very malignant nature, like the Plague, a sorrowful hearing indeed. . . .

30. . . . A List made out by William Currie and I. Catheral both M.D.s of the persons who have been sick, recovered or died of the yellow fever in the Northern parts of the City, and Norn. liberties of Philada. the present year.— 197 in all, 90 died, 79. recover'd 28. undetermin'd—those below Market street are not included. . . .

[Oct.] 2. . . . My husband has had a very trying day; distress'd by an urging and disordred bowels—his Urine bloody—and very painful to discharge—he has been about to day and eat vituals as usual, was worse after night, took 35 drops ladanum—which does not as yet ease him—'tis hard to see him in pain. . . .

13. . . . JD. says that the Doctors some of them say that it will be best to stay in the Country 'till the infection is drove away by frost—My husbands indis- possition makes us wish to be at home, otherwise we would not wish to be, as yet, in our part of the City.

14. . . . I took a walk with William and Eliza round the back meadow, to examine the varigated colours of the leaves of the trees, brought home, green, red, yellow, and purple leaves. The leaves of some trees in the fall of the year look beautiful. . . .

15. . . . Sally went on horse back 3 or 4 miles for the taylor, by herself—little Sandwith rose astride[7] and, held the briddle, while his father led the horse, up and down the lot, smartly—he will be 3 years old the 24 this month. . . .

Octor. 18. . . . John Mullen, whom my husband had partly engaged to drive one of our Carriages to town called to know when he would be wanted. HD. told him when he concluded, he would let him know so that it is given over for

7. The words "on the horse" crossed out.

the present—he sent word by JD. to Paul S. Brown to open our house, I wish he had omitted it, as Paul is but a careless boy, and may not shut it properly up again. . . .

20. . . . two letters from our Son Henry, one to his father, the other to William: with a strange, and to me, a destressing proposal, which I trust he will not put in practice.[8] . . .

22. . . . I wrote to my Son Henry. . . .

25. . . . I expect my Son will get my letter to day: I hope he will give over all thoughts of going to the East-indies if he does not, he will make me very unhappy. . . .

29. . . . Jacob Downing returned home after candle light—he brings bad accounts from our poor City—Numbers are in the Hospital tho' we have no account of them in the papers. The reports were left out just before the Election when the fever had abaited, and they dont like, I expect, to insert them again, a Man was buried from our Neighr. Haselhursts, another opposite to our house, and another between us and arch-street. . . . My husband and self being both invalides, would make home very desirable, could we be there with propriety. . . .

30. . . . The Country, to me, is delightful when in any health—but we see many humbling occurances, that are hid from us in Town—the many droves of Cattle that pass this door, sheep & Hogs also, a drove of upwards of 200 sheep past by the day before Yesterday going to slaughter, we have had very frequent dinners of the best of Beef—we hear at night of a Beef being killed, the next day we have part of it, for our dinner—the sufferings of the inferior animals, as they are called, is here more obvious—as we hear and see more of them. . . .

31. First Day: . . . I bath'd my husbands side, when he had a pain, which has been done for some time past, and he took as usual 30 drops Ladunum— he is now fast asleep. . . .

Novr. 1. . . . My husbands mind seems sett on going home, he has fixt on 4th. or 5 day for all of us to go—the last accounts we had from town were by

---

8. Henry S. Drinker apparently wanted to give up farming and try his hand as a merchant's supercargo or agent on East India voyages. The issue arises sporadically during the next few years, although Drinker would not act on his plan until 1806. His cousin by marriage, Thomas Pym Cope, who thought Drinker was already living beyond his means, called this desire "a strange infatuation hurling him to destruction" (H. S. Drinker, *Drinker Family*, 41; Harrison, *Thomas P. Cope*, 281–83).

JD. on sixth day last—and were the worst we have yet heard—but he thinks this weather will clear away all infection, I wish it may. . . .

3. . . . We left Downingtown between 8 and 9 o'clock. . . . I never choose to ride over the Bridge, HD. WD. and self took a view of the works at Schuylkill, I mean the large piers that are erecting for a new bridge, it appears to me to be a great work.—walk'd over the bridge, and mett 3 Waggons on it—I wett my feet in getting out of their way[9]—Cowards are oftenest in danger. arrived safe at home about 4 o'clock or before, found our house in good order— Our Dog Tarter was the first to welcome us, the Cat soon after. . . .

Novr. 5. . . . Our Patience came Yesterday Morning on the old terms, Paul S. Brown came this morning so that we are just as we were before we left town, Andrew excepted—the best of them all in my Oppinon, he could not wait without a place 'till we return'd, I expect he will come and offer himself again ere long. . . .

Novr. 18. . . . My husband has been unwel all this day with his gravely complaint a frequent urgeing took 40 drops ladunum, which is more than he has taken heretofore.

30. . . . We read an Advertisement in the paper of this evening which has cause uneasiness and apprehension in my mind, but my husband says I may be mistaken.[10]

[Dec.] 2d. . . . Peter went this evening to Nancys, Molly was there, Nancy sick up stairs, how sick we know not: Poor dear Nancy, Poor dear Henry, the latter would not perhaps, thank me for my pity, I feel much for him Neverthe- less—I know he loves me, his love is not lost—My Children are as dear to me, seemingly, as my existance—I believe no wife or mother, is more attach'd to her near relative[s] than myself. . . .

Decemr. 3. . . . Molly Rhoads . . . heard that a Subscription was handing about for errecting a Temple of Reason for the Deists. Oh! what will this

9. The deep, swirling waters of the Schuylkill made building piers for the permanent bridge one of the most formidable tasks faced by the bridge builders. The first stone on the eastern pier had been laid on Sept. 5, 1801, but on the western pier, where workmen were forced to dig forty feet until they came to rock, the first stone would not be laid until Christmas 1802. Some of the older floating bridges had no railings and would sink slightly under the weight of traffic (Powers, "Historic Bridges," 265–90).

10. ED feared that her son Henry had advertised himself as "having a knowledge of business and an extensive number of reputable connections" and was looking for work as a merchant's supercargo (*Gazette of the United States*, Nov. 30, 1802; see above, Oct. 20, and below, Dec. 17).

World come too!—Poor Philadelphia how art thou altred!—and where will all this end.

6. . . . A French Man who was in Amricia since the revolution—wrote an account of his travels, and among many other errors, he says, that the Quakers put on worsted Stockings on the —— day of september to a Man.[11]—he was mistaken, for I who am a quaker, have not put them on till this day, it has been such a moderate fall. . . .

7. . . . Molly Rhoads was here forenoon, she has made a beginning to wean her Son, having a great weakness in her Eyes, not sore eyes but as if they were drawn into her head, and her sight fails, she has been told it is owning to her suckling such a strong lusty boy—and was told of a person who lost her sight by it—that after her Child was wean'd, her sight was restored.[12] . . .

15. . . . I went out after 11. o'clock, called to see Becky Tompson, JJ. and CJs wife there—then went to McAlesters for Spectals[13]—order'd new glasses put into bows I had—then walk'd round to J Downings where I dined. . . .

Decr. 17. . . . WD. out towards evening, he bought pruens and call'd at Brounsons printer, he thinks by what he heard that the Advertisement in the Paper of 30 last month address'd to Merchants, was not by whom we thought, so much the better if tis so. . . .

18. . . . Sally intended to come here, but it was too cold to walk, and she could not ride with the Children, as our street is dug up, to lay the water pipes. . . .

31. . . . in about an hour and half, the new-year will commence—the idea always strikes me with a kind of awe, to think that I have lived another year and my dear family still with me—how long it will continue so, the Lord only knows!—may we be properly prepared for a seperation! . . .

11. Brissot de Warville, *New Travels* (301), states: "On the fifteenth of September Quakers put on woolen stockings. This is part of their system of discipline, which applies even to their clothing, and they attribute their longevity to the regular observance of this custom." Two English editions of Brissot de Warville's travel journal had appeared in the late 1790s in London, and several pirated editions followed in the U.S. (xxvi).

12. Alexander Hamilton, a noted Edinburgh physician and professor of midwifery at Edinburgh's famous medical school at the end of the eighteenth century, wrote in his 1792 treatise on female disorders that nursing women were susceptible to two classes of complaints "in consequence of the drain of milk proving too weakening of their constitutions." The first class included back pain, excessive daytime languor, night sweats, and "gummy" eyes. The second involved the actual inflammation of the eyes (Alexander Hamilton, *A Treatise on the Management of Female Complaints*, 6th ed. [Edinburgh: Peter Hill, 1809], 215).

13. John McAllister, though listed in Philadelphia directories as a whip and cane maker, was a well-known optician. In 1802 he was living at 48 Chestnut St. and ran his business with a partner from the house next door at number 50 (Harold E. Gillingham, "Old Business Cards of Philadelphia," *PMHB* 53 (1929): 200–201).

1803

1803. Janry. 1st. . . . Parting with the Old year is to me rather sorrowful, the commencement of the New year, is more chearful—the spending the year as we ought, is the main matter. . . .

Janry. 16.   First Day: . . . On Second day last, Nancy Skyrin was at S. Stilleys, and the Children at home with the Servants Elizath. standing too near the fire, her frock caught, and was soon in a flame, their maid Polly and little Eleanor burnt their hands in putting it out, the Skirt of her frock is so burnt that it must be repair'd by a new one, how wrong it is to dress Children in Callico in winter, many have been the instances of Children being badly hurt and some loosing their lives, yet still it is continued. . . .

17.   . . . WD. attended the sale of some land belonging to his father at the Coffee house[1]—if HD. had men as honest as himself to deal with, he would not meet with the many perplexities that he does. . . .

Febry. 1st.   . . . sent Paul when he went to his dinner to know how Nancy and Molly were—Nancy he say'd had her head bound up, she had a bad head ach, which she hoped would go off, I suppose she had taken opening pills, which has often had that effect—Molly he say'd came to the door to him, and told him that they were bravely—to come to the door, so soon after the pleurisy, was very imprudent, Those who have Children and love them, especialy married Children, have many cares—I am glad to hear that my son Henry is well. . . .

2d.   . . . Patience took Oatmeal and wine to Alice Wright to make gruel, two or 3 days ago, this morning she tells us, that Alice is so ill that the doctors say she cant recover that 5 young Doctors were there last night—for what! for no good I fear! It looks indeed as if she was not in the way of getting better— her legs are very much swel'd, her stomach also, and one breast very much enlarged—she has been blister'd, and they talk of more blisters—if the same

---

1. The sale of over seventeen thousand acres in Huntingdon County, Pa., belonging to HD took place at the coffeehouse on Second Street between Walnut and Chestnut streets (advertisement in *Poulson's American Daily Advertiser*, Jan. 4, 1803).

idea strikes her, as does me, of the visit of the young Doctors—she must feel distress'd—Poor Alice! . . .

7 . . . Wm. Ellis has named his youngest Son, now 11 months old, Henry Drinker Ellis—as a mark of respect to HD. . . .

8. . . . about an hour after I laid down HD. arose and look'd at the window, on raising my head I heard fire cry'd. it was then between 3 and 4 o'clock—we none of us got up to enquire, but in Sisters room—the bells rang best part of an hour—This morning heard it was friends Schoolhouse in fourth street— where I went many years to school to Ay. Benezet—and where my Sons went to learn Lattin—I was uneasy in the night thinking of my Children, but had they been in danger, we should soon have known it. . . .

10. . . . my husband has been ever since his little ride yesterday on business, been very poorly with his old complaint, his urine is Sangunary—and he is in pain—disorder'd in his bowels, took more than his usual dose of ladunan 45. instead of 33. . . .

11. . . . Hannah S. Drinker was here before dinner—she seem'd uneasy and said several things to very little purpose—I hope my Son will not go abroad. . . .

14. . . . William was here this Afternoon, his Aunt Betsy Smith, and Uncle James, with little Esther was with him—he took a ride, on his Uncle Williams little Horse, Peter Woodard waited on him, he was very much pleased with his short ride. . . .

21st. . . . Sally Downing was here forenoon—she inform'd us of the Death of Robt. Morgan, oldest Child of Thos. and Nancy Morgan, between 15. and 16 years of age, he died, I believe, of a mortification in his Knee, Poor Nancy! I really feel much for her, knowing her to be a very affectionate Mother, and this was a promising pritty Lad:—but what can we promise ourselves in this world of trouble. . . .

22. . . . A little Saucy girl, whom HD. had often drove from our steps, he found there again this evening and gave her 2 or 3 boxes in the ears—her Mother came very angry, but went away in rather better temper. . . .

Febry. 23. . . . poor Alice Wright, is, as Patience says, near her end, she has been one of our humble servants. . . .

Feby. 25. . . . Our Patience came this morning to inform us of the Death of

Alice Wright, who died in the Night—she came for a Windingsheet and other things to bury her in. . . .

27. First Day. . . . This is my birth Day, and the same day of the week, that I was born which is never likely to occur again.—all my mothers Children which was but 3. were born on a first Day morning. . . .

28. . . . Paul S. Brown went home this evening unwell, he said he had sat up last night with a sick Sister, and that he had a chill. . . .

[Mar.] 4. . . . Our Sally Dawson has been offering her service[s] to Phebe Waln, without consulting me, I believe she thinks she will not be free till she leaves us, poor girl she dont know what she is about, she says she shall get 1½ Dollars a week—I dont intend to say against it, but expect she will be sorry for her conduct. . . .

28. . . . I have seen no body here to day but the Doctor—and so much the better may be—as I have had a very trying day sick stomach &c—the Doctor desired me to continue the powders, they, with the Pills I took last night, made me very sick—had the pills done their office I, perhaps, should not have been so sick by the powders My Cough continues hard, I cant bare to think of any kind of food, tho' I set up and walk about the room, very seldom lay down tho' very weak. . . .

30. . . . Elizath and Eleanor were here to day, they are always pleas'd to come, but unwilling to leave us.

[Apr.] 17. First Day: . . . My husband tho' very poorly went to meeting, he has left the Harlem Oyl,[2] and took a tumbler of cold water for 2 nights past, and quit the ladunam which he has been in the practice of taking 30 drops every other night, changing hot medicines for cold, so suddenly, will not, I fear, suit him. . . .

18. . . . Elizath. Skyrin came to tell us her Sister Eleanor is very unwell with something like the bloody flux. . . .

19. . . . Elizath. Skyrin came with little Mary, I am surpris'd Nancy would trust her with the Child, she shall not take her home. . . .

2. A popular seventeenth-century British nostrum also known as Harlem Drops or Dutch Drops, this mixture of linseed oil, sulfur, and oil of turpentine was considered "serviceable for heat of urine" (La Wall, *Pharmacy*, 333–34; Committee on Recipe Book of the American Pharmaceutical Association, *The Pharmaceutical Recipe Book*, 3d ed. [n.p.: American Pharmaceutical Association, 1943], 128–29; W. Lewis, *New Dispensatory*, s.v. "oleum empyreumaticum," 268).

20. . . . My husband is gone this evening to visit our dear little Eleanor. . . .

21. . . . WD. went to know how Eleanor is, she continues better. . . .

May 1st. First Day: . . . Sall Dawson arose at 4 o'clock to go Maying—these are new airs in her. . . .

May 9. . . . Our dear little William came on Horse back by himself from North bank, with a letter from his father to his Grandmother Smith, whom he mett on the road going up, giving an account of the safe delivery of his Mother of a Daughter just before William came away about ½ past 10 or 11. forenoon, he was here, Afternoon at 5 or 6. o'clock, this intellegence was a relief to my mind, as my husband had heard since dinner from Sally N. Waln that Hannah Drinker was dangerously ill and had 3 Doctors with her. . . .

10. . . . JSs affairs in bad plight, which is not unexpected.—poor N——y.

13th. . . . settled with S Dawson, paid her off, she seems to have a great call for money—to purchase finery, she has laid out £27.6.—since she has been free, which is not quite 17. months all but 8 or 9 Dollars paid her to day. . . .

17. . . . S Brant took tea with our Sally Dawson. . . .

21. . . . I believe I must endeavour to take but very little Snuff, as I think it contributes to hurt my head and, perhaps, stomach.—obstructed bowels is another cause. . . .

27. . . . Sally Downing and Molly Rhoads were here before dinner, they had been to shops, they look well dear Creatures. . . . I have been poorly all this day, very poorly tho' not ill.

June 1 st. . . . Betsy Smith was here to day with an Iron Coller, which I lent them some years ago, for one of the Children that stoop'd. . . .

15. . . . My husband on a Committee of the landholders this evening. . . .

21st. . . . I took a walk of 8 squars this evening with William a very fine new moon light came home tired the first walk I have took since the night I came from HPs when I was taken with the sweming in my head. . . .

22. . . . Sally took Molly this Afternoon to the place where S. Rhoads is going to reside this Summer, where they were last summer in Poplar lane. . . .

24. . . . Dr. Rose dined here, as did Elizath. and Eleanor Skyrin. . . . Peter

has been to day assisting Molly to move her things out of town, where she expects to go herself this Afternoon in S.Ds Carriage; she bid us farewell last night.—several in & out the Office to day—J. Skyrin call'd for his Children about 5 o'clock. . . .

25.   . . . no account from any of our Children to day.

27.   . . . [Rey] King told HD. that he mett our Son Henry last week going to mill, driving the Cart himself, with several bags in it, he remarked, that it had a very reputable look, which I do not contridict, but at same time, I think, there is nothing disreputable in a servant doing that business where it suited. . . .

28.   . . . Jn. Hillar came by appointment to Cup me, an hour latter than he was expected, near 9 o'clock, I did not feel in the humour to have it done, as WD. was not return'd from his ride my mind uneasy on account of his being so late out. . . . it is now near 10 o'clock and William not yet returned, it is so unusual for him to be out so late on horse back, that I am realy very uneasy— it is a fine clear moon light night. may be he is at Mollys, tho' that I have no reason to suppose. he came home after ten, had been at Mollys to tea. . . .

29.   . . . This evening about Seven o'clock, John Haylor came, he fixt 7 Cups on my back, a little below the Neck, and one on each temple, or under—each cup received 16 gashes 144 in all,—those on the side of my Face hurt much worse than the others, he did not take above 4 or 5 ounces of blood, very thick, and somewhat inflam'd. . . .

30.   . . . our dear Children are all gone into the Country but William, I shall miss them. . . .

[July] 2.   . . . We were much alarmed towards evening by the loss of little Saml Rhoads, it was, perhaps, a quarter hour before he was found. the Necessary, was the most frightfull Idea, William got a long string of twine and a Candle which he let down, but could not determine the matter.—It was well, he soon after made his appearence from Race Street corner with two other Children with him—It is a shocking situation, Molly poor girl, was much distress'd for the time. . . .

8.   . . . My husband went into the tepid Bath before dinner, he handsel'd a new bathing Tub, which WD bought yesterday for 17 Dollars—made of wood lined with tin and painted—with Castors under the bottom and a brass lock to

---

let out the water.[3] . . . Sister Sall, Judy and Rose, busy upstairs Buging &c, in two of our bedsteads some bugs were found, a very uncommon occurance with us, as we are often, for years together, without seeing one, and when any make their appearence we make fuss enough, and make a throrough examination.—J Smiths Nurse, brought little Sally Drinker Henrys youngest Child for us to see, she will be two months old tomorrow, a pretty Child—looks well and healthy—I was much pleased to see her—some born, and some dieing! . . . Molly continues disorder'd in her bowels—she has always been so, in the situation I suppose her to be at this time, wish I was nearer her. . . .

11 . . . WD. and self went this evening to see Hannah Pemberton, she is going out of town, Betsy and Sally Jervis there, to enquire for John Wilson—If I was not much better than for[4] many week past, I could not have taken such a walk. . . .

16. . . . HD. and self went before dinner into the bath, *pas ensamble*, I went after him, had more warm water put into the tub. . . .

17. First day: . . . Our Rose's Sister came to say, that their little Brother Tommy is dyeing, he wanted to see Rose very much—they live 2½ miles off, I let her go, tho' I did not altogether credit the account, If crying was a mark of the truth, she cryed and so did Rose. . . . Rose came home after night, her little Brother is better, he was playing at the door when she got there. . . .

20. . . . I was taken very unwell early this morning with a violent pain in Stomach and Bowels a purdging and vomitting follow'd, WD. went or sent for Dr. Kuhn, who soon came, he ordr'd an Applycation of flannel wet with hot Brandy to the pain'd part, and to take nothing but Chicken Water during the day, if the pain increased or did not get better—we were to send a recipet he wrote to the Apothacary, &c. . . .

22. . . . I have not eaten a crum of any kind of food, nor drank any thing but Chicken water since third day last, but some molasses and water this evening I have been about house as usual, but have not walk'd as much as common being very weak. . . .

23. . . . I am rather better to day: which I wonder at, feel stronger than

---

3. Wooden bathtubs lined with metal made their first appearance in Europe in the latter half of the eighteenth century and arrived in Philadelphia shortly thereafter. The establishment of a municipal water system in Philadelphia in the first decade of the nineteenth century further encouraged the use of home bathing devices, although they did not come into widescale use until later in the century (Lawrence Wright, *Clean and Decent: The Fascinating History of the Bathroom and the Water Closet* [London: Routledge & Kegan Paul, 1960], 88, 126–38; Sidney Hart, " 'To Encrease the comforts of Life': Charles Willson Peale and the Mechanical Arts," *PMHB* 110 (1986): 330; Richard L. Bushman and Claudia L. Bushman, "The Early History of Cleanliness in America," *Journal of American History* 74 (1988):1213–38).
4. The words "any time" crossed out.

yesterday, so that I am convinced, we may live without eating, or make very little suffice, I took one dish Coffee, and a little dry bread for my breakfast—eat rost lamb in great moderation for dinner, nothing more, do I intend 'till tomorrow, unless 'tis molasses and water or an opening pill. . . .

27.   . . . It is 4 months and 11 days since our Son HSD. was here.

30.   . . . WD. MS. Sally, Rose and Tarter[5] went into the warm bath. . . .

[Aug.] 3.   . . . our dear little William Drinker is to go to a Boarding School some time in this week—his Father will miss him, young as he is, and the Child will be out of his Element. . . .

10.   . . . I went with my husband before 10 o'clock, to John Inskeeps to acknowledge a Deed before him—After my return home, and being as usual, some time up stairs, I went after William into the warm bath, as he said I stay'd too short a time in the Water Yesterday—MS. went after me—it is attended with some trouble to warm water and fill the Bath, so that we make the best of it—I have no objection to going into it after my husband or Son &c—but William and Nancy, chooses to be the first, or not to go into it at all. . . .

Augt. 11.   . . . The Yellow Fever increases in New-York, and there is some talk of its being up town in water Street. . . .

14.   First day: . . . SD. has had a party in the Kitchen this evening—Tea, pound Cake, water Mellon, &c—3 young men and 3 girls—it wont do often. . . .

29.   . . . My husband took tea at Edmd. Physicks this Afternoon.

30.   . . . tho' my husband, myself and several of our friends are unwell, yet it is a healthy Summer.

[Sept.] 10.   . . . P. S. Brown, informs us, that 4 or 5 deaths have occur'd, in Water Street between Chestnut and Market Streets, that many more are taken down, and that several families in that square have shut up their houses and left them.—this looks serious! . . . My Cough continues deep and hard, but not so frequent, nor have I quite so much fever. . . .

Sepr. 20.   . . . About 4 o'clock this Afternoon, who should come in but our Daughter Ann with her little Mary, they came in Hainss Stage, she felt uneasy not knowing how we were, and would not wait 'till fifth day, when we

5. The family dog.

generally send for them—I am pleased to see her, but am rather fearful of their coming to town at this sickly time. . . .

22. . . . a girl of the name of Hannah Stringer, an intimate of our S. Dawsons, a maid of Neighr. Campbells, has come by Salls invitation to lodge here to night &c. girls who are runing about the City at this time, without fear or care, are not desireable inmates, their foulk went away to day. I did not like to refuse her, but shall not like a long continuance of her company.

28. . . . This morning Sally Dawson was going to market, but complain'd of a pain in her head and sick stomach, Sister told her she had better lay down and not think of going out,—soon after she vomitted frequently, I sent for Dr. Kuhn, knowing how imprudent Sally had been running out of nights &c the Doctor said he hop'd it was not the Yellow fever, but might turn out an intermittent fever. . . .

29. . . . It has been a day of trouble, to us, tho' worse might have happen'd—I cant describe how I have felt this day, indeed it is what I do not at any time undertake to do—Sally continued very ill, but not so much so as to alarm me much—Docr. Kuhn came rather sooner than is common for him, he went up with me, and examin'd her Eyes which were red—on coming out of the room he told me she had the Yellow fever. . . . my husband and the Doctor talk'd of sending her to the hospital,[6] he say'd she would be taken as much care of there as she could be here, unless her mistress could attend constantly on her, which I am not qualified to do, was I in good health, and the rest of my family absent, I think I could undertake it, but that would not be allow'd of—the Doctor wrote a note to the board of health, and a Carriage was sent about 3 o'clock P.M. in which she was taken—she shifted herself and was dress'd rather smartly—stood at the kitchen door while her bed and bedcloaths was put into the Carriage. . . .

30. . . . the sending SD to the hospital, I believe was quite right, my mind is more at ease, tho' we have not heard, yet how she is. . . . Now, if I had strength of body, and firmness of mind to have undertaken the care of our SD. my family would not have suffer'd it, tho' I think with Dr. Kuhn's help, I[7] might have brought her through—but I believe we have acted for the best. . . .

6. The City Hospital, established in 1793 and since 1796 located at the Wigwam Inn, where Race Street met the Schuylkill River, was designed for yellow fever victims who could not be cared for at home—generally the sickest and poorest patients; its mortality rates approached 50 percent. The resident physician in 1803 was John Syng Dorsey, assisted by Charles Caldwell and Samuel Duffield. Sally Dawson's admission to the hospital would be recorded on Oct. 1, 1803 (Powell, *Bring Out Your Dead*, 73–74, 195–206; Rush, "Yellow Fever, 1797," 35, 52–57; Rush, "Yellow Fever, 1803," 139; Scharf and Westcott, *Philadelphia*, 1:516, 2:1666, 1676; *Poulson's American Daily Advertiser*, Sept. 15, Oct. 1, 1803).
7. The word "would" crossed out.

Octor. 1. . . . our poor Sally is very bad and delirious. . . .

Octor. 3. . . . John Alsop came forenoon, he had not been to the Hospital,
but had heard on enquiring that our Sally Dawson was gone. . . . My husband
went to fourth street meeting—brought a letter home in his pocket from Docr.
Dorsey, who stays at the hospital, Nathan Smith gave it him at meeting—
wherein he informs, . . . this morning she expired at a quarter before 6
o'clock, without having suffer'd, as she often told him, any pain, but weakness
and sick stomach. he thinks, he has seen but few cases of more malignant
disease than hirs. . . . Thus it is, a pretty girl, in the bloom of youth, with an
high and independant spirit, taken off the stage of life[8] in no more than 5 day's
illness—a lesson for the young and old. . . .

6. . . . Jacob tells us in his letter that a Waggon from Downingtown is now
here and could take any thing we wanted to send—and we could go with him
tomorrow, Sally is very much distressed at our continueing in the city.—I
ask'd my husband what he thought of Jacobs proposial, he said, nothing at
all—so that there is no probability of our leaving the City. . . .

9. First Day: . . . Tomorrow morning is a week, and but a week, since our
Sally departed—how distresss of some kind wear off the mind, 'tis a favour it
is so, sometimes, I do not feel quite as I did this day week—tho' it comes over
me at times hard enough, to think, how quick was the transition from health
to sickness, and from Sickness to death.

Octor. 10. . . . S Rhoadss family are indisposed—Sister Rhoads has a cold,
her maid Jane has a fever, Pompey the same, the two Children had yesterday a
chill followd by fever, to day the Children are about & Chearful but the
servants in bed. . . .

16. First Day: . . . My husband and Sister went to morning meeting as
usual, HD. went in the Afternoon. . . .

Octor. 21st. . . . there is such a sameness in my way of living every day, that
I have little to say. . . .

23. First Day: . . . HD. went this Afternoon to Thos. Stewardsons, he is
lately return'd from the Indian Country. . . . This is Sally Downings birth
Day, 42 years, few are favour'd to have both their parents living at that age.

[Nov.] 7. . . . I have put on most of my winter cloathing, another Jupe, and a
Grazette[9] Gown. . . .

8. The word "with" crossed out.
9. A silk and worsted dress material, often with warp of one color and weft of another
(Montgomery, *Textiles*, 243).

8. . . . Sister went to Neighr. Pratts after meeting: 'tis seldom we visit our Neighbours.—Judath and Peter went Afternoon to the Negro meeting—many will not call the black people Negros, 'tis thought by some rather a harsh appelation, but as it is a common name for them and Niger is, I believe, the lattin term for them, which is black, think there is no impropriety in it.—have they not always been so calld? Affricans, Ethiopians indeed—but those here are nither.

13. First Day: . . . HD. WD. writing this evening.

Novr. 15. . . . on first Day last I put on a flannel under garment, it is new with me.[10]

19. . . . I had a fire made in our room, but went down stairs as usual, Doctor called and said he wishd I would stay in my Chamber, the frequent passing thro' the entry and coming up and down renewed my cold, if the cough was not better in a day or two, I must loose more blood—he order'd a medecine which I took last spring to cut the Phlegm, &c. I am now up stairs, and how long I shall remain so, cannot judge. . . .

[Dec.] 2. . . . Yesterday I took the last pinch of Westons snuff,[11] that, perhaps, I shall ever take, unless by Chance, as none is to be had in this city, nor none imported—it is upwards of 50. years that I have taken snuff, more or less, and mostly of the same kind—it was more the custom when I was a girl, for young persons to take it than it is at present. . . .

3. . . . Our son HSD. bid us farewell, I had a very affecting conversation with him—they are going homeward to day. . . .

7. . . . my cough seems a little renewd, I nevertheless intend dineing down stairs to day. . . .

10. Women did not wear flannel underclothes in the 1760s, but by 1805 they had become commonplace during the winter months (Benjamin Rush, "An Inquiry into the Comparative State of Medicine, in Philadelphia, between the Years 1760 and 1766, and the Year 1805," in *Inquiries and Observations*, 4:381).

11. Probably a reference to a brand of snuff made from 1760 to 1786 by Thomas Weston (d. 1791), a London Quaker tobacco and snuff manufacturer. In England, snuff taking among women became popular with the ascension in 1760 of George III, whose wife, Queen Charlotte, was a prodigious snuff taker. Even earlier in the century, the practice was common among elite female Friends in the Philadelphia area. Either smoked or chewed, tobacco was thought to have medicinal value in evacuating phlegm (see below, Apr. 15, 1806; reference to Weston Snuff in *Pa. Journal*, July 31, 1760; information on Thomas Weston courtesy of Phyllida Melling, Guildhall Library, London; C. W. Sheperd, *Snuff Yesterday and Today* [London: G. Smith, 1963], 66–70; Weiss and Weiss, *Snuff Mills of New Jersey*, 18; Blackwell, *Curious Herbal*, vol. 1, pl. 146).

12.   . . . HD. went this evening to W Saveries—WD. to Dr. Duffields, he gave the Doctor a list of what Sally Dawson took to the Hospital, he said he would enquire after them—and further said of which I most desired to know— that Sally, when in the Hospital, made very little complaint or moaning as many others did—that she was very much dibilitated, and her blood dissolved, that she had the disorder in a very melignant degree, that it generaly prove'd fatal to Girls, that she lived but 3 days after her coming there—William ask'd him, if he thought she would have lived could she have had the best of nurseing at home, he answer'd No, she could not—all this is rather satisfactory than otherwise. . . .

Decemr. 14.   . . . John Lawless was here this evening for money to buy books to improve himself, of which there is great room. . . .

Decemr. 16.   . . . I believe I require less sleep than many others, it is yet very trying to lay for 4 or 5 hours waking after going to bed. . . .

21st.   . . . Saml Hodgson, Ebnezar Bowman, and Dr. Rose mett, HD. in our back parlor this forenoon on Business.

1804

1804.—First Day of the week, first of the month, and first of the year—if we are to spend the year as we begin it, as some say, we will—Nancy Skyrin will have a stormy year of it. . . .

[Jan.] 27. a fine winters day—Nancy spent the day agreeably with us, as much so as could be!—all things considerd—Sally Downing and her little Sally—spent the Afternoon, The family of our kitchen, Betsy, Judah, Rosee and Peter took a ride this moon light night in the Sleigh.

28. rainy morning clear'd up cold towards evening the melted snow has made the streets very sloppy, and it will be very slip'ry . . . Nancy has been at home all day, few Men who cold help it would go out to day. . . .

Janry. 30 . . . Rose's father and Stepmother, and others called.

[Feb.] 12. First Day: . . . Nancy Skyrin came in the Stage from Frankford,[1] and our Son Henry and his Son William came also in a Stage, towards evening—it is very agreeable to me to have my Children with us—they all lodge with us—clear star light night.

19. First day: William junr. went to meeting with his Grandfather. . . .

27. . . . I have passed another mile stone this morning the miles seem to shorten as we come near our journeys end.

March 4. First Day: . . . My husbands birth day. 3 score and 10—70.—we are both grown old, and feel so, tho' not so much as many of our age.

7. . . . Dr. Wm. Shippen called forenoon to inform me that he was under the necessity of going to Neshaminey to attend on his daughter in Law, who expects every hour to be taken ill, he hopes he may be back before my Molly is taken unwell, tho' her time has been some time out according to common reconing, but she has always overstay'd it 3 weeks at least. . . .

1. The Skyrins had a home in Frankford.

12. . . . Nancy & Children are come to stay sometime with us—I have seen all my Children this day but Henry. . . .

13. . . . HD. went to the burial of Charles Eddy.

22. temperate, Pompey came this morning to inform us that his mistress had been ill all night, that the Doctor and Nurse were with her—Sally Downing was sent for in the night, their Man Harry was out, they found him in a Neighbors house who has a bad black girl—I have had an anxious day—Nancy and Sister came home in the evening—Molly, dear girl, was delivered about 5 o'clock this Afternoon of a daughter by Docr. Dunlap.[2] Shippen still from home—she is as well, they think as may be, what a favour!—Sarah Rhoads, M Sandwith, Sally Downing, Nancy Skyrin, the Doctor and Nurse were with her. . . .

26. . . . WD. called forenoon at SRs Molly setting up pritty well, the baby sucks.

30 . . . no accounts from any of our Children this day, what will Sally Downing do, in a damp house, which they are cleaning—2 months hence would have been time enough for that business. . . .

[Apr.] 16. Several at breakfast, when all were gone to meeting I set of for my daughter Mollys. Elizath. Skyrin with me, I have not been from home before since last November. . . .

[May] 6. First Day: . . . I have not heard from any of my Children, this day has appeard rather long and lonesome, which is what I very rarely complain off, nor do I now, tho' all days do not appear exactly alike—I am not well, far from it.—tho' I might be worse, therefore have cause of thankfullness. . . .

7. . . . HD. MS. WD. went to quarterly meeting. the 2 latter did not stay to business. . . .

20. First Day. . . . MR. told me an affecting piece of intelligence, that My Friend Mary Penry is no more! Peggy Stocker sent her word, the particulars she has not heard—she was in her 69. year—we were acquainted upwards of 50 Years, perhaps 4 or 5. I have lost in her, I do believe, a sincere friend and an agreeable sensible coraspondant—how many of my old Friends are gone before me! . . .

2. James Dunlap's practice "was extensively and almost exclusively devoted to obstetrics" (Henry Simpson, *The Lives of Eminent Philadelphians Now Deceased* [Philadelphia: William Brotherhood, 1859], 605).

21. . . . I intended after tea to have gone to Peggy Stockers to enquire what she knew of the death and Sickness of M. Penry, but signs of rain put off my journey, a journey it would have been to me, who have not been so far, but once or twice for a twelve month past. . . .

30. . . . Nancy and her Children left us about 10 this morning I sent for John Haller to bleed me, he struck twice before he brought blood—the blood is better than last bleeding, but far from good—This has been a day of trial to me, not on account of the bleeding, that I think nothing off,[3] Peter return'd about 6 o'clock, Nancy left her Children at John Comleys at Bybary, his wife is the School Mistress, her name was Becky Budd, has been one of the mistresses at Weston School and said to be well qualified for that Business,[4] Peter Says that the dear Girls weep't when their Mother left them, the Mistress was gone to meeting—when I weigh'd the Bowl this evening in which I was bleed, found it weighd 8 ounces; with the blood in it, it weighd 20 ounces & ¾—so that instead of 8, as the Doctor order'd there was 12¾. . . .

[June] 23. . . . Sally Downing and 2 or 3 of her Children came to bid farewell as they talk of going to morrow to Downingtown. . . .

24. First Day: . . . I feel much for my Son, he talks again of going to the East Indies—which hurts my feelings. . . .

[July] 2. . . . Polly Summers a black woman who has been with us 4 weeks tomorrow, will be loath to leave us, but she knows so little of Cooking, that we cannot well make out with her. . . .

[Aug.] 2d. . . . Mary Downing was here forenoon, Eliza this evening she set her muslin Shawl on fire, it blazed up, she tore it off, and WD. put it out with his foot—he and I went home with her. . . .

6. . . . Mollys Dan was here, he says the 2 oldest Children have the Chills and fever, I sent them Century.[5]

3. More than two lines crossed out.
4. Rebecca Budd had taught arithmetic and grammar at Westtown, where she met John Comly, who was teaching reading, Latin, and grammar. They married in 1803 and a year later started the Pleasant Hill Boarding School for girls in Comly's native Byberry. Subjects taught included reading, writing, arithmetic, bookkeeping, geography, English, grammar, and needlework. The tuition was one hundred dollars, payable quarterly. The school, converted to a boys' school in 1810, would be discontinued in 1815 (Dewees and Dewees, *Centennial of Westtown*, 55; Comly, *Comly Family*, 102–3).
5. The American centaury, a bitter herb, was commonly used to alleviate remittent and intermittent fevers (Millspaugh, *Medicinal Plants*, 514).

Augt. 9 . . . Sandwith Downing came to see his cosin Mary, they had very little to say to each other.[6] . . .

13. . . . Hannah S. Drinker was deliver'd yesterday morning of 2 Children a Son and a Daughter—so that our Son Henry at present has 6 Children, and has buried two—they have been married 9 years and 8 months, nearly—O dear!

24. . . . Our maid—Nancy Stewart left us this morning before any of the family were up, she has been in ill humour for some time past, with Peter, Judia and Rose, she would not eat with Negroes which we did not desire her to do—Peter was backward in waiting upon her—she said nothing to me of any affront, but went off without giving notice—there has been two to offer their service to day. . . .

27. . . . J Downing saw Sam Rhoads who inform'd him that Molly had something of the flux. . . .

Augt. 28. . . . Molly had had a good night and is better, she was blooded yesterday—has no one with her but her family who are ignorant—a sucking child—My situation &c is such that I cannot be with her—'tis trying to be seperated from ones Children, especially in time of sickness. . . .

[Sept.] 8. . . . Clementinea is come to town to the funeral of her Sister, who has been long unwell—Nancy does not wish her return, thinks she can do better . . . I have hired Clementinea to stay with us 'till she can get a place, she does not understand cooking &c. . . .

27. . . . Hannah S Drinker, we understand was delivered of her 2 little ones before the arrival of the Doctor. 'tis a favour when it can be so, tho' alarming. . . .

Octor 2. . . . I went after dinner William with me down to Mollys, she was in her room up stairs tending the 3 Children, while the Whitewasher and her girls were cleaning the house—Molly has had a fit of Colick, but is better, the little one continues disorder'd in her bowels—We left her before sunset—came round second street, called at Emer Kimers, bought 3 little books there— stop'd at the Market, bought peaches, I have not taken such a walk for some time, 12 long squares. . . .

11. . . . E. Downg. was here this forenoon, she came from Frankford this morning says her Aunt Nancy has a bad cold, and ES. the tooth ach—My

6. This is not surprising, since Sandwith was not quite five and Mary was three.

mind would be releived of much anxiety if she and her little family were with us, it must be so, I think, she waits to hear from her husband, but she may wait, no one knows how long. . . . Peter went for Frankford before 3 o'clock—Paul Brown return'd from New York &c—Peter return'd before night brought Elizabeth with him, and a trunk of cloths &c—he is to go again tomorrow to help Nancy and bring her &c home, the thought pleases me. . . .

Octor. 27. . . . Anna Duffee called, I engaged her to come here to service on 3d. day next. Mollys man Dan came to let us know that his mistress was very unwell and wish'd to see me—I have a cold on my breast and in my head, which is generaly the case with me when the weather becomes cool—Nancy went down to know how Molly was,—she sent her Elizath. back to inform us that her Sister was very unwell WD. went with me there. . . .

30. . . . Anne Duffey came here this morning at 7/6 p week.

Novr. 1st. . . . Our Children; Elizath. and Eleanor began a quarters Schooling at the uptown school-house, they go in the forenoon to Ann Thomas to learn reading, writing &c. Afternoon to Ann Tucker to sew &c. . . . I made a pair Shoes to day for Elizabeth Rhoads. . . .

[Dec.] 11. . . . Alice Woodward Mother to our Peter died Yesterday at the Bettering-house,[7] as it is called, they buryed her in 5 or 6 hours after her decease, she has been measureably deranged for some time past.

13. . . . Eliza Downing came to invite Eleanor to the Examination of the second class—she went, and stay'd 'till 10. at night. . . .

Decr. 17. . . . Nancys chamber door open'd with the wind after 10 o'clock, I heard them shut it, and was uneasy, not knowing but something ailed one of the Children, was apprehensive if I got up of taking cold. . . .

19. . . . I went with WD. to Jos. Inskep's, he was not at home, we then went to M. Lollers Mayor, where I acknowledged a[t] Deed from HD. to Willm. Alexander—did not find the cold so hard as I expected, am favour'd, I trust, to escape taking cold. we left the Deed at the Mayors, HD. is to call there for it. I have not been abroad, before since the cold weather commenced. . . .

26. . . . Henry S. and Hannah Drinker, sup'd here, Susan Smith with them—have not seen Hannah for a long time past. . . .

7. A synonym for the Philadelphia Almshouse (Billy G. Smith and Cynthia Shelton, "The Daily Occurrence Docket of the Philadelphia Almshouse, 1800," *Pa. Hist.* 52 [1985]: 115).

1805

[Jan.] 3. . . . our Son Henry came about 3 o'clock with his William and little Js. Smith, William bid farewell, as his father is now about taking him over the river to Haddonfield and leave him to board at James Hopkinss to go to school to S. Munson Day. . . .

6. First Day: . . . the two days past have been like former winters, 'tho I cant say, as some do, that they never felt colder weather, 'tis not because I stay much in the house, I go enough about, to judge of the weather, by different things. . . .

14. . . . Peter took his Master out this¹ afternoon in the Sleigh, Nancy went on his return to Mollys, where she spent the Afternoon, Peter went for her in the evening he took Jacobs Children Sleighing forenoon, Eliza was here to ask it—This evening he took our Anna and Nancys 3 girls a mile or two—Willm. Drinker junr. came runing in after Candle light, he came over the river in a Sleigh with his School master on the ice, was in a great hurry, and a great heat, runing to see his friends, I wish he may not take cold, after being so heated. . . .

Janry. 15. . . . I sleep't none 'till after 4 o'clock this morning so had some oppertunity of seeing something of the Eclipse, the moon was totaly eclips'd about 2 o'clock or near it—being awake, and the moon shining in our room, I could plainly perceive the diminution of light as the eclipse came on, I did not arise, but being wakefull, made my observations. . . .

Janry. 18. . . . Nancy was busy all this forenoon in the kitchen making minced pies, a business she well understands. . . .

19. . . . HSD. and Esther lodges with us. dear little girl, she is a fine child, I wanted to see her—our Children are much pleased with her.

24. . . . little Wm. Drinker the beginning this week attempted to fire off a pistol loaded 6 fingers deep, it kick'd against his face, stun'd him, and wounded his face in two or 3 places—it is well it is no worse. . . .

1. The word "morning" crossed out.

Febry. 3.   First Day: . . . soon after 6 o'clock who should come in but Willm. Drinker junr.—he came from Haddonfield, part of the way in a Sleigh, he walk'd 3. miles and over the river—called at the boy's house who came with him and at his grand-father Smiths—he lodges here.—not quite clear this evening after nine o'clock Jammy Smith junr. came for WD. but his Grand-father HD. say'd he must stay here. I believe he is tired of the walk he has taken.

11.   . . . our old Neighbour and acquaintance Hannah Shoemaker departed this Life about 2 weeks ago at Germantown, she was brought to the City to be buried—aged upwards of 70 years—thus our cotemporaries move off, one after another!—This house we now live in was built by Hannah Shoemakers father, of whose hairs we bought it.[2] my Sister and self lived next door.

Febry. 12.   . . . little Mary while she was out, fell on the kitchen step, and cut her forehead, a deep wound which bleed much, Dr. Rose came in while I was about dressing it he assisted me. . . .

Febry. 20   last night, my husband was taken with disordered bowels, was up and down very often in the corse of the night, not in much pain but a great runing off . . . in the Afternoon he consented we should send for Docr. Rush—who order'd injections of flaxseed tea made strong with liquid ladunum in it, say 60 drops, and to give him ten drops every 3 or 4 hours, and 35 at bed time, which was complyed with. . . .

21st.   Nancy sat up with me last night, we were almost constantly employ'd, as my husband had frequent calls the forepart of the night and his legs so cramp'd that they were quite hard on the Calf required rubing. . . . As Nancy went to her bed at 6 o'clock this morning she said if I would go to bed this night, she could set up very well—which she did—My husband sat up the greatest part of the day—the Doctor say'd this morning he was much better, had no fever, he reads, his voice is low and weak, which I dont like—Nancy went to bed this morning also at 6 o'clock and sleep'd till about noon, when Sister arose—when I sit up a night by chance, I do not lye down in the day, as I think I feel worse for it.

23.   . . . our Son H.S.D. continues with us, he did intend going home this morning but waits to see his father better . . . he eat a bit of meat for his dinner, and smoked his pipe after it, an agreeable circumstance I always think

2. Hannah Shoemaker's father, Benjamin Shoemaker, was a mayor of Philadelphia and a member of the provincial council. He died in 1767; the Drinkers moved into the house in 1771 (Benjamin R. Shoemaker, comp., *Genealogy of the Shoemaker Family of Cheltenham, Pennsylvania* [Philadelphia: J. B. Lippincott, 1903], 36–40).

when those that use tobacco and have been too ill to take it as usual call for it—it is very mild weather wind S.W—I know not how it has been for 3 or 4 days past, what I have wrote is mostly from recollection since third day last till this day. . . .

26 and 27. . . . numbers have been to enquire how HD. is, wish we could say much better, the Doctors tell us he is so, and I hope they think as they say— but I have my fears, on 3d. day night, which was the 7th. day, I thought appeard critical, about that time the lax stoped, we thought next day he was better, but has been ill ever since. . . .

March 1st. . . . There are some things that are necessary I should attend to relative to myself, that I find difficult to accomplish at this time, but no matter, if my husband gets abroad again, I shall have more time to attend to my own concernes, and have reason to be thankful. . . .

2d. . . . The Doctors this evening order'd 40 drops of Hoffman's medicene[3] and a anodyne Pill. . . .

3d. 'Tis now between 2 and 3 o'clock First Day morning MS. is up with me, my dear husband appears in pain, with hiccops and wind, is so much under the effect of the anodyne as not to be sensible when we speak to him, he cannot sleep, or wake, I have not been so frighten'd since he was taken unwell, there is something wrong about his breast I fear; at 5 o'clock he would get up, we dressed him, his bowels were again open'd and he vomitted, the effect of the pill—he went again to bed about 6 and fell asleep, we were pleased he had been up 'tho did not approve it at the time—I lay down by him, we both sleep'd 2 hours, at 9 or 10 he arose, and seems better, the Doctors who came before he was out of bed, pronounced him so. . . .

March 4. . . . Dr. Griffits did not come this evening I suppose he intends coming but once a day—if that is the case, he undoubtedly thinks HD. much better. . . . This is my dear HDs birthday 71 years.

5. . . . HSD. and Sally Downing sat up—HD. sleep'd well the first part of the night, was restless after. . . .

9. . . . my husband continues mending, but is very weak—he has eat 2 Eggs for dinner, the Doctors were here forenoon, no kind of medicine recommended to day. . . .

3. A compound spirit of ether, also known as Hoffman's Anodyne or Hoffman's drops; used for nervous disorders, "especially low fever and stomach complaints associated with hysterical disorders" (Gould, *Dictionary of Medicine*; Estes, "Therapeutic Practice," 382).

13. . . . it is 49 years this day since the Death of my dear father—HD. was up very early, he has eat his breakfast with a relish. . . . little Mary Skyrin has taken unwell this evening she complain'd of her throat, had a fever, the mumps are very prevalent. . . . 'Tis now between 12 and one o'clock, all asleep but myself, who am scribling, must go into the Childrens room to see little Mary, before I go to bed.

15. . . . at 11 o'clock came Saml. Smith, Ann Alexander and Mary Roach, after a long silence, Ann had some things to say, *wide of the mark.* WD. had something also to say, very pertinent, which she, perhaps, will not be much pleased with—how carefull ought those to be in what they offer, who pretend to be led and guided by the truth, and call themselves Gospel ministers.[4] . . .

20. . . . Peter Woodward is this day a free man, if being 21 years of age and [out] of his time will make him so—no talk of parting yet, poor fellow I sencerly wish him well. . . .

March 23. . . . I wrote to Molly endeavouring to preswade them to have their Children Vaccinated instead of inocculated for smallpox—SR. is for the latter, which might be done afterwards, if they were in doubt . . . one Wall has mov'd next door where Lee lived, he is a chair maker, and is errecting some sort of building in the Yard, which would once have been more disagreeable to me than at present, as it probably may cut of some sky-light from us, the older I grow, the less I think of triffles—which is a favour.

25. . . . Paul S. Brown bid us farewell this even'g he is going into S. Rhoadss Counting house tomorrow, he has been with us about five years—My husband has not sufficient employ for him at this time of life, he is desirous of learning shiping business &c. . . .

31. First Day: . . . My Mollys two youngest Children were innoculated about 3d. day last by Dr. Kuhn for the Small pox—it will be an anxious time with her in which I shall participate. . . .

April 1. . . . Poor Eleanor has mett with trouble this Afternoon, she did not behave quite well, and her grandfather repremand'd her, and she had been keept at school.

---

4. Ann Tuke Alexander, a British Quaker minister traveling through the U.S. to several different Quaker meetings, would publish while in Philadelphia a condemnation of slaveholding addressed to residents of Charleston, S.C. She would return to England in December 1805 (William Alexander, *Some Account of the Life and Religious Experience of Mary Alexander, Late of Needham Market* [Philadelphia: B. and T. Kite, 1815], 48–62, 109–10, 148; Ann Alexander, *An Address to the Inhabitants of Charleston, South Carolina, Condemning the Slave Trade* [Philadelphia: Kimber, Conrad, 1805]).

2. . . . Henrys little Son is bravely—he has vaccinated 4 of his Children since he was here, they have had the disorder, and got over it finely. . . .

4. . . . John Buch called to make Peters freedom Cloths. . . .

9. . . . Nancy Skyrin very unwell this evening she has taken cold—a pain in her limbs, little chills, and pain up the side of her Neck—I bath'd her Neck with Opodeldock, she held her feet in warm water, and took Cammomile tea when in bed—she left our room this night where she has sleept ever since her fathers illness. . . .

13. . . . I went after three o'clock, Nancy Reiger with me, down to Mollys. . . . I have not been so far from home for a long time past—but 3 times out of the house, or rather from our door, 'till now, since last fall. . . .

18. . . . J Smiths Nurse was here this Afternoon with our little twin grand Daughter Hannah Drinker, she is a lovely babe 8 months old. I have never seen her before. . . .

25. . . . My husband has lately been inform'd of the Death of his old friend Fredrick Pigou. Thos. Stewardson received an account of his decease when HD. was ill in his Chamber, but as he was an old friend whom he valued, and about his age, we thought it best not to mention it 'till he was better. . . .

27. . . . Oh! my dear Children how much I feel for you, My HS.D. and Nancy—JS. wrote her that he expected to be at home the middle this month, she has since heard that it is not likely that he will arrive here for a longer time—she is perplext to know how to act—to go by herself again to Frankford, or to hire a small house in town. . . .

[May] 9. . . . WD. all day up stairs writing as usual—I pull'd out a tooth for HD. this evening—Henry & Sandwith Downing were here forenoon. . . .

May 10. . . . Our daughter Molly was here forenoon with her Son, the first time I have seen him out of Peticoats. . . . Betty Newton alias Deborah was here forenoon to take materials to make me a persian[5] gown.

May 14. . . . Nancy, and a Girl she has hired to day named Phebe Walton, and Peter, went to Frankford after breakfast to put the House in order, they return'd in the evening to late tea. . . .

5. A thin, plain silk, mainly used for linings in coats, petticoats, and gowns (Montgomery, *Textiles,* 321).

15. . . . we have our daughter with us another night, she intended to have gone to Frankford but rain prevented her—she received a letter the day before yesterday informing her that he intended being at home on sixth day next.— the letter from J Skyrin dated at New York—he was but 90. days on the pasage from Carolina to N.Y. . . .

16. . . . Nancy left us at ½ past three in Jacob Downings Carriage, her little Mary, her Maid Phebe, and Black Becky, with her Elizath. and Eleanor is to stay with us 'till seventh day—Nancy and her 3 Children and Beck have been with us 7 months and 2 weeks, we shall miss them much—Peter return'd before night, he informs that John Skyrin was at Frankford before them. . . .

May 17. . . . John Skyrin called this Afternoon, he says he left Nancy well, but little Mary has some cold. John looks very harty and well.—he has been absent 11 months. . . . Molly sent word that they had colds but were geting better, the young one has been ill for two nights past, she is cutting 2 Jaw-teeth, an early age for that business, not 14 months old.

23. . . . Our Son HS.D—left us after breakfast apparently with a very heavy heart, the weight of which I have partaken not in a small degree—he talks of selling his farm & I believe of going abroad—but we dont talk with him much about it—not knowing what he intends. . . . Betty Newton fitted my gown this forenoon. elle parler beaucoup.[6] . . .

27. . . . Nancy is low Spirited—Lord preserve our dear Children!

30. . . . WD. Nancy and self went out this evening we called to see Hannah Thomas, who is very weak and feverish—then went down to Saml Rhoadss he and Molly were abroad—sat some time to rest, then came home much tired I mean myself—it is I believe ¾ of a mile there—a mile and a half is no triffling walk for me. . . .

June 1st. . . . W.D. is also gone to take a ride on his little horse, he has not rode out on horseback for a long time past, his Saddle is new, never used before and his horse not much used, I shall be pleas'd to see him well home— he is not well. . . .

10. . . . I assisted to day doing what I never in all my life did before, drowning 3 kittins, 3 days old—the old Cat came to us 8 or 10 weeks ago, a pretty Tortise coulour'd cat.—I thought if they were sent by Petter to the river, he would see them swim ever so long.—as we managed it, the poor little things were soon out of pain lap'd them up in a Cloath and pump'd on them

---

6. She talks a lot.

I know not how it happen'd that I could have an hand in such an undertaking. . . .

15. . . . William and Nancy went this evening out to eat Ice'd cream; the eating of iced cream, or going to the ice'd cream house are two acts neither of which I admire or approve. . . .

20. . . . WD. went into the warm-bath before dinner the first time this Summer—finished making and Phil[ ]ing a quantity of Liquid Ladunum yesterday.—My husband is gone this evening to attend the sale of Atsion Iron-works at the Coffee house⁷—by which he is like to be a considerable loser but it is nissesary they should be sold. . . .

[July] 4. Annaversity of Independence as it is called. . . . Jacob Downing, his daughter Mary and Son Henry Henry Drinker junr. his Wife and 4 of their Children, sett off this morning for Atsion, quite a group. . . .

7. First Day: . . . Jacob Downing &c &c are return'd from Atsion. . . .

20. . . . William received a letter from his Brother giving an account of the illness of their twin Son, dangerously ill, dear lamb! I never saw it—or is it likely I ever shall, tho' little Children go through a great deel, sometimes and recover, and they have a skillful Doctor not far from them. . . .

[Aug.] 22. . . . John Skyrin called, he says Nancy is poorly, but not ill—How near are my Children to my heart. I must soon leave them, May the Lord preserve them! . . . WD. received a letter from his brother yesterday—he has sold his Farm, the thoughts of which adds not to my Comforts! . . .

29. . . . We understand that there is 12 new Cases of Yellow fever in Southwark. . . .

[Sept.] 5. . . . Our Baker was paid off to day, he is afraid to come with bread, as the fever is in our Neighbourhood. . . .

Sepr. 6. . . . My husband was out since night, I would best like our family to stay at home, as the evening air is stronger with any thing infectious than when the sun is up. . . .

7. Notices of the sale, with the terms of purchase, had appeared in newspapers in April. The works included a blast furnace, an air furnace, a forge, two hammers and a cinder bank, a gristmill, two sawmills, a smith's shop, numerous outbuildings, and accommodations for the smith, a clerk, and seventeen workers and their families on twenty thousand acres of land, some of which was also improved for farming (*Poulson's American Daily Advertiser*, June 13, 1805).

10. . . . I sent this morning for John Haillar, he came between 11 and 12, open'd a vein and took 11 ounces blood, I weigh'd it—John acknowledg'd that he had bleed many in the Yellow fever—said his lancet was safe—I did not altogether like it—but!. . . . It is evident that the disorder increases down town, and is, here and there, a case in different parts of the City. Our Neighbourhood appears almost forsaken, the houses generaly near us shut up—clear moon light.

Sepr. 12. . . . The burying the Dead, who dye in this disorder, so soon after the breath appears to leave the body, is an awful circumstance; indeed I have felt pain in thinking how soon, it is the custom here, to interre the nearest friends after their decease, in the old countries it is common to keep them a week, but our hot summers will not admitt it—indeed in winter, one or two days is common with some, if a person dies with us, in hot weather, the burial is invited too the same day, to be concluded the next day change or no change—now would it not be better to have a Coffin ready, and when an evident change has taken place, if there is not time for an invitation, a few relations and friends might answer as well as a long procession or so think I. . . .

16. . . . The Musquitoes are more numerous & troublesome than for some years past, the reason of their absence laterly I have imputed to the introduction of the Schuykill water, which prevents the necessity of keeping rain water standing in the yards as formerly. . . .

17. . . . The disorder seems to increase. . . .

23. . . . By the accounts in the papers, the fever dont appear to increase, but we hear of cases nearer to us. . . .

Octor 6. First day: . . . This morning on attempting to rise, found myself incapable of so doing, I dont recollect much pain, but down right weakness, I lost my recollection and nearly, if not quite fainted away. . . .

From the 6th. of this month, on which day I was taken ill, 'till this day which is the 16th. I cannot make out any regular account—I was for several days so weak as not to be able to walk to the easy chair, without help—On fourth day the 9th. Sister was taken very ill, fainty and much disordered in her bowels. . . . We have had Nancy and Molly both with us, dear girls, I know not what we should have done without them. . . . What a great consolation it is in times of sickness and distress to have a good Doctor and kind friends around one— My husband has not been neglected, the complaint in his bowels is no worse, 'tho it sometimes returns—he continues to take Sage-wine, and at times spiced Rhubarb—his appetite is good. . . . We have had a variety of operrations, performed, purging, bleeding, sweating &c &c—May we be truly thankful that we are what we are a present. . . .

Octor. 17. . . . Our dear Nancy left us about 3 o'clock, John went with her—
they went to look at a house in 11 street between Market and Arch streets,
that John talks of taking. . . .

20. First Day: . . . We are, as some say, to thank God for all things—I have
cause of thankfulness in many respects—but I am far from well—the old
obstruction in my bowels makes much against me, when a weakly person
comes to be near three score and ten, they cannot lay out for much of what is
called comfort in this world—if they can keep from a large share of bodily
pain, 'tis all that some of us ought to look for. . . .

Novr. 1st. . . . I am still under the necessity of being in my Chamber oweing
to a weakness that still continues with me, is worse than heretofore on account
of weakness and relaxsation and will continue, undoubtedly more or less
while I continue in this vale of trouble. . . .

10. First Day again: how fast the Weeks pass off. . . . I eat my dinner in my
Chamber, Sister being alone would not have the cloath laid, but din'd in the
kitchen I dont remember the like ever before happening.

Novr. 11. . . . Yesterday when H.D. was at S.Rs Molly told him that little
Sam had nearly Choak'd by swollowing a bit too large for him he was almost
black in the face, they were very much frighten'd—no wonder, every day
something.

18th. . . . Henry Cox took tea and spent the evening with us.—He says that
he really saw a Mermaid, it was dead, he had it in his Arms and examined it,
and is sure it was no deception—so that what I have look'd on as fabulous
seems to be a reality, I believe him to be a man of varicity. . . .

Novr. 21. . . . HS.D. heard, as he pass'd the Methadist meeting last evening
a noise which induced him to go in, there was 5 or 6 under conviction, as
they term it, laying on the flour screming, kicking and some groaning, numbers of the congreation were singing over them—he left them in their exta-
sies—he never saw the like before, nor have I . . . Our Peter Woodward had a
frecaus yesterday with Cake the hatter who lives next door but one to us—they
have made a practice of putting their dirt against our fence in the Alley, most
of this summer, Peter has to clean it away: Yesterday Peter shouveld it back
through the little Alley into their yard, when Cake struck him on the head and
wounded him not a little, he bleed like a Pig as the saying is; he struck Cake
and hurt his Nose, they got warrants for each other, and met at a Justices
where the matter was settled with small cost on each side—HD. told Cake if
Peter had behaved amiss to him he should have complain'd to him which he
acknow'leg'd would have been right. . . .

26. . . . little Sam Rhoads is not well 'tho his health and appetite seems good, he has a running at his Ears, and kernals[8] in his neck. Dr. Kuhn has order'd him dieted, as he is very hearty eater, he says it is humours oweing to his eating too much. their boy Dan has run away, they know not where, he has been very rough for some time past. Molly is not well her self, 'tho she always appears in good spirits—makes the best of every thing.

Decr. 1. First Day: HD. MS. went to morning meeting. we are now reduced to our old small number, four in the Parlor, 3 in the kitchen when Patience is not there. . . .

2. . . . Thos. Stewardson and Danl. Stroud in the Office with HD. on business. . . .

9. . . . I was inform'd to day by my daughter Molly, that HD. expects to lye-in next month, which I have not heard before—the ninth Child. . . .

12. . . . for 5 or 6 weeks past, we have been favour'd with uncommonly beautiful weather—how delightful must it be to those that are in health and can enjoy it—I do, 'tho in ill health and in my Chamber. . . .

13. . . . as I dont lay out for any one but some of my Children to read my silly writings, am the more free to menton bowels and obstructions, than I otherwise would do. . . . by being so, unwill, I am deprived of the pleasure of my dear little grand Childrens company as much as I should like. . . .

22. First Day: . . . spent the evening in my Chamber, my three daughters, 'tis long since they have been altogether their spending the Summer in the Country deprives me of their Company in that[9] Season—and they live so far from us that we cannot expect to see them often. . . .

25. . . . about one o'clock this morning I heard a dull heavy thumping, I could not account for after listening some time I heard musick, then con-cluded that the first Noise was a Kittle-drum—a strange way of keeping Christsmass. . . .

26. . . . I went down stairs before dinner, stay'd but a short time. It will be 3 weeks tomorrow since I was taken ill—since which I have eat no kind of meat, one dish of Coffee, morning and evening with a bit of dry toasted bread with it, turnips in Chicken water for dinner—3 times the Yolks of two eggs. . . .

Decr. 31. . . . My husband and William were this evening at Jacob Down-ings, he has been putting up a large quantity of Pork for the Iron-Works, of which concern he has become a considerable owner.

8. I.e., inflamed lymph glands (Gould, *Dictionary of Medicine*).
9. The word "Summer" crossed out.

1806

Janry. 1, 1806. . . . Peter went home with little Skyrens—he did not return, as he is engaged on a party this evening of black Baux's and Misses. . . .

2. . . . I spent most of this day down stairs—I feel more agreeable when above. . . .

8. . . . I have spent part of several days past, looking over old letters and papers. . . . Our Peter Woodward has made up his mind to go a voyage to sea, and has engaged to go in a sloop belonging to Cope and Thomas, to St. Domingo. . . . We have said all that is proper to discourage him, laying before him the risks he will run, not only in winters passage, but the danger of his being taken and made a slave of, being black, but all will not do,—he has long wished to go to sea; poor fellow!

9. . . . 50 years since the death of my dearest mother.

11. . . . Peter has got from C. Biddle what is called a protection, I wish it may prove one.[1] . . .

12. First day: . . . Sally and[2] Molly are going, I understand, this evening to visit Nancy. I like their being togeather as much as they can. . . .

15. . . . I have been looking over letters this day, from and to New York, during our Sons illness there, which has renewed old feelings—tho' 14 years has not done away my recollections of that time . . . My husband has been abroad, and WD. has been also out—my going abroad again is a thing uncertain, Sister seems as if she was almost done.

---

1. In 1796 the federal government had begun issuing to seamen protective certificates of U.S. citizenship, designed to protect seamen from impressment if vessels were seized. The documents were particularly important to African-American sailors because, in theory at least, they prevented freemen and indentured servants from being sold into slavery. Seafaring was especially important to blacks in Philadelphia, where perhaps a quarter of the black male population worked as mariners (Ira Dye, "Early American Seafarers," *Proceedings of the APS* 120 (1976): 331–34, 348–53; Nash, *Forging Freedom*, 134–36, 145–46).
2. The name "Nancy" crossed out.

18. . . . after mending Stockings, I spent the rest of this day, reading over HDs letters of the years 77 and 78. wrote in Virginia when in Banishment. . . .

24. . . . I have been employ'd for 2 or 3 days past making Pincushons for my Granddaughters; having much leisure and am thro' mercy much better, for 6 days past then before, in one respect. . . .

25. . . . WD. went to J. Downings this evening, Elizas face swelled, and no wonder, the young girls dress so ridiculously thin[3] we need not marvel that they take cold. . . .

26. First Day: . . . this was a beautiful red evening the moon shining, the evening star very [brilliant]—fine, very fine, winter weather.

Febry. 5. . . . W Drinker junr. who drove one of the waggons back from the ferry, is well, wishes to see his father, which he will not soon do, I believe, as his Mother is near her time, and Henry will not leave home.

8. . . . Our poor Peter took leave of us this evening as he expects to sail tomorrow morning at 9 o'clock. the vessel lays far down town, he appears dull on the occasion, I feel for him, his Master advis'd him to keep clear of strong drink and profane language, which I had enforced before on his mind, with several other things that I thought necessary. . . .

13. . . . The Slaughter between the Russians and French has been Shocking, when the best is made of it.[4]—will the world never be at peace.

22. . . . yesterday forenoon I was realy ill for an hour or more in pain with my old disorder, under the necessity when a little better of laying down, which is what I rarely do.

24. . . . I took several walks up and down our yard after dinner this fine day. . . .

[Mar.] 5. . . . I received a few lines from my Son Henry he tells us that Hannah was delivered yesterday of a fine girl, who with its Mother are in a good way: Nurse Kimble came the day before,—all which I am pleasd to hear. . . .

11. . . . HD. has engaged a black man of the name of John Thomas to come tomorrow, as JD. wants John Moore. . . . WD. went out this evening to the

3. The word "and" crossed out.
4. A reference to the Battle of Austerlitz, Dec. 2, 1805 (Chandler, *Campaigns*, 413–37).

University to hear good reading &c perform'd by one Js. Fennel.[5] he came home by 9 o'clock—he went yesterday to see an Ostrich exibheted in south Street—curious.

15. . . . Our Son Henry and his little girl, Thos. Cope and one of his Children set off early this morning in light waggon for the Neighbourhood of Downingtown, I believe he intends to board Esther out to a School or something like it, there away—I dont like, if it can be helped, boarding out girls anywhere. . . .

[Apr.] 5. . . . My Motto, is Je suis [Seuls][6]—or apparently so.

13. First Day: . . . Last night, or rather this morning about one o'clock I heard a loud noise in our yard like something heavy falling, I thought it might be the old spout that stood up inside the pent house,[7] or the sides of the Wheelbarrow which John had fixed carelessly against the wall—Our Dog who was in the kitchen bark'd as loud and as hard as he could, I soon after heard WD. getting up, he did not know what awaked him, but when awake, the barking of the Dog alarm'd him, he called John up, and went down stairs and in the Yard, but discover'd nothing—the faithfull Tarter when he saw that he had made report to the family was quiet, I believe he would have been noisey all night if he had not seen some of the family—This morning a Baker's Sign painted with a barrel of buescuit and loaves of bread &c was found in our Yard. It had been thrown over the fence by some mischivious person. . . .

14. . . . Sally Downing came after 9 o'clock, she says that her daughter Mary has the Itch, which I beleive is a great mistake—Eliza and Mary were here in the morning, Mary shew'd me her Arm, which is broke out on the inside, like a rash, nothing on her fingers or breast,—I think it is the Nettle rash, which the late cold weather and thin cloathing has occasion'd. . . .

15. . . . Elizath. and Eleanor Skyrin came after dinner Sister gave them and Patience money to go see an Elephant that is in town, little Wm. Cooke was with them—they were highly entertained.[8] . . . Isaac Jones was here again with 2 bottles of his best old Snuff—I wish I could easily leave it off.

---

5. James Fennell, a famous British and American stage actor, offered a course of dramatic readings and recitations for six weeks beginning Mar. 4. The readings, held at the University of Pennsylvania's building on Ninth Street every Tuesday and Thursday evening, consisted of selections from authors such as Shakespeare, Milton, Pope, Sterne, and Goldsmith (*DAB; Poulson's American Daily Advertiser*, Mar. 1, 19, Apr. 4, 1806).
6. I am alone.
7. A shed with a sloping roof, usually attached to a larger building (*OED*).
8. A live elephant had been exhibited at the George Tavern on Second and Arch streets. The price of admission was twenty-five cents, and children were admitted for half price (*Poulson's American Daily Advertiser*, Apr. 9, 1806).

16. . . . Nancy Skyrin dined with us her throat is still in a weak state, she went home before tea as her Children are going to a party this evening of [J].Cs at B.Ws I never wish'd to deprive dear little Children of innocent amusements, but dont like mixt parties &c. . . .

19. . . . I finish'd working a Queen-stitch Matt, for M. Rhoads. . . .

May 2d. . . . Our Anna has taken a House at 20 pounds a year, as she says, to keep shop and take lodgers.

3. . . . Sally Nicholdson called this morning by appointment to take muslin to make 3 Shirts for Peter, ready against his return. . . .

6. . . . I went, WD. with me afternoon to visit Tabetha and Becky Fisher, 'tis the first time that I have been out of our front door for 8 months past. . . . Our son, Henry came with his little Esther before tea. he is going to take her to board and be School'd in Chester-County, at Jams. Emerys 4 miles from Downingstown. . . .

8. . . . Our Son Henry and his daughter left us about 8 o'clock, intending for Downingtown to day: tomorrow for James Emerys, dear little Esther does not like the thought of going from home—Henry is a most kind and indulgent father to all his little ones, &c. . . .

11. First Day: . . . the cold which I have taken by carelessness, and the Change of weather, the sore throat and little fever that I have had, for some days past, and being necessitated to take a pill, all those occurances have put me out of sorts. . . .

12. . . . Settled this evening with A Duffy, she will be here 80 weeks next day after tomorrow, and has taken up but 17¾ Dollars, so that she will have a good sum due to her, but it will not go far towards furnishing a house &c—she is a saving manageing body—has money due to her in the back woods, she says 100 Dollars—I wish she may make out reputably—. WD. teaching our black John, his letters &c—he has arrived to words of one syllable. . . .

13. . . . S. Swett came to spend the day with us—she sent for Docr. Kuhn to examine a red lump on her Cheek that she has been uneasy about for some time past—The Doctor spoke of it as nothing alarming, advis'd a plaster of Goulards cerate,[9] to be renew'd morning and evening. . . .

9. An unctuous combination of wax and extract of lead, or Saturn, in alchemist's parlance, named after Thomas Goulard, a French surgeon who experimented with lead-based preparations (W. Lewis, *New Dispensatory*, 204–5; Mr. [Thomas] Goulard, *A Treatise on the Effects and Various Preparatins of Lead, Particularly of the Extract of Saturn, for Different Chirurgical Disorders* [London: P. Elmsley, 1773], 201–3, passim).

15. . . . I see my Children much seldomer than I could wish, especialy Sally, they dont consider that they will not have their mother long to visit. I dont like to tell them so, as I trust there is no love wanting.

16. . . . Doctor Redman was here forenoon, he lends and borrows books to and off us, and if he could hear well he would be a very agreeable companion, considering his age. . . .

18. First Day. . . . Our poor M.R. thinks! . . .

20. . . . a black woman came to hire, she has a husband and a child, I beleive she wont do. . . .

May 23. . . . Some weeks ago, our John was about laying a small stick of wood on the fire, I observed marks on it that I wish'd to inspect, on so doing discover'd 18 or twenty exact representations of sheafs of wheat, as well done, as if cut by an artist, with a pen-knife, it was the work of worms under the bark of hickory wood—I was showing it to S. A. Law this morning, he says, he thinks it curious enough for the museum. HD. laughs at it, as he is apt to do at all triffles. . . .

26. . . . S Swett dined here. the lump on her Cheek is more inflamed! . . .

[June] 4. . . . S. Swett came in the forenoon, she sent for Lewis Cunits, who applies Leeches, she had about a Dozen applied to her sore cheek, not all at once, he was upwards of an hour busy about it. . . .

June 6. . . . Sister went this evening to see S. Swett, and to recommend Patty Brand[10] a Docteress who has done many cures, but SS. puts off, 'tho' she thinks her face is no better.

13. . . . M. Brand was here, Abraham went with her to S. Swetts, she says she cannot pronounce the sore to be a canser, nor can she say it is not one— she is to send her an ointment which if it brings it to run good matter, she thinks she can cure it. . . .

14. . . . WD. and self went this evening to Betsy Jerviss set a short time, came home before ten—walk'd eleven squars. the longest walk I have taken since last summer. . . .

10. Martha G. Brand, a Quaker physician who may have been known for treating skin cancers (Whitfield J. Bell, Jr., "Martha Brand (1755?–1814): An Early American Physician," *JHMAS* 33 (1978): 218–19).

17. . . . Mary and Sally Downing were here, they took home some baby toys. . . .

21. . . . our black Judath was here yesterday and the day before doing days work, as she calls it, washing and Ironing, her little Michel with her. . . .

June 23. . . . Sister went this evening to visit S. Swett, her face is no better, she has applied to Dr. Catheral, who is attending at their house, he has ordred another sort of plaster; I think she has done wrong in applying to another while she was under the care of M. Brand. . . .

24. . . . Jacob had wrote for Sally, but since has countermanded his orders, as he wanted her to sign a Deed, but since finds it will do some other time. . . .

[July] 7. . . . sent this morning for Dr. Phisick, he came, told him the situation of S. Swetts face, desired him to visit her, which he did, his opinion is that the lump in hir Cheek must be cut out, nothing else can cure it and he cant say possitively that that will. I went to see her this evening Molly Rhoads with me she is to conclude ere long; and if it is to be done to send for the Doctor—she seems composed, I feel much for her. . . .

9. . . . Sally and Nancy went to see S. Swett, the poor old woman has come, I believe, to a conclusion to have the lump in her Cheek taken out, but the time is not fixt. . . .

July 10. . . . Sally Downing left home at about one o'clock for the Valley, to stay, perhaps, all summer. her Daughter Mary, her maid Polly, Elizath. Skyrin went with them to spend a little time in the country. . . .

15. . . . Our Peter Woodward came this Afternoon, he is well, and if he can get a good place wishes to stay on Shore, if not he will go to sea again—John Thomas has behaved well since he has been with us,—it would not do to turn him off. . . .

18. . . . HD. went into the warm bath, prepar'd by Peter and John for me, but I felt so weak and unwell that I could not undertake it—My husband has been twice in the french-man's bath—and William once this Summer—It is a little more expence but much less trouble for the men, than getting it ready at home. . . .

19. . . . Dr. P—— visited S. Swett, this morning he says the lump in her face must be taken out by the knife—she put him off for a day or two, when she is ready, is to send for him. . . .

July 21. . . . Robert Proud paid us a morning visit, he is in his 78th. year—complains of infirmity, but is an agreeable companion, he left with me some verses of his own making, which I intend to coppy. soon after he was gone, another Old Gentleman came in Dr. Redman, to whom I lent some extracts relative to Bishop Newton &c. . . . Our Maria came last night from Nancys.—We have suspicions that she is in a way, that will not suit, if it is so, for her to be long with us, why did she leave her own friends and Country? . . .

22. . . . I had a Conference this morning with our black woman Maria, I ask'd her the Question point-blank, she own'd it was so, says it is her husbands Child, he has been dead 6 months, that she will lye-in in less than 3 months. Why did thee come among Strangers in such a situation? because they would not pay her wages, Are they kind to thee? Yes, then go back to them and live without wages till thou art up again—she says it[11] is her father-in-Law that she lived with, but it is hard to believe any thing one hears. . . .

23. . . . Dr. Physick has, at S. Swetts desire, engaged to wait on her tomorrow morning. . . .

24. . . . I arose near an hour sooner than usual: went between 8 and nine to S. Swett. stay'd till between 12 and one, No Doctor, S.S. was disapointed—I came home to dinner—after dinner Mary Hillborn called to let me know that the Doctor would be there at 3 o'clock, I went, and he came, Dr. Dorsey with him. S. Swett appear'd undismade, sat down in the Arm Chair ready for the opperation—her face was towards the window, I sat behind her on the foot of her bed—she made some complaint in the groaning way, in the begining, but not any, or next to none afterwards; as near as I could judge he was 5. 6. or 7 minuits about it, she bore the operation with great fortitude, the Doctor thought so, as did I. the Cancer, for a Cancer, I have no doubt it was, was as big as a very large garden Bean, and the hole in her Cheek appear'd much larger, she bleed a a great deal—had to change most of her cloaths. Dr. P. said she should have Some one to sit up with her tonight, least her face should bleed, I observed he tied something with thread in two places, which I suppose was veins, that were cut and occasioned the great bleeding.—M.H. say'd she will get John [Tease's] daughter to set up with her—HD. came there after 6 o'clock, I came home with him. . . .

27. First Day: . . . A.S. went after meeting to see S.S. who is no worse—she expects the Doctor towards evening to dress her face, sent to know if I would come—After tea towards dusk, Nancy and myself went to M. Hillmans, Becky Price was upstairs, with S.S.—Dr. Dorsey had dress'd her Cheek, it is easier since, and does not appear inflamed—I was pleased to hear it was done. . . .

11. The word "was" crossed out.

Augt. 1st. . . . seven months of this year already gone, and we have not had a physician in our house on account of any of our family's being indisposed—'tho we have been often complaining.

4. . . . From the Observations that I have made there are more die in the 72d. year than in any other between 40 and 100—even more,[12] than in 63. the grand Clymactric, as tis called—but there is no age exempt. . . .

7. . . . I went into a warm bath this afternoon, HD. after me, because he was going out, Lydia and Patience went into the same bath after him, and John after them—If so many bodies were clensed, I think the water must have been foul enough. . . .

9. . . . My husband and Sister went after candlelight to see S. Swett—they found her bravely—the proud flesh lissend and her Cheek in a fair way of getting well—in time. . . .

21. . . . Our Neighbour Hahn's Wife was here this evening to enquire something concerning a Negro Doctor that our Negro man knew of, as her grand daughter is ill of swellings and pains &c. we could give her no information, Christian Hahn has lived 20 years she says, where they now are, within 3 doors of us, and I do not know that I have ever seen her before—so little notice I take of many around us. . . .

Augt 23. . . . S. Swetts cheek is a little painfull, and occasions some painful apprehensions, but she hopes it may all do well yet—poor thing I wonder not at her fear.

Augt. 27. . . . WD. gone out this beautiful moonlight night—I wish I could have gone with him, but must try to be resigned to what, I have long been used too, staying at home. . . . Saml. Rhoads gone out of town for some time.

Sepr. 1st. . . . JD. inform'd us at dinner that Saml Rhoads was gone to the Havanna expects to make a short stay, the day he went away, Molly told her Brother, she is in much trouble least he should get the yellow fever, he has no other reason for keeping he going [a sort] of secret than that he might get quietly away. . . . S.R. is gone after a vessel that is taken, his Partners wife is near lieing in so that he could not leave home.

5. . . . sent Abraham forenoon to ask S. Swett how she was, she told him that a hard lump had form'd in her sore Cheek. . . . I have not been well enough for some time past to wait on her, poor thing! I had a hard pain in my right

12. The words "I think" crossed out.

arm and Shoulder all the fore part of the day, 'tis better this evening perhaps rheumatic, 'tis a new complaint with me. . . .

Sepr. 7. First Day: . . . Thos. Reynold, Rose's father called to see her forenoon. I gave him but a poor account of her, wish'd it could be better, her Sister Mary came in the Afternoon—Rose is no changeling.

10 . . . John Skyrin was here after dinner Nancy and her 3 Children rode home in Jacob's light waggon black Becky with them, we have two less in family, Elizath. and Beck. . . .

Sepr. 11. . . . S.S. was let blood forenoon by J. Warton, she sent me word that she is better than usual to day—so am I. the cool weather, perhaps, strengthens old women, measureably.

16. . . . JD. J Skyrin his 2 eldest, MR, her [three] Children and HS.D. took tea here—they went away after night—WD. and self took a walk of 6 squares. . . .

23. . . . Our Peter, a foolish Blockhead, is married, on first Day last, to a girl of Hazelhursts, who is not free—and by accounts not so good as she ought to be—I am sorry for Peter! . . .

26. . . . Our John has been yesterday and to day cleaning &c JD. house. . . .

[Oct.] 3. . . . I had the satisfaction of seeing my daughter Molly this evening, her Sally with her—when speaking of her husband she sheads tears, I should be glad to hear of his safe arrival in Port. . . . S. Swett, her face is so painful that she puts on poltices again has sent for Dr. Physick, but has not yet seen him. . . .

Octor. 4: . . . William Drinker junr. came here from Haddonfield—went to the Bank with his Uncle, and out after with his father, to buy a new Hat. . . .

8. . . . JD. came home about 11 o'clock to a late breakfast he set up last night with Isreal Weeling who is better. . . .

9. . . . Molly Rhoads was here before dinner, she did not stay, her daughter Sally dined here as did HS.D—MS. out this Afternoon Shoping, she has done but little at that business latterly. . . .

11 . . . HS.D. out this morning very busy, but with me he talks none relative to his intended absence—it distresses me to think of it, tho I say nothing to oppose him, he thinks we injured him, by our opposition, some few years ago,

when he had laid out for a voyage to India: we could not see his reasons for it; it hurt me much. . . . WD. went home with AS. this Afternoon, they called at a house in Eighth street near race street, which John Skyrin has taken, and intends removeing thereto next week—it will be the Eighth house since they were married. . . .

13. . . . Peritt called to inform of the safe arrival of Saml Rhoads at the Havannah in[13] 29 days passage—Molly came after dinner full of Glee. . . .

Octor. 14. . . . I took a walk, a walk indeed, with my Son William, such a one as I have not taken for years—left home after three o'clock, did not stop till we came to S. Pleasants, where we stay'd above half an hour, then went on to J Skyrins, Nancy was going abroad, and as I did not intend to stay but a short time, we went over to see Tabby and Becky Fisher, who live very near, they regret loosing Nancy as a Neighbour, after a short stay we set of for home, where we arrived without stoping.—24 squares going and returning, I did not think I was equal to such an undertaking—I am tired it is true, but not as much as one quarter the way would have done in the summer—came home to tea a little after sun sett. . . .

15. . . . our HS.D. came a little before dinner from Burlington by water; he has taken a house there for his Wife and family during his absence—his going to the East-Indias seems determin'd, in a *New* Ship, when he will be likely to leave us, I have not enquired, it occasions much anxiety to my mind. . . .

17. . . . two men employ'd by one Hurley, a paper hanger,[14] have been papering our back parlor to day, it was in very bad order, or it would not have been done, as we do as little of that kind of business as we can well[15] avoid, they have not finished it, but expect to do so tomorrow forenoon,—It wants painting but that will be omitted at present. . . .

25. . . . Our Son Henry left us before dinner time for Atsion, he intends removing his family the beginning next week to Burlington, there to reside during his Absence to the East Ind[ies]. Oh dear! in a New-Ship never before at Sea.—WD. and self went this Afternoon to Nancys, found her at work with a flannel round her Neck, her throat is ulcerated, and she has some fever— I once could not have left her in such a situation—sent her Senna and Manna. . . .

13. The number "30" crossed out.
14. Thomas Hurley owned a paper-hanging manufactory at 78 Chestnut St. (*Philadelphia City Directory, 1806*).
15. The word "help" crossed out.

[Nov.] 6. . . . William went to see Nancy and Molly, the latter is more than poorly, she took an opening pill which has had no effect, has eat nothing all this day, she has a gum boil that is very troublesome occasiond by a bad tooth, when my Children are unwell, it makes me wish I could go abroad as formerly. . . .

Novr. 16. First Day . . . A particular invitation to the funeral of Nancy Redman, tomorrow afternoon at three o'clock—by a Note.—How distressed must be the Old Couple her parents, the Doctor near 85, his wife 83. Their Daughter Nancy the only Child they[16] had with them, their Eldest Daughter Coxe with her family are settled in England—Nancy was, I expect, between forty and 50, always at home with them, or nearly so, they have lived for many years very retired—I feel for them. . . .

19. . . . My husband retired at 10. his usual hour, we sat up till after 11—, when Henry left us, we soon follow'd, not on my part to sleep, till near 3 o'clock and as our dear Son was to leave us, at 9 o'clock as he said, I desired Rose to call us at seven, our people are very lazey in rising and it was a little after 8 when we came downstairs.

20 Henry was gone—my husband when he had his breakfast went down on the Warfe, he saw the New Castle boat at a distance dear Son he thought such an indirect taking leave would save some painful moments,—May the Lord be with him. this has been a painful day to me. . . .

24. . . . In a letter from Perett to his brother he informs that Saml Rhoads left the Havannah 29 ultimo intending to take shipping from another Island in 10 days—We may suppose he is now on the Sea. . . .

26. . . . We received a letter this forenoon from our Son Henry—dated Capes of Delaware, Novr. 24—not 2 days ago, in which he tells us, "Our Ship proves to be an excellent Sailor—is stiff and answers the Helm well,—the Crew appear to be orderly and the Captain obliging—We have great plenty of excellent provision—& abundance of water—As for myself I never in my Life was in better Health" &c.—could we possiably, things being as they are, have expected better inteligence—I could not help sheding tears, which is very unusual of late years with me, but I believe pleasing news would be more likely to have that effect than the reverse. . . . That state of tranquility, or equallity of mind, which good or bad fortune, as it is called, can neither exault or depress, is hard to attain. sure I am, I have not arrived at it. . . .

[Dec.] 3. . . . Nancy is too unwell if the weather was fair to come abroad,

16. The words "have with or" crossed out.

and poor Molly who was poorly last night and near her time, if she should be taken ill, I do believe she would not send for me. No mother, no Sister, no brother to go near her—it is a very gloomy night, things may ware a better aspect in a day or two.—I wish Sally Downing would come to town. If we had bad Children, such as would make our hearts ach by their ill conduct, how much worse would it be, 'tho perhaps we should not be so uneasy on account of their wellfair here—but I know not how that would be, I have reason to be thankfull on account of my dear Children and many other things. . . .

6. . . . before dinner James Smiths black man brought our dear little grandson Henry to see us, I never saw him before, he is a fine child. . . .

7. First Day: . . . James Smiths Nurse, as they call her, came forenoon with little Hanry and Mary, the latter is about 8 months old, we never saw her before, they are all fine Children. . . .

8. . . . WD. went home with Nancy, and to several other places on business. he called to enquire how MR. is, and who should he find there but Sammy, arrived this Afternoon or evening in good health.—and Molly in great Spirits, I wish she dear girl was well over her Vioage. . . .

18. . . . Elizath. and Eleanor Skyrin came to dinner they stay'd till 8 o'clock in the evening, and 'tho it drizel'd they went home in order to be timeously at school tomorrow morning . . . I gave each of them a picture work'd between 50 and 60 years ago by my dear friend Nancy Swett—they were pleased.

Decr. 20. . . . S.S. continues very poorly, her face grows worse—Oh! what a world of destress we live in—WD. went this evening to JDs—Sally had sent to Dr. Kuhn as her throat is sore and the glans in her Neck or throat swell'd the Doctor order'd loosing blood, or having leaches, she prefer'd the latter. . . .

24. . . . It is a month this day since our son left us—Our John, and Jacobs John Moore, have been cutting up, and salting pork at JDs store.—I made gingerbread. . . .

25. Christsmass. . . . last night or rather this morning I heard the kettle-drum for a long time it is a disagreeable noise in my ears, it was after one o'clock, and at two, I sat up, and took a pinch of snuff, which I do not do, but when I feel unwell and uncomfortable—I had sleep't none, nor for some length of time after. . . .

27. . . . Dr. Dorsey called for an Order to bury a Son of Dr. Physick, Saml.

Emlen Physick aged 5 months. he inform'd me that he had told S. Swett, or very near it, that nothing to purpose could be done for her. he thought she bore it with fortitude. . . .

30.   . . . A Saml. Wilson a black man, whom S. Swett is desirous of seeing, as he is a Cancer Doctor,—called here, I had some discourse with him, and find, it was he that cured Patience Gibbs of a Cancer on the back of her neck, it was taken away by a plaster, I saw it after it was extracted—. if he can cure SS. he will do wonders, as I fear it is in her constitution. . . .

1807

[Jan.] 2. . . . few days have lately past but we have heard of the death of one or more of those we knew. what so common as coming into, and going out of this world—the former sometimes the cause of the latter!—night brings a gloom over my mind, on my dear Mollys account.

12. . . . Jacob Downing and his daughter Mary came. I was sorry to see a coolness between S.R. and JD—Sally is I fear, more poorly than we are aware off. . . .

15. . . . poor Molly is still about, and no ways low Spirited—she has a fire upstairs as she is asham'd, she says, to be seen, she cuts such [a] figure—but goes up and down stairs frequently. Oh! how pleas'd should I be, if she was safe in bed with her babe by her side. . . .

17. . . . I went after dinner Eleanor with me to Saml Rhoadss Molly insists upon it that she is bravely—it is high time she was otherwise. . . .

19. . . . S.R. sent their black Jim to inform me that Molly was taking unwell about 12 last night, that the Doctor and Nurse were with her—I would have gone immediately, but was not allow'd to walk there, sent for Sally Downings Carriage, as our horses are at present, rather too frolicksome—before he came SRs Frank came with the agreeable intelligence that his mistress was brought to bed of a Daughter. when Harry came with the Carriage I went, stay'd an hour or two, Dr. Dunlap was at dinner with S.R. he said every thing was safely settled—how thankfull ought I to be—but what is the reason that my Joy at the event, is not equal to my fears before it occur'd, perhaps it is, that I do not know how she may yet be, or the indispossition of my other dear Children keeps my mind in suspence, just before I came away, Molly took an [anidoyne] to ease after pains—may it please the Lord to be with her. . . .

24. . . . It is two months this day, since HS.D. left the Capes.

25. First Day: . . . I wrote this Afternoon to Hannah S. Drinker. . . .

Janry. 29. . . . I was very desirous of going to visit my Children but WD. almost insisted on my staying at home—as it is wett under foot. . . .

30. . . . Sally Downing came in her Carriage, Nancy Skyrin, and Eliza Downing with her, for MS. to go with them to visit Molly Rhoads, whom they found bravely—she had been in the front room, where there has been[1] no fire—she talks of coming down stairs—I dread her venterous conduct. . . .

[Feb.] 2. . . . Eliza went with me after dinner to visit poor S. Swett, her face looks badly to me, the black Doctor says it is in a good way . . . upon the whole, I think her in a very critical situation. . . .

Febry. 3. . . . sent a note to Molly. . . . I intended to have spent this day with her—but it has been too cold for me to venture. . . .

4. . . . Nancy has had Dr. Physick to look at her Eye lids, he says, he has seen such before, that they sometimes go away of themselves—she ask'd him if they were of the Wen-kind, he said sometimes, what then must be done to them? cut them out was answered, he cured his Sister of the same complaint &c. it is distressing to think of it! . . .

5. . . . Our black Judith came to ask a character to get some wood &c—she says so many ordinary people apply that she was afraid to ask without some recommendation—I gave her a Certificate of her honesty and sobriety as far as I knew, and I thought as I wrote—her poor little Son Michel is likely to loose one of his eyes by a cold—how many poor creatures suffer for want of the necessities of life, while others live in affluence and superfluitey—it has always been so!—Jacob Downing called—Sally is about appleing to a Dutch Doctor for the swelling in her Neck. . . . I received a letter today from Hannah Drinker giving an account of her families health. . . .

Febry. 8 First Day: . . . Our foolish John inform'd Sister that he was going to be married, to a cleaver woman that has a Son, her Man has left her, some time ago, I rather think that matrimony is not the plan,—be that as it may, I believe he will not long do for us. . . .

13. . . . I wrote a Note to S. Swett, informing her that I could not with propriety attend on her this rainey day: but have sent twice there, it seems the Doctor applied the burning plaster on her cheek, which she took off before two minuits elapsed, said it was as hard to bear as if live coals had been put on her face. . . . Sally has been Cup'd this Afternoon by Dr. Kuhn orders. The disorder she labours under, is very prevailent at present. . . .

23. . . . Sister's Nose bleed this evening a very uncommon circumstance, it was but a little, she will not consent to be bleed or to take physick, 'tho we

1. The word "in" crossed out.

think the bleeding at her Nose, little as it was, indicated a fullness of blood. . . .

24. . . . it is 3 months this day, since HS.D. left the Capes. . . .

28. . . . poor S. Swett very weak, her face worse. WD. junr. went out after breakfast, we know not where, his Uncle Js. Smith was here to look for him after he was gone out—he is not come home yet, between 8 and 9. William comes not home to night, I wishd to send to his Grandfather Smiths but it is thought by us that he is there without doubt—I should be best pleas'd to be sure of it. . . .

[Mar.] 3. . . . Nancy Skyrin came from meeting, she dined here. She wares a black patch on each eye-lid—of the lead-plaster. . . . WD. was abroad this Afternoon, he heard from Sisr. Rhoads, that Nancy Warner was dangerously ill—Sister and WD. went to know how she was this evening was inform'd that she departed this life at 4 o'clock this Afternoon—she has been one of my old acquaintances that I have seemingly neglected laterly. my Sister and self, lived with her near four years, we boarded with her mother, A. Warner, before I was married, when she lived next door, where H. Pratt now dwells—she was upwards of 63 years of age. . . .

5. . . . I finish'd working a large Matt to cover a bowl of fruit &c. in my seventy second year. needlework in silk or worsted was always pleasing to me.—I have done much of it in my time.

6. . . . what I should have mention'd first I have left for the last, not that I have forgot it, but I begun wrong—My husband was this morning let blood, having been unwell for a day or two past, and as he practises it about this time every Spring, John [Uull] opperated. he seems bravely this evening.

11. . . . about 12 o'clock Sally Downing came by herself. Anna Clifford had been riding with her—she stayd near an hour—then rode home—her face continues swell'd and pain in her Ear. . . .

13. . . . It is 51 years this day since the death of my dear father. S.S. better, my husband was there, I could not go, he left money with her. . . .

16. . . . I went after dinner to see S. Swett—poor thing she is almost constantly confin'd to her bed. . . .

22 First Day: . . . Dr. Kuhn called WD. had desired him so to do, he advised me to loose 8 or 10 ounces blood, which I propose doing. . . .

24. . . . We received a letter this forenoon from our dear Henry dated at Sea, Longitude 29° west—Latitude 23.—South. Janry. 11. A whaler spoke them and by sending their boat, gave an oppertunity of sending us word that he is in perfect health. (What a favour). . . .

26. . . . A Negro man from Js. Smith came forenoon to inform us of the death of his wife Esther Smith, awefull information! a woman not much past the prime of life. . . . how fluctuating and uncertain is everything in this transitory world. H S. Drinker Hannah I mean, this morning 'tis likely received the letter with good intelligence from her husband, she will, proba-bly, this evening hear of the death of her poor mother! . . . S.S. after lieing very still for several days, is become very restless, which I think indicates a lasting stillness to follow. . . .

27. . . . before dinner one of Prices daughters came to inform us that S. Swett was near her end. . . . she departed about one o'clock.—a happy release I trust!—aged 85 years and 3 months. . . .

[Apr.] 7. . . . Our dear Sally is very poorly, I have hopes that warm weather, when she may go more abroad, will be beneficial to her. . . .

9. . . . poor dear Sally has another blister on her face by Dr. Kuhn's orders—. Oh dear my poor Child must suffer much, she bares it as well as^2 any body would, having a remarkable flow of Spirits, but that cannot always hold out. I wish I could be always with her, but that cannot be, as I grow old and infirm, and have to attend to myself in some respects, which I could not do there. . . .

12. First Day: . . . have not heard from our daughter Molly for 2 or 3 days past; she is the farthest from us, and is I hope in usual health—I cannot go to my Children, nor can I have them with me, which is the case of many other Mothers.

18. . . . WD. went home with Hannah, he called at Jacob Downings, poor dear Sally was under the opperation of leaches when he went. . . .

25. . . . our John is gone to be married this evening poor creature, he knows not what he is about—he and the woman will, I beleive, each have but a bad bargin—William brought a affecting account of our dear Sally, she has another blister on her face, and has been blooded.—I know no one more afraid of the latter opperation than she is. . . .

2. The word "most" crossed out.

26. First Day: . . . Nancy Skyrin was there, one of the lumps on her eye lids has become a stie, came to a point and descharg'd some matter, which looks well, I hope they will all go away in time. . . .

[May] 2. . . . black John Woodward, our Peters brother, came to ask for an order to the Despensary, as he has a sore tongue, I know not wether it is a Canker or Aptheys, HD. gave him an order. . . .

3. First Day: . . . My husband stay'd all day at home, a very uncommon circumstance. . . .

May 7. . . . Issabella Price the woman with whome S. Swett boarded, came this morning with an Account against S.S—an exorbitant one, HD. thought he had paid her sufficent for her extra trouble—he would not pay her. . . .

8. . . . Isabella Price was here again to day insisting on having her unreasonable demand paid, I was not at home, but HD. told her, she should prove her account before a Magistrate, which she said she would not. she had been told that she should have all friend Swetts furniture that was in her house. HD told her that she had a long tongue, aye said she, and a good deal of Spirit also, as he should find—She came again in the Afternoon and brought the Widdow Bolton and M. Hillborn with whome S.S. had boarded with her, they went into the office, what past there I have not heard, but that they said her demand was not out of the way—. cloudy evening—low people generally hang in a string, as it suits their purposes—this I.P. is a very low body. . . .

15. . . . I went after dinner, Abraham with me to Jacob Downings, spent the Afternoon alone with Sally—she is very poorly. . . .

17. First Day: . . . Sally Downing is no worse, she expects the Doctors there tomorrow to make a Seton[3] in the back of her neck, poor dear, I wish I could be with her. . . .

18. . . . I went soon after 9 o'clock to J Downing the Doctors had been there, and perform'd the opperation under her left ear; it hurt her more than she expect'd she has been more chearful this day than I have seen her for a long time past. . . .

22. . . . I went this morning before breakfast to JDs had some discourse with Dr. Kuhn before Physick came, nothing done to Sally but leaches order'd,

3. A thread, piece of tape, or the like (such as a piece of silk), drawn through a fold of the skin to maintain an issue or opening for discharges (*OED*).

Jacob came home with me before noon, we called at Cunetess the woman said they were out looking for leaches. . . .

May 25.   . . . I went after dinner to my poor dear Sally, she is I fear rather worse than better. . . .

30.   . . . Sally much destress'd by fear of another Seton being made, as the Doctors have recommended—Cunets widdow apply'd twenty odd leaches, she was two hours about it. . . .

May 31.   First Day: . . . last week a trench was dug in our alley and pipes put down to convey the water as far up as the livery Stables &c—it was filled up with earth yesterday, the rain this afternoon soften'd it, a horse in a Chaise going up not long before night, sunk in, they ungear'd him and with some difficulty got him out, poor thing while he was in the clay, he snorted and seem'd frighten'd . . . how much that part of Creation will bare! and how much more than is necessary they are made to bare. . . .

June 6.   . . . A Hydrant was fixt up in our Wash-house Morning.

June 13.   . . . I have sent twice to Sally. She is poorly indeed—Dr. Kuhn has advised her to go to the sea shore—which I cant bare to think of—I would much rather have her here at our house, where every thing could, I trust, be done for her, the minutia attended to, but I am opposed, more is the pity—my mind is greatly distressed. . . . O. my poor Sally!

June 15.   . . . I went about 10 o'clock to Jacob Downings—found Sally more chearful and apparently better than common . . . Sally and self took a ride of 5 or 6 miles. came back between one and two o'clock—Sally was tired and laid down and sleep't which she is very apt to do, being very weak. . . . It is several years since I have been in a Carriage, John Moore appears to be a careful driver, and the horses behaved very well—but I do not like riding—but as Sally wish'd it, I complied. . . .

June 16.   . . . The Days are now at the longest or very [nearly so], they will be stationary for 14 or 15 days; a season, I once much loved—as I always prefer'd light to darkness, and rather be up, and on my feet, than lolling; or in bed. . . . Sally gone to bed in pain.—who knows! but it may please the Lord to raise our dear Sally again—women at her time of life, sometimes go thro' many trying scenes &c. . . .

June 23.   . . . I sent Abraham this[4] forenoon for Dr. Kuhn, he came, and

4. The word "After" crossed out.

when he came, I had not courage to ask him those questions which I intended relative to Sally, he appears to think that she should by all means go to the shore. . . .

June 25. . . . Elizath. Skyrin came after dinner, her Uncle is about teaching her the rudiments of Latin she took her first lesson this Afternoon. . . .

June 28. First Day: . . . Sally has been very poorly indeed this Afternoon, the right side of her face has become painfull—Dr. Kuhn was there this Afternoon he seems to wish her on the way to the shore. . . .

29. . . . the usual account from Sally this forenoon, I intended to have gone there after breakfast, 'tho very unwell, but MS. told me she would go and bring her[5] after dinner, which put me off from going, I much fear it will not turn out so—but I much acquisesce in it—I could have wish'd to have had her with me a little time before her leaving us, to have fitted her, in body and mind, as much as I could, for such an undertaking—to leave us, we know not how long—perhaps?!—but it wont bare thinking of. . . .

[July] 7. . . . Received a letter from Jacob Downing, dated yesterday at Longbranch,[6] wherein he tells us that they arrived there on sixth day last, about 2 o'clock afternoon, Sally bore the Journey wonderfully—she has not used the salt water, otherwise than by a little application to her face—he says she sleeps much better, breaths freer, and he thinks complains rather less of pain. . . . They have excellent accomodations at McKnights, very little company there as yet. . . .

12. First Day: . . . we received letter from J. Downing dated 10th. instant, Sally had been twice bath'd in a tub, I fear she took cold, for she has had much pain in the side of her face, and apply'd a blister, which in measure releived her . . . we understand that Hy. Pratt and others are going to longbranch to McKnights, a house of great resort, very unfitt in my oppenion, for a person so much of an invalied as S.D. is. . . .

20. last night I was taken with a griping and lax, & vomitting . . . William went, unknown to me for Dr. Kuhn—he said I had little or no fever. advis'd me to live this day upon Chicken Water, half a Chicken boil'd in half gallon water for half an hour—which I have done. . . .

5. The word "here" crossed out.
6. Long Branch, N.J., had become a summer resort for Philadelphians in 1788, when Eliston Perot first boarded there. The house in which he stayed was purchased in the winter of 1790–91 by Lewis McKnight, who, with help from Perot, improved it and turned it into a popular summer resort for Philadelphia families (Franklin Ellis, *History of Monmouth County, New Jersey* [Philadelphia: R. T. Peck, 1885], 756).

24. . . . Received a letter this Afternoon from J. Downing with serious information, that our dear Child is discouraged, and intends coming home in a day or two, she thinks she is rather worse than better, and wishes to be at home. . . .

27. . . . we expected Sally &c home this evening but Jacob and his Daughter Mary arrived before tea. They left my poor dear child at Trentown at one Higbeys to lodge by her own desire to be under the care of Dr. Bellville: We know not what is for the best, but must trust in kind Providence, the Doctor intends to give her callomille and poltice her face with Hemlock bark[7] which is poison—he says it is not the Scroffula she has, that he had cured a woman that was much worse, who had 5 Tumors as hard as bone—Jacob and his Son Henry lodges at their house, Mary with her Aunt here, Wm. Drinker junr. return'd from his Grandfather Smiths, went out again—I suppose there—but did not say so. . . .

31. . . . Our Son William left us about 10 o'clock this forenoon, in Sulkey, for Wilksbarre, the beach-woods &c. . . .

Augt. 1st. . . . my dear WD. has been gone 24 hours. he intended to lodge last night at Trentown, that he might visit his Sister, it is many miles out of his way, but he was desirous of knowing how she was, before he proceeded further. . . . No accounts from Sally, she told Jacob if he did not hear from her he might conclude she was better. I am not of a very sanguine dispossition, but apt to fear the worst, unless circumstances tend to the contrary. . . .

2. First Day: . . . Nancy Skyrin and her 3 daughters and little Beck, dined here—Jacob Downing & Son also.—when shall we hear from our absent Children? . . .

5. . . . I told JD. to day at dinner, that it is ten days since he left his wife—he has not concluded that I see, when he shall go.—If I could but fly, I would be with her for 12 hours at least. . . .

6. . . . JD. and Son are preparing for Trenton, I have wrote a few lines to my afflicted daughter—They left us after eleven o'clock in a Chaise. . . .

Augt. 9. First Day: . . . we received a letter this evening from Jacob Downing, dated at Trenton this morning wherein he says—"I mean to leave

---

7. In the late eighteenth century, small doses of hemlock, administered as an extract or in powdered form, were thought especially helpful in cases of glandular tumors (Buchan, *Domestic Medicine* (1793), 318–19; Thacher, *New American Dispensatory*, 195–97).

this place after dinner, shall get as far as B. Wilsons, and breakfast with you tomorrow morning if nothing unforeseen should turn up to prevent." . . .

Augt. 10. . . . Jacob Downing and Son Henry arrived here before nine o'clock—from B. Wilsons where he lodg'd last night—his account of our dear Sally, is to me very distressing, of her weakness &c—she dont wish to leave the Doctor as yet, and to urge her so to do, dont seem quite right—but I sincerly wish she was here—or I able to be with her. . . .

11. . . . about 7 o'clock this evening our Son WD. return'd to us in quite as good health as he left us. . . .

12. . . . I settled with Lydia Atkinson this evening paid her off and took a receipt—she has left 33 Dollars under MSs care to keep 'till she returns—she is going on a visit to her Father and her Son &c. . . .

14. . . . JD. has heard that Sally is no better, she wishes to come to town . . . WD. out this evening Jacob and Nancy and Mary took tea here, none other here this day that I recolect, many have colds like the influenza, what a world of trouble is this!

15. . . . Jacob Downing and Nancy Skyrin went this morning for Trenton— Our John did not leave our house 'till after Six o'clock. he was in a ill humour, having been in liquor some time past, and not got over the effects of it: I wish he may behave as he ought. . . . WD. gone to visit his neices Elizath. and Eleanor Skyrin.

17. . . . after we had dined, Jacob and Sally Downing & Sandwith, Nancy Skyrin, Lydia who tends SD. John Moore and our John arrived here about 3 o'clock, they all dined here—My poor Child is very poorly indeed, but not so much so as I expected. . . .

19. . . . Sally has spent this day, quite as well as yesterday. she was down stairs 2 hours, went into the garden with help—'tis hard to think of, but she cannot walk by herself. . . .

Augt. 20. . . . It is 9 months this morning since our HS.D. left this house— I have fear that he will never see his Sister Sally again, at other times have hopes. . . .

24. . . . Our dear Sally has spent this day much as yesterday, not worse she had a very poor night last, I was 3 or 4 times in her room, she hawks and spits abundance. . . . Jane Tunnis was here Afternoon, she has been ill of the

prevailing disorder and several of her family. No one that calls, but has some of their household troubled with it. . . .

Augt. 26. . . . our dear Sally very unwell this day, and a poor prospect, I fear, of her getting better for a long time, if ever—tho I am not without hope. . . .

Sepr. 2. . . . My husband very unwell in his bowels, he voids blood in his stools,—sent for Dr. Rush this evening who ordred a blister applied to his side, supposing he has something of the Pleurisey, but to me it appears to be a kidney complaint, we applied the blister, and gave him near 100 drops of asthmatic Ellexer.[8] . . .

Sepr. 3. . . . Richd. Downings wife and Richd. Thomass wife, came here before tea to visit our dear Sally, they lodge here to night—it is a pleasure to see kind friends, but at this time, every addition makes more to do. . . .

Sepr. 4. . . . My head and heart achs.

5. . . . Nancy Skyrin was here this Afternoon and evening she assisted me in putting on 2 blisters on my Husbands wrists by Dr. Rushs advise, and [giving] him two injections, he has sleep't a long time in the course of this day—and I hope he is rather better than worse. . . .

Sepr. 8. . . . Jacob sent his Carriage for Nancy Skyrin, who came, and intends staying here all night—she is very helpfull to me, last night I slept more than any night since our dear Sally has been here, oweing to Nancys being with us. . . .

11. . . . Nancy Skyrin came Afternoon to stay with us all night, M. Rhoads here this evening—her daughter Sally with her—I feel, almost over-done, mind and body—My husband and Child are both in bed, but in a very poor way. . . .

Sepr. 12. . . . Nurse Amy Wascot came to day to attend our dear Sally—she appears as far as we have seen cleaver. . . .

15. . . . Sally, I think grows weaker, finds it hard to leave her bed—has been

8. Asthmatic, or paregoric, elixir was a liquid preparation consisting of flowers of benzoine or benzoic acid, opium, oil of aniseed, some form of alcoholic spirits, and one or two other ingredients, depending on local custom. It was given to soothe scratchy throats, quiet coughs, and clear congested chests. The recommended dosage for children was five to twenty drops; for adults, twenty to one hundred drops (W. Lewis, *New Dispensatory*, 325–26; Estes, "Therapeutic Practice," 375).

purged this morning—she takes as much liquid food as we can expect—she cant chew anything of substance. . . .

16. . . . Our poor Child is, I think as unwell to day as at any time yet, her Doctors were here this Afternoon, order'd a small dose Rhubarb, she seems at times unconnected, talks in her sleep—and is very low Spirited—I am so weak that I feel ready to fall at times. . . .

20. First Day: . . . Sally takes little or no notice of any thing that occurs, nor wishes to see any one that calls, the lumps in her neck are evedently less, as their Lydia who dress'd 'em and was here this Afternoon plainly perceived, If they are going away; I fear, she will go with them, but the Lord only knows! . . .

21st. . . . My husband had a good night, he rode out in Carriage about 3 or 4 miles WD. with him. . . .

22. . . . Our dear Sally was so very low this night that Jacob and her Children, his 3 Daughters stay'd all night, the disorder in her bowels continues, she is too weak to bring up the Phlegm as heretofore, and takes no nourishment, without a Change for the better e're long, I fear she cannot hold out but a short time. . . .

23. . . . My husband continues poorly.—his Doctors has order'd him to take a dose of Rhubarb wine—and to take a ride—. his hicough has left him, and in many other respects he is better, yet still he is far from well. . . .

Septr 24. . . . My husband is better to day. . . . Sally very poorly indeed all night.—the Doctors were here forenoon—'tis plain to me that they think our dear Child in a dangerous way. . . .

From the 24. to the 28th. I cannot recollect in any order.

Sepr. 28th. second day My beloved Sally is in her grave, since yesterday between 12 and one o'clock—she departed this life on sixth day morning about, or rather before, 6 o'clock. in the 46th. year of her age—she was very quiet, did not appear in any pain, without any strugle, sigh or grown—a great favour! . . . Oh! what a loss! to a mother near 72 years of age, My first born darling,—My first, my 3d. my 5th, 7th. and 9th. are in their graves,—my 2d. 4th. 6th. and 8th. are living, if Henry is yet spared to us. . . . Great numbers have been here within the few last days, few of whom I have seen—Hannah S. Smith, our Hannah Drinker, Becky Thompson, Polly Drinker, Phebe Pemberton, Polly Pleasant and many men have been here to day. . . .

29. . . . Oh my dear Sally! I trust and beleive thou art accepted: May it be my case when it pleases the Lord to call me hence. . . .

Octor. 9. . . . It is 2 weeks this morning since we parted with our dear Child, I wont say we lost her, I trust she is not lost—she enjoy'd while here, all that is, or ought to be, desireable in this world, and was happy and contented— a good and kind Husband, 5 dear Children, and every conveniency her heart could wish—which she left without murmering. . . .

Octor. 10. . . . Sister had a violent spell of coughing indeed for which she will do, nothing, and scarcely take anything. . . .

Octor. 12. . . . Our Jude, whom we sold 51 years ago when she was a Child, was here this Afternoon, I thought she was dead, as we have not seen her for many years, she is now, not far from sixty years of age—when we sold her, there was nothing said against keeping or selling Negros—but as we were going to board out knew not what to do with her—some time after we were more settled in our minds, were very sorry we had sold the Child to be a slave for life, and knew not what would be her fate, we went to Springfield to repurchase her, but her mistress a very plausable woman refused to sell her 'tho we offer'd 40 pounds, and had sold her 2 months before for 25—some time afterwards her mistress sold her to Parson Marshal, it was several years, when she was grown up, and when much talk was, of the inequity of holding them in bondage—My husband[9] called on her Master, and had some talk with him, he did not see the matter as[10] he did, but at his death left her free. . . .

Octor. 15 . . . I have had this morning a fit of griping which is always trying in a pecililar manner to me, and have a bad pain in my back, cannot stoop but with difficulty, and am hard set to 'rise when I do—Our dear Sally has escaped the pains of old-age, and if at rest with her Maker, 'tis well, which I hope and trust she is! . . .

18th. First Day: . . . Nancy Skyrin, her 3 Daughters Sally Downing and Beck dined here—Thos. Scattergood here this evening he had something to offer in the testimonial line to HD. chiefly—very kindly. . . .

24. . . . About 11 o'clock, I was upstairs as I generally am at that time, busy, step'd back, and my heel struck or hitch'd agains a brick or one of 4 End-irons that was behind me, so as to occasion a fall. . . . WD. went for Dr. Kuhn, who advis'd the parting with 10 ounces blood, which I would not comply with, perhaps actuated by a whim, be that as it may, it was not done,

9. The words "& Sister" crossed out.
10. The word "they" crossed out.

he then desired me to take a dose of Physick, which I told him I had not done since I was ill 2 years ago. I have taken no kind of Physick, but prunes or peaches &c!—so got off of that. . . .

26. . . . Dr. Kuhn called unexpectedly, I was pleased to see him, he advised bleeding again, which was perform'd near one o'clock by John Uhle, the blood when seperated was enflam'd and buffey—shew'd the necessety of loosing it— the Doctor order'd 9 or 10 ounces, Sister told J.U. to take but 7. I who was acquainted with the Bowl knew there was more than 10, when I told him to stop it—and when I weigh'd it found there was 12½ ounces. JD. here as usual. . . .

[Nov.] 3. . . . Our old Friend & acquintence Samuel Pleasants departed this life last night about 10 or 12 o'clock, I was much surpris'd as well as Shock'd when I heard it, 'tho he had been ill for a week past—we had not heard of his indispossion 'till yesterday—he and wife have been married between 45 and 6 years. . . .

5. . . . Saml. Pleasants was about 71. years of age; little did I think, last sixth day week, when he was talking with us, in this parlor, that I should never see him again—How uncertain is life. . . .

8. First Day: . . . My husband, Nancy and William went to Afternoon meeting, Nancy left us soon after meeting, as it sprinkled rain, little Mary with her, she took some salts with her for Eleanor, who has a swelling in her cheek—JD. took tea here—We all, under our roof, are better than we have been some time back thro' favour! . . .

11. . . . Last night I sleep't but little was at the window after one o'clock, the moon was near setting very red—the lamp going out, so that we were soon in darkness. . . .

12. . . . Jacob Downing left town about 11 o'clock A.M.—for the vally, intending to bring home his Daughters. . . .

13. . . . HD. was abroad this forenoon—and in the Afternoon also—he brought a letter from Thos. Cope from our HS.D. dated at Calcutta June the 16th. p Oliver Ellsworth, Capt. Ely—The capt. in his letter to T.C. says they are all well, dont expect to sail 'till August—" to hear he is well, is the chief matter at present to me. . . .

Novr. 16. . . . Elizath. Skyrin came after dinner to say her lattin lesson. . . .

17. . . . we found our WD. junr. when we came down stairs, he was all night

---

on the water—he came on an errent to his Uncle from his mother—he inform'd me that his little brother Henry was very unwell, by the effects of the peach stones that he swallow'd several weeks ago. . . . Ezra Comley came with a letter from Js. McIn[tire] the manager at the Iron Works, wherein he says, that Peter Woodward and wife behave well, and are very serviceable and handy—I am pleased to hear it. . . . William thinks that winter has set in, it has been snowing all round the country in many places—If winter has set in, it is a month sooner than usual—It is very cold in our back Parlor, tho' we burn [sea] cole with wood.

18. Clear and cold all day wind N.W. [Our] little William, little is improper, for [he is] a stout boy, he left us before 11 o'clock—[with] a good wind—WD. went this Afternoon to JDs and JSs—they were well, only E. Downing had something of the toothach—it clear'd up last night before 11.—a clear moon light night.[11]

11. The word "this" crossed out. This is the last entry in ED's diary. The following obituary appeared on Dec. 2: "Departed this life, on the 24th ultimo, in the seventy-third year of her age, Mrs. Elizabeth Drinker, the wife of Henry Drinker Esquire; a lady whose sweetness of disposition, and singular propriety of conduct, endeared her through life to all who had the happiness of knowing her. In her youth she possessed uncommon personal beauty, which the gentleness of her temper preserved, in a great degree, to the last; for her countenance was a perfect index of a mind, whose feelings were all attuned to harmony. She had received an education much superior to what was common for young ladies, in the country sixty years ago; and the writer of this article can most feelingly attest, how much her conversation abounded with proofs that 'the heart of the wise teacheth the mouth and addeth learning to the lips.' Her chief happiness consisted in the discharge of her domestic duties; and in every part of her conduct she might be pointed out as an example of the affectionate wife and tender mother. At the same time that she was perfectly free from all bigotry of sentiment, or narrowness of feeling, she was a firm believer in the doctrines of Christianity, and studiously inculcated them into the minds of her children, not only as a rock of salvation in another world, but as a harbour of refuge from the cares and afflictions of this. Her fondness for literature she always retained, and for many years amused herself with recording in the evening, her reflections during the day. In a diary which she kept, nearly from the time of her marriage to the evening preceding her last illness, it may safely be asserted, that there is not to be found a single misrepresentation or illiberal observation; for her words flowed from her heart, and that was a source which was ever pure and serene. In truth, to no one can be applied, with more perfect propriety, the inspired language of the Scriptures, that 'Her ways were the ways of pleasantness, and all her paths were peace' " (*Poulson's American Daily Advertiser*, Dec. 2, 1807; the obituary, with minor variants of spelling and punctuation, also appeared in *Bronson's United States Gazette* and can be found in H. S. Drinker, *Drinker Family*, 44–45).

Biographical Directory

Elizabeth Drinker recorded the names of several thousand people over the nearly fifty-year period during which she penned her entries. Some, such as her husband and children, were mentioned almost daily, others less frequently, and many only sporadically. The directory has been compiled for the purpose of identifying as many people as possible in all three categories. A surprising quantity of biographical information has surfaced in the attempt, although the amount and nature of that information vary from person to person.

Where feasible, birth, death, and marriage dates have been included, as well as occupation, public roles, religion, and relationship to the Drinkers. Some dates are prefaced by a *c.*, which means that the genealogical source was ambiguous. Thomas Coombe, for example, "d. 1799 in the 79th year of his age," and his birthdate, therefore, is listed as "c. 1720." Although some of the information obtained from the various sources is suspect, the editor has attempted to amend the reference material only when ED herself inscribes a birth or death date that conflicts with secondary evidence.

Because of the length of the diary and its eighteenth-century qualities, certain problems arise of which the reader should be aware. Most important, family members with the same last name frequently had the same given name even within a single generation, and as Drinker herself realized, "several of one name in a family occasions confusion and mistake—oftentimes." To compound matters, ED knew a number of distantly related or unrelated people with similar names. Thus, when she refers simply to Ann Emlen, for example, it is sometimes unclear whether she has Ann Emlen Mifflin or Ann Emlen Pleasants in mind. (The former married in 1788, the latter in 1796.) Where the context makes it possible to narrow the choice to a specific person, or where two or three equally strong candidates seem likely, the alternatives have been included in the directory. Where, however, there are several possibilities but no clue to a positive identification, the name has been omitted from the directory altogether. Jacob Taylor is a case in point: three men of that name were members of the Northern District Monthly Meeting during the late eighteenth century, but no supporting evidence exists to indicate which one appears in the diary.

Spelling variations have been cross-indexed. The main entry may be found under the currently accepted spelling of the name; ED's departures are included as guides to the main entry, since some bear little similarity to contemporary references.

Since the diary covers nearly five decades, many women appear in it under two names: their name at birth and their name after marriage. In the directory, the full identification may be found under the name by which a subject first appears in the diary. A cross-reference under the married name will direct the reader to the name at birth if the full entry appears at the latter location. A word of caution, however: given the relative similarity of first names (the profusion of Sarahs, Marys, and Anns is bewildering), and the frequency of intermarriage among people who answered to no more than six different surnames, it is possible that in a few cases the cross-reference may not be to the same person, as intended, but rather to a mother or cousin with the same name.

The directory entry for each person always refers to the subject's formal name. ED, however, referred to many acquaintances by their diminutives. The following list, therefore, provides the reader with the nicknames that appear most often in the diary:

Ann	Nancy
Catherine	Caty, Katy
Dorothy	Dolly
Eleanor	Nelly
Elizabeth	Betsy, Betty, Eliza
Esther	Hetty
Frances	Fanny
Hester	Hetty
Jane	Jenny
Margaret	Peggy
Martha	Patty
Mary	Molly, Polly
Rebecca	Becky
Sarah	Sally
Susannah	Suky, Sukey
Thomasine	Tammy
Edward	Ned, Ted
James	Jemmy
Joseph	Josey
William	Billy

In the interests of conserving space, the entries do not include source references. (A list of the principal sources may be found in the three-volume edition of the complete diary.) Likewise, the following abbreviations allow the material to be presented in the most concise form possible.

ABBREVIATIONS

admin.	administration
aft.	after
Am.	America(n)
assoc.	associate, associated, association
asst.	assistant
atty. gen.	attorney general
b.	born
btw.	between
c.	circa
capt.	captain
co.	county, company
Cong.	Congress
Cont. Cong.	Continental Congress
d.	died, death
dept.	department
e.	east(ern)
ED	Elizabeth Sandwith Drinker
esp.	especially
est.	established, establishment
gen.	general
HD	Henry Drinker (1734–1809)
incl.	including
m.	married, marriage
M.P.	member of parliament
mtg.	meeting
n.	north(ern)
nw.	northwest(ern)
NYC	New York City
Phila.	Philadelphia
prob.	probably
pub.	published
R.	River
rd.	road
s.	south(ern)
soc.	society
st.	street

---

twp.	township
univ.	university
w.	west(ern)

ADLUM, John. 1759–1836. b. York Co., Pa.; in Muncy, Pa. (1790s). Appointed associate judge of Lycoming County, Pa. (1796). A close friend of Samuel Wallis; active in surveying, scientific farming, viniculture.

AFFLECK, Thomas. d. 1795. Eminent Phila. cabinetmaker; b. Aberdeen, Scotland; trained in London; to Phila. (1763). Shop on Second St., near Drinker home. Commissioned to furnish Congress Hall and to design pieces for wealthy Phila. families. One of a group of Quakers arrested as British sympathizers (Sept. 1777); exiled to Winchester, Va., for more than seven months.

ALEXANDER, Ann. Quaker minister. Resident of Suffolk Co., England; sister of Quaker minister Mary Alexander.

ALLEN, Margaret Hamilton. d. 1760. Daughter of Speaker of Pa. Assembly Andrew Hamilton and Anne Brown Preeson Hamilton; sister of James Hamilton; m. William Allen (1734); six surviving children.

ALSOP, Othniel. 1770–1836. b. Colchester, England; to Phila. (1793) with his brother Ruhamah John Alsop. Trained as a staymaker; worked for a short while in HD's countinghouse; later a merchant and vinegar manufacturer. Minister, Phila. N. District Monthly Mtg. m. Hannah Brown (1806); six children; m. Sarah Waring (1824).

ARMITT, Elizabeth Howell. c. 1742–1808. Daughter of Joseph HOWELL (1719–90) and Hannah Hudson Howell; m. John Armitt (1763).

ARMITT, Elizabeth Lisle. d. 1802. Daughter of Maurice or Morris Lisle, a Phila. Quaker; m. (1739) Joseph Armitt, a Phila. Quaker merchant (d. 1747); at least two surviving daughters: Elizabeth (m. Richard WALN [1760]), Mary (m. Elijah BROWN [1761]).

ARMITT, Sarah. 1733–87. Daughter of Phila. Quakers Stephen (1705–51) and Sarah Whitpain Armitt; m. (1766) James LOGAN (1728–1803); no children.

ASHBRIDGE, Elizabeth Fletcher. m. (1760) William Ashbridge (1734–75); five children.

ASHBRIDGE, Sarah James. d. 1801. Of Welsh Quaker descent; parents lived in Willistown, Chester Co., Pa.; m. (1757) at Goshen Mtg. Jonathan Ashbridge (1734–82), who had been disowned from the Chester Mtg. and had moved to w. Pa. after the Revolution; 11 children. To Upper Canada (now Ontario) with some of her family (1793).

ASHBRIDGE, Sarah Leonard. m. George Ashbridge (b. 1769).

ASHBRIDGE, Sarah Vernon. Sister-in-law of Sarah James ASHBRIDGE; m. David Ashbridge (d. 1788) as his second wife (1783). Because the ceremony was performed by a minister, the couple was disowned by Goshen Mtg.

ASHBY, William. Quaker; merchant tailor.

ATKINSON, Lydia. From a N.J. Quaker family; her mother, Rachel (d. 1758), lived in Chester Twp., N.J.

BACON, David. 1729–1809. Hatter; active Quaker. b. N.J., where parents belonged to Salem (Co.) Monthly Mtg.; to Phila. (1749); m. (1751) Mary Trotter (d. 1793); ten children.

BAKER, George Adam. 1756–1816. Son of Hilary Baker (1705–83) and Catherine Reinke Baker; m. Anna Klink; seven children. Officer, Am. army, Revolution; after war, to Phila.; businessman; member, Phila. Common Council (1801–3); Phila. city treasurer (1803–13).

BAKER, Hilary. 1746–98. Son of Hilary Baker (1705–83) and Catherine Reinke Baker; educated at father's school in Germantown, Pa.; m. Anna Marie Kreiden (1783). Clerk for HD; businessman; interpreter and notary public during Revolution; mayor of Phila. (1796). d. yellow fever.

BALDERSTON, John. 1740–1821. Quaker farmer, Solebury Twp., Bucks Co. m. Deborah Watson (1767); eight children; m. Elizabeth Langdale, or Langdon, the daughter of a Quaker minister, at Phila. mtg. (1797).

BARTRAM, Elizabeth Budd. d. 1808. b. N.J.; m. (1764) Moses BARTRAM; 12 children.

BARTRAM, John. 1743–1812. Apothecary. Son of John Bartram (1699–1777) and Ann Mendenhall Bartram; inherited Bartram Botanical Gardens; m. first cousin, Elizabeth Howell (1771). Disowned by Phila. Monthly Mtg. (1789).

BENEZET, Anthony. 1713–84. Quaker teacher and abolitionist. b. into French Huguenot family; to England; joined the Soc. of Friends; to Phila. (1731); m. Joyce Marriott (1736); taught in Germantown, Pa., in Friends' Public School in Phila. (1742–54), in his own school for girls. Wrote and spoke out against slave trade and slavery; worked to promote peace with Indians.

BENEZET, Joyce Marriott. 1713–86. Burlington, N.J., Quaker minister; daughter of Mary Owen Marriott and Samuel Marriott; m. Anthony BENEZET (1736); two children; d. in infancy.

BIDDLE, Clement. 1740–1814. Partner with father, John Biddle, in Phila. shipping business; later partner with brother Owen BIDDLE; deputy quartermaster gen., Pa. and N.J. militia (1776); commissary gen. (1777–80) and quartermaster gen. (1781) of Pa. militia. Disowned by Soc. of Friends, eventually reinstated. U.S. marshal of Pa. (1793). m. Mary Richardson (d. 1773); m. Rebekah Cornell (1773); 13 children.

BIDDLE, Owen. 1737–99. Son of Sarah Owen Biddle and John Biddle; m. Sarah Parke; ten children. Phila. clock and watchmaker, merchant; delegate, Pa. Constitutional Convention (1776); deputy commissioner of forage (1777); surveyor (1782); member, Am. Philosophical Soc., Soc. for Encouraging the Culture of Silk in Pa. Disowned by Soc. of Friends for war efforts; founding member of Soc. of Free Quakers (1781); received back by Phila. Monthly Mtg. (1783); instrumental in est. of Quaker school in Westtown, Pa.

BOLSBEY, Thomas. A N. Liberties farmer.

BOND, Phineas. 1749–1815. Son of Phineas Bond and Whilliamina Moore Bond. Phila. lawyer, loyalist; exiled (1777); joined British forces invading Phila.; after Howe's evacuation (1778), to N.Y., then to London. British consul to U.S., in Phila. (1787–1810); d. London.

BOWMAN, Ebenezer. Attorney, Wilkes-Barré, Pa.; represented Luzerne Co. in state legislature (1793); local counsel for a landholders assoc. whose members included HD (1801).

BRADFORD, William. 1719–91. Printer; b. N.Y.; publisher, *Pa. Journal and Weekly Advertiser;* m. Rachel Budd (1742).

BRADFORD, William. 1755–95. Son of William BRADFORD (1719–91); Princeton-educated lawyer; colonel, Continental Army; U.S. attorney gen. (1794–95); contributed to revisions of Pa. criminal jurisprudence; m. Susan Vergereau Boudinot.

BRAND, Martha Gardiner (Patty). c. 1755–1814. Phila. Quaker physician; daughter of Mary Gardiner Brand (d. 1791).

BRINGHURST, Elizabeth. 1723–90. Daughter of John Bringhurst and Mary Claypoole Bringhurst.

BROWN, Elijah. 1740–1810. Quaker, b. Nottingham, Pa.; nephew of William Brown and John Churchman; to Phila. (1757); m. Mary Armitt at Phila. Mtg. (1761); eight children, including novelist Charles Brockden Brown. Conveyancer; managed Armitt family real estate. Exiled to Va. with HD and other Quaker leaders (1777–78).

BROWN, Mary Armitt. d. 1825. Daughter of Phila. Quakers Joseph Armitt and Elizabeth Lisle ARMITT; m. Elijah BROWN (1761); eight children.

BROWN, Phoebe. b. c. 1733. Daughter of William and Susannah Brown; m. (1761) Israel MORRIS (1738–1818).

BROWN, Sarah Cooper. 1722–74. Quaker, b. Haddonfield, N.J.; sister of James Cooper (1720–89); m. John Brown at Chester Mtg., Moorestown, Burlington Co., N.J. (1746).

BUCKLEY, Hannah. Member, Phila. Monthly Mtg.; m. John Gardner (c. 1752); censured for marrying against Quaker discipline; at least five children; m. Thomas Buckley (1775).

BUDD, Rachel. 1750–1805. Daughter of Thomas Budd and Rebecca Atkinson Budd SAY; b. Mt. Holly, N.J.; to Phila. in childhood to reside with stepfather Thomas SAY; sister of Elizabeth Budd BARTRAM; aunt of Rebecca Budd COMLY; m. Quaker printer Isaac Collins (1771); to N.Y. (1796); d. yellow fever.

BUNTING, Joseph. 1758–1830. Disowned by Falls Monthly Mtg., Bucks Co., for joining local militia (1775); m. Phoebe Moon (1783); to Lower Dublin Twp., Phila. Co. Stabled horses.

BUNTING, Philip Syng. 1763–1826. Phila. grocer and merchant; raised Anglican; joined Northern District Monthly Mtg. following m. to Elizabeth Tompkins (1788). Related to John Syng DORSEY and Philip Syng Physick.

BURGE, Beulah Shoemaker. d. 1820. Daughter of Phila. Quaker Benjamin Shoemaker; m. Samuel Burge at Phila. Mtg. (1758); seven children.

CALLENDER, Hannah. 1737–1801. Daughter of William CALLENDER and Katherine Smith Callender; diarist (1758–62); m. (1762) Samuel SANSOM (1739–1824); five children; member, Phila. Monthly Mtg.

CALLENDER, William. 1703–63. b. Barbados to Quakers William Callender and Hannah Callender; to Phila.; m. Katherine Smith (1731); helped organize

Fellowship Fire Co., Phila. (1738); member, Pa. Assembly (1754, 1755); resigned in protest of French and Indian War (1756).

CANAN, John. 1746–1831. HD's agent in Huntingdon Co., Pa.; officer, Pa. Line, Revolutionary War; member, Pa. Assembly (1791–93); member, state senate (1794); associate judge, Huntingdon Co. (1791).

CANNON. See CANAN.

CARLISLE, Abraham. 1720–78. Quaker; neighbor of ED; m. Ann Brooks at Phila. Mtg. (1748). Master builder, lumber merchant; member, Carpenter's Co. of Phila. Accepted post in Loyalist civil administration during British occupation of Phila.; indicted for treason (Sept. 1778); executed (Nov. 1778).

CARLISLE, Ann Brooks. c. 1723–87. Quaker; m. (1748) Abraham CARLISLE.

CARMALT, Jonathan. 1765–1830. Phila. currier. Son of James Carmalt and Susannah Say Carmalt; m. Hannah Hewlings at N. District Mtg. (1789); at least six children. Member, Abington Mtg.

CASH, Thomas. 1726–75. Member, Schuylkill Fishing Co., founded by father, Caleb Cash, a Phila. coroner; m. Cynthia Van Histe.

CATHERALL, Hannah. 1736–1806. Quaker; Phila. schoolmistress. Daughter of Edward Catherall and Rachel Herring Catherall. Clerk, Women's Yearly Mtg. (1778–94); disciplined by Soc. of Friends for inebriation; reinstated (1797).

CATHERALL, Hannah Coffin. c. 1730–1816. Sister of Rebecca Coffin WALN; m. Isaac CATHERALL (1733–99) at Phila. Mtg. (1758); eight children. Member, N. District Monthly Mtg.

CATHERALL, Isaac. 1733–99. Phila. cooper. Son of Edward Catherall and Rachel Herring Catherall; m. Hannah Coffin (1758); eight children. Member, N. District Mtg.

CATHERALL, Isaac. 1763–1819. Quaker physician. Son of Isaac CATHERALL (1733–99) and Hannah Coffin CATHERALL. Studied medicine with John REDMAN, Phila.; studies in Edinburgh, London, Paris; to Phila. to start practice (1793). Research in epidemiology, pathology, anatomy.

CHOVET, Abraham. 1704–90. Phila. physician. b. London; to Phila. from Jamaica (1774); famous for anatomical studies and lectures; founder, College of Physicians.

CHURCHMAN, George. 1730–1814. Son of John Churchman (1705–75) and Margaret Brown Churchman; m. Hannah James (1752); eight children. Associated with Westtown School; clerk, Nottingham Monthly Mtg.

CLARKSON, Jacob. 1768–1832. Phila. merchant. Son of Dr. Gerardus Clarkson; m. Jane Stevenson (1795); nine children.

CLARKSON, Matthew. 1733–1800. Phila. merchant; b. N.Y.; to Phila. following mother's marriage to Presbyterian minister Gilbert Tennent. Alderman; mayor of Phila.; director, Library Co.; treasurer, Am. Philosophical Soc.; vestryman, Christ Church. m. Mary Boude (1758); seven children.

CLIFFORD, Anna. See Anna RAWLE.

COBBETT, William. 1763–1835. b. Farnham, England; to Am. (1792); to Phila. (1794). Journalist, pamphleteer, reformer; pseud. Peter Porcupine. Federalist.

COLLINS, John. d. 1817. Son of Burlington, N.J., Quakers Francis Collins and Ann

Collins; m. (1807) at Redstone Monthly Mtg., Fayette Co., Pa., Esther Roberts Hunt, daughter of Enoch and Rachel Roberts.

COLLINS, Stephen. 1733–94. Phila. Quaker merchant. b. Lynn, Mass.; m. Mary PARISH (1761); three children. Am. sympathizer, Revolutionary War.

COMLY, Ezra. 1787–1824. One of 16 children of Phila. Quakers Hannah Comly and Ezra Comly; superintendent of an ironworks.

COMLY, John. 1773–1850. Quaker educator and minister, Byberry, Pa.; surveyor; publisher (with his brother, Joseph Comly [1775–1854]) of journal, *Friends Miscellany*. m. Rebecca Budd (1803); five children.

COMLY, Rebecca Budd. 1773–1832. Daughter of Mt. Holly, N.J., Quakers Stacy Budd and Sarah Budd; m. (1803) at Mt. Holly Mtg. John COMLY, whom she had met when teaching at Quaker boarding school, Westtown, in Chester Co.; five children. Ran boarding school at Comly ancestral home in Byberry, Phila. Co. (1804–17). Member, Byberry Mtg.

COOMBE, Thomas. c. 1720–99. Customs official, colonial Phila.; Anglican; m. Sarah Rutter (c. 1744); father of Thomas COOMBE (1747–1822).

COOMBE, Thomas. 1747–1822. Clergyman, author. b. Phila.; graduate, College of Phila. (1766); studies for Anglican ministry, England; to Phila. (1772). Asst. minister, united ministries of Christ Church and St. Peter's Church, Phila. (1773–78). m. Sarah Ann Leake Badger (1773). Loyalist; exiled to N.Y. (1778); to Ireland (1780), later to England.

COOPER, William. d. c. 1770. Haddonfield, N.J., Quaker; m. Abigail Metcalf; m. Mary Rawle (1732); to Phila. (N. Front St.); five children.

COPE, Thomas Pym. 1768–1854. Wealthy Phila. Quaker merchant and diarist. Son of Caleb Cope and Mary Mendenhall Cope; apprenticed to uncle, Thomas Mendenhall of Phila. (c. 1785); m. (1792) ED's niece Mary DRINKER (1766–1825); six of their eight children survived; m. Elizabeth Stokes Waln, widow of Joseph Waln (1829). Member, Phila. city council, Pa. Assembly.

CORNWALLIS, Charles. 1738–1805. To Am. (1776); led British forces against Washington at Trenton and Princeton, and against Gates at Camden and Guilford Court; defeated at Yorktown; returned to Europe. d. India.

COX, Henry. d. 1822. Irish nobleman. b. Henry Hamilton; took surname Cox to gain inheritance from grandfather. Fled debt-encumbered estates to York Co., Pa. (1799); adopted Quaker habit and guise; member, York Monthly Mtg.; to E. Marlboro, Chester Co. (1813); member, London Grove Mtg.; on return to Ireland (1817), dropped Quaker ways.

CRESSON, Caleb. 1742–1816. Son of Quakers James Cresson and Sarah Emlen Cresson; with brother, Joshua Cresson, raised by John Armitt and Mary Emlen Armitt after parents' death. Member, Phila. Monthly Mtg. Apprenticed to Quaker merchant Thomas Clifford, but did not pursue mercantile career; m. (1767) Sarah Hopkins (1748–69); to Haddonfield, N.J.; back to Phila. (after 1769); m. Annabella Elliott (1772); m. Jane Cox Evans (1795). Administered family properties and trusts for Soc. of Friends, kept burial register, Phila. Monthly Mtg.

CROSSFIELD, Jane Rowlandson. 1712–84. Quaker minister. b. England; m. George

Crossfield of Westmoreland (1746). Several trips abroad to preach (1748–72); to Phila. accompanied by George Mason and Irish Quaker preacher Susannah Hatton (1760).

CURRIE, William. 1754–1823. Physician. b. Chester Co.; son of clergyman William Currie (d. 1803); studied medicine with John Kearsley and at forerunner of Univ. of Pa. Medical School; served in Am. military hospitals, Revolutionary War; practiced medicine, Chester Co.; to Phila.; strong advocate of smallpox vaccination.

DAVIS, Elizabeth. c. 1738–95. Eldest child of George Davis and Jane Currie Davis; m. banker John Nixon (1765); five children; buried in St. Peter's (Anglican) churchyard, Phila.

DAY, Stephen Munson. c. 1776–1812. Quaker schoolmaster, minister, Burlington, N.J.; to Haddonfield, N.J.; m. (1805) Sarah Redman, daughter of Thomas Redman (1742–1823); at least one son.

DEBRAHM, John Gerar William. 1717–99. Astronomer, philosopher, mystic. Surveyor general of N. America before settling in Phila. (c. 1790). To Bristol Twp., Phila. Co. (by 1795); purchased Clearfield, HD and ED's 39-acre Germantown estate, which he renamed Bellair and bequeathed to his wife, Mary Drayton Fenwick DeBrahm. In later years, attended Quaker meetings, dressed plain, published several mystical religious books.

DICKINSON, William. c. 1734–76. Phila. Quaker schoolmaster; member, N. District Monthly Mtg.

DINSMORE (Dinsmoor), Silas. 1766–1847. b. N.H.; graduate, Dartmouth College (1791); agent to Cherokee Indians (from 1794); served on board naval vessel *Gen. Washington*; agent to Choctaw Indians during Jefferson's administration.

DORSEY, John Syng. 1783–1818. Surgeon. Son of Leonard Dorsey and Elizabeth Physick Dorsey. Educated, Friends schools; studied medicine with uncle, Philip Syng Physick, and at Univ. of Pa.; further medical studies, London, Paris; back to Phila. (1804). m. Maria Ralston (1807).

DOWNING, Elizabeth. 1789–1882. Daughter of Jacob DOWNING and Sarah DRINKER Downing (1761–1807); m. Robert Valentine Sharples (d. 1822) at Arch St. Mtg. (1810); member, Downingtown Mtg.; farm in Aston Twp.

DOWNING, Elizabeth Reese. 1753–1840. Daughter of Quakers David Reese and Mary Garrett Reese, Newtown, Pa.; m. (1771) Richard DOWNING (1750–1820); seven children; to Bucks Co.; to Downingtown, Pa. (1778).

DOWNING, Henry. 1795–1854. Son of Jacob DOWNING and Sarah DRINKER Downing (1761–1807); m. (1818) Rachel Chew (d. 1825) of Forestville, Pa.; two children; m. Christine Gruner of Bethany, Pa.

DOWNING, Hunt. 1757–1834. Son of John Downing and Elizabeth Hunt Downing; m. Deborah Miller (1760–1833), daughter of Quakers Joseph Miller and Mary Williams Miller; three children. Tavernkeeper, Gen. Washington inn, Downingtown; first postmaster, Downingtown; quartermaster to local troops, Whiskey Rebellion (1794).

DOWNING, Jacob. 1756–1823. Son of Richard DOWNING (1719–1803) and Mary Edge Downing; b. family homestead, Downingtown, Chester Co.; to Bucks

Co.; member, Falls Mtg.; to Phila. (1778); flour merchant; m. (1787) Sarah DRINKER (1761–1807); six children, five of whom survived to adulthood. Bought Atsion Ironworks from father-in-law, HD.

DOWNING, Jane Ashbridge. 1764–aft. 1819. Daughter of George Ashbridge and Rebecca Garrett Ashbridge; m. Samuel DOWNING at Uwchlan Mtg. (1790); one child, a son (b. 1802).

DOWNING, Joseph. 1734–1804. Landholder, E. Caln, Pa. Brother of Richard DOWNING (1719–1803); uncle of Jacob DOWNING; m. Mary Trimble at Bradford Mtg., Chester Co. (1755); 11 children. Parted company with Soc. of Friends over his support of Am. Revolution. Daughter Ann Downing Todd accidentally shot and killed her sister's husband, Samuel Kennedy (1801).

DOWNING, Joseph R. 1765–1855. Fuller. Brother of Jacob DOWNING; m. at Chester Mtg. Ann Worrall, daughter of William Worrall and Phebe Grubb Worrall (1791).

DOWNING, Mary. 1792–1879. Daughter of Jacob DOWNING and Sarah DRINKER Downing (1761–1807); m. (1822) George Valentine (1788–1856); six children.

DOWNING, Phebe. 1786–1845. Daughter of Richard DOWNING (1750–1820) and Elizabeth Reese DOWNING; m. Quaker schoolmaster Jesse Meredith.

DOWNING, Richard. 1719–1803. b. England to Quakers Thomas Downing (1691–1772) and Thomasine Downing; to E. Caln Twp. (later Downingtown), Chester Co., Pa., in childhood; m. Mary Edge at Uwchlan Mtg. (1741); 12 children. Overseer, Uwchlan Mtg. (from 1763); large landholder.

DOWNING, Richard. 1750–1820. Son of Richard DOWNING (1719–1803); brother of Jacob DOWNING; inherited much of father's land and mill holdings in Downingtown, Pa., vicinity; m. Elizabeth Reese at Newtown Mtg. (1771); seven children; in Bucks Co. (1773–78); member, Falls Mtg.; back to Downingtown. Delegate, Pa. Convention, which ratified U.S. Constitution (1787); member, Pa. Assembly (1788–92).

DOWNING, Samuel. 1763–1819. Maltster, farmer, Downingtown, Pa. Brother of Jacob DOWNING; m. Jane Ashbridge at Uwchlan Mtg. (1790); one son, George.

DOWNING, Sandwith. 1799–1847. Son of Jacob DOWNING and Sarah DRINKER Downing (1761–1807); superintendent, McMinn's mills, in Valley Creek, E. Bradford Twp., Chester Co.; m. Lydia Smedley (1829); one son; after wife's death, to family lands in Susquehanna Co. originally purchased by HD.

DOWNING, Sarah. 1797–1843. Daughter of Jacob DOWNING and Sarah DRINKER Downing (1761–1807); m. Reuben Bond Valentine; three children.

DOWNING, Thomas. 1773–1811. Son of Richard DOWNING (1750–1820) and Elizabeth Reese DOWNING; m. Mary Spackman (1794); six children; d. Baltimore.

DRINKER, Ann. 1764–1830. Second daughter of ED. m. John SKYRIN at N. District Mtg. (1791); three daughters. To Cincinnati, Ohio (c. 1829), with two unmarried daughters to join married daughter, Eleanor SKYRIN Drinker, and son-in-law, Joseph Drinker.

DRINKER, Charles. 1781–84. Last of the nine children born to ED.

DRINKER, Daniel. 1735–1815. Phila. shopkeeper, merchant. Brother of HD; m. Elizabeth Hart at Phila. Mtg. (1760); at least three children; m. Hannah White Prior (1796); d. Burlington, N.J.

DRINKER, Elizabeth. 1801–74. Daughter of Henry S. DRINKER and Hannah SMITH Drinker; m. (1827) at Arch St. Mtg. Samuel C. Paxson, a NYC Quaker merchant; to NYC; eight children.

DRINKER, Esther. 1798–1856. Daughter of Henry S. DRINKER and Hannah SMITH Drinker; m. (1841) Israel Pemberton Pleasants, a Phila. stockbroker; one child.

DRINKER, Hannah. *See also* Hannah SMITH (1774–1830).

DRINKER, Hannah. 1760–1806. Daughter of John DRINKER and Rachel Reynear DRINKER; m. John THOMAS at Phila. Mtg. (1783); at least two sons.

DRINKER, Hannah Hart. Daughter of Philadelphian Thomas Hart; cousin of Elizabeth Hart Drinker; m. Joseph DRINKER, HD's brother (1760); at least ten children.

DRINKER, Hannah White Prior. 1740–1824. Daughter of Josiah White and Rebecca Foster White; m. Thomas Prior (1762); four children; m. Daniel DRINKER (1796); d. Burlington, N.J.

DRINKER, Henry. 1734–1809. Son of Henry Drinker (d. 1746), a scrivener, and Mary Gottier Drinker (m. Burlington, N.J., 1731; d. c. 1750), of French Huguenot ancestry; reared, with his brothers, by grandmother, Mary Janney Drinker, a devout Quaker; apprenticed to George James (d. 1746), a Phila. Quaker merchant (1744–48); eventually entered into mercantile partnership with James's son, Abel JAMES. m. (1757) Ann Swett (d. 1758), daughter of Benjamin SWETT (d. 1774), at New Castle (Del.) Mtg.; following a trading voyage to England, m. Elizabeth Sandwith at Phila. Mtg. (1761); five of nine children survived to adulthood. Phila. merchant; interests in iron mining; exiled to Va. during Revolution; after Revolutionary War, involved in land speculation in n. Pa. Leading figure in Phila. Quaker community; served N. District Mtg. and Phila. Yearly Mtg. in various capacities.

DRINKER, Henry. 1757–1822. Phila. Quaker merchant. Sometimes called Henry Drinker, Jr. Son of John DRINKER and Rachel Reynear DRINKER; ED's nephew; m. (1782) Mary HOWELL; five children. Cashier, Bank of N. Am. (1800–1822); active in Phila. politics.

DRINKER, Henry. 1797–1798. Son of Henry S. DRINKER and Hannah SMITH Drinker.

DRINKER, Henry. 1804–68. Son of Henry S. DRINKER and Hannah SMITH Drinker; m. Frances Morton (1845); three children. Resided in Montrose, Susquehanna Co., Pa., where HD had owned property.

DRINKER, Henry Sandwith. 1770–1824. Son of ED; m. (1794) Hannah SMITH (1774–1830) at Phila. Mtg.; eight of 14 children survived to adulthood. In mercantile business with father, who gave him (1794) North Bank, a farm at Pennsbury Manor in Bucks Co.; sailed as supercargo on voyage to Calcutta (1806); after return to Phila., helped manage father's investments.

DRINKER, James. 1800–1801. Son of Henry S. DRINKER and Hannah SMITH Drinker.

DRINKER, John. 1733–1800. Brother of HD. Hatter; later shopkeeper, merchant; wrote newspaper articles and pamphlets supporting Soc. of Friends; clerk,

Phila. Yearly Mtg. (1782–86). m. Rachel Reynear, sister of Hannah Reynear Clifton, at Phila. Mtg. (1756); six children.

DRINKER, Joseph. d. 1809. Phila. cooper. Brother of HD. m. Hannah Hart at Phila. Mtg. (1760); at least ten children.

DRINKER, Joseph D. 1764–c. 1833. Phila. merchant. Son of John DRINKER and Rachel Reynear DRINKER; m. Ann Bartow, a grandniece of Anthony BENEZET, at Phila.'s Moravian Church (1795); disowned by Soc. of Friends for marrying out of unity; nine children.

DRINKER, Mary. *See also* Mary HOWELL (1759–1821).

DRINKER, Mary. 1761–aft. 1819. Daughter of Joseph DRINKER and Hannah Hart DRINKER; m. John James (1801); at least one child, Rachel (b. 1802).

DRINKER, Mary. 1766–1825. Daughter of John DRINKER and Rachel Reynear DRINKER; m. Thomas Pym COPE (1792); six of their eight children survived.

DRINKER, Mary. 1774–1856. Youngest surviving child of ED; eloped (1796) with Samuel RHOADS (1774–1810); disciplined by N. District Mtg., but not disowned; first child stillborn (1797); four more children.

DRINKER, Mary S. 1806–1879. Daughter of Henry S. DRINKER and Hannah SMITH Drinker; resided in Phila.

DRINKER, Rachel Reynear. 1730–1822. Daughter of Phila. Quakers Joseph Reynear and Mary Reynear; m. (1756) John DRINKER, HD's brother; six children.

DRINKER, Sarah. 1761–1807. Eldest child of ED; m. Jacob DOWNING (1787); five of six children reached maturity; d. cancer.

DRINKER, Sarah. 1803–77. Daughter of Henry S. DRINKER and Hannah SMITH Drinker; m. (1828) James Canby Biddle (d. 1841), a Phila. attorney; six children; to Montrose, Pa., where the Drinker family had extensive landholdings; back to Phila. (after 1841).

DRINKER, William. 1767–1821. Son of ED; b. and d. in Phila.; began mercantile career with father; contracted tuberculosis and thereafter seems to have led a more retiring life; helped father and aunt, Mary SANDWITH, with their landholdings; organized family papers; seems also to have done some writing on his own.

DRINKER, William. 1795–1836. Eldest child of Henry S. DRINKER and Hannah SMITH Drinker; m. (1818) Eliza G. Rodman, daughter of Gilbert Rodman and Sarah Gibbs Rodman of Bucks Co.

DUFFIELD, Benjamin. 1753–99. Phila. physician. Received medical training at College of Phila. (1774); founding member, College of Physicians; at Bush Hill emergency hospital during 1793 yellow fever epidemic; disagreed with Benjamin RUSH's use of bloodletting to treat yellow fever; lectured privately on midwifery and other medical subjects (1790s).

EDDY, Charles. c. 1754–1804. Phila. Quaker merchant. Son of James Eddy and Mary Darragh EDDY; inherited father's mercantile and ironmongering businesses. Suspected loyalist, exiled to Va. (1777); later allowed to go to N.Y.; from there to England and Ireland on business; married and lived temporarily in England; back to Phila. (c. 1796); member, S. District Monthly Mtg.; wife, Mary, and at least five children.

EDDY, George. c. 1763–1810. Phila. Quaker merchant and broker. Son of James Eddy and Mary Darragh EDDY; m. Hester Lewis (c. 1791); ten children.

EDDY, Mary Darragh. d. c. 1788. Affluent Irish Quaker. m. James Eddy (d. c. 1769) in Dublin (c. 1742); 16 children; to Phila.; admitted to Phila. Mtg. (1753).

ELLIS, William. 1751–1806. Close friend of HD. b. Chester Co.; taught school in Md.; m. Mercy Cox (1785); following mother's death, sold his property in Chester Co. and moved to Muncy, Pa. Member, Catawissa Monthly Mtg.; clerk, Muncy Monthly Mtg. Supervised HD's real estate interests near Muncy; named one son Henry Drinker Ellis. Large family; sent several children to school at Westtown.

ELLIS, William Cox. 1787–1871. Lawyer, Muncy, Pa. Son of Quakers William ELLIS and Mercy Cox Ellis; student at Westtown; became an Episcopalian; m. Rebecca Morris of Phila. (1810). Member, Pa. legislature, U.S. Congress.

EMLEN, Ann. d. 1815. Daughter of George Emlen and Ann Reckless Emlen; sister of George EMLEN; m. Warner MIFFLIN at Phila. Mtg. (1788); three children.

EMLEN, Elizabeth. *See also* Elizabeth MOODE.

EMLEN, Elizabeth. c. 1773–1820. Daughter of Quaker minister Samuel EMLEN (1730–99) and Sarah MOTT Emlen; m. (1800) Philip Syng Physick, "Father of American Surgery"; seven children.

EMLEN, George. c. 1741–1812. Eldest son of Phila. Quakers George Emlen and Ann Reckless Emlen; spent much of adulthood managing vast estate inherited from father, including Emlenton, country estate in Whitemarsh Valley, Pa. Interested in the occult, but remained a Quaker. m. (1775) Sarah Fishbourne (b. 1756); eight children.

EMLEN, Joshua. 1701–76. One of three Quaker brothers who established the Emlen family in Phila. Tanner; served intermittently on Phila. Common Council (1742–56). m. Mary Holton; m. Deborah Powell; one surviving son, Samuel EMLEN (1730–99).

EMLEN, Samuel. 1730–99. Phila. Quaker minister. Son of Joshua EMLEN and Deborah Powell Emlen. Though apprenticed in a countinghouse, had the financial means to devote himself to Quaker activities; well versed in modern and classical languages; traveled to Great Britain to preach. m. Elizabeth MOODE (1761); one son, Samuel EMLEN (1766–1837), reached maturity; m. Sarah MOTT (1770); two daughters.

EMLEN, Samuel. 1766–1837. Son of Samuel EMLEN (1730–99) and Elizabeth MOODE Emlen; m. Susannah Dillwyn (1795); to Burlington, N.J. Founded Emlen Institute for Indians and blacks, later merged into the Colored Normal School at Cheney, Chester Co., Pa.

EMLEN, Sarah. *See* Sarah MOTT.

ESTAUGH, David. c. 1728–87. Phila. Quaker physician; member, N. District Monthly Mtg.

EVANS, Cadwalader. 1749–1821. Phila. merchant. Son of Rowland EVANS and Susanna Foulke Evans.

EVANS, Cadwalader. 1762–1841. Son of John Evans and Margaret Foulke Evans. b.

family homestead in Gwynedd, Montgomery Co., Pa. Trained as a surveyor; member, Pa. Assembly, (1790–98, 1802, 1805); Speaker of the House (1798); to Phila. (1812); director, Bank of the U.S., Schuylkill Navigation Co.

EVANS, Enoch. c. 1744–1818. N.J. Quaker; a founder, Cropwell Meeting. m. twice; five children.

EVANS, Hannah Walton. d. 1801. Daughter of Phila. Quaker Michal Walton; m. (1740) Jonathan EVANS (c. 1714–95); seven children.

EVANS, Jonathan. c. 1714–95. Phila. wine merchant. Son of Evan Evans; brother of David Evans; m. Hannah Walton (1740); seven children.

EVANS, Jonathan. c. 1758–1839. Son of Jonathan EVANS (c. 1714–95) and Hannah Walton EVANS; m. Hannah Bacon. Fined and jailed for refusing military service (1781); overseer (c. 1782), elder (c. 1794), Phila. Monthly Mtg.

EVANS, Rowland. c. 1717–89. Brother of Cadwalader EVANS (1716–73); m. Susanna Foulke; two children. Member, Pa. Colonial Assembly (1761–63, 1765–71). Maintained homes both in Phila. and in Old Forge, along Schuylkill R.

FALCONER, Nathaniel. d. 1806. Pa. ship captain. Numerous voyages btw. Phila. and London (1765–74). Member, Pa. Council of Safety (1775). Active in naval affairs during Am. Revolution. Warden, port of Phila. (1778–90), and later its surveyor.

FENNO, John Ward. 1778–1802. Phila. newspaper publisher. Son of newspaper publisher John Fenno and Mary Curtiss Fenno; took over publication of *Gazette of the United States* (1798) following father's death from yellow fever; sold the newspaper to Caleb Parry Wayne (May 1800). His daughter Harriet later became a contributor to *The Port-Folio*.

FISHER, Elizabeth. *See also* Elizabeth RHOADS (c. 1770–96).

FISHER, Elizabeth. b. 1760. Daughter of William FISHER (c. 1713–87) and Sarah Coleman FISHER; apparently d. in infancy.

FISHER, Esther. 1734–95. Daughter of Quakers Joshua FISHER and Sarah Rowland FISHER; m. Samuel Lewis (1793).

FISHER, James Cowles. c. 1754–1840. Phila. merchant. Son of William FISHER (c. 1713–87) and Sarah Coleman FISHER; second cousin of HD; m. (1785) Hannah Wharton (1753–95); one son; m. her cousin, Ann Wharton (1804).

FISHER, Joshua. 1707–83. Founder of one of Phila.'s great Quaker mercantile firms of the colonial era, Joshua Fisher & Sons. b. Del.; to Phila. (1746); m. Sarah Rowland (1733); seven children; his business was confiscated during Revolutionary War.

FISHER, Miers. 1748–1819. Phila. Quaker lawyer. Son of Joshua FISHER and Sarah Rowland FISHER; read law with Benjamin Chew; admitted to bar (1769); m. (1774) Sarah Redwood, daughter of Abraham Redwood, a leading Quaker of Newport, R.I.; 16 children, seven of whom reached adulthood. During Revolutionary War, exiled to Va. along with two brothers and other Quaker leaders, incl. HD; after the war, resumed his law practice; active in local politics and Soc. for the Abolition of Slavery; director, Bank of N. Am.

FISHER, Rebecca. d. 1824. Daughter of Quakers William FISHER (c. 1713–87) and Sarah Coleman FISHER.

FISHER, Samuel Rowland. 1745–1834. Phila. Quaker merchant. Son of Quakers Joshua FISHER and Sarah Rowland FISHER; exiled to Va. with two brothers and HD during Revolutionary War; abolitionist; m. (1793) Hannah Rodman, from a prominent Newport, R.I., Quaker family; five children.

FISHER, Samuel W. c. 1765–1817. Phila. Quaker merchant. Son of William FISHER (c. 1713–87) and Sarah Coleman FISHER; m. Elizabeth RHOADS (c. 1770–96); four children; m. (1803) Sarah West Cooper, of a Gloucester Co., N.J., Quaker family; four children. Manager, Phila. and Lancaster Turnpike Co., Pa. Hospital.

FISHER, Sarah. 1757–62. Daughter of William FISHER (c. 1713–87) and Sarah Coleman FISHER.

FISHER, Sarah Coleman. c. 1718–1806. Sometimes referred to by ED as Aunt Fisher or Cousin Fisher; m. (1738) William FISHER (c. 1713–87); at least eight children.

FISHER, Sarah Rowland. 1716–72. Daughter of Lewes, Del., Quakers Thomas Rowland and Sarah Miers Rowland; m. (1733) Joshua FISHER; to Phila. (1746); seven children.

FISHER, Tabitha. c. 1744–1814. Daughter of Quakers William FISHER (c. 1713–87) and Sarah Coleman FISHER.

FISHER, Thomas. 1741–1810. Phila. Quaker merchant. Son of Joshua FISHER and Sarah Rowland FISHER; directed family business after father's death; among the Quakers exiled to Va. during Revolutionary War. Founding member, Am. Philosophical Soc.; manager, Pa. Hospital; founding member, Quaker boarding school, Westtown. m. (1772) Sarah Logan (1751–96); five children; resided at Wakefield estate, an inheritance through the Logan family.

FISHER, William. c. 1713–87. Mayor of Phila. (1773); merchant; trading partner of Abel JAMES (c. 1724–90). Grandson of a Quaker emigrant to Phila. of the same name; his mother, Tabitha Janney Fisher, was sister of Mary Janny, who had married Joseph Drinker, HD's grandfather. m. Sarah Coleman (1738); at least eight children.

FISHER, William. c. 1747–84. Son of William FISHER (c. 1713–87) and Sarah Coleman FISHER.

FOULKE, John. 1757–96. Phila. Quaker physician. Son of Judah FOULKE and Mary Bringhurst FOULKE. Served in hospitals of Am. forces, Revolutionary War; medical education at College of Phila. (Univ. of Pa.); travels abroad; back to Phila.; at 107 N. Front St. (near ED); m. Ellenor Parker (1788).

FOULKE, Judah. 1722–76. Quaker. b. Gwynedd, Pa.; to Phila. in childhood; collector of excise (1745–50), sheriff, Phila. City and Co. (1770–73); m. Mary Bringhurst (1743); at least four children; friend of Abel JAMES (c. 1724–90); resided at 34 N. Front St.

FOULKE, Mary Bringhurst. c. 1720–98. Daughter of Mary Claypoole Bringhurst and John Bringhurst; m. Judah FOULKE (1743); at least four children.

FOX, Joseph. 1709–79. Phila. Quaker carpenter and landowner. Son of Justinian Fox and Elizabeth Yard Fox; m. Elizabeth Mickle at Phila. Mtg. (1746). Member, Pa. Assembly (1750, 1753–71); Speaker, Pa. Assembly (1764–66).

Disowned by Soc. of Friends (1756) for advocating defensive measures during French and Indian War.

FRANKS, David. 1720–94. Phila. Jewish merchant. b. NYC; to Phila. (1740); m. Margaret Evans. Loyalist; supplier to British prisoners of war during Revolution; banished from Phila. to NYC (1780), although his property was not confiscated; later to England.

GIBBONS, James. c. 1731–1810. Son of Joseph Gibbons (1712–c. 1781) and Ann Marshall Gibbons; m. Deborah Hoopes (1756); 12 children; from family homestead at Westtown, Pa., to lands owned by his father in Lancaster Co., Pa.

GIBBONS, James. 1736–1823. First cousin of James GIBBONS; reared at family homestead in Westtown, Chester Co. Quaker scholar, farmer, surveyor; for a short while kept a school in Phila.; back to Chester Co.; sold land at Westtown for Quaker boarding school (1795). Treasurer, Chester Co.; representative, Pa. Gen. Assembly (1773–76). m. Eleanor Peters (1756); 12 children.

GILLINGHAM, John. 1710–93. Phila. Quaker joiner.

GILPIN, Thomas. 1727–78. Inventor, engineer. Son of Jane Parker Gilpin and English-born Quaker Samuel Gilpin; m. (1764) Lydia Fisher (1736–1807); three children. Founding member, Am. Philosophical Soc., to which he presented a model of his hydraulic pump. One of a group of Quakers exiled to Va. by Pa. government, Revolutionary War; d. in exile.

GOSNOLD, Mary c. 1722–92. Phila. Quaker.

GREENLEAF, Catharine Wistar. b. 1730. Daughter of Quaker merchant and glass manufacturer Caspar Wistar (1696–1752) and Catharine Jansen Wistar; m. (1753) Isaac Greenleaf (1715–71); five children.

GREENLEAF, Catharine. 1756–83. Daughter of Catharine Wistar GREENLEAF and Isaac Greenleaf.

GRIFFITTS, Abigail Powel. 1735–97. Daughter of Phila. Quakers Mary Morris Powel and Samuel Powel; m. William Griffitts (1752); four children.

GRISCOM, Rebecca. 1745–1807. Mantua and/or miniature maker, 221 N. Front St. First cousin of Rebecca GRISCOM (1747–98), with whom she was reared.

GRISCOM, Rebecca. 1747–98. Daughter of Samuel Griscom and Rebecca James Griscom; sister of Betsy Ross; censured and disowned by Soc. of Friends for excessive drinking (1785).

HAGA, Godfrey. 1747–1825. Phila. merchant. b. Germany; to Phila. as a redemptioner. Manager, Phila. Dispensary; member, Phila. Select Council, Pa. legislature. m. Hannah Mozer, a Moravian (1777); joined Moravian Church.

HAHN, Christian. c. 1736–1806. Chocolate and mustard manufacturer at 104 N. Front St. (1793–1806); wife, Hannah, and six children. Neighbor of ED's.

HAILER, Frederick. Phlebotomist at 24 Arch St., Phila.

HAILER, John. Phlebotomist at 159 S. Front St.; nephew of Frederick HAILER.

HAINES, Catherine. 1761–1808. Daughter of Quakers Reuben HAINES and Margaret Wistar Haines; m. Richard HARTSHORNE (1798); joined Concord Mtg.; later to Rahway (N.J.) Mtg.

HAINES, Reuben. 1728–93. Phila. Quaker brewer; m. Margaret Wistar at Phila.

Mtg. (1760); active in civic affairs; real estate in Phila. and elsewhere in Pa.; disowned by Soc. of Friends (1783); d. yellow fever; buried in Friends Burial Ground.

HALL, David. 1714–72. Printer, bookseller, newspaper publisher, partner of Benjamin Franklin. m. Mary Leacock (1748); five children.

HARPER, Robert Goodloe. 1765–1825. b. Va.; to N.C. in childhood; 15-year-old soldier, Revolution; graduate, Princeton College; to S.C.; admitted to bar. Took over Alexander Gillon's seat in U.S. Cong. after Gillon's death (1794); Federalist leader, House of Representatives (1794–1801); to Md.; practiced law in Baltimore; served briefly in U.S. Senate (1816).

HARPER, Samuel. c. 1736–aft. 1790. Son of Robert Harper (d. 1765) and Sarah Buzby Harper; m. Ann Powel at Christ Church, Phila. (1758); m. Ann Roberts Shoemaker, widow of Isaac Shoemaker, at Oxford Mtg. (1767); six children; lived in various twps. in Phila. Co.; in Bristol (1790).

HART, Seymer. c. 1734–1819. Phila. Quaker lumber merchant. Owned property in Phila., Passyunk, and Bristol, Pa.; bequeathed land to Soc. of Friends to use as a school, and securities to aid the insane.

HARTSHORNE, Catherine. See Catherine HAINES.

HARTSHORNE, Elizabeth Field. d. 1802. Daughter of Elijah Field and Mary Field; m. (1790s) John Hartshorne (1763–1849).

HARTSHORNE, Pattison. 1745–1828. Quaker merchant, 119 N. Front St., Phila. Son of Hugh Hartshorne and Hannah Pattison Hartshorne; nephew of Robert HARTSHORNE; m. Susannah WALN (1776); five children. Member, Pa. Prison Soc.

HARTSHORNE, Richard. 1750–1836. Son of Quakers Hugh Hartshorne and Hannah Pattison Hartshorne; brother of Pattison HARTSHORNE; m. (1772) Jane Large (d. 1783); four children; m. (1785) Isabel Smith (d. 1793); m. (1798) Catherine HAINES; from Bucks Co. to Phila. (c. 1786); later to Rahway, N.J.

HARTSHORNE, Robert. 1721–1801. Son of Quakers William Hartshorne and Elizabeth Lawrence Hartshorne; lived on family estate in Monmouth Co., N.J.; m. (1744) Sarah Saltar, sister of Lucy Saltar Hartshorne; nine children.

HARTSHORNE, Susannah. See also Susannah WALN.

HARTSHORNE, Susannah. b. 1784. Daughter of Quakers Pattison HARTSHORNE and Susannah WALN Hartshorne; d. young.

HATTON, Susannah. 1720–81. Irish Quaker minister, m. Thomas Lightfoot; settled in N. Am. (1764).

HAVILAND, Daniel. 1746–1829. N.Y. Quaker minister; blind for many years before his death; ministerial travels to Ga., Pa., N.J.

HAZELMAN, Jerome. See Jerome HEINTZELMAN.

HAZLEHURST, Isaac. 1742–1834. Phila. merchant. Neighbor of ED; b. England; to Phila. (c. 1768); m. Joanna (Juliana) Purviance; father-in-law of Benjamin Latrobe.

HAZLEHURST, Joanna (Juliana) Purviance. 1741–1804. Daughter of Phila. merchant Samuel Purviance; m. Isaac HAZLEHURST.

HEINTZELMAN, Jerome. 1730–96. b. Hieronimus Heintzelman, in Germany; to

England; first lieutenant, "Royal American" regiment (1756); served at Manheim, Lancaster Co., Pa.; m. Catharine Elizabeth Wagner; at least five children.

HICKS, Elias. 1748–1830. Long Island Quaker minister; leader of the liberal Hicksite branch of Soc. of Friends during doctrinal split (1827–28); m. Jemima Seaman; 11 children.

HICKS, Hannah. 1733–83. Early friend of ED; daughter of Quaker Augustine Hicks (d. 1769); m. Charles Jones (1761); m. (1770) Robert STEVENSON, her first cousin; disowned by Soc. of Friends for this breach of discipline; four children.

HIL(L)BORN, John. c. 1741–1826. b. Bucks Co.; captive of Indians for two years during Revolutionary War; HD's land agent in Susequehanna Co.; a manager, Union Farm. First Friends meeting in Harmony, Pa., was held in his home.

HOPKINS, Catherine. *See* Catherine HOWELL.

HOPKINS, Hannah. 1764–1838. Daughter of John Estaugh Hopkins and Sarah Mickle Hopkins.

HOPKINS, James. 1763–1826. Son of John Estaugh Hopkins and Sarah Mickle Hopkins; m. (1784) Rebecca Clement, daughter of Samuel Clement and Beulah Evans Clement. Member, N.J. senate; judge, Gloucester Co., N.J.; first president, Haddonfield (N.J.) Library Co.

HOPKINS, Johns. b. 1751. Son of Md. Quakers Johns Hopkins and Mary Richardson Crockett Hopkins; m. Elizabeth Harris (1775); m. Catherine HOWELL at Phila. Mtg. (1779); to Charleston, S.C.

HOPKINS, Samuel. 1743–aft. 1798. Son of Samuel Hopkins and Sarah Giles Hopkins, Md. Quakers of Harford Co. m. (1765) Hannah Wilson, daughter of George Wilson and Mary Rakestraw Wilson, at Phila. Mtg.; perhaps seven children; to Md. (1768); to Philadelphia; member, N. District Monthly Mtg.; may have been potash maker.

HOWARD, John. 1727–1809. Phila. Anglican joiner. Quaker mother, Anglican father; m. Sarah Bunting, a Quaker (1749); 12 children; of eight who reached maturity, four were Anglican, four Quaker. Back to Phila. (1753); later a fishtacker; engaged in land speculation.

HOWELL, Catherine. d. 1793. Daughter of Joshua HOWELL and Catherine Warner HOWELL; to Phila. (1773); m. Johns HOPKINS (1779).

HOWELL, Catherine Warner. c. 1737–1810. Elder, Phila. Mtg.; m. Joshua HOWELL (1753); three children survived to maturity.

HOWELL, Deborah. b. 1757. Daughter of Samuel Howell (1719–80) and Ann Evans Howell; m. (1778) Daniel MIFFLIN (1754–1812); seven children.

HOWELL, Isaac. 1722–97. Brother of Joshua HOWELL; m. Mary Bartram (1745); four children; m. Patience Roberts Gray (1759); one child; from Chester Co. to Phila. (1759). Member, Committee of Correspondence, Revolutionary War; disowned by Soc. of Friends (1776); joined Free Quakers. Judge, Court of Common Pleas and Quarter Sessions, Phila. Orphans Court (1777; recommissioned, 1793); Phila. alderman (1796).

HOWELL, Jacob Samuel. 1749–93. Phila. Quaker. Son of Samuel Howell (1719–80) and Ann Evans Howell; m. Mary Carmalt at Phila. Mtg. (1772); two children.

Secretary, Council of Safety (1776–77); receiver gen. of clothing, Continental Army (1778–79). d. yellow fever.

HOWELL, Joshua. 1726–1797. Phila. Quaker merchant. Son of Jacob Howell and Sarah Vernon Howell; m. Catharine Warner (1753); three children reached maturity. Manager, Pa. Hospital (1779–82); member, Am. Philosophical Soc.

HOWELL, Joshua Ladd. 1762–1818. Son of John Ladd Howell and Frances Paschall Howell. Member, N.J. Assembly; various military posts. m. (1786) Anna Blackwood (1769–1855); 11 children.

HOWELL, Mary. c. 1759–1821. Daughter of Abraham Howell, a Phila. Quaker; m. (1782) ED's nephew Henry DRINKER (1757–1822) at Phila. Mtg.

HOWELL, Sarah. d. 1759. Daughter of Joshua HOWELL and Catherine Warner HOWELL. Another daughter of same name (1759–62).

HUDSON, Martha. See Martha LLOYD.

HUNT, Isaac. c. 1742–1809. Phila. loyalist lawyer, political pamphleteer. To England at beginning of Revolution; ordained minister, Church of England (1777). m. sister of Benjamin West; father of poet and essayist Leigh Hunt (1784–1859).

HUNT, John. 1712–78. Phila. Quaker minister, businessman. b. England; arrested with other Phila. Quakers and exiled to Va. (1777–78); d. in exile.

HUNT, Rachael Hudson Jorey. 1723–1806. Phila. Quaker. Daughter of William Hudson and Jane Evans Hudson; m. John Jorey (1741); m. John Hunt (1769).

HUTCHINSON, James. 1752–93. Physician. Army surgeon, Revolution; surgeon gen. of Pa. (1778–84); professor of science, Univ. of Pa.; member, Am. Philosophical Soc.; surgeon, Pa. Hospital. m. Lydia Biddle (1779); m. Sidney Howell.

INSKEEP, John. 1757–1834. Son of Gloucester Co., N.J., Anglicans Abraham Inskeep (d. 1780) and Sarah Ward Inskeep; m. Sarah Hulings; at least five children. Soldier, Continental Army, Revolution; owner of the George Tavern, Phila. (1785); china and glassware merchant (1790s); mayor of Phila. (1800, 1805); assoc. judge, Court of Common Pleas (1802–5); trustee, Mutual Assurance Co.; director, Insurance Co. of N. Am.

JACKSON, William. 1746–1834. Public Friend. b. London Grove, Chester Co., Pa.; m. (1778) Hannah Seaman of Westbury, N.Y.; to Westbury (1778); back to Chester Co. (1780); travels to Quaker mtgs. in England and Ireland (1802–4); visits to mtgs. throughout U.S. e. seaboard.

JAMES, Abel. c. 1724–90. HD's business partner in the mercantile firm of James and Drinker. Son of Phila. Quakers George James and Susannah Hinkson James; m. (1747) Rebecca Chalkley, a substantial property owner; at his death, their estate included his home in N. Liberties, large land holdings in Phila., and ironworks and sawmills in Goshen, N.J.; member, Pa. Assembly (1770–71).

JAMES, Chalkley. 1754–1825. Son of Able JAMES and Rebecca Chalkley JAMES; m. (1787) Sarah Huston (1766–1823); at least seven children; in Burlington, N.J.; to NYC (1796).

JAMES, George. d. 1781. Surviving son of Martha Livezey James and Phila. tailor Joseph James (d. 1745), younger brother of Abel JAMES.

JAMES, Rebecca. 1753–1837. Daughter of Abel JAMES and Rebecca Chalkley JAMES; m. (1782) John Thompson (1744–1819) at Oxford Mtg.; eight children.

JAMES, Rebecca Chalkley. c. 1721–95. Daughter of Quaker minister Thomas Chalkley (1675–1741) and Martha Brown Chalkley (d. 1749); m. (1747) Abel JAMES; 10 children.

JAMES, Susannah. 1757–74. Daughter of Abel JAMES and Rebecca Chalkley JAMES.

JAMES, Thomas. Son of Joseph James and Martha Livezey James; m. (1764) Ann Lownes Page (c. 1721–84?), who was disowned by Phila. Monthly Mtg. for marrying contrary to discipline (1765).

JAMES, Thomas Chalkley. 1766–1835. Physician. Son of Abel JAMES and Rebecca Chalkley JAMES; graduate, Univ. of Pa. (1787); to London and Edinburgh to study obstetrics (1787); back to Phila. (1793); received M.D., taught obstetrics, Univ. of Pa.; president, Phila. College of Surgeons; founder, Historical Soc. of Pa.; m. Hannah Morris (1802); seven children.

JARDINE, Lewis. d. aft. 1812. Physician. To Pa., prob. from England (1795); a farm, Richland, on Delaware R. near Bristol, Bucks Co.; practiced medicine in area (1795–1802); to Liverpool, England (1802).

JERVIS, Charles. 1731–1806. Phila. Quaker hatter and merchant. Son of John Jervis (c. 1705–85) and Rebeccah Walton Jervis; ED's first cousin; m. Elizabeth Boore at Christ Church (1766); disciplined by Soc. of Friends for marrying out of meeting; five children. Overseer of the poor (1767); exiled to Va. with HD, others (1777–78).

JERVIS, Elizabeth. 1733–1809. Quaker. Daughter of John Jervis (c. 1705–85) and Rebecca Walton Jervis.

JONES, Absalom. 1746–1818. Phila. African-American leader. b. into slavery on Del. plantation of Wynkoop family, wealthy merchant-planters; brought to Phila. at age 16; attended night school taught by an Anglican minister; purchased his freedom (1784); with Richard Allen, a leader of Free African Soc.; minister, Phila.'s first African church, St. Thomas's African Episcopal Church (founded 1794).

JONES, Aquilla. c. 1724–1800. Phila. Quaker of Welsh descent. Son of Griffith Jones. m. (1759) Margaret Evans (d. 1765) in Gwynedd, Pa.; two children; m. (1767) Elizabeth Cooper of Haddonfield, N.J.; at least two daughters; to Haddonfield (1768); back to Phila. (1791).

JONES, Hannah. 1749–1829. Daughter of Owen Jones (1711–93) and Susannah Evans JONES; m. (1779) at Phila. Mtg. Amos Foulke (d. 1791), a Phila. merchant whose brother Caleb had m. Jones's sister Jane; three children; d. husband's hometown of Gwynedd, Pa.

JONES, John. 1729–91. Quaker physician. b. Jamaica, N.Y.; studied medicine in Phila. under Thomas Cadwallader; medical degree, Rheims (1751); back to N.Y.; practice in obstetrics and surgery; professor of surgery, Kings College (later Columbia Univ.); author of first Am. textbook on surgery; to Phila. (1780); attending physician, Pa. Hospital; first vice president, College of Physicians.

JONES, Rebecca. 1739–1817. Quaker minister and educator. Daughter of William Jones and Mary Jones, an Anglican who ran a school in her home; attended Quaker school run by Anthony BENEZET; first appearance in Quaker ministry

(1758); acknowledged a minister (1760); took over her mother's school (1761–aft. 1781). Ministerial travels in England (1784–88); shopkeeper, Phila. (aft. 1788); founder, Westtown School.

JONES, Richard. Wealthy Quaker lumber merchant, Merion, Pa.

JONES, Susannah. 1747–1828. Daughter of Owen Jones (1711–93) and Susannah Evans JONES; m. John Nancarrow at Phila. Mtg. (1779); one son; d. Burlington, N.J.

JONES, Susannah Evans. 1720–1801. Daughter of Quakers Hugh Evans and Lowry Evans of Merion, Pa.; m. (1740) Owen Jones (1711–93); to Phila.; ten children.

KEARSLEY, John. d. 1777. Phila. physician. Nephew of John Kearsley (1684–1772); Loyalist; placed under house arrest by Phila. Council of Safety (1775); sentenced to Carlisle Jail; wife, Mary, and five children.

KUHN, Adam. 1741–1817. Phila. physician, botanist. Studied medicine at Uppsala Univ. under Linnaeus (1761), London (1764), and Edinburgh (M.D., 1767); professor of botany, College of Phila.; physician, Pa. Hospital; founder, president (1808), Phila. College of Physicians.

LAMPLEY, Sarah. Ran a boardinghouse on Market St., Phila. (1790–91).

LARGE, John Baldwin. Son of Ebenezer Large; m. Rebecca Hartshorne at N. District Monthly Mtg. (1806); at least three children.

LARGE, Sarah. 1779–1856. Daughter of Ebenezer Large and Dorothea Sparks Large; m. (1799) Thomas Mifflin, son of Martha Morris Mifflin and George Mifflin, a merchant who had been disowned by Soc. of Friends (1794) for participating in military activity during the Whiskey Rebellion; disowned for marrying contrary to discipline; eight children.

LEWIS, Jacob. 1713–74. Wealthy Phila. Quaker carpenter; m. Hannah Wood at Darby, Pa. (1735); two children; m. (1759) Sarah MIFFLIN at Phila. Mtg.

LEWIS, Robert. 1715–90. Phila. Quaker merchant. b. Chester Co.; member, Pa. Assembly (1745–46); m. Mary Pyle at Concord Mtg. (1733); 12 children.

LEWIS, Sarah. See Sarah MIFFLIN.

LEWIS, William. c. 1747–1801. Son of Robert LEWIS and Mary Pyle Lewis; m. Rachel Wharton (1781).

LEWIS, William. 1751–1819. Jurist. Son of Chester Co. Quakers Josiah Lewis and Martha Allen Lewis(?); as attorney, represented many Friends accused of treason; state legislator (1787–91); U.S. attorney for Pa. (1789); federal judge (1791–92). m. Rosanna Lurt; three children; m. Frances Durdin.

LIPPINCOTT, William. c. 1735–c. 1802. Phila. Quaker merchant. Son of N.J. Quakers Jacob Lippincott and Mary Burr Lippincott; m. Sarah Bispham (1771); three children; member, N. District Monthly Mtg. (from 1800).

LLOYD, Hannah Fishbourne. 1711–86. Daughter of Phila. Quakers William Fishbourne and Hannah Carpenter Fishbourne; m. (1733) Mordecai Lloyd (d. 1750), son of Thomas Lloyd, formerly of London, at Phila. Mtg.; at least five children.

LLOYD, Martha. d. 1780. Daughter of Rees Lloyd and Sarah Cox Lloyd; m. Samuel Hudson (1761).

LLOYD, Mary. d. 1762. m. John SEARSON (1759); daughter, Sarah Searson (b. 1760).

LLOYD, Sarah. 1736–59. Quaker. Daughter of Mordecai Lloyd and Hannah Fishbourne LLOYD. Disowned (1758) for marrying out.

LOGAN, James. 1728–1803. Son of James Logan and Sarah Read Logan; m. Sarah ARMITT (1766). Cultural and literary activities, Phila.

LOGAN, James. 1780–1805. Son of Charles Logan and Mary PLEASANTS Logan; d. at sea.

LOGAN, Sarah. *See* Sarah ARMITT.

LYNN, Hannah. 1741–60. Daughter of Phila. Quaker shipwright and real estate investor Joseph Lynn and Sarah Hutchinson Norwood Lynn.

MALLERIVE, Gasper. French ice cream maker. From Saint-Domingue (Haiti) to Phila. with his sister, Emilia (1790s).

MARRIOTT, Martha. 1747–1826. b. Trenton, N.J.; daughter of Thomas Marriott and Sarah Smith Marriott; m. William Canby at Bristol Mtg., Bucks Co., Pa. (1774); six children.

MARRIOTT, Sarah. 1711–70. Burlington, N.J., Quaker. Sister of Joyce Marriott BENEZET.

MARSHALL, Christopher. 1740–1806. Son of Christopher Marshall (1709–97) and Sarah Thomson Marshall; took over his father's apothecary shop with his brother Charles Marshall when their father retired (1772). m. Ann Eddy (1760); m. (1777) Elizabeth Flower (d. 1781); m. Margaret Roberts (1783): 12 children. Lived at 24 Strawberry St.

MASON, George. 1706–74. Quaker minister, landowner, New Garden Mtg., Chester Co.; travels in England.

MASTERMAN, Thomas(?). From Yorkshire, England, to Phila. (c. 1757); m. Mary Stiles at Phila. Monthly Mtg. (1759); at least seven children.

MATLACK, Timothy. 1736–1829. Son of Timothy Matlack and Martha Burr Matlack; b. Haddonfield, N.J.; m. (1758) Ellen Yarnall (d. 1791); five children; m. Elizabeth Claypoole Copper (1797). Disowned by Soc. of Friends (1765); leader, Free Quakers; army colonel; clerk, Cont. Cong. (1776); member, U.S. Congress (1780).

MENDENHALL, Jonathan. 1759–95. Son of Chester Co. Quakers. Disowned from Bradford Mtg. for marrying his first cousin, Martha Mendenhall; three children.

MIFFLIN, Ann. *See* Ann EMLEN.

MIFFLIN, Charles. d. 1783. Quaker. Son of George Mifflin and Anne Eyre Mifflin of Phila.; m. (1777) Mary Waln (1755–86).

MIFFLIN, Daniel. 1754–1812. Kent Co., Del., merchant. Son of Daniel Mifflin (1722–95) and Mary Warner Mifflin; m. (1778) Deborah HOWELL; seven children. Abolitionist; travels to Quaker mtgs., N.Y., R.I., Pa.; elder, Murderkill (Del.) Mtg.

MIFFLIN, Deborah. *See* Deborah HOWELL.

MIFFLIN, Esther Cordary. 1692–1776. Daughter of Deborah Cordary and Hugh Cordary; m. George Mifflin at Phila. Monthly Mtg. (1713); six children, three reached maturity.

MIFFLIN, Sarah. 1718–95. Phila. Quaker. Daughter of George Mifflin and Esther

Cordary MIFFLIN; m. Jacob LEWIS (1759). Possibly an earlier(?) m. to William Powell (Price?); five children.

MIFFLIN, Warner. 1745–98. Son of Daniel Mifflin (1722–95) and Mary Warner Mifflin; b. Accomac Co., Va.; m. Elizabeth Johns; m. (1788) Ann EMLEN. Representative, Quaker peace testimony, Revolutionary War; visited both Howe and Washington on behalf of Friends (1777). Abolitionist; manumitted his slaves (1774–75). Author, *A Serious Expostulation* . . . (1793) and *A Defence of Warner Mifflin* (1796). Contracted yellow fever, Phila.; d. near Camden, Del.

MITCHELL, Abraham. 1710–88. Phila. Quaker hatter. m. Sarah Robins (1734); six daughters reached maturity.

MITCHELL, Ann. d. 1778. Daughter of Abraham MITCHELL and Sarah Robins MITCHELL; m. Joseph POTTS at High St. Mtg. (1774); two children, both d. young.

MITCHELL, Sarah. 1739–1825. Daughter of Abraham MITCHELL and Sarah Robins MITCHELL; m. (1759) Isaac Parish (c. 1734–1826) at Phila. Mtg.; 11 children. Elder, Phila. Mtg. (1796).

MITCHELL, Sarah Robins. c. 1711–88. Phila. Quaker. m. Abraham MITCHELL (1734); 12 children, of whom six daughters reached maturity.

MOODE, Elizabeth. d. 1767. Phila. Quaker. Close friend of ED; sometimes called Baubette in the diary. m. (1761) Samuel EMLEN (1730–99); three children, one reached maturity. To England (1764); d. Bristol.

MOODE, Hannah. d. 1791. Sister of Elizabeth MOODE; m. (1762) Henry Haydock (d. 1798) at Phila. Mtg.; nine children. To NYC; clerk, N.Y. Women's Yearly Mtg. (1778–88).

MORGAN, Ann. *See* Ann WALN.

MORGAN, Robert. c. 1788–1803. Son of Thomas MORGAN and Ann WALN Morgan. Member, N. District Monthly Mtg.

MORGAN, Thomas. c. 1756–1804. Phila. merchant. m. Ann WALN at N. District Mtg. (1786); at least seven children.

MORRIS, Benjamin. 1762–1825. Quaker. Son of Samuel Morris and Rebecca Wistar Morris; m. Mary Wells (1785); to her family home, Wellsborough, in Tioga Co., Pa.

MORRIS, Israel. 1738–1818. Phila. merchant. Son of William MORRIS and Sarah Dury Morris; b. Trenton, N.J.; m. Phoebe BROWN (1761); m. Sarah Bond.

MORRIS, Israel. 1741–1806. Phila. Quaker merchant. Son of Anthony Morris (c. 1705–80) and Sarah Powell Morris. m. (c. 1774) Mary Harrison (d. c. 1775). Prob. accompanied ED to Reading, Pa. (1778), where his brother Samuel Morris had relocated during the British occupation of Phila.

MORRIS, Richard Hill. 1762–1841. Quaker judge, Chester, Delaware cos., Pa. Son of William Morris (1735–66) and Margaret Hill Morris; m. (1786) Mary Mifflin (d. 1789); m. (1798) Mary Smith (1778–1848); three children.

MORRIS, Sarah. c. 1702–75. Phila. Quaker minister. Daughter of Anthony Morris and his fourth wife, Elizabeth Watson Morris; ministerial travels to R.I. (1764), to Great Britain with niece Deborah Morris (1772–73); d. Phila.; left money to several Quakers, incl. HD, to distribute to "reputable housekeepers needing help."

MORRIS, Thomas. c. 1745–1809. Son of Quakers Anthony Morris (c. 1705–80) and Sarah Powell Morris. House carpenter. Managed the family brewery. Overseer, Phila. public schools (1782); manager, Pa. Hospital (1793–1809). m. Mary Saunders (1768); four children.

MORRIS, Thomas. 1774–1841. Quaker. Son of Thomas MORRIS (c. 1745–1809) and Mary Saunders Morris; m. (1797) Sarah Marshall; eight children. Managed family brewery business with brother Joseph S. Morris. Member, Phila. Common Council; manager, Pa. Hospital (1817–40); treasurer, Phila. [Public] Library.

MORRIS, William. 1695–1776. Trenton, N.J., Quaker merchant, judge, city councilman. Son of Anthony Morris and Mary Howard Coddington Morris; m. (c. 1718) Sarah Dury (1694–1750); m. (1752) Rebecca Cadwallader, whose sister Hannah Cadwallader m. Samuel Morris (1711–82).

MOTT, Huldah. c. 1747–1825. Daughter of Quakers Asher Mott and Deborah Tallman Mott of Monmouth Co., N.J.; to Phila. in childhood.

MOTT, James. 1742–1823. N.Y. Quaker merchant and author. Son of Richard Mott and Sarah Mott of Long Island; m. (1765) Mary Underhill (d. by 1776), daughter of Samuel Underhill and Ann Mott Underhill of N.Y.; at least five children; to Purchase, N.Y. (1776).

MOTT, Sarah. c. 1744–96. Sister of Huldah MOTT; m. (1770) Samuel EMLEN (1730–99) at Phila. Mtg.; two daughters.

NEWTON, Elizabeth. d. 1765. Member, Phila. Monthly Mtg.; was condemned by Soc. of Friends for marrying out of unity (1751).

NICHOLSON, Content. d. 1763. Received by Phila. Mtg. (1748); formerly a member of mtgs. in Del. and in Chester Co., Pa.

OL(L)IVER, Benjamin. d. 1802. Coachman and horsekeeper. Neighbor of ED. Following his marriage, went into business for himself, aided by HD, hiring out horses. d. yellow fever.

PARISH, Abigail Halloway Bissell. d. 1796. Daughter of Quaker Tobias Halloway; m. Samuel Bissell (1756); m. John Parish at Phila. Monthly Mtg. (1773); to N. District Monthly Mtg. (1774).

PARISH, Mary. 1738–1808. Sister of Isaac Parish (c. 1734–1826); m. Stephen COLLINS at Phila. Mtg. (1761); to Phila.; three children.

PARISH, Mary Wilson. 1733–1801. Phila. Quaker. m. Robert Parish (1760); eight children.

PARISH, Sarah. See Sarah MITCHELL.

PARKE, Thomas. 1749–1835. Phila. Quaker physician. Son of Chester Co. Quakers Thomas Parke and Jane Parke; m. (1775) Rachel Pemberton, daughter of James PEMBERTON and Hannah Lloyd Pemberton, at Phila. Mtg.; five children. Medical degree, College of Phila. (1770); studied medicine in London and Edinburgh (1770–73); practice in Phila. with Cadwalader Evans (1716–73); assumed his practice when Evans d. a few months later. Physician, Phila. Almshouse (1773), Pa. Hospital (1777–1827). Founder (1787), president (1818–35), College of Physicians; curator, Am. Philosophical Soc. (1795); director, Library Co. of Phila. (1778–1835).

PARKE, Thomas. 1776–1840. Son of Thomas PARKE (1749–1835) and Rachel Pemberton Parke.

PARKER, Elizabeth. b. 1750(?) in Montgomery Co., Pa.; daughter of Alexander Parker; m. (1777) Andrew Porter, a career officer; at least eight children. A talented needleworker.

PARR, Margaret Cadge. d. 1772. m. William PARR (1750).

PARR, William. d. 1786. b. England; to N. Am.; settled in Lancaster, Pa.; lawyer; held several public offices in Phila. and Lancaster Co.; proprietor, N. Liberties tavern, The Sign of the King of Prussia; m. Margaret Cadge (1750); m. Grace Powell (c. 1776).

PARRISH. *See* PARISH.

PARROCK, John. Quaker. m. Mary Bell. Owned a wharf, several brick stores, a lumberyard, and a plantation in Richmond, Pa.; partner of Abel JAMES; member, with James and HD, Fishing Co. of Fort St. Davids (1763). Loyalist; appointed superintendent of the navy by Adm. Howe when British occupied Phila. (1777); accompanied British to N.Y. (1778); back to Phila. (1784); to Halifax; entered the whaling business.

PAUL, John. 1731–80. Quaker farmer, Jenkintown, Pa. Son of James Paul (1692–1761) and Ann Jones Paul of Merion (Pa.) Mtg.; m. Sydney Roberts (1754); nine children. Purchased land and the Wagon Inn in Mooreland Twp. (1767); operated a stagecoach line; acquired Phila. tavern The Indian King, Am. Revolution.

PEMBERTON, Hannah. 1755–88. Daughter of James PEMBERTON and Hannah Lloyd Pemberton; m. Robert Morton (1784).

PEMBERTON, Hannah Zane. 1734–1811. Daughter of Isaac ZANE (1711–94) and Sarah Elfreth Zane, m. John PEMBERTON (1766).

PEMBERTON, Israel. 1715–79. Wealthy Quaker landowner, reformer; clerk, Phila. Yearly Mtg.; member, Pa. Assembly (1750–51). Imprisoned and exiled to Va. with HD and others (1777). Son of Israel Pemberton and Rachel Read Pemberton; m. (1737) Sarah Kirkbride (1714–46); m. (1747) Mary Stanbury Jordan Hill; six children reached maturity.

PEMBERTON, James. 1723–1809. Phila. Quaker merchant. A founder, Pa. Abolition Soc.; member, Pa. Assembly (1756), from which he resigned; exiled to Va. (1777). Son of Israel Pemberton and Rachel Read Pemberton; m. Hannah Lloyd (1751); m. Sarah Smith (1768); m. Phoebe Lewis Morton (aft. 1773).

PEMBERTON, John. 1727–95. Traveling Quaker minister and author. Exiled to Va. (1777); son of Israel Pemberton and Rachel Read Pemberton; m. Hannah Zane (1766); d. on a ministerial visit to Pyrmont, Germany.

PEMBERTON, Mary. 1738–1821. Daughter of Israel PEMBERTON and Sarah Kirkbride Pemberton; m. (1762) Samuel PLEASANTS (1736?–1807); ten children.

PEMBERTON, Mary Stanbury Jordan Hill. 1704–78. Daughter of Quakers Nathan Stanbury and Mary Stanbury; m. Richard Jordan; m. Capt. Richard Hill; m. (1747) Israel PEMBERTON; one child.

PEMBERTON, Phoebe Lewis Morton. 1738–1812. Daughter of Robert LEWIS and Mary Pyle Lewis; m. Samuel Morton; three sons; m. James PEMBERTON (aft. 1773).

PEMBERTON, Sarah. 1741–1810. Daughter of Israel PEMBERTON and Sarah Kirkbride Pemberton; m. (1765) Samuel RHOADS (1740–84); three children.

PENINGTON, Edward. 1726–96. Phila. Quaker merchant. Son of Isaac Penington and Ann Biles Penington; m. Sarah Shoemaker at Bank Mtg. (1754). Member, Pa. Assembly (1761); judge, Court of Common Pleas (1761); member, Am. Philosophical Soc. (1768); manager, Pa. Hospital (1773–79); city councillor (1790). Exiled to Va. (1777).

PENN, Richard. 1735–1811. Grandson of William Penn; m. Mary Masters at Christ Church (1772). Lieutenant governor, Pa. (1771–73); commissioned as naval officer (1773); carried Olive Branch Petition to England (1775); M.P.

PENRY, Mary. 1736–1804. Girlhood friend of ED. b. Wales, educated in Phila.; joined the Moravian settlement at Bethlehem (1757); to Lititz, Pa. (1774); skilled seamstress; diarist for the Moravian community.

PERKINS, Elisha. 1741–99. b., medical training and practice, Conn.; invented "metallic tractor" (1795), two pieces of connected metal drawn or stroked over affected part of the body. To Phila. (1796), d. yellow fever.

PEROT, Elliston. 1747–1834. Phila. Quaker merchant in E. India trade. b. to a Huguenot family in Bermuda; trader, NYC (1772); mercantile business with brother John Perot, Phila. (from 1781); held important civic positions. Joined Soc. of Friends (1786); m. Sarah Sansom (1787); five children.

PINES, Elizabeth. m. (1772) at Christ Church Matthew Whitehead, later a singing instructor at St. Peter's Church (1783).

PLEASANTS, Charles. 1772–1827. Son of Samuel PLEASANTS (1736?–1807); and Mary PEMBERTON Pleasants. m. (1796) Ann EMLEN (c. 1774–1844); ten children.

PLEASANTS, Israel. 1764–1843. Phila. merchant. Son of Samuel PLEASANTS (1736?–1807) and Mary PEMBERTON Pleasants; m. (1788) Anne Paschall Franklin; 14 children. President, U.S. Insurance Co., Phila.; manager, Pa. Hospital (1796–1800); business relationship with brother John Pemberton PLEASANTS in Baltimore; to Northumberland, Pa.

PLEASANTS, James. 1782–1829. Son of Samuel PLEASANTS (1736?–1807) and Mary PEMBERTON Pleasants.

PLEASANTS, John Pemberton. 1766–1825. Son of Samuel PLEASANTS (1736?–1807) and Mary PEMBERTON Pleasants; m. Ann Cleves Armistead (1793); five children; m. Mary Hall (1816); one child. Established a business in Baltimore with his brother Israel PLEASANTS.

PLEASANTS, Mary. See also Mary PEMBERTON.

PLEASANTS, Mary. d. c. 1800. Daughter of John Pleasants and Mary Pleasants of Henrico Co., Va.; niece of Samuel PLEASANTS (1736?–1807); m. Charles Logan at Phila. Mtg. (1779); six children. Manumitted her slaves (1779); to Bellmeade, Powhattan Co., Va. (1782); disowned by Cedar Creek Monthly Mtg. for "non-attendance and inconsistent conduct" (1788); m. Robert Cary Pleasants, a cousin (1795).

PLEASANTS, Samuel. 1736?–1807. Phila. Quaker merchant. b. Va.; to Phila. (c. 1762); m. (1762) Mary PEMBERTON; ten children. Exiled with HD and other Quakers to Winchester, Va. (1777–78). Manager, Pa. Hospital (1779–81).

PLEASANTS, Samuel. 1771–97. Phila. physician. Son of Samuel PLEASANTS (1736?–1807) and Mary PEMBERTON Pleasants; d. yellow fever.

PLEASANTS, Sarah. 1767–1825. Daughter of Samuel PLEASANTS (1736?–1807) and Mary PEMBERTON Pleasants; m. Samuel Mickle FOX (1788); 13 children.

PLEASANTS, Thomas. d. c. 1803. Quaker landowner, Goochland Co., Va. First cousin of Samuel PLEASANTS (1736?–1807); m. Elizabeth Brooke of Md. (1761); nine children. Member, Cedar Creek Mtg.; representative, Va. Yearly Mtg. Manumitted his slaves.

POTTS, Joseph. 1742–1804. Phila. merchant, mill owner, Quaker minister. Brother of Isaac Potts. Involved in a land dispute with HD (1800); m. Mary Morris (1764); m. Sarah Powel (1768); m. Ann MITCHELL (1774); m. Mary Kirkbride (1780); ten children.

PRATT, Henry. 1761–1838. Phila. merchant. Neighbor of ED on Front St. Son of painter Matthew Pratt and Elizabeth Moore Pratt; m. Frances Moore (d. 1785); m. Elizabeth Dundas; m. Susanna Care; eight children.

PRESTON, Samuel. 1756–1834. Bucks Co. Quaker. Surveyor for HD (1780s); agent for HD in Stockport, Wayne Co., Pa. (1787); assoc. judge, Wayne Co. (1798). m. housekeeper, Marcia Jenkins (1795); disowned by Phila. Mtg. for marrying contrary to discipline; four children.

PRICE, Isabella. 1728–1808. Phila. shopkeeper. m. George Price.

PRICE, Sarah. d. c. 1818. Phila. schoolmistress and shopkeeper with kinswoman Rebecca Price. School on Race St.; shop on Market St.

PROUD, Robert. 1728–1813. Historian; master, Friends Public School. b. Yorkshire, England; to Phila. (1759). Author, *The History of Pennsylvania in North America* (1797–98).

PUSEY, Mary. 1742–1823. Daughter of Joshua Pusey and Mary Miller Pusey; m. Joseph Husband; m. Daniel Mifflin (1722–95).

RAWLE, Anna. 1757–1828. Daughter of Francis RAWLE and Rebecca Warner RAWLE; m. John Clifford (1783).

RAWLE, Francis. 1729–61. Attorney. Son of Phila. Quakers William Rawle and Margaret Hodge Rawle; m. Rebecca Warner (1757); three children; d. accidental gunshot wound.

RAWLE, Rebecca Warner. d. 1819. Daughter of Phila. Quakers Edward Warner and Anne Coleman WARNER; m. Francis RAWLE (1757); three children; m. Samuel SHOEMAKER (1767); one child. Loyalist; remained in Phila. while husband was in NYC, then England (1778–86).

REDMAN, John. 1722–1808. Phila. Presbyterian physician. Son of Joseph Redman and Sarah Leader Redman. Apprenticed to John Kearsley (1684–1722), practiced medicine in Bermuda; medical studies in Edinburgh; M.D., Leyden (1748). Advocated use of saline purges rather than bleeding for yellow fever; strong advocacy of inoculation for smallpox. First president, Phila. College of Physicians (1786–1804); consulting physician, Pa. Hospital (1751–80). m. Mary Sobers (1751); one child.

REDWOOD, Hannah. 1759–96. Daughter of William Redwood and Hannah Holmes Redwood; b. Newport, R.I.; m. Charles Wharton at Phila. Monthly Mtg. (1784); six children.

REED, Joseph. 1741–85. Lawyer, iron manufacturer, land speculator, Trenton, N.J., and Phila.; m. (1770) Esther DeBerdt (d. 1780); from Trenton to Phila. (1770). George Washington's military secretary, adjutant gen. of Continental Army, Am. Revolution; delegate, Cont. Cong. (1777–78); president, Supreme Executive Council of Pa. (1778–81).

RHOADS, Elizabeth. c. 1770–96. Daughter of Samuel RHOADS (1740–84) and Sarah PEMBERTON Rhoads (1741–1810); m. Samuel W. FISHER; four children.

RHOADS, Elizabeth. 1804–82. Daughter of Samuel RHOADS (1774–1810) and Mary DRINKER Rhoads (1774–1856).

RHOADS, Mary. 1738–79. Daughter of Samuel RHOADS (1711–84) and Elizabeth Chandler Rhoads; m. (1764) Thomas Franklin (1734–97); three children.

RHOADS, Mary. d. 1788. Daughter of Samuel RHOADS (1740–84) and Sarah PEMBERTON Rhoads.

RHOADS, Mary. 1807–85. Daughter of Samuel RHOADS (1774–1810) and Mary DRINKER Rhoads (1774–1856); m. Tobias Wagner, a Phila. merchant (1841).

RHOADS, Samuel. 1711–84. Phila. Quaker master carpenter, merchant. Son of John Rhoads and Hannah Willcox Rhoads. Member, Phila. Council (1741); alderman (1761); member, Pa. Assembly (1762–64); delegate, first Cont. Cong.; mayor, Phila. (1774). Joined other members of Am. Philosophical Soc., incl. HD and Israel PEMBERTON, in the creation of a silk manufacturing co. (1770). m. Elizabeth Chandler (1737); three children.

RHOADS, Samuel. 1740–84. Phila. Quaker merchant. Son of Samuel RHOADS (1711–84) and Elizabeth Chandler Rhoads; m. (1765) Sarah PEMBERTON (1741–1810) at Phila. Mtg.; three children.

RHOADS, Samuel. 1774–1810. Son of Samuel RHOADS (1740–84) and Sarah PEMBERTON Rhoads; m. (1796) Mary DRINKER (1774–1856); disciplined by N. District Mtg. for marrying without parents' consent; four surviving children. Merchant; assigned his property to pay off creditors (1810); d. on a voyage from Montevideo to Havana.

RHOADS, Samuel. 1801–20. Son of Samuel RHOADS (1774–1810) and Mary DRINKER Rhoads (1774–1856).

RHOADS, Sarah. *See also* Sarah PEMBERTON.

RHOADS, Sarah. 1798–1811. Daughter of Samuel RHOADS (1774–1810) and Mary DRINKER Rhoads (1774–1856).

RICHARDSON, Joseph. 1711–84. Phila. Quaker silversmith. Member, Friendly Assoc. for Preserving Peace with the Indians. m. Hannah Worrel; m. Mary Allen; seven children.

RICHE, Thomas. c. 1728–92. Phila. Anglican merchant. Serious losses during Seven Years' War; sheep farmer, N.J. (1770s). m. Sarah Peel at Christ Church, Phila. (1751); at least five daughters.

RITTENHOUSE, David. 1732–96. Astronomer, engineer, mathematician. Son of Welsh-born Quaker Elizabeth Williams Rittenhouse and Mennonite minister-manufacturer William Rittenhouse. Produced one of first Am. telescopes (c. 1768–69), which he used to chart Venus's orbit. To Phila. (1770). Member, Pa. Assembly, Board of War; state treasurer. Professor of astronomy, Univ. of Pa.; president, Am. Philosophical Soc. (1791–96); first director, U.S. mint.

ROBERTS, John. c. 1721–78. Quaker miller, Merion, Pa. Executed for treason for guiding British foraging parties and for negotiating with Gen. Howe to intercept and rescue Quaker exiles en route to Va. m. Jane Downing (1743); 12 children.

ROBESON, Andrew. 1752–81. Phila. Anglican attorney. Son of Peter Robeson, a coroner and justice of the peace. m. Mary Stocker (1779); two children, d. in infancy. Admitted to bar (1771); officer, Revolutionary War; member, Court of Admiralty.

ROSE, Robert H. 1766–1842. Agent for HD, Susquehanna Co., Pa. b. Chester Co.; studied medicine, Univ. of Pa.; m. Jane Hodge (1810).

RUSH, Benjamin. 1745–1813. Physician. m. Julia Stockton (1776). Signer, Declaration of Independence; member, Congress; taught, Univ. of Pa.; treasurer, U.S. Mint (1797–1813). Author, *Medical Inquiries and Observations* (1789), *Essays, Literary, Moral, and Philosophical* (1798), first American chemistry textbook; established first free dispensary in U.S. HD's physician.

SALTAR, Dorothy Gordon. 1738–1781. Half sister of Frances Gordon Edwards; m. Lawrence SALTAR in Phila. (1769).

SALTAR, Elizabeth Gordon. 1752–c. 1818. Sister of Dorothy Gordon SALTAR; m. John SALTAR (1774); seven children.

SALTAR, Hannah. 1770–1855. Daughter of Joseph Saltar and Huldah Mott Saltar; lived in Shrewsbury, N.J.

SALTAR, John. 1733–1802. Phila. merchant. Son of Richard Saltar and Hannah Lawrence Saltar of Monmouth Co., N.J.; m. (1765) Rachel Rheese (d. 1770); m. Elizabeth Gordon (1774); seven children.

SALTAR, Lawrence. 1737–83. Brother of John SALTAR; m. Mary Tremain; m. Dorothy Gordon at Christ Church, Phila. (1769); m. Sarah Howard at Christ Church (1782).

SALTAR, Margaret. 1769–1860. Daughter of Joseph Saltar and Huldah Mott Saltar; sister of Hannah SALTAR; lived in Shrewsbury, N.J.

SANDWITH, Mary. 1732–1815. Older sister of ED. Owned considerable property in and outside Phila., stock in various canal and turnpike companies; invested in Henry Sandwith DRINKER's voyage to Calcutta (1807). Left most of her estate to ED's children and grandchildren; property she left for Mary DRINKER Rhoads and Ann DRINKER Skyrin was put in trust so that it could not be used by their husbands or creditors of their husbands. Active on Quaker committees; left £10 in trust to N. District Monthly Mtg. of Women Friends.

SANSOM, Hannah. *See* Hannah CALLENDER.

SANSOM, Joseph. 1767–1826. Son of Quakers Samuel SANSOM (1739–1824) and Hannah CALLENDER Sansom; m. Beulah Biddle (1798). Artist; produced Quaker silhouettes (HD was one of his subjects), designed commemorative medals. Joined John Parish in negotiations with Five Nations Indians (1791). Member, Am. Philosophical Soc.

SANSOM, Samuel. 1707–74. Phila. Quaker merchant. Son of English Quakers John Sansom and Elizabeth Conyers Sansom; to Phila. (1732); m. Sarah Johnson at Phila. Mtg. (1737); seven children.

SANSOM, Samuel. 1739–1824. Phila. Quaker merchant; sold Manchester goods at his store on Front St. Son of Samuel SANSOM (1707–74) and Sarah Johnson SANSOM; m. Hannah CALLENDER at Phila. Mtg. (1762); five children.

SANSOM, Sarah Johnson. 1706–68. Daughter of London Quaker emigrant Joshua Johnson of Phila.; m. (1737) Samuel SANSOM (1707–74); seven children.

SANSOM, William. 1763–1840. Phila. Quaker real estate developer and investor. Son of Samuel SANSOM (1739–1824) and Hannah CALLENDER Sansom. Apprentice in HD's iron business (1782). m. Susannah Head, daughter of his former partner (1788); two daughters. Active in charitable associations; served on the boards of banks and insurance companies.

SAVERY, William. 1750–1804. Quaker minister and tanner. Son of William Savery (1721–87). Ministerial travels in U.S., Canada, Europe; mission to Nw. Indians, Sandusky, Ohio (1793); to Six Nations Indians, Canandaigua, N.Y. (1794). m. Sarah Evans, daughter of Pennell Evans of Berks Co., Pa. (1778).

SAY, Rebecca Atkinson Budd. 1716–95. Daughter of Samuel Atkinson; m. (1739) Thomas Budd (d. 1751); four children; m. (1753) Thomas SAY (1709–96); two children.

SAY, Thomas. 1709–96. Phila. Quaker druggist. Son of Quakers William Say and Mary Paschall Say; m. Susannah Catherine Sprogel (1735); eight children; m. Rebecca Atkinson Budd (1753); two children. Noted for mystical religious visions, ability to effect medical cures, and benevolent activities on behalf of blacks, widows, orphans, and refugees.

SAY, Thomas. 1740–59. Son of Thomas SAY (1709–96) and Susannah Catherine Sprogel Say.

SCATTERGOOD, Rebecca Watson. d. 1800. m. (1736) Joseph Scattergood (1714–c. 1754); reprimanded by Phila. Monthly Mtg. for marrying contrary to discipline; to Burlington (N.J.) Mtg. (1746); at least five children.

SCOTT, Joseph. c. 1707–81. Rahway, N.J., Quaker; to Phila. (1771).

SEARSON, John. m. Mary LLOYD at Christ Church, Phila. (1759).

SEARSON, Mary. See Mary LLOYD.

SHARPLES, Joshua. 1747–1826. Chester Co. Quaker b. Middletown; m. Edith Yarnall, later a Quaker minister; eight children; to Kennett Twp. (1769); active in New Garden Mtg. in its attempts to abolish slaveholding among Friends. To Concord (1779); overseer, Concord Mtg. (1784). To Birmingham (1789); elder, Birmingham Mtg. (1786). With second wife, Ann Trimble, superintendent of Westtown School (1800–1811); two children with his second wife.

SHARPLES, Mary. 1756–1839. Daughter of Joseph Sharples and Mary Pyle Sharples; m. Morris Truman, a Darby miller, at Middletown Mtg. (1781); six children. To Darby (1781); in Phila. (1786); to Fayette Co., Pa. (1807); member, Redstone Mtg.

SHIPPEN, William. 1712–1801. Phila. druggist, physician. Son of Joseph Shippen and Abigail Grosse Shippen; m. (1735) Susannah Harrison (1711–74); four children. Pharmacy on Market St. opposite prison. Physician, Pa. Hospital.

SHIPPEN, William. 1736–1808. Phila. Presbyterian physician. Son of William SHIPPEN (1712–1801) and Susannah Harrison Shippen; m. Alice Lee, of the Va. Lee family (1762). Graduate, College of N.J. (1754); studied medicine with his father; M.D., Univ. of Edinburgh; to Phila. (1762). Founder, Univ. of Pa. medical school; lecturer in surgery, anatomy, and obstetrics. One of the first Am. physicians to specialize in obstetrics, particularly skilled in the use of forceps.

SHOEMAKER, Elizabeth. *See* Elizabeth WARNER.

SHOEMAKER, Hannah. c. 1732–1805. Daughter of Benjamin Shoemaker, prominent Phila. Quaker who served as provincial councillor of Pa. and mayor of Phila., and Sarah Coates Shoemaker.

SHOEMAKER, Hannah. 1754–79. Quaker. Daughter of Samuel SHOEMAKER and Hannah Carpenter Shoemaker.

SHOEMAKER, Rebecca. *See* Rebecca Warner RAWLE.

SHOEMAKER, Samuel. 1725–1800. Phila. Quaker merchant. Son of Phila. mayor and Quaker merchant Samuel Shoemaker (1704–67); m. Hannah Carpenter (1746); at least two children; m. Rebecca Warner RAWLE (1767); one child. Mayor of Phila. (1769, 1771); member, Pa. Assembly (1771, 1773). Loyalist; sailed for NYC when British evacuated Phila. (1778); to England (1783); to U.S. (1786); in Burlington, N.J.; back to Phila.

SKYRIN, Eleanor. 1795–1877. Daughter of John SKYRIN and Ann DRINKER Skyrin; m. (1826) in Phila. her non-Quaker second cousin, Joseph D. Drinker, grandson of John DRINKER; six children. To Cincinnati, Ohio (c. 1829), where her husband was a clerk at the U.S. Bank; back to Phila. (by 1840), where he was a broker. To Montrose, Pa. (c. 1843), where a number of Drinker relatives had settled on land owned by HD.

SKYRIN, Elizabeth. 1793–btw. 1829 and 1843. Daughter of John SKYRIN and Ann DRINKER Skyrin; to Cincinnati, Ohio (c. 1829); not mentioned in the 1843 division of HD's estate among his surviving heirs.

SKYRIN, John. d. c. 1824. Phila. Quaker merchant. b. England; to Phila. (c. 1783); m. Ann DRINKER (1791); three daughters. Traded in bonds (1790s); serious business reversals (early 1800s); to Frankfort, Ky. (c. 1824).

SKYRIN, Mary. 1801–aft. 1843. Daughter of John SKYRIN and Ann DRINKER Skyrin; to Cincinnati, Ohio (c. 1829); m. Henry Clark, a druggist from Conn. (c. 1833); at least one child. Disowned by Cincinnati Mtg. for marrying out of unity.

SLEESMAN, Henry. c. 1733–1805. Tailor, 98 N. Front St., Phila.; wife, Catherine, and children.

SLEIGHMAN, SLESMAN, SLIGHSMAN. *See* SLEESMAN.

SMITH, Catherine. 1741–83. Daughter of Quakers Robert Smith (1698–1781) and Elizabeth Bacon Smith; b., d., Burlington, N.J.; in Phila. (1760–63).

SMITH, Elizabeth. b. 1790. Daughter of James SMITH and Esther Hewlings SMITH; m. Mordecai Lewis at Mulberry St. Mtg. (1808).

SMITH, Esther Hewlings. c. 1752–1807. Daughter of William Hewlings; m. James SMITH (1772); condemned by Burlington Monthly Mtg. for marrying contrary to Quaker discipline (1773); 11 children. d. in Phila.

SMITH, Hannah. *See also* Hannah STEVENSON.

SMITH, Hannah. 1774–1830. Daughter of James SMITH and Esther Hewlings SMITH;

b. Burlington, N.J.; to Phila. (1784); m. Henry Sandwith DRINKER at Phila. Mtg. (1794); 14 children, incl. two sets of twins, nine of whom reached maturity.

SMITH, James. 1750–1833. Burlington, N.J., Quaker. Apprentice to HD. m. (1772) Esther Hewlings, contrary to Quaker discipline; 11 children. To Phila. (1784).

SMITH, John. 1722–71. Phila. Quaker merchant. b. N.J.; son of Richard Smith and Abigail Raper Smith; m. Hannah Logan (1748); six children. Partnership (1741–62) with Abel JAMES. First secretary, Pa. Hospital; member, Pa. Assembly; justice of the peace; county judge. To N.J. (1761); member, N.J. Council.

SMITH, John Rubens. 1775–1849. Portrait, miniature, and topographical painter; engraver; lithographer; drawing teacher. b. London; in Boston (1809); school in Brooklyn; school in Phila. (1830s).

SMITH, Richard. 1735–1803. Son of Richard Smith and Abigail Raper Smith. Member, N.J. Assembly, Cont. Cong. Studied law under Joseph Galloway; practice in N.J. and Phila. m. Elizabeth Rodman (1762).

SMITH, Samuel. 1737–1817. Quaker minister, N. District Monthly Mtg. Ministerial travels to New England and Great Britain. Son of Robert Smith and Phoebe Smith; m. Mary Woolston at Middletown Mtg.

SMITH, Samuel J. b. 1755. Poet. Son of Joseph Smith and Mary Burling Smith; m. Abigail Schooley.

SPAVOLD, Samuel. 1708–95. English Quaker minister.

SPICER, Abigail. aft. 1743–1807. Daughter of Samuel Spicer, a surveyor in Waterford Twp., Gloucester Co., N.J., and Abigail Willard Spicer; first cousin of Jacob Spicer; m. (1771) in Phila. English-born John Kibble (Keble, Kible, Kimble [c. 1744–1807]), benefactor of St. Paul's Church and Pa. Hospital.

SPICER, Sylvia. 1736–1802. Sister of Jacob Spicer; m. Welsh minister Samuel Jones, later Pa. state chaplain (1776); in Phila.; many children, only one reached maturity.

STAMPER, Sarah. Anglican Daughter of Joseph Stamper and Sarah Maddox STAMPER; m. Thomas Lloyd Moore (1782).

STAMPER, Sarah Maddox. d. 1827. Daughter of Joshua Maddox; m. Joseph Stamper (1755).

STANBURY, Sarah. c. 1770–1810. m. (1791) John Stille (1767–1842); ten children.

STANTON, Daniel. 1708–70. Phila. Quaker minister. Ministerial travels in Am. colonies, Caribbean, Europe. Son of Daniel Stanton and Abigail Stanton; m. (1733) Sarah Lloyd (d. 1748); seven children, only two reached maturity.

STEER, James. Son of Chester Co. Quakers John Steer and Rachel Evans Steer; to Va. (1749); m. Abigail Edgerton (1761); nine children.

STEVENSON, Hannah. *See also* Hannah HICKS.

STEVENSON, Hannah. b. 1774. Daughter of Hannah HICKS Stevenson and Robert STEVENSON; m. Clifford Smith (1794); three children; m. Owen Jones (1755–1825).

STEVENSON, Robert. 1722–96. Son of Quakers William Stevenson and Hannah Hicks Stevenson of Newtown, Long Island. With brother Cornelius Stevenson made a fortune in W. Indies sugar trade. To Phila.; m. his first cousin Hannah HICKS (1770); four children. To Hopewell, N.J., Am. Revolution.

STEWARDSON, Thomas. c. 1762–1841. Phila. merchant, Quaker elder. b. England; to Phila. (1790s). m. Anna Head (1796).

STILES, Edward. c. 1722–1804. Neighbor of ED. b. Bermuda; merchant-shipper, before Am. Revolution. Dealt in real estate, n. sections of Phila., aft. Am. Revolution. m. Mary Murray in Bermuda; one son; m. Mary Chappell Meredith (1796).

STILLE, Sarah. *See* Sarah STANBURY.

STOCKER, Margaret. 1737–1821. m. Anthony Stocker, a Phila. merchant.

STROUD, Daniel. 1772–1864. Son of Jacob Stroud and Elizabeth McDowell Stroud. Classical education; studied law with Jared Ingersoll, Phila.; m. (1792) Elizabeth Shoemaker (d. 1809), who would be disowned by Soc. of Friends for this marriage; 12 children. Practiced law in Easton, Pa.; back to Stroudsburg (1800). Joined Soc. of Friends (1802); stopped the practice of law because of oath-taking; gave up tavern he inherited from his father. m. Mary Paul, another Quaker (1811); one child.

SWETT, Benjamin. d. 1774. Father of Ann Swett, HD's first wife. b. Del., where an earlier Benjamin Swett, prob. his grandfather, had come from New England and helped found New Castle (Wilmington, Del.) Mtg. In Phila., Chester Co., Pa., and Burlington, N.J. (1760s). m. Susannah Siddon (1760); Ann Swett was his daughter from an earlier marriage.

SWETT, Benjamin. c. 1739–1819. Nephew of Benjamin SWETT (d. 1774); prob. b. New Castle, Del.; given a certificate by Phila. Mtg. to a London Mtg. (1759); m. Mary Howell (aft. 1737–1821) at Phila. Mtg. (1762); to Burlington, N.J.; to Haddonfield, N.J. Member, Phila. Yearly Mtg.'s Friends' Indian Committee; left money to Soc. of Friends for care of the insane.

SWETT, Susannah Siddon. d. 1807. Daughter of Philadelphia Quaker Thomas Siddon; m. Benjamin SWETT (d. 1774) at Phila. Mtg. (1760).

TALLMAN, Sarah. b. 1740. Daughter of Job Tallman and Sarah Scattergood Tallman of Mansfield, Burlington Co., N.J.; m. (1760) Joseph Wharton (1734–1816). Member, S. District Monthly Mtg.

TAYLOR, Mary Richardson. 1750–1835. Phila. Quaker elder. Daughter of Joseph RICHARDSON and Mary Allen Richardson; m. Samuel Taylor at Phila. Mtg. (1781); seven children. Clerk, Women's Phila. Yearly Mtg. (1800–1805).

TEAS, John. c. 1749–1809. Quaker; wife, Rachel, and seven children. Member, Darby Monthly Mtg. (to 1790); to Salem Monthly Mtg. (1790); to N. District Monthly Mtg. (1792).

THOMAS, Ann Waln. d. 1785. Daughter of Richard Waln (1717–64) and Hannah Hilles Waln; m. Elisha Thomas of Horsham, Montgomery Co., Pa.

THOMAS, Hannah. *See* Hannah DRINKER.

THOMAS, John. Phila. merchant. Son of Phila. Quakers Arthur Thomas and Sarah Thomas; m. Hannah DRINKER (1783). Partner with brother-in-law Thomas Pym COPE (1803–7); Henry Sandwith DRINKER sailed in one of their vessels (1806).

THOMAS, Richard. 1744–1832. Brother of George Thomas (1746–93); m. Thomasine Downing, a sister of Jacob DOWNING, at Uwchlan Mtg. (1774). Colonel,

Revolutionary War; disowned by Uwchlan Mtg. although his family remained in the Society. Member, Pa. Assembly; Federalist member, U.S. House of Representatives (1795–1801).

THOMAS, Richard. 1775–1836. Chester Co. Quaker miller. Son of Richard THOMAS (1744–1832) and Thomasine Downing THOMAS; m. Rebecca Malin at Goshen Mtg. (1799); two children; m. his first cousin Sarah Thomas; three children. President, Bank of Chester Co. Member, Downingtown Mtg.

THOMAS, Thomasine Downing. 1754–1817. Sister of Jacob DOWNING; m. (1774) Richard THOMAS (1744–1832) at Uwchlan Mtg.; nine children, eight reached maturity.

THOMPSON, Rebecca. *See* Rebecca JAMES.

TILGHMAN, Tench. 1744–86. Phila. merchant. Son of James Tilghman and Ann Francis Tilghman. Graduate, Univ. of Pa. (1761). Aide-de-camp to George Washington (1776–81). m. his cousin Ann Maria Tilghman (1783). Partner of Robert Morris (1734–1806).

TODD, William A. d. before 1811. Downingtown, Pa., physician. m. (1789) Ann Downing, daughter of Joseph DOWNING and Mary Trimble Downing.

TRIMBLE, Daniel. 1745–1807. Son of Irish-born Quaker William Trimble and Ann Palmer Trimble; m. Mary Downing (d. 1779), sister of Jacob DOWNING, at Uwchlan Mtg. (1776); two children. To Concord, Pa.; to Bucks Co., Pa.; member, Falls Mtg.; m. Phebe Jones; m. Ann Warner.

TRIMBLE, Samuel. 1741–1818. Brother of Daniel TRIMBLE. Apprenticed to a hatter in Nottingham, Pa.; to Phila.; back to Concord (1764). m. Esther Brinton at Concord Mtg. (1767); five children. Overseer (1774–81), elder (1775–87), Concord Mtg.; recommended as a minister (1788).

TROTTER, Daniel. 1747–1800. Phila. Quaker cabinetmaker. Son of William Trotter and Elizabeth Hoodt Trotter; m. Rebecca Canarroe at N. District Mtg. (1773); seven children. Friend and neighbor of ED. Member, Pa. Abolition Soc., Phila. Library Co.

VALENTINE, Robert. 1717–86. Chester Co. Quaker minister. b. Ireland; to Chester Co. in childhood; m. Rachel Edge at Uwchlan Mtg. (1747); ten children. Ministerial travels in Va., England, and Ireland.

VALENTINE, Robert. 1752–1803. E. Caln, Pa., miller. Son of Robert VALENTINE (1717–86) and Rachel Edge Valentine; m. Ann Bond (1773); 11 children.

VAUX, Ann Roberts. 1753–1814. Daughter of Hugh Roberts and Mary Calvert Roberts; m. Richard Vaux (1751–90), brother of James Vaux, at Phila. Monthly Mtg. (1784); at least two children. Member, N. District Monthly Mtg.

WALMSLEY, Sarah Titus. 1712–1763. b. Long Island; m. William WALMSLEY (1735); five children; at Walmsley family farm, Byberry Twp., Pa.

WALMSLEY, William. 1709–73. Farmer. Clerk, elder, and overseer, Byberry Mtg., Phila. Co.; m. Sarah Titus (1735); five children; m. Susanna Mason Comly (1764).

WALN, Ann. 1760–1814. Daughter of Robert WALN (1721–84) and Rebecca Coffin WALN; m. Thomas MORGAN at N. District Mtg. (1786); at least seven children.

WALN, Elizabeth Armitt. d. 1790. Quaker. Daughter of Joseph Armitt and Elizabeth Lisle ARMITT; m. (1760) Richard WALN; eight children.

WALN, Hannah. d. 1820. Phila. Quaker. Daughter of Robert WALN (1721–84) and Rebecca Coffin WALN; m. Gideon Hill Wells (1790); eight children. Member, N. District Mtg. (until c. 1805); to Trenton, N.J.

WALN, Jesse. c. 1750–1806. Phila. merchant. Cousin of Richard Waln (1717–64) and Nicholas WALN (1742–1813); in business with uncle Robert WALN (1721–84); wife, Rebecca (d. 1820), and seven children.

WALN, Mary. 1765–1844. Daughter of Richard WALN and Elizabeth Armitt WALN; m. Thomas Wistar (1786); 13 children.

WALN, Nicholas. 1742–1813. Phila. Quaker minister. Son of Nicholas Waln and Mary Shoemaker Waln; m. Sarah Richardson, daughter of Quaker merchant Joseph Richardson (1772); six children. Abandoned successful legal career for ministry (1773).

WALN, Nicholas. 1763–1848. Son of Richard WALN and Elizabeth Armitt WALN. Spent his entire life at family estate, Walnford, near Crosswicks, N.J.; ran mill; m. Sarah Ridgway of Burlington (1799); seven children.

WALN, Phebe Lewis. 1768–1845. Of Welsh Quaker descent; m. Robert WALN (1765–1836), Phila. merchant, son of Robert WALN (1721–84) and Rebecca Coffin WALN, at Pine St. Mtg. (1787); nine children.

WALN, Rebecca. 1760s–85. Phila. Quaker. Daughter of Robert WALN (1721–84) and Rebecca Coffin WALN; m. Ezra Jones (1784).

WALN, Rebecca Coffin. d. 1798. Neighbor of ED. Sister of Hannah Coffin CATHERALL; m. (1746) Robert WALN (1721–84); condemned by Phila. Mtg. for marrying contrary to Quaker discipline; at least 11 children. Member, N. District Mtg.

WALN, Richard. c. 1737–1809. Phila. Quaker merchant. Brother of Nicholas WALN (1742–1813); m. Elizabeth Armitt at Phila. Mtg. (1760); eight children. To estate, Walnford, near Crosswicks, N.J. (1774).

WALN, Robert. 1721–84. Merchant. Son of Phila. Quakers Richard Waln and Ann Heath Waln; m. Rebecca Coffin (1746); marriage contrary to Quaker discipline, but retained membership in Soc. of Friends; at least 11 children.

WALN, Robert. 1765–1836. Quaker merchant. Son of Robert WALN (1721–84) and Rebecca Coffin WALN; m. Phebe Lewis (1787).

WALN, Susannah. d. 1828. Daughter of Robert WALN (1721–84) and Rebecca Coffin WALN; m. Pattison HARTSHORNE (1776); five children.

WARDER, Ann Head. 1758–1829. Daughter of London Quakers; m. John Warder; ten children. To Phila. (1788); lived at first with widowed mother-in-law Mary Head Warder on N. Third St.; member, N. District Monthly Mtg. Her diary, kept during first few years in Phila., notes aspects of Am. Quaker life, mentions the Drinker family.

WARDER, Jeremiah. 1744–1822. Phila. merchant. Son of Jeremiah Warder (1711–83) and Mary Head Warder; m. Deborah Roberts (1772); one child; m. Hannah Moore (1780).

WARNER, Anne (Anna) Coleman. d. c. 1787. Prob. daughter of William Coleman and Rebecka Coleman of Phila.; m. Edward Warner (d. 1754), a Phila. carpenter and merchant, at Phila. Mtg. (1733); at least six children.

WARNER, Elizabeth. d. before 1823. Daughter of Edward Warner and Anne Coleman WARNER; m. Benjamin Shoemaker at Phila. Mtg. (1773); four children.

WATSON, John. d. 1799. Bucks Co. Quaker poultry dealer. m. Rachel Paxson (1764); two children.

WATSON, John. d. 1818? Quaker physician, Buckingham Twp., Bucks Co., Pa.; Son of Joseph Watson and Alice Mitchell Watson; grandson of John Watson (1697–1760); m. Mary Ham(p)ton at Wrightstown Mtg. (1772); at least one child.

WATSON, John. 1768–1844. Son of John WATSON (d. 1799) and Rachel Paxson WATSON; m. Lydia Blakey at Middletown Monthly Mtg. (1799); seven children, incl. three sets of twins.

WATSON, Rachel Paxson. 1744–1800. Daughter of Buckingham, Bucks Co., Quakers Thomas Paxson and Jane Canby Paxson; m. (1764) John WATSON (d. 1799); two children. Elder, Buckingham Mtg.

WAY, Nicholas. c. 1747–97. Wilmington, Del., physician; practiced in Phila.; treasurer of the Phila. Mint (1794); d. yellow fever.

WELLS, Hannah. *See* Hannah WALN.

WELLS, Rachel Hill. 1735–96. Quaker. Daughter of Dr. Richard Hill and Deborah Moore Hill; m. Richard WELLS (1759); 11 children.

WELLS, Rachel Lovell. d. 1795. Wax sculptor; taught her sister, Patience Lovell Wright; exhibited her work in Phila. (1760s–70s). Daughter of Quakers who moved from Oyster Bay, L.I., to Bordentown, N.J. (1729); m. James Wells, a Phila. shipwright (1750); back to Bordentown (c. 1785).

WELLS, Richard. 1734–1801. Phila. Quaker merchant; cashier, Bank of N. Am.; secretary, Am. Philosophical Soc.; director, Library Co. of Phila.; b. England; to N. Am. with parents, Gideon Wells and Mary Partridge Wells (1750); m. Rachel Hill (1759); 11 children.

WEST, William. 1724–1808. Brother of painter Benjamin West; b. Upper Providence, Pa. Member, Goshen Mtg. (from 1752); Phila. cooper. Back to Del. Co. (1765); member, Pa. Assembly. m. twice; nine children.

WHARTON, Hannah Owen Ogden. 1721–91. Daughter of Phila. Quakers Robert Owen and Susanna Owen; m. (1740) John Ogden (d. 1742); m. (c. 1753) Joseph WHARTON; seven children.

WHARTON, John. c. 1732–99. Son of John Wharton and Mary Dobbins Wharton; nephew of Joseph WHARTON; m. Rebecca Chamless; two children. Member, N. District Monthly Mtg. City directories list his occupation as hairdresser (1785), barber (1791), bleeder and tooth drawer (1799), surgeon barber (1800).

WHARTON, Joseph. 1707–76. Phila. Quaker merchant. Son of Quaker tailor Thomas Wharton and Rachel Thomas Wharton, early Pa. settlers; m. (1730) Hannah Carpenter (1711–51); 11 children; m. Hannah Owen Ogden (c. 1753); seven children. Retired to family estate, Walnut Grove, Southwark, Pa.

WHARTON, Robert. 1757–1834. Federalist mayor of Phila. (1798–1824). Son of Joseph WHARTON and Hannah Owen Ogden WHARTON; m. by Bishop William White to Salome Chancellor, daughter of William Chancellor and Salome

Wister Chancellor Morgan; two children. Apprenticed to a hatter; entered mercantile business of half brother Charles Wharton; subsequently a flour merchant and wholesale grocer. Member, Phila. City Council (1792–96); alderman (1796). Elected mayor (1798) because of his success in quelling a riot at Walnut St. Prison during the yellow fever epidemic.

WHARTON, Sarah. *See* Sarah TALLMAN.

WHARTON, Sarah Lewis. c. 1739–1835. Daughter of Stephen Lewis and Rebecca Hussey Lewis of Wilmington, Del.; m. (1755) Samuel Wharton (1732–1800); at least six children. Member, S. District Monthly Mtg.

WHARTON, Thomas. 1735–78. Son of John Wharton and Mary Dobbins Wharton; first governor of Pa. under Constitution of 1776; disowned by Friends; presided over the exile of Quaker leaders, incl. HD and his own cousin, Thomas Wharton (1731–82), to Va. (1777). m. Susannah Lloyd (1762); five children; m. Elizabeth Fishbourne (1752–1826), daughter of William Fishbourne and Mary Tallman Fishbourne; three children.

WHEELING. *See* WHELAN.

WHELAN, Israel. 1752–1806. Phila. shipping merchant, Federalist politician. b. Chester Co.; supported Americans during Revolution. To Phila. after the war; country home in Chester Co. Member, state senate; president, Lancaster Turnpike Co.; m. Mary Downing (1772); 11 children.

WHELAN, Mary Downing. 1751–1831. Daughter of John Downing and Elizabeth Hunt Downing; m. Israel WHELAN (1772); 11 children.

WHITE, Esther Hewlings Newman. d. 1790. b. Burlington, N.J.; m. John Newman; m. (1747) at Christ Church Col. Thomas White (to Phila. from Md. [c. 1745]); mother of William White and Mary White Morris.

WIDDOWS, Peter. fl. 1796–c. 1833. Phila. Quaker schoolteacher. b. Ireland; to Long Island (1794); to Phila. (1796); HD's clerk. Master, boys' grammar school on Front St. near Arch St. (after 1800). Disowned by Soc. of Friends for marrying out of unity (1810); wife, Mary, later joined the Hicksite Quakers.

WILSON, Benjamin. Phila. Quaker merchant, shopkeeper. Of Irish descent. Friend of William DRINKER (1767–1821).

WISTAR, Richard. 1756–1821. Phila. hardware merchant. Grandson of Phila. glass manufacturer Caspar Wistar; son of Quakers Richard Wistar and Sarah Wyatt Wistar. Disowned by Soc. of Friends for war activities, Am. Revolution; became a Freemason (1779). Manager, Phila. Hospital (1803–6). m. Sarah Morris (1782); four children.

WOODCOCK, Bancroft. 1732–1817. Quaker gold- and silversmith, Wilmington, Del. Son of Robert Woodcock and Rachel Bancroft Woodcock. m. Ruth Andrews (1759); two children. To Bedford Co., Pa. (aft. 1797).

YERKES, Hannah. Daughter of Joseph YERKES and Hannah Ashton YERKES; married name was Tomkins; two children.

YERKES, Hannah Ashton. d. 1802. m. Joseph YERKES (1767); two children.

YERKES, Joseph. c. 1746–1807. Phila. schoolmaster (c. 1768–1800). Son of Quakers Anthony Yerkes and Jane Yerkes of Moreland, Pa.; m. Hannah Ashton (1767).

ZANE, Isaac. 1743–95. Son of Isaac ZANE (1711–94) and Sarah Elfreth Zane. To

Barbados and Europe as a young man; settled near Winchester, Va. (early 1770s); owned Marlboro Ironworks, plantation. Member, Va. House of Burgesses; disowned by Phila. Monthly Mtg. for taking oath of office (1774). Supported Americans during Revolution; aided Phila. Quakers exiled in Winchester. Manumitted his adult slaves at his death. Father of Isaac Zane (d. 1799), son of his longtime housekeeper, Elizabeth McFarlane.

ZANE, Jonathan. 1706–78. Phila. Quaker merchant. Brother of Isaac ZANE (1711–94); b. N.J.; m. Mary Shenton (c. 1728); 13 children. Founder, Fellowship Fire Co.; one of Phila.'s first fire wardens.

ZANE, Sarah. b. 1754. Phila. Quaker. Daughter of Isaac ZANE (1711–94) and Sarah Elfreth Zane. To Va. (aft. 1795) to settle estate of brother Isaac ZANE (1743–95); back to Phila.

Index of Names

Abraham (servant), 108, 282, 285, 295, 296
Adams, John, 187
Adlum, John, 127, 308
Affleck, Thomas, 61, 76, 308
Aimes, M., 154
Airs, Benjamin, 198
Alexander, Ann Tuke, 271, 308
Alexander, William, 267
Allen, Margaret, 14, 308
Allen, Richard, 199
Alsop, John R., 154, 260
Alsop, Othniel, 211, 246, 308
Amos, 54
Andrew (servant), 250
Ann (servant), 68, 69, 71
Anna (servant), 268
Anthony (servant), 128
Ardey, Benjamin, 47
Armitt, Elizabeth, 69, 308
Armitt, Sarah. *See* Logan, Sarah
Ashbridge, Elizabeth (Lizey), 33, 308
Ashbridge, Sarah (Sally), 101, 308
Ashby, William, 177, 308
Atkinson, Lydia (servant), 232, 285, 299, 301, 308

Bacon, David, 145, 309
Baker, Dr. (dentist), 88, 101
Baker, George, 44, 309
Baker, H., 105
Baker, Hilary, 162, 309
Balderston, John, 79, 99, 173, 309
Baley, Mary, 139, 152
Barbauld, Anna Laetitia, 161
Barns, Isaac, 186

Barret, Ty, 51
Bartram, Elizabeth, 170, 309
Batts, Tom, 170
Batts, Tom, wife of, 170
Bedford, Mistress, 218
Bekey, Jacob, 137
Belville, Dr., 184, 298, 299
Benezet, Anthony, 57, 73, 97, 98, 253, 309
Benezet, Joyce, 29, 309
Bensel, M., 200
Bensel, Widow, 199, 200
Benson, George, 144, 149
Berkeley, Bishop George, 191n
Betty (servant), 25
Bicknell, Peter, 234
Biddle, Clement, 278, 309
Biddle, Owen, 76, 309
Bingham, A. W., 180
Black Arch, 16
Black Becky, 273, 286, 298, 302
Black Charles, 214, 216, 217
Black Hannah, 160
Black Harry, 247
Black Jacob. *See* Turner, Jacob
Black Jim, 291
Black John, 236, 238, 239
Black Joseph, 113
Black Jude, 14, 15
Black Jude, 302
Black Judith (Judey), 212, 257, 261, 263, 266, 283, 292
Black Nedd, 29
Bolingbroke, Viscount Henry Saint-John, xiv, 229
Bolsbey (Bowlsby), Thomas, 13, 29, 309

Index of Names

Evans, Jonathan, 145
Evans, Jonathan, Sr., 144, 318
Evans, Rowland, 45, 318
Evans, Sally, 168

Falconer, Nathaniel, 9, 318
Fanny (servant), 238, 243
Feating, Henry, 59
Fennell, James, 280
Fenno, John, 182, 224, 318
Ferguson, Agnes (servant), 32, 33, 38, 40
Ferman, Samuel, 101
Fifer, Ned, 99
Fisher, Elizabeth, 14, 126, 161, 318
Fisher, Esther (Hetty), 73, 318
Fisher, James, 73, 128, 167, 318
Fisher, John, 27
Fisher, Joshua, 73, 318
Fisher, Miers, 61, 318
Fisher, Nurse, 155
Fisher, Rebecca, 168, 281, 287, 318
Fisher, Samuel, 57n, 61, 85, 130, 134, 319
Fisher, Samuel W., 161, 167n, 319
Fisher, Sarah (Sally), 12, 13, 14, 17, 20, 27,
    73, 84, 90, 103, 104, 130, 207, 209,
    319
Fisher, Tabitha (Taby), 104, 168, 281, 287,
    319
Fisher, Thomas, 57n, 60–61, 199, 319
Fisher, William, 12, 17, 84, 191, 319
Fletcher, Japhat, 103
Folwell, Becky, 84
Fordam, Sarah, 36
Fordham, Betsy, 126, 150
Fortune, George, 31
Foulke, Dr. John, 113, 127, 319
Foulke, Judah, 4, 14, 15, 28, 33, 53, 319
Foulke, Mary (Molly), 4, 8, 9, 12, 15, 28,
    29, 30, 319
Fox, Joseph (Josey), 74, 97, 107, 319–20
Frank (Rhoads servant), 291
Franklin, Benjamin, 9n, 57n
Franks, Betsy, 138, 165
Franks, David, 28, 320
Frederick. See Hailer, Frederick
Friend, Captain, 15
Fry, Betsy, 152
Fry, George, wife of, 147, 149
Fry, John, 101, 191

Gallatin, Albert, 182, 188n
Galloway, Joseph, 80n
Gardette, Js., 165
Gardiner, Bill, 59
Gardner, Archibald, 97, 98
Gardner, Eve, 42
Gardner, Sally, 40, 42, 211
Garrigues, William, 232

George (gardener), 136, 139
George II, 19
George III, 20, 261n
Gibbons, Abraham, 75
Gibbons, James, 75, 76, 320
Gibbs, Absolem, 232
Gibbs, Hannah, 141
Gibbs, Jane (servant), 218
Gibbs, Joe (servant), 110, 112, 128, 132,
    144, 145, 148
Gibbs, Patience (Skyrin servant), xiii, 148,
    193, 212, 226, 227, 232, 250, 252, 253,
    277, 280, 285, 290
Gibbs, Rebecca (servant), 148
Gilbert, 131
Gillingham, John, 69, 320
Gilpin, John, 84, 320
Gilpin, Thomas, 61
Gordon, Colonel, 77
Gordon, Polly, 79
Gosnold, Mary (Molly), 54, 320
Gothrope, Thomas, 68
Grant, Betsy, 210, 213
Grant, General James, 66
Green, Racl., 204
Greene, Nathanael, 75
Greenleaf, Catharine, 95, 320
Greenleaf, Catharine Wistar, 81, 95, 320
Griffits, Dr. Samuel, 270
Griffitts, Abigail, 171, 320
Grigory, Peggy (nurse), 22
Griscom, Rebecca, 159, 320
Guilliams, Lewis, 157

Haga (Hagger), Godfry, 186, 320
Hahn, Christian, 285, 320
Hahn, Hannah, 285
Hailer, Fredrick, 80, 90, 146, 157, 161,
    176, 239, 320
Hailer, John, 256, 265, 275, 320
Haines, Catherine (Caty), 90, 193, 320
Haines, M., 68
Haines, Reuben, 90, 320–21
Hall, Mary, 44
Harper, Nanny, 31, 34, 36
Harper, Robert, 33
Harper, Robert Goodloe, 182, 321
Harper, Samuel, 31, 36, 321
Harry (servant), 47, 52, 53, 61, 65, 68, 70,
    264, 291
Hart, Mart., 176
Hart, Peggy, 79
Hart, Seymer (Seamor Heart), 105, 321
Hartshorne, Neighbor, 162, 210
Hartshorne, Pattison (Patterson), 83, 106,
    125, 131, 167, 321
Hartshorne, Rebecca, 95, 194
Hartshorne, Richard, 193, 321

Hartshorne, Robert, 191, 321
Hartshorne, Suckey, 95, 98, 131, 210
Hartshorne, Susan, 194
Hartshorne, Susannah, 98, 321
Hartshorne, William, 120n
Hatton, Susannah, 17, 321
Haviland, Daniel, 224, 321
Haydock, Henry, 108, 121
Haylor, John. *See* Hailer, John
Hazlehurst, Isaac, 249, 321
Hazlehurst, Joanna, 249, 321
Hazlehurst, Tom, 93
Hazleman, Jerome. *See* Heintzelman, Jerome
Heart, Seamor. *See* Hart, Seymer
Heintzelman, Jerome, 45, 321–22
Henny (Skyrin servant), 191, 212, 213, 226, 232, 236, 238, 240, 243
Hensel, Molly (servant), 82, 87, 160
Heritta (stable boy), 72
Hervey, Jonathan, 149
Hesser, George, 111, 115, 116, 201
Hicks, Elias, 86, 322
Hicks, Hannah, 6, 10, 19, 322
Hicks, Jos., 8
Hillar, John. *See* Hailer, John
Hillborn, John, 105, 322
Hillborn, Mary, 284, 295
Hillman, M., 284
Hodgson, John, 207
Hodgson, Samuel, 262
Holker, Jean, 87n
Holloway, Molly, 19
Hopkins, Catherine (Caty) Howell, 82, 83, 86, 322
Hopkins, Hannah, 58, 98, 156, 322
Hopkins, James, 268, 322
Hopkins, John, 98, 99, 102
Hopkins, Johns, 83, 322
Hopkins, Joshua, 86
Hopkins, Samuel, 54, 97, 322
Hopkinson, Caleb, 114
Howard, John, 95, 322
Howard, Sarah (Sally), 93
Howe, Lord William, 58, 63, 66
Howell, Abigail (Abey), 51
Howell, Catherine (Caty), Jr. *See* Hopkins, Catherine (Caty) Howell
Howell, Catherine (Caty, Katty), 9, 12, 15, 17, 30, 69, 73, 82, 322, 323
Howell, Deborah, 81, 322
Howell, Edward (Neddy), 80
Howell, Elizabeth (Betsy), 90, 117, 156
Howell, Hannah, 98
Howell, Isaac, 13, 136, 322
Howell, Jacob, 7, 322–23
Howell, Joshua, 4, 7, 9, 12, 14, 17, 19, 61, 68, 69, 81, 82, 84, 91, 323

Howell, Nurse, 154
Howell, Sarah (Sally), 7, 143, 323
Hudson, Martha Lloyd (Patty), 74, 323, 325
Humphreys, Mary (Molly), 192
Hunt, Isaac, 54, 323
Hunt, John, Jr., 40, 60, 74, 75, 323
Hunt, Rachel, 73, 74, 323
Hurley, Thomas, 287
Hutchinson, Dr. James, 112, 114, 323
Hutchinson, Governor Thomas, 51

Ingel, Joseph, 63
Inskeep, John, 258, 323
Inskeep, Jos., 267
Israel, Israel, 190, 191

Jackman, John, 14
Jackson, William, 67, 323
James, Abel, 21, 25, 26, 27, 28, 29, 30, 32, 33, 34, 35, 36, 44, 47, 49, 51, 54, 68, 74, 77, 79, 83, 96, 323
James, Chalkley, 66, 68, 73, 88–89, 96, 323
James, George, 26, 58, 323
James, Jacob, wife of, 79
James, James, 10
James, Joseph, 49, 57, 86, 88–89
James, Josh, 91
James, Patty, 25, 29, 32, 40
James, Rebecca (Becky), 25, 28, 29, 36, 40, 53, 324
James, Rebecca (Becky), Jr., 93, 323
James, Susannah (Sucky), 51, 324
James, Thomas, 53, 84, 91, 94, 324
James and Drinker, 49n–50n, 50
Jaquet, Susanna, 44
Jardine, Dr. Lewis, 186, 223, 233, 324
Jardine, Mary, 233
Jeffory (servant), 248
Jervis, Charles, 14, 61, 324
Jervis, Elizabeth (Betsy), 32, 183, 257, 282, 324
Jervis, John, 5, 6, 7, 8, 12, 13, 14, 15, 16, 17, 18, 21, 29, 36, 69, 76
Jervis, John, 51
Jervis, Rebecca, 9, 21, 144
Jervis, Sally, 257
Jess, James, 160
John (gardener), 128, 129, 137, 154, 176
Johnson, Jervis (Gervais), 164
Johnson, Sally, 133, 138, 148, 159, 162–63, 164, 204
Jolliffe (Jolloff), Richard, 48
Jones, Absalom, 209, 324
Jones, Aquilla, 219, 324
Jones, Charles, 12, 14
Jones, Hannah, 27, 36, 324
Jones, Isaac, 280

Merrifield, Joseph, 143
Merriott. *See* Marriott
Mickle, Betsy, 58
Miers, Mrs., 107
Mifflin, Ann (Nancy), 227, 317, 326
Mifflin, Charles, 90, 326
Mifflin, Daniel, 81, 326
Mifflin, Deborah Howell, 81, 322, 326
Mifflin, Esther, 11, 326
Mifflin, Sarah, 8, 326–27
Mifflin, Warner, 79, 140, 148, 189, 191, 327
Miller, Mark, 195
Miller, Robina, 166
Mitchell, Abraham, 8, 327
Mitchell, Ann (Nancy), 36, 327
Mitchell, Henry, 57
Mitchell, Sarah, 54, 327
Molesworth, James, 59
Moode, Elizabeth (Betsy), 5, 7, 8, 15, 18, 18n, 219, 327
Moode, Hannah, 9, 10, 11, 12, 13, 14, 15, 16, 17, 18, 19, 20, 21, 22, 25, 26, 27, 327
Moode, Nelly, 11, 14, 15, 20, 25, 91
Moore, John (Downing servant), 279, 289, 296, 299
Moore, Joseph, 120n
Moore, Mary (Molly), 42
Moore, Polly (servant), 92
Moore, T., 12
More, Hannah, 166n
Morgan, Ann Waln (Nancy), xii, 17, 113, 145, 194, 223, 230, 253, 327, 338
Morgan, Benjamin R., 190, 191
Morgan, C., 13
Morgan, Colonel, 77
Morgan, Elizabeth, 13
Morgan, Robert, xii, 253, 327
Morgan, Thomas, xii, 253, 327
Morris, Benjamin, 95, 327
Morris, Israel, 19, 74, 75, 327
Morris, Jacob, 101, 151
Morris, Molly (nurse), 91
Morris, Phoebe, 29, 31, 33
Morris, Richard, 149, 158, 327
Morris, Robert, 189n
Morris, Sally, 152
Morris, Sarah (Sally), 6, 12, 13, 19, 28, 327
Morris, Thomas, 170, 328
Morris, William, 14, 328
Mott, Huldah, 111, 127, 132, 134, 328
Mott, James, 86, 328
Mott, Sarah (Sally), 219–20, 328
Moyes, Dr. Henry, 100
Mullen, Caty, 119
Mullen, John (HD's servant), 248
Mullen, Patty, 147

Murry, Parson, 79
Musser, John, 76

Needham, Sarah (servant), 190, 198, 199, 206, 208–9, 210, 218
Newgent, Polly. *See* Noble, Polly Nugent
Newport, Molly, 20, 99, 106
Newton, Elizabeth (Betty), 193, 272, 273, 328
Nice, William, 164
Nicholson, Content, 5, 6, 328
Nicholson, Sally, 281
Noble, Polly Nugent (servant), 90, 94, 98, 145, 165, 242
Norton, Margery, 97
Norton, William, Jr., 79
Nugent, Polly. *See* Noble, Polly Nugent

Oat, George, 47, 49
Oat, Nanny, 48, 51, 52, 63, 67, 78
Oat, Sally, 45, 47
Oberlin, J. F., 46
Oliver, Benjamin, 104, 155, 175, 176, 184, 199, 206, 328
Oronoko (Noke; servant), 164, 213
Oxon, B., 25

Paine, Thomas, 195
Pantlif, Mr. and Mrs. (neighbors), 93, 97, 98
Pappin, Peter, 14
Parish, Abigail (Abey), 73, 328
Parish, Anne, 156n
Parish, John, 120n
Parish, Mary (Polly), 13, 18, 19, 328
Parish, Samuel, 93
Parish, Sarah (Sally), 14, 36, 327, 328
Parke, Dr. Joseph, 52, 73, 248
Parke, Thomas, Jr., 189, 328
Parker (servant), 186
Parker, Billy, 107
Parker, Elizabeth (Betsy), 15, 18, 44, 329
Parker, Sally, 106
Parker, Samuel, 143
Parr, Ann (Nancy), 6, 26, 27, 36
Parr, Caleb, 18, 27, 45
Parr, Caley, 18
Parr, Margaret (Peggy), 4, 6, 8, 13, 14, 15, 18, 26, 27, 28, 29, 37, 45, 47, 329
Parr, William (Billy), 6, 8, 9, 11, 13, 15, 16, 18, 25, 29, 30, 36, 44, 45, 329
Parrock, John, 34, 50, 329
Paterson, Caty (servant), 87
Paul (servant), 223, 227
Paul, John, 14, 329
Payne, Walter, 96, 98, 99
Peale, Charles Willson, 80n, 96, 102, 150, 207
Pemberton, Hannah, 69, 71, 73, 74, 104,

Smith, William, 61, 79, 80, 112
Smith, William D., 61
Snowden, Leonard, wife of, 148
Snyder, G. W., 195
Spain, Widow, 78
Spavold, Samuel, 6, 336
Spicer, Abigail (Abby), 41, 336
Spicer, Sylvia, 25, 336
Sprig, Sam, 127, 133, 134, 155, 164
Stamper, Sarah, 244, 336
Stanbury, Sally. *See* Stille, Sarah Stanbury
Stanton, Daniel, 4, 12, 13, 336
Stanwick, John, 189n
Steel, H., 10
Steel, Jemmy, 10
Steel, R., 9, 10
Steer, James, 80, 336
Steer, Joseph, 80
Stevens, Richard, 189
Stevenson, Hannah, 52, 95, 322, 336
Stevenson, Hannah, Jr., 52, 336
Stevenson, Robert, 57, 336
Stevenson, Robert, Sr., 163
Stevenson, Susanna, 95
Stewardson, Thomas, 120, 143, 185, 225, 260, 272, 277, 337
Stewart, Nancy (servant), 266
Stiles, Edward, 98, 191, 337
Stille, Emma, 244
Stille, Mary, 244
Stille, Sarah Stanbury (Sally), 91, 244, 252, 336
Stocker, Margaret (Peggy), 264, 265, 337
Storor, John, 13
Street, James, 93
Stretch, Lidia, 78
Stretch, Molly, 54
Stringer, Hannah (servant), 259
Stroud, Daniel, 277, 337
Summers, Polly (servant), 265
Sutton, Oswin, 26
Swett, Ann (HD's first wife), 3, 193n
Swett, Benjamin, 6, 9, 17, 18, 19, 25, 54n, 337
Swett, Nancy, 289
Swett, Susannah, 54, 58, 61, 73, 79, 83, 109, 120, 126, 137, 157, 158, 161, 162, 164, 168, 178, 218, 219, 223, 229, 235, 237, 281, 282, 284, 285, 286, 289, 290, 292, 293, 294, 295, 337
Swift, Neighbor, 44

Tallman, Sarah. *See* Wharton, Sarah
Tasker, James, 20
Taylor, A., 54
Taylor, Mary (Molly), 170, 337
Teas, John, 284, 337
Thomas, Ann, 267, 337

Thomas, Arthur, 131
Thomas, Hannah, 126, 273, 337
Thomas, John (servant), 279, 280, 281, 282, 283, 285, 286, 289, 292, 294, 299
Thomas, John, 131, 338
Thomas, John, Jr., 131
Thomas, Nancy, 100
Thomas, Richard, 214, 222, 337–38
Thomas, Thomasine, 300, 338
Thomas, Tom (Black Tom), 93
Thompson, Rebecca (Becky), 204, 251, 301, 323, 338
Thomson, John, 83
Thomson, Peter, 9
Tilghman, Edward, 243
Tilghman, Tench, 75, 338
Todd, Dr. William, 202, 214, 338
Tomkins, Sarah, 174
Townsend, Susanna, 14
Trapnal, Benjamin (servant), 16, 28, 30, 31, 33, 52
Trimble, Daniel, 137, 338
Trimble, Esther, 125
Trimble, Peggy, 125
Trimble, Samuel, 78, 86, 338
Trotter, Rebecca, 12, 13
Trotter, Rebecca Canarroe, 175, 338
Tucker, Ann, 267
Tunnis, Jane, 299–300
Turner, Jacob (servant), 26, 48, 52, 53, 146, 166, 173, 176, 180, 184, 185, 189, 190, 191, 194, 197, 199, 206, 208–9, 212, 213, 221, 223, 224
Turner, Sarah Needham (servant), 190, 198, 199, 206, 208–9, 210, 218
Tylee, T., 144

Uhl, John, 293, 303

Valentine, Robert, 78, 338
Vanaken, Widow, 31
Vaux, Ann Roberts, 110, 338

Wall, Richard, 271
Wallover, Peter, 99
Walmsley, Sarah, 7, 10, 338
Walmsley, William, 10, 338
Waln, Ann, 80, 338
Waln, Elizabeth (Betsy), 25, 30, 38, 40, 45, 48, 100, 338
Waln, Elizabeth, 40
Waln, Hannah, 102, 339
Waln, Jesse, 107, 339
Waln, Mary (Polly), 100, 101, 339
Waln, Nancy, 52, 53, 79, 102
Waln, Nicholas, 30, 73, 79, 126, 140, 339
Waln, Phebe, 254, 339
Waln, Rebecca, 83, 339

Subject Index

Aloe trees, 80
American Revolution, 54, 87, 88, 91–92,
    127
  Continental Congress, 61, 62, 72, 78
  Fort Mercer, 66n, 67n
  Fort Mifflin, 64n, 67n
  Hessians, 66, 72
  hospitals for soldiers, 65
  Independence, celebration of, 60, 78,
      151–52, 184, 195, 234, 274
  Monmouth, Battle of, 78
  Mud-Island Battery, 64, 67
  Pennsylvania Supreme Executive Coun-
      cil, 61, 62, 75, 76, 82
  and Philadelphia
    anti-Quaker feeling in, 54, 91–92
    British evacuation, 77
    British invasion, 62, 63–64
    celebration of independence, 60, 78,
        151–52, 184, 195, 234, 274
    celebration of Yorktown victory, 91–92
    Congress returns to, 78
    illuminated because of repeal of Stamp
        Act, 36
    inspectors take inventory of provisions
        in, 84
  quartering soldiers, 59, 69–70, 71, 72, 74
  and Society of Friends, 54, 60, 73, 91–
      92, 191
  Stamp Act, 36
  tea, 49, 50
  Yorktown, Battle of, 91
Animals, 111, 157, 280
  cats, 138–39, 191, 199, 250, 273–74
  cattle, 249
  dogs, 91, 93, 199
  elephants, 166, 171, 280
  frogs, 133, 153
  hogs, 249
  horses, 87, 95, 179, 182, 190, 291, 296
  insects, 133, 157, 174, 213, 227, 247, 275
  mermaids, 276
  moles, 129
  pig, learned, 239
  sheep, 249
  spiders, 227
  Tarter (ED's dog), 250, 258, 280
Ann (ship), 31
Apothecary shop, 228, 244, 257
Assaults, 224–25
Astronomy and astrology, xvi, 157, 172,
    175n, 179n, 238n. *See also* Moon
Atsion Ironworks, 49, 51, 58, 88, 136, 274,
    277, 287, 304
Austerlitz, Battle of, 279n

Baboon, 111
Baking, xvi, 131, 236, 268

Balloons, 98
Banishment, 61–62
Bank of the United States, 199
Bankruptcy, 189
Bathing, 142
  bathtub, xv, 256–57, 258, 274, 283, 285,
      297
  cold baths, 100
  in river, 211
  shower, 131, 197, 211, 215, 226
  "washing frolic," 16
  See also Medications and treatments
Baths, 44, 45, 100, 185, 197, 215, 226, 283
Beef, xvi, 82, 131, 249
Beer, 234, 244
Beggar, 136
Bethlehem, Pa., 45
Bettering-house, 267
Bible, 234
Blankets, 60, 63, 66
Bleeders
  Cunits, Lewis, 282, 296
  Hailer, Frederick, 80, 90, 146, 157, 176,
      239, 272
  Hailer, John, 256, 265, 275
  Uhl, John, 293, 303
Bloodletting, 7, 18, 37, 38, 40, 47, 48, 90,
    91, 93, 97, 109, 119, 126, 127, 130,
    137, 141, 146, 153, 157, 161, 162, 163,
    172, 175–76, 195, 196, 201, 235, 239,
    243, 261, 265, 266, 275, 286, 293, 294,
    302, 303
  in childbirth and pregnancy, xii, 7n, 216,
      235
  cupped, 7n, 127, 226, 256, 292
  disposal of blood, 141
  with leeches, 7n, 282, 289, 294, 295, 296
  and phases of the moon, 175n
  and pregnancy, 7n, 176n, 196
  refusals to be, 172, 292–93, 302
  with thumb lancet, 214
  and yellow fever, 275
Boating, 16
Boston, Mass., 13, 50. *See also* Hutchinson,
    Governor Thomas
Boxing, 94
Breast-feeding, prevention of pregnancies
    by prolonged, xviii, 216. *See also*
    Weaning
Bridge (over Schuylkill), 250
Bristol, Pa., baths, 44, 45
Bugging (of bedding), 257
Burglary, 90n, 194
Burlington Yearly Meeting, 19
Burness Tavern, 168

Cancer, xviii, 282n
  of breast, 36, 88, 90

of the neck, 290, 292, 301
tumor in cheek, 281, 282, 283, 284, 285, 292, 293
Wilson, Samuel (cancer doctor), 290, 292
Candle making, 84
Cap François, Hispaniola, 108
Cards, pictured, 230
Cats, 138–39, 191, 199, 250, 273–74
Cattle, 249
Celebrations
of independence, 60, 78, 151–52, 184, 195, 234, 274
of Yorktown victory, 91–92
Cemetery, 234
Negro, 15, 53
visits to, 8
Chalkley (ship), 50, 51, 52, 54
Chambering, 243, 276
Charity, 156, 170, 179–80, 217, 227
Cherries, 127–28
Chester, Pa., 50
Childbirth, xiii, xiv–xv, xvii, 4, 14, 18, 27, 30, 40, 42, 48, 51, 52, 86, 91, 93, 95, 98, 135, 140, 147, 154, 155–56, 180, 180–82, 184, 194, 196, 202, 203, 215, 215–17, 223, 226, 235, 235–36, 237–38, 241, 255, 264, 266, 279, 291
and bloodletting, xii, 7n, 216, 235
death of child in, xiii, 95, 181, 210, 235
death of mother in, 42, 95, 115, 144, 159, 161
and easy chair, 155
fainting after, 181, 182
inhibiting milk production, 182, 183
nursing as a means of birth control, xviii, 216
and phases of the moon, 178–79
triplets, 164
twins, 144, 266
and yellow fever, 115
Chimney sweeps, 127
Chocolate, 40
Christmas, 158, 230, 277
Cleaning house, xvi, 30, 40, 48, 110, 127, 163, 164, 203, 264, 266, 286. *See also* Bugging; Curtains; Ironing; Washing clothes
Clearfield, 128
sale of, xi, 159, 164, 165
Clock, 171, 229
Clothing
aprons, 145, 160
baby clothes, 178
body lining, 11
bonnet, 13
breeches, 206
cap, 160, 215
cloak, 80, 159, 241

coat, 139, 172, 206
coat and breeches (for boy), 47, 54, 215
dresses, children's, 244
flannel, 169, 177, 261
garter, 209
gloves, 221, 222
gown skirt, 230
gowns, 15, 29, 33, 137, 143, 162, 193, 223, 241, 260, 272, 273
handkerchiefs, 227
hat, 111, 286
locket buttons set in gold, 224
mittens, 12, 21
neckerchief, 160
petticoat, 15, 76, 160, 161, 241, 272
pocketbook, 238
purse, 15
shifts, 160, 193, 242
shirts, 145, 191, 192, 281
shoes, 19, 74, 120, 214, 217, 233, 239, 267
stockings, 158, 161, 178, 206, 251, 279
suit of clothes (man's), 177
undergarments, 156, 215, 261
vest, 206
wedding dress, 125
See also Ironing; Knitting; Sewing; Washing clothes
Coinage, 194–95
College and Academy of Philadelphia, 12
Committee for the Civilization and Welfare of the Indian Natives, 160
Confiscation, of horses, 87
Congress, 187–88
Continental Association, 54
Continental Congress, 61, 62, 72
returns to Philadelphia, 78
Counterfeiting, 54
Courting, 132
Criminal activities
burglary, 194
counterfeiting, 54
drunkenness, 160, 163, 170, 178, 186, 238, 299
fighting, 150, 226, 276
misprision of treason, 85
plundering, 66, 69
rape, 100n
robbery, 47, 69, 89, 90n, 98, 131
stabbings in Philadelphia, 224–25
suicide, 130
theft, 60, 62, 69, 90, 92, 131, 194
treason, 59n, 80, 81, 82
See also Banishment; Hangings; Imprisonment; Jail; Martial law
Currant jelly, xvi, 28, 129, 130
Currants, 16
Curtains, 157

Deists, 250
Delaware (frigate), 64
Dentistry
  sore gums, 215
  teeth cleaning, 101, 165
  tooth aches, 3, 6, 9, 17, 73, 88, 161, 169,
    188, 245, 266, 288, 304
  tooth cutting by infants, 28, 30, 33, 36,
    39, 49, 97, 114, 151, 184, 219, 245,
    273
  tooth pulling, 6, 43, 80, 90, 165, 169,
    214–15, 225, 226, 236, 237, 272
  tooth replacing, 6, 222
Diseases. *See* Illnesses and diseases
Divine Will, resignation to, 187, 201, 232,
  246
Doctors. *See* Doctors *in Index of Names. See
  also* Bloodletting; Dentistry; Health
  care; Hospitals; Illnesses and diseases;
  Medications and treatments
Dogs, 199
  bites from, 93
  rabid, 91
  Tarter (ED's dog), 250, 258, 280
Dolls, 159, 206, 228
Domestic Medicine (William Buchan), xiii,
  169, 173, 185
Draymen, 127
Drunkenness, 160, 163, 170, 178, 186, 238,
  299

Earthquake, 25
Easy chair, 155
Elections, 169, 190, 229, 230
Electricity, 12, 13
Elephants, 166, 171, 280
Elopement. *See* Rhoads, Mary Drinker
Executions. *See* Hangings
Eyeglasses, 218, 251

Female Society for the Relief and Employment of the Poor, 156
Fights, 150, 226, 276
Figs, 248
Fires, 8, 11, 17, 38, 65, 67, 87, 94, 97, 98,
    125, 136, 170, 190, 210, 211, 253, 291
  in Boston, 13
Fireworks, 130. *See also* Independence,
  celebration of
Fishing, xvii, 34, 52, 53, 202, 215
Flies, 174, 227, 247
Fly (sloop), 64n
Food and drink
  baking, xvi, 131, 236, 268
  beef, xvi, 82, 249
  beer, 234, 244
  cherries, 127–28
  chocolate, 40

currant jelly, xvi, 28, 129, 130
currants, 16
figs, 248
fruit trees, 113, 199, 248
gingerbread, 161, 194, 289
grapes, 229, 248
green peas, 128
ice cream, 169, 174, 274
minced pies, 268
peach blossom syrup, 127
peaches, 248, 266, 303, 304
pears, 16
pies, xvi, 268
pineapples, 16
pork, cutting and salting, 289
potatoes, 137
prunes, 251, 303
rennet whey, 244
strawberries, 3, 127, 128, 132, 246
tea, 49, 50
Fort Mercer, 66n, 67n
Fort Mifflin, 64n, 67n
Fortepiano, 233
France, 150, 279
Freedom dues, 63, 78, 163, 272
French lessons, 94
Frogs, 133, 153
Fruit trees, 113, 199, 248

Gardens, 13, 16, 80, 139, 162, 176, 223,
  248, 299
German servant trade, 54
Ghost, 230
Gingerbread, 161, 194, 289
Glass manufacturing, 45
Glasses (eyeglasses), 218, 251
Gospel ministers, 271
Gossiping women, 202, 207, 223, 233
Grand Climactic, 175, 285
Grapes, 229, 248
Grays Ferry, Pa., 149
Green peas, 128

Hand organ, 144
Hangings, 59, 66, 82, 90, 98, 100
Haunted house, 230
Havana, Cuba, 27, 285, 287, 288
Health care, xii–xiii. *See also* Accidents;
  Bloodletting; Dentistry; Doctors;
  Hospitals; Illnesses and diseases;
  Medications and treatments
Hearing trumpet, 143
Hessians, 66, 72
Hispaniola, 108
Hogs, 249
Homer, *Iliad*, 11
Horseback riding, xv, 49, 52, 53, 248, 253,
  256, 273

hiccups, 270, 301
hives, 106, 221, 240
hysteria, 183
ill taste in mouth, 243
influenza, 121, 299
insomnia, 88
itch, 87, 90, 280
jaundice, 138
kidney problem, 300
knees, 142, 210, 243–44, 253
languor, 183, 210
lax, 33, 42, 165, 189, 239, 270, 297
legs, 292, 269
lethargy, xviii, 124
lice, 140
light-headedness, 41
limbs
    loss of use of, 121
    sore, 168, 241, 272
lips, sore, 222
liver, 121, 138
lungs, ruptured blood vessel in, 108
lymph glands, inflamed, 277
measles, 48, 163, 242, 245
memory loss, 275
mouth
    bad breath, 84
    ill taste in, 243
    mortification of the (pleurisy), 7
    sore, 77
    sore lips, 222
    uncommon taste in stomach and, 138
mumps, 271
neck
    glands swollen in, 277, 289
    pain in, 272
    swollen, 292, 301
nervous fever (typhus), 8
nettle rash, 106, 116, 128, 280
nosebleed, 37, 292–93
old-age pains, 302
pain and soreness
    arm, 285–86
    back, 242, 302
    bones, 95, 147
    breast, 99, 100, 127, 146, 158, 168,
        232, 242
    ears, 154, 293
    eyes, 30, 110, 154, 173, 238
    finger, 196
    flesh, 147
    gums, 215
    hard retchings and, 138
    headaches, 9, 14, 82, 95, 116, 126,
        155, 164, 184, 220, 228, 229, 230,
        234, 236, 238, 241, 252, 259, 300
    knee, 142, 210, 243–44
    limbs, 168, 241, 272

lips, 222
mouth, 77
neck, 272
old-age, 302
shoulder, 286
side, 73, 243, 249
swellings and, 285
throat, 7, 19, 21, 22, 32, 33, 51, 109,
    121, 172, 271, 281, 289
tongue, 295
wrist, 213
palsey, 226
phlegm, 97, 126, 134, 146, 261, 301
pleurisy, 7n, 19, 119, 146, 252, 300
pulse, lack of, 228
purging, 27, 28, 33, 257
putrid fever, 112–13
putrid sore throat, 116, 244
quinsy, 121
rash, 51, 84
    hives, 106, 221, 240
    itch, 87, 90, 280
    nettle, 106, 116, 128, 280
retchings and pain, 138
rheumatism, 74, 162, 286
St. Anthony's Fire, 57
scarlet fever, 244
scrofula, 298
shoulder pain, 286
side pain, 73, 243, 249
soft palate (uvula), inflammation of, 22
spitting up blood, 121, 130
stagnation in feet, 185
stomach, 131
    cold in, 7
    cramps, 42
    disordered, 131
    sick, xiii, 52, 78, 90, 95, 98, 110, 116,
        121, 190, 193, 234, 254, 255, 257,
        259
    swollen, 252
    uncommon taste in mouth and, 138
stools, blood in, 300
stooped condition, 255
suffocation, feeling of, 209
sweat, 116, 151
swelling under the arms, 84
swellings and pain, 285
swimming in head, 255
tenesmus, 236
throat
    putrid sore, 116, 244
    sore, 7, 19, 21, 22, 32, 33, 51, 109,
        121, 172, 271, 281, 289
    spasms, 228
    ulcerated, 287
tongue, 165, 295
tumors, 298

physic, 48, 51, 60, 186, 222, 292, 303
pills, 254
plaster, 183n, 239, 281, 283, 285, 290, 292, 293
poultice with hemlock bark, 298
powders, 254
purging, 37, 84, 127, 275, 300–301
rhubarb, 48, 78, 84, 90, 171, 228, 275, 301; wine, 301
sage wine, 275
sago tea, 190
Saint-John's-wort, 112, 117, 130n
salts, 9, 303
seton, 295, 296
spirits of nitre, 236
starving, 186
strawberries, brandy, and loaf sugar, 246
surgical removal of tumor, 283, 284
sweating, 275
tansy, 34
tar water, 191
tarred rope, 113
Turlington's Balsam, 34
venice treacle, 34–35
vinegar, 117, 209, 238
vomiting, 37, 78
warm water, 152
wean baby to restore mother's eyesight, 251
worm powder, 31
wormwood, 34, 113
See also Accidents; Bloodletting; Dentistry; Doctors (*in Index of Names*); Hospitals; Illnesses and diseases
Mermaids, 276
Methodists, 228, 276
Microscope, 13
Militia, 85
Minced pies, 268
Miscarriages, 23, 28, 30, 40, 126
Mobs, 91–92, 127
Moles, 129
Money, 85, 194–95
Monmouth, Battle of, 78
Montgomery (ship), 64n
Moon, 134, 177, 179n, 180
 and childbirth, 155, 178–79, 184, 237, 238
 eclipse of, 132, 179n, 268
 and fevers, 179n, 279n
 and sex of a child, 154
Moravians (Bethlehem, Pa.), 46
Mosquitoes, 227, 275
Mud-Island Battery, 64, 67
Music, 144, 277

Nag's Head (inn), 45
Necessaries (outhouses)
 blood thrown into from bloodletting, 141

cleaning out, 207–8
 falling into, 107, 256
Needlework, xvi, 3, 14, 200, 281, 293
New York City, and yellow fever, 115, 258
Nonassociation fines, 85

Old age, 158, 302
Ostrich, 280
Outhouses. *See* Necessaries

Parties, mixed-gender, 281
Peach blossom syrup, 127
Peaches, 248, 266, 303, 304
Pears, 16
Pennsbury Manor, 118, 121
Pennsylvania Supreme Executive Council, 61, 62, 75, 76, 82
Philadelphia
 almshouse, 267
 American army re-occupies, 77
 anti-Quaker feeling in, 54, 91–92
 British evacuation of, 77
 British invasion of, 62, 63–64
 celebrates independence, 60, 78, 151–52, 184, 195, 234, 274
 celebrates Yorktown victory, 91–92
 College and Academy of Philadelphia, 12
 Congress returns to, 78
 dispensary, xiv
 hospitals, 65, 187, 199, 249, 259, 262
 illuminated because of repeal of Stamp Act, 36
 inspectors take inventory of provisions in, 84
 Irish-town, 117
 packet (ship), 17
 shops ordered closed for inventory, 77
 smallpox epidemic in, 9
 smells of, xviii
 stabbings of women in, 224–25
 street lamps, 151, 180, 303
 visiting time in, 149
 water pipes being laid, 251, 275, 296
 yellow-fever epidemics in, xii, 27n, 112, 113–18, 185–87, 197–202, 209, 211, 213, 214, 248, 274
Physicians. *See* Doctors *in Index of Names*
Pig, learned, 239
Pincushions, 279
Pineapples, 16
Pipe smoking, 269–70
Plundering, 66, 69
Poetry, 30, 103, 106, 140, 145, 157–58, 161, 284. *See also* Reading
Point No Point, Pa., 13
Pork, cutting and salting, 289
Portraits, 166, 218, 231
Post office, 198
Potatoes, 137